T0334292

The Problem-solving Capacity of the Modern State

The Problem-solving Capacity of the Modern State

Governance Challenges and Administrative Capacities

Edited by
Martin Lodge and Kai Wegrich

OXFORD
UNIVERSITY PRESS

Great Clarendon Street, Oxford, OX2 6DP,
United Kingdom

Oxford University Press is a department of the University of Oxford.
It furthers the University's objective of excellence in research, scholarship,
and education by publishing worldwide. Oxford is a registered trade mark of
Oxford University Press in the UK and in certain other countries

First Edition published in 2014
Impression: 2

Published in the United States of America by Oxford University Press
198 Madison Avenue, New York, NY 10016, United States of America

British Library Cataloguing in Publication Data
Data available

Library of Congress Control Number: 2014938176

ISBN 978–0–19–871636–5

Printed and bound by
CPI Group (UK) Ltd, Croydon, CR0 4YY

Preface

Bureaucracy tends to be spoken of in negative terms, usually associated with 'too much', 'too slow', or 'too burdensome'. The reputation may be deserved in some cases. But imagine public services without the street-level public servant working through the requirements to determine whether an individual is eligible for benefits, without the standards that indicate how a policy should be implemented at what level of quality, without the knowledge of who should be or is being served and with what effect, or without the interaction of various departments to ensure adequate coverage. Regardless of different understandings of the appropriate size or even role of the state, bureaucracy (or, to put it in more palatable terms, public administration) plays a key role in developing, implementing, and evaluating policy decisions and is the backbone of any governance regime.

This volume and its companion, *The Governance Report 2014*, highlight the administrative capacities that may be required of states to be able to meet the demands of today's public problems. How much 'muscle' is left during the current 'age of austerity' after waves of reforms that have changed the architecture of the state? How can or should states usefully draw on non-state actors to act upon and address the pressing problems of our time?

The volume stems from an interdisciplinary effort led by the Hertie School of Governance in Berlin, Germany to examine the state of the art of governance at the local, national, and transnational levels, and by looking at governments, public administration, business corporations, and civil society. In doing so, the Governance Report initiative enlists experts from the Hertie School but also from other institutions. Special attention is paid to institutional designs and approaches, changes, and innovations that state and non-state actors have proposed or adopted in response to the shifts that have been occurring. This applies to the profound geopolitical changes that are likely to gain momentum and become more entrenched in the future, as it does to the world's financial architecture and smaller, often more incremental developments at local levels, be they the spread of new approaches to public administration, the role of information and communication technology, or the capacities of civil society to support municipal governance.

The results of this effort are available in an annual series that includes an edited volume, a compact edition (both published by Oxford University Press), and a dedicated website at <http://www.governancereport.org> that offers access to additional background information, a governance innovations database, and our growing set of governance indicators. Together, these various outputs and outlets are designed to provide both policy-makers and analysts ideas, knowledge, and tools to consider and implement policies and programmes that lead to better solutions to public problems.

Launched in 2013, the first set of outputs, including *The Governance Report 2013* and the companion edited volume, *Governance Challenges and Innovations: Financial and Fiscal Governance*, examines the challenges of governing financial and fiscal crises, proposes a new paradigm—'responsible sovereignty'—for tackling global issues, highlights selected governance innovations, and introduces a new generation of governance indicators. Upcoming editions will cover the future of the European Union as a governance innovation in and of itself, the progress and setbacks in energy and infrastructure policy, and the challenges presented by the mass collection and use of data, as well as the rights and obligations that go along with them.

Many people have been involved in the Governance Report effort. Among them are members of the Report's International Advisory Committee who have offered input at various stages of the project:

Craig Calhoun	London School of Economics
William Roberts Clark	University of Michigan
John Coatsworth	Columbia University
Ann Florini	Singapore Management University & Brookings Institution
Geoffrey Garrett	Australian School of Business, University of New South Wales
Mary Kaldor	London School of Economics
Edmund J. Malesky	Duke University
Henrietta Moore	Cambridge University
Woody Powell	Stanford University
Bo Rothstein	Quality of Government Institute, University of Gothenburg
Shanker Satyanath	New York University
James Vreeland	Georgetown University
Kent Weaver	Georgetown University
Arne Westad	IDEAS, London School of Economics
Michael Zürn	Wissenschaftszentrum Berlin

The Hertie School community, especially the faculty, has also engaged in many ways. Working with the authors at various stages has been an active team of research assistants and associates including Alieza Durana, Mark Fliegauf, Sonja Kaufmann, Olga Kononykhina, Julia Kropeit, Dennis Mwaura, Christian Ruiz, Nathalie Spath, Ramsey Wise, and Christopher (CJ) Yetman. Thanks are also due to David Budde, Zora Chan, Magriet Cruywagen, Regine Kreitz, Iseult Rea, and Simone Dudziak. We also wish to think the Board of the Hertie School of Governance for encouraging this effort, and for providing critical feedback and direction.

Finally, we wish to acknowledge especially the support of the Hertie Foundation and the additional financial resources provided by Evonik and Stiftelsen Riksbankens Jubileumsfond that made this effort possible.

Helmut K. Anheier and Regina A. List

Berlin
March 2014

This book [illegible] especially the [illegible] [illegible] has [illegible] of [illegible] including [illegible] [illegible] Thanks are also due to [illegible] [illegible] We also wish to thank the [illegible] the Hertie School of Governance for [illegible] this effort, and for providing critical feedback and direction.

Finally, we wish to acknowledge especially the support of the Hertie [illegible] and the [illegible] [illegible]

[illegible]

[illegible]
March 20[illegible]

Table of Contents

List of Tables and Figures

List of Acronyms

ALMP	active labour market policies
AMC	Administrative Management Capacity
AOSIS	Alliance of Small Island States
BRICS	Brazil, Russia, India, China, and South Africa
BSE	bovine spongiform encephalopathy ('mad cow' disease)
CCBA	Community and Biodiversity Alliance
CDM	Clean Development Mechanism
CEC	Commission of European Communities
CFCs	chlorofluorocarbons
COCOPS	Coordinating for Cohesion in the Public Sector of the Future
CPI	climate policy integration
DDT	dichlorodiphenyltrichloroethane
DG	Directorate General
DG Employment	Directorate General for Employment, Social Affairs, and Inclusion
DG Markt	Internal Market and Services Directorate General
DG Regio	Directorate General for Regional and Urban Policy
DAE	Digital Agenda for Europe
EIA	environmental impact assessment
EPA	Environmental Protection Agency (USA)
EPI	environmental policy integration
ESF	European Social Fund
ETS	emission trading scheme
EU	European Union
FATF	Financial Action Task Force
FSC	Forest Stewardship Council
G33 (WTO Context)	Group of 33
G7	Group of Seven
G77	Group of 77

G8	Group of Eight
GDP	gross domestic product
HR/HRM	human resources/human resources management
IBEI	Institut Barcelona d'Estudis Internacionals
ICANN	Internet Corporation for Assigned Names and Numbers
IMF	International Monetary Fund
IMI	Internal Market Information System
IOSCO	International Organization for Securities Commissions
ISA	Inter-operability Solutions for European Public Administrations
ISO	International Organization for Standardization
JI	joint implementation
LEED	Leadership in Energy and Environmental Design
MbO	management by objectives
MEP	Ministry of Environmental Protection (China)
MSC	Marine Stewardship Council
MSI	multi-stakeholder sustainability initiative
NAPs	national allocation plans
NEPIs	new environmental policy instruments
NGO	non-governmental organisation
NPM	New Public Management
OECD	Organisation for Economic Co-operation and Development
OMC	Open Method of Coordination
PPPs	public–private partnerships
R&D	research and development
REDD+	Reducing Emissions from Deforestation and Forest Degradation
RSPO	Roundtable on Sustainable Palm Oil
SAC	Sustainable Apparel Coalition
SARS	severe acute respiratory syndrome
SD	sustainable development
SDTs	sustainable development technologies
SEA	strategic environmental assessments
SIGMA	Support for Improvement in Governance and Management
SRU	Sachverständigenrat für Umweltfragen (Germany)
TAIEX	Technical Assistance and Information Exchange
UN	United Nations

UNICEF	United Nations International Children's Emergency Fund
USAID	United States Agency for International Development
VCS	Verified Carbon Standard
WCED	World Commission on Environment and Development
WHO	World Health Organization
WRR	Scientific Council for Government Policy (Netherlands)

About the Contributors

Gerhard Hammerschmid (Dr. soc. oec., Vienna University of Economics and Business) is Associate Dean and Professor of Financial and Public Management at the Hertie School of Governance. He is Director of the School's Executive Master of Public Management programme and coordinator of the EU FP7 research project Coordinating for Cohesion in the Public Sector of the Future (COCOPS). His research spans public management (reform), performance management, comparative public administration, personnel management, and institutional theory.

Eva G. Heidbreder (PhD, European University Institute) is Junior Professor for Political Science (European integration) at the Heinrich Heine University Düsseldorf. She worked previously at the Hertie School of Governance (Berlin) and Free University Berlin and had visiting professorships at the Humboldt University Berlin and the University of Konstanz. Her current research concentrates on EU public and administrative policy and civil society participation.

Michael Hill is Emeritus Professor of Social Policy of the University of Newcastle and Visiting Professor at the University of Brighton. He has written on many aspects of the policy process and social policy. He is author of *The Public Policy Process*, *Implementing Public Policy* (with Peter Hupe), *Social Policy in the Modern World*, and *Understanding Social Policy* (with Zoë Irving). In 2009 he was given the Social Policy Association's lifetime award.

Peter Hupe is Associate Professor in the Department of Public Administration at Erasmus University Rotterdam. In 2012–13 he was Visiting Fellow at All Souls College, Oxford. His research focuses on the theoretical-empirical study of the policy process, particularly implementation and street-level bureaucracy. In a long-standing collaboration he and Michael Hill have published articles in *Public Administration*, *Public Management Review*, and *Policy and Politics*. With Aurélien Buffat, they edited *Understanding Street-Level Bureaucracy* (forthcoming).

Jacint Jordana (PhD, University of Barcelona) is Professor of Political Science and Public Administration at the Universitat Pompeu Fabra. His main research focus is the analysis of public policies, with special emphasis on regulatory policy and regulatory governance. He has also published extensively on collective action, policy diffusion, and social capital. His most recent publication, co-edited with Andrea Bianculli and Xavier Fernandez-Marin, is *Accountability and Regulatory Governance: Audiences, Controls and Responsibilities in the Politics of Regulation* (Palgrave, 2014).

Michaela Kreyenfeld (PhD, University of Rostock) is Head of the Research Group on Life Course, Social Policy, and the Family at the Max Planck Institute for Demographic Research in Rostock and Professor of Sociology at the Hertie School of Governance. Her main areas of research are family sociology, life course research, and the relationship between social policies and demographic behaviour.

Nico Krisch (PhD, University of Heidelberg) is ICREA Research Professor at the Institut Barcelona d'Estudis Internacionals (IBEI) and a Fellow at the Hertie School of Governance. His most recent book, *Beyond Constitutionalism: The Pluralist Structure of Postnational Law* (2010), was awarded the 2012 Certificate of Merit of the American Society of International Law. He is a member of the Executive Board of the European Society of International Law and of the Council of the International Society for Public Law.

Andrea Lenschow (PhD, New York University) is Full Professor of European Politics and Integration at Osnabrück University. Her research interests include structures and dynamics of policy-making in the European Union and in comparative perspective, especially in environmental policy and sustainable development. Her most recent publication, co-edited with Helge Jörgens and Duncan Liefferink, is *Understanding Environmental Policy Convergence. The Power of Words, Rules and Money* (Cambridge, 2014).

Martin Lodge (PhD, University of London) is Professor of Political Science and Public Policy in the Department of Government and Director of the Centre for Analysis of Risk and Regulation at the London School of Economics and Political Science (LSE).

Kira Matus (PhD, Harvard University) is Assistant Professor of Public Policy and Management in the Department of Government at the London School of Economics. She is co-Director of the Innovation and Access to Technologies for Sustainable Development Project at Harvard University's Sustainability Science Program. Her research focuses on innovation policy and green technologies, the role of voluntary governance in sustainable development, and the interactions between science and policy.

Salvador Parrado (PhD, University Complutense, Madrid) teaches in the Department of Political Science and Public Administration at the Spanish Distance Learning University (UNED), Madrid, and is adjunct faculty of the Hertie School of Governance (Berlin). He has published on comparative administrative systems, the civil service, inter-governmental relations, and public sector reform. His current research focuses on public management and regulatory policies. At present, he is European Editor of the journal *Public Administration* and Director of Governance International (<http://www.govint.org>).

Anika Rasner (PhD, Berlin University of Technology) is Research Associate at the DIW Berlin working on the German Socio-Economic Panel Study (SOEP). Her main area of interest is in retirement and life-course research, in particular the interplay of institutions and individual work and family choices.

Eva Sørensen (PhD, University of Copenhagen) is Professor in Public Administration and Democracy at the Department of Society and Globalisation, Roskilde University.

She is Director of a large-scale research project on Collaborative Innovation in the Public Sector and Vice-Director of the Centre for Democratic Network Governance. Her research interests include public innovation, network governance, and political leadership.

Vid Štimac is Research Associate at the Hertie School of Governance. He studied econometrics and operations research at the University of Amsterdam. Previously he worked at the European School of Management and Technology (ESMT), the Amsterdam Institute for Advanced Labour Studies (AIAS), and the Amsterdam Institute for International Development (AIID). His current research concerns public performance management practice and reform.

Jacob Torfing (PhD, University of Essex) is Professor of Politics and Institutions at the Department of Society and Globalisation, Roskilde University. He is Director of the Centre for Democratic Network Governance and Vice-Director of a large-scale research project on Collaborative Innovation in the Public Sector. His research interests include administrative reforms, public innovation, and interactive forms of governance.

Marco Verweij (PhD, European University Institute) is Professor of Political Science at Jacobs University in Bremen, Germany. He is the author of *Clumsy Solutions for a Wicked World: How to Improve Global Governance* (Palgrave Macmillan, 2011) and editor (with Michael Thompson) of *Clumsy Solutions for a Complex World: Governance, Politics and Plural Perceptions* (Palgrave Macmillan, 2006).

Kai Wegrich (Dr. rer. pol., Potsdam University) is Professor of Public Administration and Public Policy at the Hertie School of Governance. Prior to this position, he was Fellow at the London School of Economics and Senior Researcher at RAND Corporation in Berlin and Cambridge. He is European Editor of *Public Administration* and co-editor of the book series on 'Executive Politics & Governance' (with Palgrave). His main research interests are regulation, executive politics, and public sector reform.

1

Introduction

Governance Innovation, Administrative Capacities, and Policy Instruments

Martin Lodge and Kai Wegrich

Introduction

The early 21st century has presented considerable challenges to the problem-solving capacity of the contemporary state in the industrialised world. Among the many uncertainties, anxieties, and tensions, three particular challenges stand out:

- The year 2012 was recorded as being the warmest in history. In the UK, it was also on record as the second wettest. This further underpinned concerns as to how politics and policy should tackle the issue of climate change, whether through prevention or mitigation (Deutscher Bundestag; U.S. Global Change Research Program). Such questions received further urgency in the aftermath of the Typhoon Haiyan that devastated parts of the Philippines in November 2013 just as another intergovernmental climate change conference was about to convene in Warsaw.
- In 2012, an official report for the federal German government suggested that by 2060, a third of the population would be over 65 years old, with considerable implications for the way the welfare state could meet demands of health, care, or pensions-related expenditures. An ageing society also pointed to a future of employment shortages (Kock, Bruckner, and Schaible 2012). Elsewhere, related concerns were raised about demographic developments in Japan and South Korea, while observers of

the Chinese economy were also puzzling over the effects of a rapidly ageing population as a result of the 'one child policy' (which was somewhat relaxed in late 2013).

- If these were not enough, the ongoing sovereign debt and financial crisis challenged the way in which government could possibly generate economic activity, while also addressing climate change and welfare state-related problems (Howell 2013).

These challenges to contemporary systems of governing have occupied armies of expert commissions, think tanks, and consultancies. Summits and conferences have been pondering them as well. The OECD has responded by establishing the Observatory of Public Sector Innovation to look for options that may 'reduce costs, improve public sector productivity and help to sustain trust in government' (OECD). Consultancies, too, have sought to display their public spiritedness by issuing reports featuring various former politicians (for example, McKinsey, PWC, Ernst & Young). The World Economic Forum has also paid increased attention to issues of 'governance' (World Economic Forum).

Policy-related debates have sought to respond (at least in part) to the above three background conditions. These debates include in particular infrastructure-, social security-, and social integration-related, and sustainability-oriented policies. First, in the area of infrastructure, questions about future capacity needs were raised across policy domains. In energy, infrastructure capacity issues related to debates about the mix of sources through which future energy needs should be addressed. These, in turn, triggered debates about the type of infrastructure required to connect energy generation to users. In communications, infrastructure capacity was particularly related to issues of access conditions and incentives for encouraging investment. In transport, repeated debates were conducted about how sustainability could be enhanced through encouraging mobility. Debates therefore involve issues such as enhancing (or not) different modes of transport and dealing with capacity bottlenecks, whether at the local or national level. Across all these infrastructure domains, political urges existed to indulge in mega projects, especially airports. Across these infrastructure-based industries, debates included issues regarding ownership, operation, regulation, and financing.

Second, in the area of social security, ageing populations challenged welfare states, not just in terms of the changing ratio between those in work and those receiving pensions, requiring health care, or receiving other forms of social assistance. Demographic change therefore raised concerns about how the financing and operation of public services could be adjusted to reflect the changing population profile. The future financing of an elder-care system represented a particularly pertinent issue given projections about rising life expectancy (with the cost of looking after increasingly Alzheimer-ridden societies or of medical-technical treatments). It was unlikely that such demands on health-care budgets could easily be accommodated through innovative and low-cost breakthrough technologies (such as telemedicine).

Third, in the area of social integration, international population mobility and ageing demographic profiles accentuated the political salience of immigration. States sought to attract particular groups of migrants to maintain their economic competitiveness. Free movement in the European Union and immigration more broadly became an increasingly prominent issue in domestic politics (such as in the UK). In addition, social integration also featured in debates about limited socioeconomic mobility among particular segments of society. Increasingly heterogeneous societies, furthermore, prompted broader questions about how public services could be delivered. Finally, social integration also involved law and order-related debates, especially the monitoring of individuals suspected of plotting terrorist activities. Again, debates explored how to organise, fund, and control social integration-related activities.

Finally, in the area of sustainability, it was widely questioned whether 'sustainable capitalism' was an appropriate (and feasible) strategy for dealing with the kind of catastrophic climate change projections that were put forward by most (if not, all) scientists. Others argued that different kinds of economic growth models were required to encourage long-term sustainability. However, regardless of such debates between advocates of various shades of green, sustainability-related policy debates focused on the way in which reduced resource intensity could be built into diverse policy areas in order to reduce the consumption of or the strain on (natural) resources. This, again, raised issues about funding, regulation, and the way sustainable policies could be organised.

Cross-cutting controversies concerned the appropriate level at which certain decisions should be taken or how much discretion could be given to states and private actors. In addition, governance debates considered whether more capacity to address these problems rested in decentralised, private, or hybrid regimes, or whether the 'hierarchical' force of states was required. Furthermore, attempts at addressing these policy questions also challenged contemporary orthodoxies regarding 'good governance'. For example, after three decades in which the independence of monetary policy (and thus also of central banks) was celebrated, the early 2010s gave rise to arguments that questioned whether central bank independence was still relevant as fiscal and monetary policies had become increasingly entwined. Similarly, after three decades during which 'independent regulators' were seen as a critical part of the administrative infrastructure of the state, the boundary lines of what 'independent regulation' should constitute became increasingly porous in the area of energy policy in particular. For example, political guarantees that offered minimum prices to particular energy providers (whether solar or nuclear) challenged the autonomy of regulatory decision-making.

While these problems were widely seen as being of a global nature, the individual and aggregate pressures constituted by these challenges differed across countries (see Lodge and Hood 2012). For some countries, the outlook in terms of financial austerity following the crisis of the late 2000s and early 2010s remained grim as ageing populations and limited sustainability added to the financial burden of dealing with depleted public finances. Other countries were arguably less exposed to these pressures, given their demographic profile or their sustainability needs.

At the heart of these debates are concerns about states' problem-solving capabilities. How states, markets, and communities are able to innovate within the setting of liberal democracy and capitalism to address long-term issues and vulnerabilities has been a source of continued debate since the late 1960s at least. These debates have returned to the forefront since the financial crisis and point to two further aspects. One is how three decades of supposed state reform have led to increasingly dispersed forms of governing (often called 'hollowing out'; see below). Another is the kind of institutional vulnerabilities that are caused by politico-administrative and economic decision-making structures. For example, federal systems such as that characterising Germany place different demands on political and bureaucratic actors when compared to so-called Westminster systems (Lijphart 1999). Equally, so-called liberal market economies display different innovation patterns from coordinated market economies (see Hall and Soskice 2001).

This volume contributes in a number of ways to debates regarding the problem-solving capacity of contemporary states. One contribution is to focus on how different regimes (at the international or national level) have sought to address some of the challenges noted above. Thus, this volume asks whether there have indeed been innovative interventions and how transferable these might be for other areas.

A second feature is the focus on the capacity of the state itself, in particular in terms of administrative capacity. It is often said that states are poor at innovation. Broad comparisons between dominantly state-, community-, or market-led strategies have been drawn to highlight differences in regimes and innovation cycles. However, such debates often neglect that market- or community-based systems also require bureaucracy. This volume considers what kind of administrative capacities have been required to encourage and sustain particular attempts at solving key governance problems.

A third contribution is to bring together different sectoral accounts of governance challenges. Contemporary debates have usually focused on one particular area (mostly the financial crisis, whereas the welfare literature is interested in retrenchment of the welfare state, and the global governance literature in climate change). It is, however, the cumulative challenge of financial austerity, demography, and environment that presents the key test for contemporary states. Some accounts highlight innovative governance devices without linking these to wider questions about the way in which critical problems can be overcome. Other, more upbeat, accounts point to sources of learning and innovation, whereas sceptical accounts regard contemporary states as incapable of overcoming their dependence on outside forces. Accordingly, states lack the necessary resources to innovate themselves out of the contradictions of contemporary governing in an international capitalist economic system.

This volume and its companion volume *The Governance Report 2014* (Hertie School of Governance 2014) therefore advance the debate, first, by moving towards a cross-sectoral perspective that takes into account the cumulative nature of the contemporary challenge to governance; second, by considering innovations in terms of governance that sought to add problem-solving capacity; and third, by exploring the kind of administrative capacities required to encourage and sustain innovative problem-solving.

Innovation and problem-solving capacity

The tone of this chapter's introductory paragraphs may be considered as too alarmist. However, the consequences of the financial crisis, the ageing population profile, and the implications of climate change are predicted to generate a considerable (financial) burden on states over the coming decades. Most of all, these three challenges cannot be tackled sequentially; they impact cumulatively on public finances. These demands are occurring at a time when existing problem-solving devices, whether domestic or international, are not perceived as being particularly apt at addressing these contemporary challenges. Calls for more than just 'policy as normal' have therefore become prevalent. The challenges strain the traditional problem-solving capacities of contemporary states, thus encouraging the search for solutions outside the comfort zone of established decision-making patterns.

At the same time, the search for governance innovation and thus problem-solving is often said to be troubled by features of the political process. These debates will not be unfamiliar to those acquainted with the wider field of executive politics (Lodge and Wegrich 2012a, 2012b; Lodge 2013). The literature on executive politics highlights the tensions between demands for long-term solutions within short-termist political time horizons. Similarly, tensions exist between those transboundary problems that require a degree of inter-state collaboration and the electoral dynamics that have increasingly seen the demand for a 're-nationalisation' of politics. Furthermore, tensions exist between the growing differentiation of social systems, the demand for 'decentralised' solutions, and calls for overall coordination. Finally, innovation is required as traditional problem-solving devices are under challenge, especially as the resources of traditional institutions (such as trade unions, churches, or political parties) decline.[1]

Innovation in governing approaches, therefore, has become a dominant demand as the prerequisites for traditional problem-solving devices appear to be no longer present. Innovation, of course, is a highly controversial term as it is usually associated with benevolent types of change. It is, furthermore, also debatable whether it is possible to clearly distinguish innovative from non-innovative types of change. For us, innovation denotes, at its most basic level, a degree of change that goes beyond the familiar and that is being replicated intentionally.

Innovation, defined in this way, can occur in a number of ways. One is in terms of actual problem-solving devices. For example, innovative devices include forms of ownership, funding mechanisms, or oversight arrangements. Another type of innovation is procedural, such as in the ways in which different actors ('stakeholders') are involved in co-deciding on, co-creating, and co-producing public services; one example might include the use of crowdsourcing-type mechanisms for online deliberations, also for unconventional topics, such as the use of extensive on- and offline consultation on dog law in Berlin that began in 2012 (the 'Bello Dialog'; the result of which was inconclusive). Similarly, political parties have increasingly sought to inform policy discussions by going outside their own membership.

Innovation, therefore, is discussed here at the level of policy regimes and instruments and not at the level of so-called paradigms that establish the wider context in which policy regimes and instruments are developed (see Hall 1993). Innovation is understood as an attempt at constructive and intentional problem-solving (in the substantive or procedural sense). Thus, in contrast to the literature that looks at national innovation systems, we are not interested in innovation in terms of the encouragement of new technologies per se. Instead, we are interested in innovation in the technologies of governing.

As noted, the debate between those that emphasise the possibility of innovation and problem-solving and those that are highly critical of the capacity of contemporary states to solve acute and latent crises is not one that is novel to the contemporary context. Such debates have gone through at least three generational cycles. First, during the late 1960s and 1970s, 'active' policy-making was seen as an essential ingredient in overcoming the limits of traditional policy approaches. For example, Renate Mayntz and Fritz Scharpf (1975) highlighted how 'negative coordination' within the German federal bureaucracy could be addressed through organisational devices that overcame organisational turf battles and lowest-common-denominator decision-making.

[1] The diagnosis of the decline of traditional governing institutions is not intended to represent a statement of regret.

A contrasting perspective pointed to the limitations, if not seemingly inevitable collapse, of the 'late capitalist' democratic state. A number of strands in this sceptical perspective can be distinguished. Implementation-interested research emphasised the perverse results that welfare-oriented policies had generated (Pressman and Wildavsky 1973). Later work by Scharpf (Scharpf, Reissert, and Schnabel 1976; Scharpf 1985) noted the inherent limitations generated by self-interested actors within interwoven political decision-making systems, the 'joint-decision trap' (*Politikverflechtungsfalle*). Other strands focused more on the seemingly inescapable legitimacy and organisational crises that state interventions generated in their attempts to compensate for the instabilities of capitalist economies (Offe 1972; Habermas 1973). Similarly, the need to contain the accelerating costs of welfare states was said to place ever-growing burdens on the capitalist economy, thereby creating a mutually reinforcing cycle of self-destruction (O'Connor 1973). This first generation was therefore increasingly shaped by the perception of the inability of states to 'innovate' to address economic instabilities. States were inevitably on a road to failure, doomed in their incapability to address the inherent tensions between democracy and capitalism.

The second-generation literature responded to public sector reforms during the 1980s. The labels of 'New Public Management' (NPM) (Hood 1991) and 'regulatory state' (Majone 1997) were coined to account for these observed changes. The reforms appeared to signal that states had a considerable capability to reform themselves in order to get out of the crisis of the 1970s. Privatisation, the 'agencification' of the state through the creation of executive and regulatory agencies, and the use of (quasi-)markets for the delivery of public services were seen as ways in which states innovated and sharpened their capability. In addition, potential capacities of hybrid and collaborative forms of governing were given increased prominence (McGuire and Agranoff 2011). This interest in 'collaboration' emphasised further the blurring of private and public actors in executing governance.

This innovative potential came as a surprise and challenge to those accounts that had focused on the lack of capacity only a few years earlier. For example, the UK, argued to be a basket case equipped with only very limited state capacity to drive through industrial policy (see Hayward 1976), suddenly emerged as 'hyper-innovative' in the 1980s (Moran 2003). Observers pointed to the UK's political system with its low number of veto points as a key explanatory variable for such extensive change. How the same political structure can encourage stagnation and innovation at the same time remains a matter of contention. For example, Mick Moran (2003) has traced the source for 'hyper-innovation' to the breakdown of elite consensus and growing internationalisation. The rise of the 'public management' field also offered accounts that usually addressed the possibility of overcoming governing limitations, whether in terms of strategic management (Barzelay and Campbell 2003), coordination (Bardach 1998), or the ability to define 'public value' (Moore 1995).

In contrast, others saw the state reforms of the 1980s as a 'hollowing out' during which states were selling off their 'family silver' (and too cheaply at that). Public sector reforms were seen as fatally undermining states' steering capacity: outsourcing, privatisation, and delayering of the administrative machinery were said to have reduced the capacity of the state to steer the economy, reinforcing a dependency on the private sector and enhancing the possibility of policy failure (see Dunleavy 1995; Rhodes 1997).

The context of the financial crisis and subsequent sovereign debt crisis provided the background for the third-generation debate. The immediate fallout of financial market meltdown which was characterised by bank bail-outs, industrial rescue packages, and other desperate measures seemed to point to considerable state resources and capacities. The 'hollowed out' state was seemingly far from hollow; instead it could 'fill in' rather quickly in the hour of perceived need (see Matthews 2012). However, as the Noughties turned into the Teens, the literature has become increasingly dominated by voices that highlight the dependence of the state on financial markets (Streeck 2012, 2011, 2010). States are seen as hardly responsive to any element of the electorate but the very top (Winters and Page 2009), while reforms have been 'strangulated' by a variety of institutional and political constraints (Carpenter 2010). In many ways, therefore, the debate has returned to the scepticism of the first generation (Lodge 2013): the state is incapable of necessary fundamental reform, captured by dominant interests, and structurally dependent on markets.

This much-simplified account highlights a number of themes that cut across these various generations. The more sceptical literature includes three strains. One strain emphasises states' dependence on international (financial) markets as well as their inability to compensate for the volatilities that are inherent in capitalist markets. States' resources, whether of a material kind or more generally in terms of their legitimacy, are too depleted to address the demands placed upon them. A second strain focuses on the inherent limitations due to bounded rationality in individual and organisational decision-making. Thus, ambitious large-scale calculative planning and complex programming are inherently limited and bound to generate unintended consequences (see Merton 1936; Simon 1946; Sieber 1981; Hood 2010).

A third strain focuses on the limits of hierarchical control. At its extreme, the diagnosed trend of highly differentiated, unsteerable, and closed systems describes a world where the state is not hierarchically superior to any other social system and where interventions will, at best, produce an irritant effect (Teubner 1998). More generally, targeted populations respond in often creative ways to intended policy interventions. One strategy is therefore to rely on 'reflexivity' by setting the appropriate framework conditions, enabling organisations and systems to reflect on themselves in ways that lead to beneficial results overall. This has given rise to ideas regarding 'regulated self-regulation' and 'meta-governance'.

In contrast, others have suggested that capacities within political–administrative systems (or states) exist in order to come up with innovative problem-solving approaches. These accounts point to the potential resources that can be utilised when admitting to the inherent limits of administration. For example, the field of public management illustrates the importance of collaborative and communicative 'communities of practice' (Wenger 1999), the significance of strengthening 'mindfulness' (Weick and Roberts 1993) that might turn organisations into 'high reliability organisations' (Frederickson and La Porte 2002), and various learning, lesson-drawing, and extrapolation strategies (Rose 1991; Bardach 2004). The capacity of individual policy entrepreneurs or collaborative decision-making systems to overcome widely diagnosed challenges of governing has been stressed (Bardach 1998; Barzelay and Campbell 2003). In contrast, Pressman and Wildavsky's (1973) basic insight was to 'keep it simple' and 'direct'. Others have placed their faith in the power of technological change, especially information technology (see Dunleavy et al. 2006).

A second upbeat argument acknowledges that political authority is inherently negotiated and mediated. Ideas stressing cooperative administration, informal networks, and collaborative governance have suggested that problem-solving capacity can be enhanced by linking state and non-state actors. This allows for the utilisation of private and para-public institutions' capacities and resources. Such strategies require organisations that are capable and willing to co-govern, as noted in the literature on (liberal) corporatism. The failed attempts of western European tripartite agreements to deal with stagflation during the 1970s have illustrated how demanding these prerequisites are.

This volume is therefore situated within a set of debates that have regained increased urgency and currency as a result of the financial crisis. Innovation, in the sense of the utilisation of non-familiar solutions, is considered within wider debates that critically engage with the problem-solving capacity of the contemporary state. Still, we are not claiming that one innovation is more likely to be effective than others. For some, 'think big' solutions are the only way to deal with the likely impending peril of climate change, whereas others argue the case of small decentralised systems, whether in terms of localised decision-making systems (Ostrom 1990) or in terms of market-based decisions relying on the price signal. Instead, we are interested in the ways in which the resources of the state, in all their variety, are being utilised and how these resources are linked to particular administrative capacities (see Wise, Wegrich, and Lodge 2014 for examples). Focusing on capacities in this way adds an additional dimension to contemporary debates about problem-solving capacity.

The rest of this chapter prepares the ground for the subsequent contributions by looking at two key aspects. First, we consider four administrative capacities. In an age in which state and non-state actors are involved in governing (at local, national, and transnational levels), it is essential to recognise the different ways in which administrative capacities are required to address governance challenges, and how the reliance on particular mixes of administrative capacities triggers its own (unintended) consequences. In addition, any discussion of administrative capacities needs to consider the ways in which this capacity is exercised. Thus, the discussion in the following part moves to a consideration of four policy instruments.

Administrative capacities

Much attention has been paid to substantive and procedural policy innovations. Much less interest has been channelled into the kind of capacities that are required to 'launch' and sustain particular types of governance innovations. Such concerns about capacities link to earlier debates about the supposed 'hollowing out' of the state and whether the state, after a period of 'dispersion', has lost its central steering capacity.

The literature on state capacities hardly enters the territory of considering different types of capacity. One exception is Matthews (2012), who distinguishes between framing, controlling, and delivery capacities: The state may have 'lost' its capacity to deliver goods and services directly, but may have 'strengthened' its capacities in terms of controlling powers instead. Similarly, the argument that states have the capacity to frame debates has been widely contested. For example, the power of social media and the ability of alternative media channels to circumvent any attempt by the state to maintain a central nodal position in the trafficking of information have been used to suggest that the state has lost its central framing capacity.

This section discusses four types of administrative capacity that are central to any attempt at problem-solving, namely delivery, coordination, regulatory, and analytical capacities. These capacities can be differently organised, financed, and staffed, and they will vary according to functional needs and to the dominance of particular doctrines over others. Any debate about administrative capacity needs to consider these four capacities. Furthermore, any (mix of) policy intervention strategy or instrument requires an understanding of the required administrative capacities that enable these instruments to have their intended effect.

Delivery capacity

Delivery capacity is defined as the capability to 'make things happen'. It is therefore directly related to the resources available to ensure that populations receive services, that revenues are extracted, and that public order is maintained.

Debates about delivery capacity relate to the long-standing literature on street-level bureaucrats, their (discretionary) resources, and coping mechanisms (Mechanic 1962; Lipsky 1980; Hawkins 1984). Whereas the basic questions regarding the discretionary application of power by such street-level actors have arguably not changed, there are a number of ways in which the context in which this power is exercised has indeed changed. One is the way in which the status of street-level bureaucrats has transformed, given the rise of outsourced social services in particular. Another contextual change is that street-level bureaucrats have become increasingly exposed to different logics of action. For example, the rise of performance management and other managerial tools has arguably given rise to a growing demand for 'accounting' for performance and the need to benchmark activities. Similarly, a growing internationalisation of policy agendas and approaches (for example, in education or food safety) has meant that street-level bureaucracies are increasingly connected to international policy developments. Finally, technology has also challenged the traditional discretion of street-level bureaucracy, whether in the context of IT-driven automation of processes or the growing observability of discretionary behaviours (with devices such as GPS or small cameras).

Moreover, delivery capacity is about indirect and background powers to 'make things happen'. When private services fail, then public administration is required to step in to ensure that the trains keep running (for example, this is the case in the UK when railway franchises fail financially), to maintain prisons, or to ensure that elderly people are receiving care. In other words, delivery capacity is not just about the people actually 'doing work'; it is also about the resources that are deployed to ensure that certain services are at least maintained when private providers fail or are found wanting.

Regulatory capacity

As noted in the literature on the 'rise' of the regulatory state, one of the key trends in contemporary government has been the growth of oversight bodies and functions at a time of overall reduction in civil service numbers (see Hood et al. 1999). For some, the ever-growing expansion of synoptic control has penetrated ever more domains that have previously been outside the grasp of the state, such as in those areas formerly reserved to professional self-regulation. For others, the rise in importance of the control capacity has gone hand in hand with the idea that states should separate production (or delivery) from control functions.

More broadly, the control capacity of the state is said to be undergoing a number of challenges. One is due to the internationalisation of business activities and the complexity of production processes. This has made the regulation of business an ever more critical part of the 'competitive advantage' of states; in other words, the 'commitment problem' in regulation, namely, how regulated fields are insulated from governments that are likely to suffer from time inconsistency, has become more salient.

At the same time, the 'agency problem', namely, the way in which regulated activities can be controlled, has become more prominent. One reason is the complexity of the regulatory process. For example, in food safety, the regulatory problem of having to move from 'sniff and poke' to far more laboratory-intensive strategies has also triggered a shift towards a management-based regulatory strategy in which firms themselves primarily self-regulate critical production aspects under the supervision of the state. This has required regulation to be able to detect the capacity and motivation of companies to practise internal control, as well as an understanding of the actual substance itself. The difficulties of such a regulatory strategy were evident in various food-related regulatory 'scandals'. Indeed, the highly complex production chains in food production and the subsequent problems in detecting sources of contamination were illustrated during the E. coli outbreak in Germany in 2012. In this case, contamination was initially and wrongly blamed on Spanish cucumbers. Similarly, the 2013 European-wide scandal when products were found to contain horsemeat highlighted how differentiated the food production chain had become.

A second challenge to the regulatory capacity of the state has been the problem of maintaining its capacity in an age when international business is able to poach regulatory staff and where regulators have trouble retaining institutional memory and expertise. Such problems with control capacity have been widespread. Lacking expertise has been blamed for failures related to the initial 'contract', while lack of institutional memory is blamed for failings in the ongoing oversight of regulated activities. Such continued oversight is particularly challenged in the light of internationalised business activities and budget cuts that affect enforcement capacities. Similar problems regularly occur in procurement, especially in large projects where 'delayered' bureaucracies face highly concentrated and well-resourced private companies.

A third regulatory capacity challenge relates to the inherent dispersion of functions and competencies. Dispersion of regulatory functions raises boundary-spanning issues as to how different regulatory bodies execute their tasks when regulatory regimes are fragmented across different bodies, often with different jurisdictional backgrounds. Furthermore, there are debates about the 'appropriate' organisation of control capacity. The past three decades have emphasised the importance of 'independence', often contrasting the value of independence with the demand for more accountability (to the political domain in particular). However, the financial crisis in particular has raised concerns about whether 'independence' should be seen as a value per se. It has also challenged one further 'orthodoxy', namely, that private organisations are capable of and motivated in policing their own behaviour and that therefore the state could concentrate on the 'regulation of self-regulation'. Instead, the financial crisis highlighted that private organisations (i.e. banks) were not capable of controlling their highly complex operations. More broadly, studies elsewhere noted the intra-organisational problems of relying on organisational self-control (Gunningham and Sinclair 2009).

Coordination capacity

Among the many long-standing concerns in public administration is the issue of coordination. Particular coordination problems arise from 'multi-organisational sub-optimisation' in which different agencies fail to communicate (Hood 1974), and from 'negative coordination' (or lowest-common-denominator decision-making) in government where concern with bureaucratic jurisdiction and turf outweighs any interest in tackling the actual problem at hand. Dispersion due to internationalisation, decentralisation, and agencification has arguably further aggravated the issue of coordination capacity. It is therefore not surprising that one of the key themes of the so-called 'post-NPM' literature has been the re-centralisation of governmental bodies in order to advance central governments' capacities to coordinate.

Coordination capacity goes beyond the organisation of the executive and the allocation of formal capacities to bang heads together. Coordination capacities apply to those areas where collaborative governance is supposed to take place and where, therefore, coordination is about bringing together and aligning organisations from different backgrounds under often tricky conditions. Moreover, coordination capacities are also about the competencies of individuals. For example, the literature on leadership has increasingly focused on the importance of 'boundary-spanning', i.e. the ability of individuals to be able to access different social systems, and to bring these dispersed and diverse forms of expertise and experience together. In short, therefore, coordination capacity is not just about the ability to hierarchically impose ways of 'working together', but it is about a non-hierarchical facilitating role (or 'orchestrating' role). Furthermore, coordination capacity is about individual capabilities to operate in dispersed systems, in terms of both being regarded as a 'partner', but also being able to navigate the difficult issues that arise in mediating agreements.

Analytical capacity

The above three capacities have attracted widespread interest in a variety of literatures in executive politics, public administration, and public management. Arguably less attention has been paid to analytical capacity, namely, the way in which executive governments are informed about future projections and current developments.

It is somewhat trivial to state that governments require information. Traditional sources of policy expertise, i.e. civil servants, are said to be increasingly contested, for example, by the internationalisation of expertise. Even if it is questionable whether any national bureaucracy may have had 'best in world' knowledge about a particular policy issue at any one time, the past three decades have challenged the idea of 'experts in government'. This trend places demands on the way in which executives organise their analytical capacities. One demand is the boundary-spanning need to bring different sources of expertise into government. The other is about ensuring transparency and legitimacy in the light of popular scepticism regarding the application of knowledge, often in the face of competing claims.

Other developments present further challenges to the way in which analytical capacity is organised. One is the growing distrust by the political class of traditional sources of advice, especially the sitting army of bureaucrats. This has raised the profile of specialist advisers and other alternative forms of receiving advice on policy and wider issues. Another trend has been the rise of the think-tank world and consultancies seeking to offer 'public governance'-related advice. These offer alternative sources of information, while some are more interested in ensuring re-election than others. To what extent any of these trends are fundamentally challenging the way in which governments access and digest information is an empirical question. However, similar to the dashed hopes of the 1970s when West European national governments were said to be dreaming of heightened analytical capacities through the creation of evaluation units close to the heart of the executive, the demand for analytical capacity and the long-standing wish for 'evidence-based policy' raise issues about how such analytical capacity should be organised, how it is financed, and how information is being accessed and disseminated (Parrado, this volume).

Summarising the four capacities

As noted, these administrative capacities are at the heart of public problem-solving. The extent to which they take on one form but not another, and are critical for addressing particular issues, depends on circumstances. However, whatever the particular governance issue, these four capacities are required, and thus any discussion about governance innovation needs to take administrative capacities seriously. In other words, administrative capacity, as understood in this chapter, operates at two levels. At one level, it points to inherent requirements that are at the heart of any policy domain. At a separate level, these four capacities also point to the need to consider the ability of bureaucratic organisations to deliver in an age, as noted above, where such capacities have become increasingly contested.

At the same time, it is difficult to 'measure' these four capacities, as noted by the various chapters in this volume. There are no agreed output or outcome indicators that would point to the presence of particular administrative capacities. Even where it may be possible to measure outputs and outcomes, such as tax offices as an example of so-called production agencies (Wilson 1989), the measurement of these indicators tells us little about how capable the actual organisations are. Similarly, knowing particular input numbers, such as the number of analysts in government or street-level bureaucrats delivering public services or inspecting businesses, offers some comparative insights about the availability of particular resources, but does not tell us about capacity per se. Instead, the debate about administrative capacities has to focus on the kind of demands that particular decision-making systems and policy-instrument innovations place on bureaucracy.

Policy instrument innovation

As noted, it is not sufficient to look at administrative capacities in isolation. Instead, in order to extrapolate from the various chapters that follow this introduction, it is necessary to consider the substantive ways in which resources are being utilised, namely through the use of distinct policy instruments. In other words, we are interested in the ways in which state and non-state actors have innovated and sought to address particular challenges. This, then, allows the discussion to reflect on the kind of administrative capacities that are required to promote and sustain such innovative practices.

As 'informal institutions', instrument choice is inherently about political values and conflicts. At the same time, the choice of (mix of) instruments also shapes the wider setting of politics. Furthermore, developing a generic typology of instruments reveals the inherent resources of the state. Following Hood (Hood 1983; Hood and Margetts 2007), these resources are information, authority, finance, and organisation.[2] The rest of this section sets out four broad instruments or tools that are based on these particular resources of the state. We argue that by focusing on innovation in these instruments (and in a

[2] We use a simplified account of Hood's (1983) NATO scheme and do not utilise the original terms nodality, authority, treasure, and organisation.

combination thereof), we can learn about problem-solving capacity. Four different types of policy instruments can be distinguished:

- **Information**: This set of instruments emphasises the importance of benchmarking and other types of 'information'-driven interventions that are supposed to steer behaviours. This area is said to have become increasingly important in the age of 'performance management'. Similarly, international ranking exercises have been used at the national level to encourage policy change, as perceived 'poor' performance is seen as encouraging reform developments.
- **Authority**: This set of instruments points to issues of control and oversight. Again, the area of authority and control has gained increasing significance in terms of international agreements and conventions. Similarly, at the domestic level, there has been a growing prominence of authority as witnessed in the rise of devices such as impact assessments and other 'meta-instruments'.
- **Finance**: It is often said that the past three decades have witnessed a decline in the direct use of public finance to change behaviours or make investments. However, finance still is a critical aspect of state intervention, and there have also been various 'innovative' schemes to facilitate investment, such as the use of 'public–private partnerships' or the use of private ownership more directly.
- **Organisation**: The past three decades are said to have seen a growth in indirect organisation, whether in terms of agencification or in terms of the rise of 'non-state' actors providing organisational resources for the delivery of public services.

Table 1.1 illustrates these four types of interventions and how these generic terms can be applied to examples of substantive and procedural instruments.

Table 1.1. Four policy instruments

Information	Finance
Substantive: Use of communication and other informational tools to change behaviours *Procedural*: Reliance on decentralised adjustment processes in light of benchmarking	*Substantive*: Payment and other monetary incentive systems *Procedural*: Use of third parties for distribution of financial resources
Authority	**Organisation**
Substantive: Exercise of regulatory and other oversight powers, need for registration *Procedural*: Procedural provisions, 'deck-stacking'	*Substantive*: Use of staff, direct provision of services and types of public organisation *Procedural*: Creation of fora for consultation and decision-making across different participants

The way in which these substantive and procedural instruments are used will depend on dominant ideas and functional demands that are determined by specific problem constellations. Instruments will differ across settings. For example, settings can be distinguished between those areas where the state abandons its responsibilities due to lack of resources,[3] those where the dominant form of engagement is in collaboration with third parties (such as private or charitable organisations) in the delivery of public services, or those areas characterised by the use of market-based mechanisms.

The relationship between policy instruments and administrative capacities is twofold. On the one hand, (combinations of) policy instruments require particular (mixes of) administrative capacities. Thus, any discussion about sustainable innovation at the policy instrument level needs to consider the kind of underlying administrative capacities that are likely to support the particular innovation. On the other hand, the way in which administrative capacities are enacted requires a mix of policy instruments as well. For example, analytical capacity may be ensured through the direct use of organisation, through the use of funding, or through the use of information collection. In other words, by viewing instruments as resources, we are able to explore how different resources are used to address (or attempt to address) particular governance challenges.

However, looking at innovation in policy instrument is not without its potential criticisms. First of all, it requires agreement as to what an innovation is. Second, any attempt at classifying innovations is confronted with a large number of diverse experiences, unique contextual constellations, and other peculiar conditions (Salamon 2002). Third, any attempt at a more generic typology or classification will be faced with criticisms regarding oversimplification. However, it allows us to explore the specific interventions that feature in the various chapters that follow.

Conclusion

This chapter has sought to develop three themes. First, it has emphasised the importance of focusing on problem-solving capacity of the state by highlighting three areas of challenge in particular, namely that of the financial crisis, that of climate change and sustainability, and that related to demographic

[3] Debates about voluntary abandonment to turn coastal areas into wetlands involved Fox Beach, New York state (see Wright 2013). See also the front-line abandonment due to financial crisis-induced redundancies in Camden, New Jersey (Zernike 2012).

change. These three background conditions place considerable requirements on states and demand a search for sustainable policy approaches. The debate about innovative forms of problem-solving, and the likelihood of such strategies achieving intended and effective outcomes, has witnessed constant attention over the past three decades.

In order to move beyond these debates that either deny the autonomy of the state to overcome structural constraints or stress the internal capacities to develop novel forms, this chapter has stressed another two separate but related themes. The first is to suggest that any domain requires administrative capacities in four key areas: analytical, coordination, regulatory, and delivery. Regardless of how these capacities are organised, these capacities are essential within organisations as well as domain-wide in order to address governance challenges. Second, governance innovation relates to the deployment of four key resources, information, authority, organisation, and finance. Again, variations exist as to how these resources are deployed in terms of policy instruments. However, any discussion about the problem-solving capacities of the state needs to address the mutual interdependence of administrative capacities and policy instruments. Therefore, when talking about innovative governance, we need to consider not just the manner in which ways of problem-solving have been changing, but also the ways in which administrative capacities are being addressed (or not).

Accordingly, the rest of the volume seeks to address these questions by looking at three distinct concerns. First, this volume turns to administrative capacities, the way in which these capacities have become stretched, and how they have been adjusted, given the changing conditions. These chapters also consider how the four capacities might be measured, given that simple and straightforward output or outcome measurements might not be available.

Second, this volume looks at the way in which different states have addressed particular governance challenges. The primary concern here is with the way in which states have responded. Particular attention is paid to innovation at the level of policy instrument and the required administrative capacities, without ignoring how different state and economic market structures might facilitate the use of some forms of policy instruments rather than others.

Third, this volume recognises that governance capacities also lie outside the boundaries of the state. The literature has increasingly highlighted that states are not autonomous; instead they are tied into a network of public and private governance systems that cut across boundaries.

References

Bardach, E. (1998). *Getting Agencies to Work Together: The Practice and Theory of Managerial Craftsmanship*. Washington, DC: Brookings Institution Press.

Bardach, E. (2004). 'The Extrapolation Problem: How Can We Learn from the Experience of Others?' *Journal of Policy Analysis and Management*, 23(3): 205–20.

Barzelay, M., and Campbell, C. (2003). *Preparing for the Future: Strategic Planning in the U.S. Air Force*. Washington, DC: Brookings Institution Press.

Carpenter, D. (2010). 'Institutional Strangulation: Bureaucratic Politics and Financial Reform in the Obama Administration', *Perspectives on Politics*, 8(3): 824–46.

Deutscher Bundestag [website]. Deutscher Bundestag: Enquete-Kommission 'Wachstum, Wohlstand, Lebensqualität—Wege zu nachhaltigem Wirtschaften und gesellschaftlichem Fortschritt in der Sozialen Marktwirtschaft'. Retrieved from <http://webarchiv.bundestag.de/archive/2013/1212/bundestag/gremien/enquete/wachstum/index.html> (accessed 16 May 2014).

Dunleavy, P. (1995). 'Policy Disasters: Explaining the UK's Record', *Public Policy and Administration*, 10(2): 52–70.

Dunleavy, P., Margetts, H., Bastow, S., and Tinkler, J. (2006). 'NPM is Dead, Long live Digital Era Governance', *Journal of Public Administration Research and Theory*, 16(3): 467–94.

Ernst & Young [website]. Government and Public Sector. Retrieved from <http://www.ey.com/UK/en/Industries/Government–Public-Sector> (accessed 15 January 2014).

Frederickson, H. G., and La Porte, T. R. (2002). 'Airport Security, High Reliability, and the Problem of Rationality', *Public Administration Review*, 62: 33–43.

Gunningham, N., and Sinclair, D. (2009). 'Organizational Trust and the Limits of Management-Based Regulation', *Law & Society Review*, 43(4): 865–900.

Habermas, J. (1973). *Legitimationsprobleme im Spätkapitalismus*. Frankfurt a. M.: Suhrkamp.

Hall, P. A. (1993). 'Policy Paradigms, Social Learning, and the State: The Case of Economic Policymaking in Britain', *Comparative Politics*, 25(3): 275–96.

Hall, P. A., and Soskice, D. W. (2001). 'An Introduction to Varieties of Capitalism', in P. A. Hall, and D. W. Soskice (eds), *Varieties of Capitalism: The Institutional Foundations of Comparative Advantage*. Oxford: Oxford University Press, 1–70.

Hawkins, K. (1984). *Environment and Enforcement: Regulation and the Social Definition of Pollution*. Oxford: Clarendon Press.

Hayward, J. (1976). 'Institutional Inertia and Political Impetus in France and Britain', *European Journal of Political Research*, 4(4): 341–59.

Hertie School of Governance (ed.) (2014). *The Governance Report 2014*. Oxford: Oxford University Press.

Hood, C. (1974). 'Administrative Diseases: Some Types of Dysfunctionality in Administration' *Public Administration*, 52(4): 439–54.

Hood, C. (1983). *The Tools of Government*. Basingstoke: Macmillan.

Hood, C. (1991). 'A Public Management for All Seasons?' *Public Administration*, 69(1): 3–19.

Hood, C. (2010). *The Blame Game: Spin, Bureaucracy, and Self-Preservation in Government.* Princeton: Princeton University Press.

Hood, C., and Margetts, H. (2007). *The Tools of Government in the Digital Age*. Basingstoke: Palgrave Macmillan.

Hood, C., Scott, C., James, O., Jones, G., and Travers, T. (1999). *Regulation inside Government: Waste-Watchers, Quality Police, and Sleaze-Busters*. Oxford, New York: Oxford University Press.

Howell, W. L. (2013). *Global Risks 2013*. 8th edn. Geneva: World Economic Forum.

Kock, F., Bruckner, J., and Schaible, J. (2012) [website]. Bevölkerungsentwicklung—Wie der demografische Wandel Deutschland verändert. Retrieved from <http://www.sueddeutsche.de/leben/bevoelkerungsentwicklung-wie-der-demografische-wandel-deutschland-veraendert-1.1486334> (accessed 15 January 2014).

Lijphart, A. (1999). *Patterns of Democracy: Government Forms and Performance in Thirty-Six Countries*. New Haven: Yale University Press.

Lipsky, M. (1980). *Street-Level Bureaucracy: Dilemmas of the Individual in Public Services*. New York: Russell Sage Foundation.

Lodge, M. (2013). 'Crisis, Resources and the State: Executive Politics in the Age of the Depleted State', *Political Studies Review*, 11(3): 378–90.

Lodge, M., and Hood, C. (2012). 'Into the Age of Multiple Austerities? Public Management and Public Service Bargains across OECD Countries', *Governance*, 25(1): 79–101.

Lodge, M., and Wegrich, K. (2012a). 'Introduction: Executive Politics in Times of Crisis', in M. Lodge, and K. Wegrich (eds), *Executive Politics in Times of Crisis*. Basingstoke: Palgrave Macmillan, 1–18.

Lodge, M., and Wegrich, K. (2012b). 'Conclusion: Executive Politics in a Changing Climate', in M. Lodge, and K. Wegrich (eds), *Executive Politics in Times of Crisis*. Basingstoke: Palgrave Macmillan, 284–96.

Majone, G. (1997). 'From the Positive to the Regulatory State: Causes and Consequences of Changes in the Mode of Governance', *Journal of Public Policy*, 17(2): 139–67.

Matthews, F. (2012). 'Governance, Governing, and the Capacity of Executives in Times of Crisis', in M. Lodge, and K. Wegrich (eds), *Executive Politics in Times of Crisis*. Basingstoke: Palgrave Macmillan 217–38.

Mayntz, R., and Scharpf, F. W. (1975). *Policy-Making in the German Federal Bureaucracy*. Amsterdam: Elsevier.

McKinsey & Company [website]. McKinsey Center for Government from the Public Sector Practice. Retrieved from <http://www.mckinsey.com/client_service/public_sector/mckinsey_center_for_government> (accessed 15 January 2014).

McGuire, M., and Agranoff, R. (2011). 'The Limitations of Public Management Networks', *Public Administration*, 89(2): 265–84.

Mechanic, D. (1962). 'Sources of Power of Lower Participants in Organizations', *Administrative Science Quarterly*, 7(3): 349–64.

Merton, R. K. (1936). 'The Unanticipated Consequences of Purposive Social Action', *American Sociological Review*, 1(6): 894–904.

Moore, M. H. (1995). *Creating Public Value: Strategic Management in Government*. Cambridge: Harvard University Press.

Moran, M. (2003). *The British Regulatory State: High Modernism and Hyper-Innovation*. Oxford, New York: Oxford University Press.

O'Connor, J. (1973). *The Fiscal Crisis of the State*. London: Macmillan.

OECD (Organisation for Economic Co-operation and Development) [website]. OECD Observatory of Public Sector Innovation. Retrieved from <http://www.oecd.org/gov/public-innovation/observatory-public-sector-innovation.htm> (accessed 15 January 2014).

Offe, C. (1972). *Strukturprobleme des kapitalistischen Staates*. Frankfurt a. M.: Suhrkamp.

Ostrom, E. (1990). *Governing the Commons: The Evolution of Institutions for Collective Action*. Cambridge: Cambridge University Press.

Pressman, J. L., and Wildavsky, A. B. (1973). *Implementation: How Great Expectations in Washington Are Dashed in Oakland*. Berkeley: University of California Press.

PricewaterhouseCoopers [website]. Government & Public Sector. Retrieved from <http://www.pwc.co.uk/government-public-sector/index.jhtml> (accessed 15 January 2014).

Rhodes, R. A. W. (1997). *Understanding Governance: Policy Networks, Governance, Reflexivity, and Accountability*. Buckingham: Open University Press.

Rose, R. (1991). 'What is Lesson-Drawing?' *Journal of Public Policy*, 11(1): 3–30.

Salamon, L. M. (ed.) (2002). *The Tools of Government: A Guide to the New Governance*. Oxford, New York: Oxford University Press.

Scharpf, F. W. (1985). 'Die Politikverflechtungs-Falle. Europäische Integration und deutscher Föderalismus im Vergleich', *Politische Vierteljahresschrift*, 26(4): 323–56.

Scharpf, F. W., Reissert, B., and Schnabel, F. (1976). *Politikverflechtung: Theorie und Empirie des kooperativen Föderalismus in der Bundesrepublik*. Kronberg/Ts: Scriptor-Verlag.

Sieber, S. D. (1981). *Fatal Remedies: The Ironies of Social Intervention*. New York: Plenum Press.

Simon, H. A. (1946). 'The Proverbs of Administration', *Public Administration Review*, 6(1): 53–67.

Streeck, W. (2010). 'Noch so ein Sieg und wir sind verloren: Der Nationalstaat nach der Finanzkrise', *Leviathan*, 38(2): 159–73.

Streeck, W. (2011). 'The Crisis in Context: Democratic Capitalism and its Contraditions', MPIfG Discussion Paper 11/15. Cologne: Max-Planck-Insitut für Gesellschaftsforschung.

Streeck, W. (2012). 'Markets and Peoples: Democratic Capitalism and European Integration', *New Left Review*, 73: 63–71.

Teubner, G. (1998). 'Legal Irritants: Good Faith in British Law or How Unifying Law Ends Up in New Differences', *Modern Law Review*, 61(1): 11–32.

U.S. Global Change Research Program [website]. 'Federal Advisory Committee Draft Climate Assessment'. Retrieved from <http://ncadac.globalchange.gov/> (accessed 15 January 2014).

Weick, K. E., and Roberts, K. H. (1993). 'Collective Mind in Organizations: Heedful Interrelating on Flight Decks', *Administrative Science Quarterly*, 38(3): 357–81.

Wenger, E. (1999). *Communities of Practice*. Cambridge: Cambridge University Press.

Wilson, J. Q. (1989). *Bureaucracy: What Government Agencies Do and Why They Do It.* New York: Basic Books.

Winters, J. A., and Page, B. I. (2009). 'Oligarchy in the United States?' *Perspectives on Politics*, 7(4): 731–51.

Wise, R., Wegrich, K., and Lodge, M. (2014). 'Governance Innovations', in Hertie School of Governance (ed.), *The Governance Report 2014*. Oxford: Oxford University Press, 77–109.

World Economic Forum [website]. Global Risks. Retrieved from <http://www.weforum.org/issues/global-risks> (accessed 15 January 2014).

Wright, R. (2013). 'Storm-Hit Staten Island Throws in Towel', *Financial Times*, 11 February: 6.

Zernike, K. (2012). 'To Fight Crime, a Poor City Will Trade in Its Police', *New York Times*, 29 September: A1.

Part I
Administrative Capacities

2

Delivery Capacity

Peter Hupe and Michael Hill

Introduction

Once upon a time, the post was delivered twice a day. The postman, who was often a woman, knew you by name, and you knew him or her. Post deliverers carried their post, bundles of letters and packages, in a large leather bag. They operated from the local post office. In general, you were happy to see them approaching your door. In the face of bad news, they often spoke comforting words.

The concept of delivery

This picture may sound nostalgic. Yet the reality it describes is one from a recent past. It is clear that much has since changed. The description invites at least two observations. First, the practice of postal delivery is different nowadays. In the Netherlands, the post comes more than once a day at varying times. Several companies are charged with a postal delivery task and the locations from which they operate are unknown. Because a diversity of personnel is being employed, not only the contents of the post but also by whom it will be delivered are a daily surprise. Second, as a result of the new reality described above, the word 'delivery' has proliferated. In a style guide British civil servants are warned against a too liberal usage of the word. 'Pizzas, post and services are delivered—not abstract concepts like "improvements" or "priorities"' (Gov.uk 2013). Therefore a clarification of the meaning of the concept is needed here.

In its everyday usage in the English language, the term 'delivery' indicates an essentially late stage in an output process. When speaking of the delivery of letters, the term refers to an activity that has been preceded by posting, collecting, and sorting. However, in its contemporary usage, 'delivery' encompasses a wider range of activities. It is often synonymous with 'administration' in the politics/administration distinction, with 'implementation' in the stages picture of the policy process, and also with 'performance' in the study of public management. That being so, we use the term in this chapter while looking at what happens where public policies are being implemented.

The example of postal delivery suggests a simple process, focused on a straightforward product of a policy. Extending that assumption to other policy issues involves what Stone (2002) has called 'the rationality project', in which the model of policy-making is a production model: 'policy is created in a fairly orderly sequence of stages, almost as if on an assembly line' (Stone 2002: 10). In the same way, Brodkin (1990: 109) identifies a prevalent view of bureaucracy 'as [the] production agent for social policies established by authoritative policy-making institutions'.

However, such an approach can be misleading. In their book *Beyond Delivery*, Peck and 6 (2006) challenge the idea that policy delivery is essentially simple. Translating a policy into action may be complex. A 'stage' in the policy process is involved where, in effect, street-level actors ordered to 'do as they are told' may not be readily identifiable. By the same token, designing a delivery system may be difficult. There may be a continuing interaction between aspects of the policy formation and implementation parts of the policy process. This consideration is important for what we have to say below, and an issue to which we return at the end of the chapter.

In this sense we need to recognise that policies differ in terms of *what* they deliver. Here both Lowi's policy typology and 'instrument choice' theory help us to recognise differences (Lowi 1972; Hood 1986, 2007; Howlett 1991). These categorisations indicate that delivering post or providing cash benefits is to be seen as a very different activity from delivering education or health services. It can be acknowledged that, in a certain sense, regulation is also 'delivered'. Given these considerations, we stress the need to see delivery in terms of a continuum, with strictly rule-based delivery at one end and high levels of discretion at the other. In real-world policy processes, both extremes of this continuum are often absent. Policy-makers are faced with questions regarding where to establish rule-based output goals, and where to allow discretionary power. Hence it should be noted that usage of the term 'delivery' inevitably mixes simple and complex aspects of implementation as the final part of the policy process.

After this examination of what we mean by delivery this chapter continues with an exploration of what may be meant by the term *delivery capacity*. The distinction between rules and discretion is used to outline factors that may affect that capacity. Delegated delivery is looked at, highlighting its widespread incidence and its effect on both vertical and horizontal inter-organisational relationships. Next, the empirical reality of the modern world is addressed 'beyond the Weberian model'. In this third section we particularly examine the factors influencing forms of delegation in the context of the increasing importance of contracting processes. The 'personalisation agenda' places individual citizens in the role of public service purchasers, a development beyond the original notion of delegation as an inter-organisation issue. In the fourth section we elaborate on aspects of the discussion so far, emphasising issues of policy contingencies, institutional arrangements, and ideology. We do so by focusing on the many factors influencing change in two specific policy areas: support for unemployed people and the provision of health and social care. Delivery is not just a matter of selecting the appropriate technology; rather, it must be seen as a political issue. This view is underlined in the concluding section.

Delivery and delegation

Delivery capacity

If what is to be delivered differs, so too must *delivery capacity*. Questions about the delivery capacity of a postal system can be explored principally in terms of the availability and functioning of forms of comparatively simple technology (vehicles and sorting machines) and staffing. Accusations about a lack of delivery capacity then centre upon comparatively straightforward resourcing issues. Alternative delivery modes may be chosen, although they vary little from one another.

However, even in this case the issues surrounding delivery capacity are not independent of policy issues. National letter delivery services are alternatives to private ways of delivering messages (of which there are many possibilities today). There are obvious political questions about whether there is a case for state-provided, and perhaps subsidised, services. If, then, there is a capacity shortfall, the response may not only be, as suggested above, to provide better resourcing, but to let the service wither using delay as a form of rationing, and perhaps as an incentive to alternative providers.

If, however, what is to be delivered is complicated, then these questions surrounding delivery capacity are more difficult given the greater range of possibilities of both policy responses and choice of alternative delivery modes. Whilst there is extensive controversy about delivery modes—particularly about delegated delivery where forms of privatisation are involved—there is an absence of systematic evaluation of the desirability or strength of the particular modes.

Variation in policy delivery may be the product of error or even deliberate rule bending. In all cases, however, it is the result of more or less constrained actions by various actors in given contexts. As such, discretion 'as used' needs to be distinguished from discretion 'as granted'. For any systematic examination of reasons for variation there is a need to analyse policies in terms of the extent to which they allow for discretionary action by actors who are supposed to deliver them. There is an extensive literature about discretion in public policy delivery, especially driven by a normative argument that discretion should be minimised. Davis (1969: 27) argues: 'Our governmental and legal systems are saturated with excessive discretionary power which needs to be confined, structured and checked.' That position, particularly taken by legal scholars like Davis, is countered by two kinds of arguments. One is similarly normative, stressing that discretion is important in fitting policy to cases in the real world. The other concentrates rather more upon the feasibility of tight regulation, particularly where policy delivery activities are relatively invisible to management systems and depend upon expert judgements. The two arguments against strong regulation and narrow discretion come together in the defence of professionalism. There, concerns about trusting those who use expertise to deliver policy appear as arguments in favour of high levels of discretion.

Delegated delivery

While some forms of delegation, especially to for-profit providers, draw particular attention in contemporary political debates, it is important to recognise that delegation of policy delivery is ubiquitous and has a long history. Here we concentrate on the issues around modern forms of delegation which can be described in purchaser/provider terms: central state-made policy delivered by other bodies (local state, for-profit, or voluntary).

Delegation may be conceptualised in terms of the concerns of two or more actors in the delivery process, who are connected vertically in the hierarchy (for example: education department—local education authority—school). In this respect, Pressman and Wildavsky's classic analysis (1973) of deficits in long 'vertical' delivery chains applies. In a delegation process there may also be horizontal organisational relationships involved. This is the case inasmuch as delivery depends upon collaboration between two or more parallel organisations (for example: hospital—community health service—social care authority). In the conclusion of their empirical study, Smith et al. argue: 'When the problem is amorphous and there are multiple agencies involved in implementation, the ability to deliver can be severely compromised' (2011: 998).

There are some interesting issues here about forces driving towards, or away from, centralisation. Barbieri and Salvatore argue that '(w)hen it is difficult to monitor or measure the performance of the service delivery, governments increase the use of joint contracting and internal service production' (2010: 360; see also Brown and Potoski 2003).

Relevant here too is the 'territorial justice' agenda—colloquially the 'postcode lottery'—pushing delegated systems towards uniformity. At the same time, concerns about the productivity of public agencies inspire the quest for organisations that may deliver services more efficiently than government departments (see Dunleavy and Carrera 2013).

There is a related question concerning whether delegation to voluntary organisations is different from delegation to for-profit organisations. In the United Kingdom it has been argued that where any form of competitive tendering is involved, an expectation of a 'level playing field' leads voluntary organisations to behave very similarly to for-profit ones. Elsewhere, however, particularly where there are very well-established patterns of state–voluntary sector partnership (particularly patterns involving religious organisations), as in Germany and the Netherlands, the situation may be rather different.

Delivery contracted out

Beyond the Weberian model?

The way in which delegation has been discussed so far does not explicitly challenge the model in which a 'top' organisation is seen as specifying tasks for subordinate organisations and expecting to maintain overall control. Two insights have been gained, however, which suggest that this may not be a simple matter: the acknowledgement of the fact that many tasks involve substantial discretion, and the fact that task performance may involve horizontal collaboration. Both suggest that there may be problems about the effectiveness of simple hierarchical models.

Elsewhere we have raised questions about the extent to which, even in the context of expectations of overall hierarchical control, there may be choices about how that control should be exercised (Hill and Hupe 2014: 181–94). We did so, following Etzioni's (1961) famous model of congruent and incongruent organisational arrangements. That model is, in essence, about the extent to which it is feasible to constrain some kinds of policies by strict rule structures. We identified three modes of control, in only the first of which rule structures are central. The three alternatives are:

1. Determination of inputs;
2. Expectations of outputs;
3. Efforts to share in the determination of outcomes.

These issues are not just about the most efficient mode of control, but rather about governance itself. Complex forms of governance, within and beyond the traditional nation state, may be at stake. Here we do not need to spell out in detail the importance of the fact that accountability needs to be conceptualised in multiple forms, and that citizenship can involve 'choice' and 'voice' in ways that supplement or replace simple representative government.

In this context, two developments impact the choice for those to whom policy delivery is important. One of these is the emergence of alternative, and perhaps competing, providers. The other is electronic technologies that simplify delivery and provide information that may facilitate 'choice', make monitoring more effective, and make 'voice' (feedback and complaints) more feasible.

The role of contracting

In a relationship where one organisation delegates a task to another, the crucial device is the contract. Is a contract any different from the imposition of a set of rules? Contracting may be more likely to involve the specification of desired outputs, as an alternative to input rules. That is, contracting ensures a specific end rather than the means to the end. The problem here is the need for a clear view of the forms outputs must take. As far as the more complex activities are concerned, strict prescriptions for specific outputs may themselves distort performance. A particular problem relating to outputs in systems of delegation is what has been called 'gaming', where the focus turns to phenomena that can be measured at the expense of those that cannot.

Discussing regulation in the context of developing public–private partnerships, Majone argues:

> The old approach relied on specification standards, which tended to stultify innovation; the new approach uses performance standards, which foster flexibility and innovation, cut down red tape, and reduce costs.
>
> (Majone 2011: 47)

This perspective may be entirely satisfactory for the development of a partnership approach to inter-organisational relationships, but it also reinforces the high discretion model. Much of the debate about new approaches to these issues involves the fact that, as Majone says:

> [N]ew-governance methods such as public–private partnerships and co-regulation imply that each party has a hand in delineating not only the means, but also certain aspects of the goal itself.
>
> (Majone 2011: 47)

Hence for Majone:

> A possible response is relational *contracting*, where the parties do not agree on detailed plans of action, but on general principles and procedures, on the criteria to be used in deciding what to do when unforeseen contingencies arise, on who

> has what powers to act and the range of actions that can be taken, and on dispute resolution mechanisms to be used if disagreements do occur.
>
> (Majone 2011: 49)

Majone is describing an approach to contract specification that transfers substantial power to the contractor. Hence we may conclude that whilst contracting may be examined in terms of traditional notions of hierarchy, in terms of policy delivery it may have features which contribute to variation in performance and to the diffusion of modes of control over it.

The personalisation agenda

Privatisation usually refers to the contracting out of government services to business corporations. However, it takes on another meaning when services are contracted out to individuals rather than corporate entities. In relation to the delivery of state-provided or supported services—health care, social care, education, and social housing—a 'personalisation agenda' has emerged. It suggests that individuals should be given cash payments or vouchers enabling them to purchase services for themselves. This has been a particularly significant development in the United Kingdom. In the development phase of the British welfare state between the 1940s and the 1970s, an emphasis was placed upon direct state provision. In countries where social insurance has been more widely used, or where delivery through voluntary and faith-based organisations has long been important, personalisation provides a less direct challenge to institutionalised modes of delivery.

While a contract between a government agency and a private organisation may be a complex document with—as noted above—clauses that facilitate forms of hierarchical control, a payment that simply enables a citizen to go into the 'marketplace' involves a much greater relaxation of state control. Issues emerge regarding regulation. If citizens receive state support to buy education or social care, is there a need for the state to monitor service quality, prevent inappropriate provisions, and protect those who have difficulty in making choices for themselves? If so, what forms do these activities take?

Contextualising delivery analysis

The above discussion suggests that questions about delivery capacity need to be addressed in terms of the nature of the policy and the contingencies likely to be faced by those who deliver it. These are then constrained by an institutional and cultural context, and are the subject of ideologically driven choices. Since it would not be instructive to continue this analysis in general terms, we have chosen to explore two policy issues in greater detail by drawing from our own experience and the availability of comparative research. Below we will explore one area which, prima facie, seems comparatively simple—the provision of support for unemployed people—and one that is inherently complex—the provision of health. We chose the latter with particular reference to the way it is complicated by issues of social care for adults.

'Mathematics' plus 'moralities'

There is a wonderful quotation from a memo written by the young Winston Churchill in 1909 in respect of the planned unemployment insurance scheme for the UK (itself influenced by previous German developments). In the memo, Churchill argues that issues about behaviour should not affect benefit entitlement:

> [H]e has insured himself against the fact of unemployment, and I think it arguable that his foresight should be rewarded irrespective of his dismissal . . . I do not like mixing up moralities and mathematics.
>
> (cited in Fulbrook 1978: 137–8)

That view was not accepted, and the UK unemployment insurance scheme was hedged by rules entailing benefit loss punishments for those who were considered to blame for their job loss and, in the long run perhaps more importantly, not making efforts to obtain work. In a study of Swiss employment insurance, Buffat (2011) provides a good example of how modern schemes combine fairly strict rules with clauses to deal with this phenomenon that require discretionary—and therefore varied—decisions. Interestingly, in a comparative study that makes particular reference to Germany, Jewell (2007) argues that complex rule structures do not avoid this problem; rather they impose problems about interpreting between rules.

Churchill's approach could only have worked in a context where unemployment was essentially an occasional interlude in a work life. 'Moralities' have inevitably entered into the treatment of unemployed people, linking concerns about job search with the issues about support. In practice, widespread and prolonged unemployment has undermined strict unemployment insurance rules almost everywhere they have been introduced. States have had to determine how to deal with hardship stemming from prolonged unemployment, way beyond the limits initially imposed to protect insurance funds, or from difficulties in getting people into the workforce in the first place. Alternatives have been the creation of separate provisions or the extension of unemployment support funds. In the UK, the 'unemployment benefit' has been renamed the 'job seeker's allowance'. This development has further been influenced by views that, regardless of the demand for labour, the qualifications, attitudes, and behaviour of the labour supply matters too. Hence in the modern world three related policy issues come together: support for the unemployed, labour market policy, and education and training policy (for a comparative discussion of the implications of this see Iversen and Stephens 2008).

Thus, we see a variety of contingencies modifying support policies for unemployed people. This has the effect not only of complicating basic policy delivery, but also of adding to the range of agencies concerned with the topic. An examination of contemporary policy delivery reveals issues of official discretion (Osiander and Steinke 2011; Van der Aa 2012), as well as issues of delegation to specialist agencies (both public and private) to deal with the complexities of training and job placement (May and Winter 2009). In this context, contract issues arise, and, inasmuch as contracts depend upon performance, there are issues about performance measurement that may have impacts upon how policy is delivered. In the UK press there have been allegations that staff performance quotas have been used inappropriately by private contractors.

Paradoxically, in this area of policy we see mass schemes that in the electronic age are dependent upon 'mathematics' and a range of issues about 'moralities'. Concerns about delivery capacities push towards an emphasis on the former, and efforts are made to hive off the latter in various ways that entail the use of specialist (sometime private) agencies.

Boundary issues

Turning now to health and social care, it is contended that in those countries in which universal health-care entitlements are established, much of the subsequent political debate addresses the modes of delivery. There is no question that delivery issues are complex. However, very often delivery solutions are sought which cannot solve what are, at heart, unresolved problems of state health-care coverage.

When the UK health service was established in the 1940s, there was a naive expectation that there would be an initial backlog of hitherto unmet need after which, as the nation's health improved, demand would fall. On the contrary, demand for health services rose steadily and continues to do so. Adequately explaining this rise would require a massive digression here. What can be said is that it involves defining and placing limits on needs, rising expectations, and progressing medical technologies. This has been addressed as a capacity problem within health-care systems beyond the UK as well: how to get health professionals to deliver more. Complicating this problem is the fact that health professionals are the definers of need within the system. This has resulted in a search for managerial approaches as a means of curbing the capacity of health professionals to determine both needs and the services they provide in response to those needs. The irreducible element of discretion in health-care decision-making tends to undermine this search.

In Lipsky's analysis of street-level bureaucracy, the problem of discretion is contextualised by an observation that 'theoretically there is no limit to the demand for free public goods' (1980: 81). That reference reminds us that in market systems, prices impose limits. This brings us to the fundamental, underlying policy issue that state health services have been developed to try to take health care out of the marketplace. Nevertheless, one response to the quest for enhancing delivery capacity has been efforts to put some aspects of health care back into the market, through limitations to what may be provided or through co-payments.

Rationing may be possible by granting gatekeepers powers of denial, or through the queuing that logically follows from limited capacity. Here, an important comparative issue arises regarding the gatekeeper role within state health-care systems between those countries with single-payer (tax-funded or highly integrated insurance) schemes and those with social insurance systems. In a sense, the latter are competitive, although concerns about inequalities between systems have tended to eliminate this (see the discussion of German health insurance in Clasen and Freeman 1994). Nevertheless, questions arise about the extent to which approaches to capacity issues—and thus ultimately cost issues—are even more driven by the professional providers than in single-payer systems (Ham, Robinson, and Benzeval 1990).

The presence of models of health-care provision in which there is a clear independent purchaser is a reminder that in single-payer systems there may be independent providers. This leads to efforts to 'mimic' a market system by forcing decision-makers within the system to make choices about how they use limited budgets. While describing the 'mimic' system as a 'quasi-market' is debatable, the use of the term clearly highlights rationing and choice issues. In the context of efforts to widen competition, as encouraged in national and European Union legislation, efforts to regulate the health sector in this way create opportunities for private providers. Inasmuch as this happens, issues of contracting become important.

The explosion of health service demand has been exacerbated by a variety of issues on the boundaries of what can be considered basic health care—for example, impotence, infertility, personal appearance problems—where rules about availability may curb demand. The so-called 'lifestyle issues' are arguably more complicated when the means to prevent the emergence of health problems exist (for example, addictions and, more contentiously, obesity). An interesting issue emerges here when a distinction is made between service delivery and policy delivery. The latter may imply the responsibility of health professionals to provide advice or even participate in the regulation of behaviour.

The most salient, and perhaps most difficult, boundary issue for health services is that with social care. If we are incapacitated by a disease or accident, we may well need more than immediate medical attention. There is no simple formula to define where health care ends and social care begins. Of course, what we are talking about here is various ways in which we may need aid for daily living—feeding ourselves, washing and dressing, shopping, and so on. All is further complicated by the extent to which these needs may be met either within or outside institutions. The latter raises questions about the expected roles of families and friends. We may see these issues exacerbated by two things: the growth in the relative size of the older population likely to suffer from chronic health conditions and the falling expectations that extended family members will play social care roles. As a result, states are engaged in drawing boundary lines between health and social care in defence of health service capacity. In this respect, the evolution of social care insurance systems alongside health insurance ones (as in Germany and Japan) is a fascinating development. However, in countries with tax-funded health services, it is politically difficult to develop such devices in the face of expectations of free health care.

We return then to the personalisation issues mentioned above. There seems to be an obvious case for providing financial support through cash payments in care insurance systems. Without insurance, care provision is complicated by means testing. In both cases, regulatory questions arise. Is a payment just a sum of money for a person in need of care to spend as they wish? Are there any problems with its use for family care, and is this an arena in which the state should interfere? If there is an arrangement for the employment of a carer, how are work conditions, labour relations, minimum wages, payment of taxes, and insurance contributions to be addressed? Finally, are there issues to be addressed regarding the need for 'agents' (local authorities, voluntary organisations, or even private agencies) to assist where the beneficiaries (who may, for example, be suffering from dementia) cannot manage payments unaided? These issues are discussed in Ungerson (1994, 1995).

Delivery complexities

As in the discussion of support for unemployed people, our aim has been to illustrate delivery complexities. As far as policy delivery is concerned, health policy is one of the most contested areas. High demands are made of the state. Cost and control issues are salient, but so are issues about choice. Privatisation is a particularly emotive issue here. It seems to offer an approach to choice and a way to curb the capacity of self-interested professionals to dictate the agenda (Le Grand 2010). Yet privatisation is seen as carrying the threat of a reversion to an age when state involvement was only marginal and concentrated upon the provision of second-class services for the poor. The contemporary United States, notwithstanding recent reform efforts, stands as a warning of that threat.

The elaboration of the unemployment and health policy examples in this section shows two things. First, it highlights how policy choice issues and delivery issues interact. In the UK reforming governments, particularly those seen as more favourable to private provision, have repeatedly asserted that they are not opposed to the principle of a free health service. Hence their response to what may be called *policy* capacity issues is to respond to these as *delivery* capacity issues, searching for more efficient modes of delivery. In that process, increasing distrust of professional control over delivery is salient. Second, when delivery modes and delivery capacity imply more than questions about the best way to deliver public policy, studying them implies a contextual analysis. Only then can the role of policy contingencies, institutional arrangements, and ideology be taken into account.

Conclusion

Delivery and politics

Approaching implementation as 'policy politics', Brodkin (1990: 116) states:

> Ultimately, policies can be no more resolute and precise than the political processes that produce them.

For the 'delivery capacity' of government, this means there are limits to the degree to which problems in society can be managed, let alone 'solved'. These limits exist to the extent that problem-solving is 'troubled by features of political processes'. Besides, there are limits to the possibilities of problem-solving as such. It is false to assume that governance innovation can enhance the problem-solving capacity of the modern state in such a way that any problem can be solved. In fact, a technocratic ideal is lurking here.

A term like 'innovation' can easily be employed as a magic concept, aimed to ward off the unpredictable character and uncontrollable aspects of the human condition (Pollitt and Hupe 2011). The idea that climate change, demographic developments, and financial crises can be countered by enhancing administrative capacities and using appropriate policy instruments is attractive. Yet recognition of the many micro-processes entailed in service delivery highlights an understanding that responses to macro-problems such as these rest upon securing acceptance of the delivery of very specific policy changes. Responses to ageing, for example, involve changes to pension arrangements, new ways of sharing the burden of social care, and so on. Even more complicated is the delivery of policies changing consumption practices often involved in efforts to curb global warming. Of course, one is obliged to admit that more could be done—the number of political–administrative flaws and shortcomings is endless. However, the possibility of objective, fundamentally constraining limits may not be excluded. In the study of government and politics, relevant insights have been gained about limits inherent to cognitive capacities (cf. Simon 1957; Lindblom 1959), social interaction (Lindblom 1965), and the power mechanisms of politics (Edelman 1988; Machiavelli 2011; also Allison 1971)—not to mention the pertinent limits provided by natural forces.

Has the problem-solving capacity of the modern state then grown or diminished? It seems a fact that street-level bureaucrats are not necessarily doing what they want, but generally do what they can (Brodkin 1997). There is no reason to assume they are the only ones acting like this in public administration. Of course, there will be differences across political systems, but in democracies checks and balances will, more or less effectively, dampen the possibilities—and certainly the effects—of unaccountable behaviour of both political representatives and political authorities. Therefore, politics needs to be approached in the way it deserves: as the locus and focus via which the common good and the general interest are being served (cf. Stone 2002), rather than as a hindrance to technically optimal solutions.

Capable delivery

Pierre (2009: 591) observes that western democracies are currently implementing governance reform 'without much reflection on the democratic ramifications of reform'. What this implies for the role of representative government is pertinent. Paradoxically, the choice agenda is being promoted by highly centralising governments in the UK. It is in this sense that we conclude that it is difficult to separate issues about different forms of delivery from wider issues about the distribution of power.

In situations of delegated delivery, separating the specific delivery issues from the wider policy process may be problematic. Inasmuch as such differentiation is seen to be desirable, problems need to be faced about the extent to which there is a legitimate search for ways of constraining some of the discretion of public service workers, particularly professionals. It is not self-evident that placing them in organisations that are required to compete offers a way to deal with this issue. It may make it harder to solve. Moreover, it may add to issues with managerial unaccountability.

In this discussion we have described policy delivery as more than the solution of technical problems. We have suggested that the discretionary element in policy delivery, although varying from policy area to policy area, is essentially pervasive. We have indicated that delegated delivery models are not new, but have become more important. This development cannot simply be attributed to the emergence of, or awareness of, 'wicked problems' (see Chapter 10 for more on 'wicked problems'). Nor can it be seen solely as a consequence of the desire to innovate or to explicitly limit the role of the state, or as a product of a privatisation ideology. There are many ways of delivering policy, influenced by the interaction of many factors. At the same time, it has to be acknowledged that there is little evidence of the efficacy of the various approaches. In many ways, actors find themselves using ideologies to justify some models and cast doubt on others. The delivery itself, then ultimately 'at the street level', comes down to the capability of the actors involved.

References

Allison, G. T. (1971). *Essence of Decision: Explaining the Cuban Missile Crisis*. Boston: Little Brown.

Barbieri, D., and Salvatore, D. (2010). 'Incentive Power and Authority Types: Towards a Model of Public Service Delivery', *International Review of Administrative Sciences*, 76(2): 347–65.

Brodkin, E. Z. (1990). 'Implementation as Policy Politics', in D. J. Palumbo, and D. J. Calista (eds), *Implementation and the Policy Process: Opening up the Black Box*. New York: Greenwood Press, 107–18.

Brodkin, E. Z. (1997). 'Inside the Welfare Contract: Discretion and Accountability in State Welfare Administration', *Social Science Review*, 71(1): 1–33.

Brown, T. L., and Potoski, M. (2003). 'Transaction Costs and Institutional Explanations for Government Service Production Decisions', *Journal of Public Administration Research and Theory*, 13(4): 441–68.

Buffat, A. (2011). 'Pouvoir discrétionnaire et redevabilité de la bureaucratie de guichet. Les taxateurs d'une caisse de chômage comme acteurs de mise en oeuvre. [Discretion and Accountability of Street-Level Bureaucracy: Swiss Taxing Officers of an Unemployment Insurance Fund as Implementing Actors]', PhD Thesis (Université de Lausanne. Lausanne).

Clasen, J., and Freeman, R. (eds) (1994). *Social Policy in Germany*. New York: Harvester Wheatsheaf.

Davis, K. C. (1969). *Discretionary Justice: A Preliminary Inquiry*. Baton Rouge: Louisiana State University Press.

Dunleavy, P., and Carrera, L. (2013). *Growing the Productivity of Government Services*. Cheltenham: Edward Elgar.

Edelman, M. J. (1988). *Constructing the Political Spectacle*. Chicago: University of Chicago Press.

Etzioni, A. (1961). *A Comparative Analysis of Complex Organizations: On Power, Involvement, and Their Correlates*. New York: Free Press.

Fulbrook, J. (1978). *Administrative Justice and the Unemployed*. London: Mansell.

Gov.uk (2013) [website]. *Government Digital Service Content Style Guide*. Retrieved from <https://www.gov.uk/design-principles/style-guide> (accessed 12 August 2013).

Ham, C., Robinson, R. V. F., and Benzeval, M. (1990). *Health Check: Health Care Reforms in an International Context*. London: King's Fund Institute.

Hill, M. J., and Hupe, P. L. (2014). *Implementing Public Policy: An Introduction to the Study of Operational Governance*. 3rd edn. Los Angeles, London: Sage.

Hood, C. (1986). *The Tools of Government*. Chatham: Chatham House.

Hood, C. (2007). 'Intellectual Obsolescence and Intellectual Makeovers: Reflections on the Tools of Government after Two Decades', *Governance*, 20(1): 127–44.

Howlett, M. (1991). 'Policy Instruments, Policy Styles, and Policy Implementation. National Approaches to Theories of Instrument Choice', *Policy Studies Journal*, 19(2): 1–21.

Iversen, T., and Stephens, J. D. (2008). 'Partisan Politics, the Welfare State, and Three Worlds of Human Capital Formation', *Comparative Political Studies*, 41(4–5): 600–37.

Jewell, C. J. (2007). *Agents of the Welfare State: How Caseworkers Respond to Need in the United States, Germany, and Sweden*. 1st edn. New York: Palgrave Macmillan.

Le Grand, J. (2010). 'Knights and Knaves Return: Public Service Motivation and the Delivery of Public Services', *International Public Management Journal*, 13(1): 56–71.

Lindblom, C. E. (1959). 'The Science of "Muddling Through"', *Public Administration Review*, 19(2): 79–88.

Lindblom, C. E. (1965). *The Intelligence of Democracy: Decision Making through Mutual Adjustment*. New York: Free Press.

Lipsky, M. (1980). *Street-Level Bureaucracy: Dilemmas of the Individual in Public Services*. New York: Russell Sage Foundation.

Lowi, Theodore, J. (1972). 'Four Systems of Policy, Politics, and Choice', *Public Administration Review*, 32(4): 298–310.

Machiavelli, N. (2011). *The Prince*. London: Penguin.

Majone, G. (2011). 'The Transformations of the Regulatory State', in L. Leisering (ed.), *The New Regulatory State: Regulating Pensions in Germany and the UK*. Houndmill, New York: Palgrave Macmillan, 31–56.

May, P. J., and Winter, S. C. (2009). 'Politicians, Managers, and Street-Level Bureaucrats: Influences on Policy Implementation', *Journal of Public Administration Research and Theory*, 19(3): 453–76.

Osiander, C., and Steinke, J. (2011). 'Street-level bureaucrats in der Arbeitsverwaltung. Dienstleistungsprozesse und reformierte Arbeitsvermittlung aus Sicht der Vermittler', *Zeitschrift für Sozialreform*, 57(2): 149–73.

Peck, E., and 6, P. (2006). *Beyond Delivery: Policy Implementation as Sense-Making and Settlement*. Basingstoke, New York: Palgrave Macmillan.

Pierre, J. (2009). 'Reinventing Governance, Reinventing Democracy?' *Policy and Politics*, 37(4): 591–609.

Pollitt, C., and Hupe, P. (2011). 'Talking About Government: The Role of Magic Concepts', *Public Management Review*, 13(5): 641–58.

Pressman, J. L., and Wildavsky, A. B. (1973). *Implementation: How Great Expectations in Washington Are Dashed in Oakland*. Berkeley: University of California Press.

Simon, H. A. (1957). *Administrative Behaviour: A Study of Decision-Making Processes in Administrative Organization*. 2nd edn. New York: Macmillan.

Smith, M. J., Richards, D., Geddes, A., and Mathers, H. (2011). 'Analysing Policy Delivery in the United Kingdom: The Case of Street Crime and Anti-Social Behaviour', *Public Administration*, 89(3): 975–1000.

Stone, D. A. (2002). *Policy Paradox: The Art of Political Decision Making*. Rev. edn. New York: Norton.

Ungerson, C. (1994). 'Morals and Politics in Payments for Care', in A. Evers, M. A. Pijl, and C. Ungerson (eds), *Payments for Care: A Comparative Overview*. Aldershot, Brookfield: Avebury, 43–8.

Ungerson, C. (1995). 'Gender, Cash and Informal Care: European Perspectives and Dilemmas', *Journal of Social Policy*, 24(01): 31.

Van der Aa, P. (2012). 'Activeringswerk in uitvoering: Bureaucratische en professionele dienstverlening in drie sociale diensten. [Activation Services in Practice: Bureaucratic and Professional Service Delivery in Three Social Assistance Agencies]', PhD Thesis (Utrecht University. Utrecht).

3

Coordination Capacity

Kai Wegrich and Vid Štimac

Introduction: two tensions of coordination

Coordination is a long-standing concern in public administration and executive government. To align the activities of a range of organisations and units that follow distinct worldviews and policy preferences is the everyday concern of the core executives, but also of leaders at departmental level. The difficulty of that task becomes obvious when things go wrong, be it at the street level when different agencies fail to align their activities and place conflicting demands on citizens or 'outsource' coordination to them, or at the executive government level when turf wars abound or cross-cutting issues do not receive attention beyond the symbolic. Given the significance of coordination for public administration and public policy, attempts to improve the capacity of government systems to coordinate are a recurring theme on the agenda of governmental reform policies. At least since the wave of government reforms guided by ideas of political planning of the early 1970s, coordination is the subject of dedicated reform programmes. At the same time, governments' capacity to coordinate is shaped by the fundamental changes in the 'habitat' of governance, in particular the dispersion of authority and the increasing complexity of policy-making. In addition, the changes in the architecture of the public sector itself, in particular those changes that are associated with so-called New Public Management (NPM) type of reforms, are said to influence (i.e. reduce) governmental capacities to coordinate.

Under these conditions, attempts to improve the coordination capacity of governments—understood here as an institutional trait, a structural asset to align the activities of organisational units in the design and implementation of public policies—need to come to terms with two types of tensions related to coordination: one related to the type of coordination problem that should be addressed and one related to determining the most appropriate way to coordinate. In terms of the first, the coordination problem is generally considered to be the result of functional differentiation and hence specialisation—both in society and within government, which at least partly reflects the increasing differentiation of society. However, specialisation leads to two very different types of coordination problem. One results from the selective perception of specialised units that leads to a lack of attention to issues that are not within the jurisdictional boundaries ('underlap') (see Hood 1974). The other and more frequently discussed coordination problem refers to overlapping jurisdictions, which often come with divergence in preferences or ideological approaches to one issue between involved organisational units (such as in 'classic' conflicts between units responsible for social regulation and those dealing with the same regulatory issue from an economic perspective).

Different types of coordination problem might require different ways to achieve coordination. Thus, the second tension in debates about coordination capacity surrounds how to coordinate governmental activities across organisational boundaries in today's world of more complex governance settings. The key question is how to coordinate effectively, given the limits to hierarchical coordination. For many, dispersion of authority via internationalisation, decentralisation, and agencification has resulted in a 'hollowed out' state that has lost its central steering capacity (see, for example, Rhodes 1997; Matthews 2012). Policy-making is happening in decoupled networks of sectoral actors that are not concerned with externalities of 'their' policies materialising in other domains. For others, those developments point to the changing role of the state and a shift from hierarchical to more collaborative or network forms of governance. While usually not couched in terms of coordination, these debates regard the inclusion of societal actors and the mediating role of the state as an enhancer of governing capacities (cf. Ansell and Gash 2008; McGuire and Agranoff 2011). 'Collaborative management' is seen as increasingly important, but also doable given the benefits of collaboration.

Somewhat contradictory advice for enhancing coordination capacities emerges from these two perspectives. For those that consider the changing context of governance mainly as a loss of steering capacity, the key aim of reforms is to get central capacities 'into shape', i.e. by strengthening monitoring and intervention capacities at the centre of government, through mergers of fragmented administrative structures, etc. For those that see collaborative governance as an opportunity, coordination capacity is enhanced through inclusive procedures and mediation across a range of 'stakeholders'. In other words, the issue of coordination capacity is situated between the poles of central control and more collaborative forms of 'bringing together' organisational activities. Debates on coordination capacities and attempts to develop respective indicators have mainly focused on hierarchical coordination and the ability of the centre to control departments (Bertelsmann Stiftung 2009, 2011).

This chapter explores these two tensions of coordination. It does so by extending the conceptual debate outlined above and by drawing on data from a large-scale survey of senior executives in Europe, the COCOPS executive survey.[1] We will use the survey data in particular to explore the relevance of different modes of coordination in government and to discuss what drives the capacity of governments to achieve 'coordination'. The data come with all the limitations of perception-based survey data, but they allow us to make a distinct contribution related to two factors, namely 'reforms' seeking to improve coordination capacity and the underlying 'coordination culture' of a governmental system.

Before we move to these issues, the chapter will first introduce the two types of coordination problem outlined above and next link these problems to different modes of coordination. We will discuss the 'fit' of four distinct modes of coordination to the different types of coordination problem. Here we already draw on the COCOPS data to explore the significance of different modes of coordination (although the data allow only discussion of the two widely discussed modes—hierarchical and horizontal coordination). These data will be further explored in the subsequent section, where we extend the discussion about different modes of coordination by linking these to the perceived level of coordination capacity in the 14 countries covered in the COCOPS survey.[2] The brief conclusion highlights the chapter's key arguments.

Two types of coordination problem

Today's world of governance is said to be increasingly characterised by 'wicked' problems (Rittel and Webber 1973; see also Verweij in this volume). Problems such as climate change, an ageing population, or migration/integration are highly complex, uncertain, and transversal. In contrast to 'tame' problems, applying well-known policy solutions to these issues does not seem to be sufficient for dealing with them. Such problems require input

[1] The research leading to these results has received funding from the European Community's Seventh Framework Programme under Grant Agreement No. 266887 (Project Coordinating for Cohesion in the Public Sector of the Future—COCOPS), Socio-economic Sciences and Humanities.

[2] The 14-country sample used in this chapter consists of 7,737 respondents. The survey was sent out to 28,302 senior public managers, implying an overall response rate of 27.3 per cent. For more information about the COCOPS project, see <http://www.cocops.eu>.

from various perspectives in order to respond at a level of complexity and variety that meets the complexity of the issue at hand.

However, government policy-making is a business divided into branches and organisational units that are set up in order to deal with a very specific aspect of some wider policy domain (such as a unit for coal in an energy department in a ministry for economics). Moreover, specialised units deal with that problem from a particular perspective, one that is the result of the institutional definition of the task, the professional training of the civil servants, and the interaction with the client network of societal actors and specialised politicians at various levels of government (Jann and Wegrich 2008). The result of specialisation in government is selective perception, and its consequence the prevalence of coordination problems. Hence a common way to define coordination relates the activity of coordination to interdependence, as for example in the definition by Simon: 'Coordination simply means organizing activity in such a way as to handle the problems that arise because the behaviour of each participant depends in some ways on the behaviours of the others' (Simon 2000: 750).

Specialisation is a precondition for policy-making based on *Fachkompetenz*—technical and subject expertise. Moreover, the legitimacy of government units also (of course, not only) derives from representing some relevant societal interest within the governmental setting. But specialisation alone is not inherently problematic for coordination in executive government; it is the critical role of 'turf' for organisational maintenance and the resulting effect of 'bureaucratic competition' that lead to the coordination problem (Wilson 1989). Organisational boundaries matter for how managers and higher-level bureaucrats behave in executive politics. From an institutionalist perspective, specialisation (and recruitment and promotion patterns attuned to specialisation) shapes specialists' worldviews, leading to (at least) ignorance towards concerns that lie outside the responsibility of a particular organisational unit. Such 'selective perception' (Dearborn and Simon 1958) is reinforced by managerial strategies for organisational survival and maintenance. Managers defend their turf because contestation of the organisation's jurisdiction or open turf wars put at risk political support as the most important external resource for survival. From an internal perspective, defending the turf, as well as denying responsibility for tasks that are outside the 'core mission', i.e. do not fit the dominant understanding of the key task of the organisation, reduces the need to control the activities of employees. In other words, specialisation and attention to turf are key preconditions for organisations, and in particular public organisations, to perform—one that is overlooked in frequent wailing about bureaucratic 'silo mentality'.

Of course, specialisation creates problems when there is interdependence. In particular, when the interdependence is structured in a way that makes it difficult to cluster high levels of interdependencies within organisational units, such a 'near decomposability' of tasks (Simon 1962) would be a precondition for limiting coordination problems to the management of hierarchical coordination (see below). Yet tasks cannot always be divided in a way that reciprocal interdependence is clustered within organisational units and 'external' coordination is limited to issues of sequential and pooled interdependence (see Scharpf 1997 based on Thompson 1967). If the diagnosis of the increasing prevalence of 'wicked' policy issues holds true, governments face an increasing number of issues that cannot be effectively dealt with within single organisational units, and possibly also not with coordination mechanisms that have been developed to deal with tame problems, i.e. issues characterised by sequential interdependence.

While the resulting coordination problems are unlimited, two generic types can be distinguished (cf. Lodge 2013), namely the problem of 'underlap' and the problem of 'overlap'. The notion of 'underlap' refers to the situation when a particular policy issue falls between the jurisdictional boundaries of different governmental organisations so that it becomes the responsibility of none. On the level of policy implementation, typical examples of underlap are cases of denial of responsibility for a particular 'case' that does not fit into the defined categories that allocate responsibility, for example, young offenders under the age of criminal responsibility. In policy-making the problem of underlap refers to issues that are usually considered as being of general interest but no department considers them as being at the core of its task structure and organisational mission. Examples of those issues, often called cross-cutting, include demographic change, cutting red tape, gender equality, sustainability, and migration.

Take the issue of migration/integration. In the German context, there is no ministry with comprehensive responsibility for the issue, but a range of departments possess jurisdiction for specific aspects of the issue area—for example, the ministry of the interior is responsible for citizenship (or 'naturalisation') and related aspects of language training, etc.; the ministry of labour and social affairs for issues related to the inclusion of migrants on the labour market. The important issue of education (school and early childhood) of migrants has no dedicated organisational responsibility within the federal government since education is mainly under the jurisdiction of the federal states (*Länder*).

The point is not that the units responsible for the parts of the wider issue area are not dedicated to this particular task. Rather, it is that orchestrating these diverse units across organisational boundaries is problematic, since their perception of the issue is shaped by the particular 'slice' of the wider issue area and their embeddedness within a department with a core responsibility and mission in another policy area. A ministry for social affairs might support objectives of improving the position of migrants on the labour market, but these concerns might not be the main priority of the ministry or even an individual division given the key issues of overall employment rates, the costs of social benefit systems, etc. To somewhat overstate the point: cross-cutting policy issue areas such as migration/integration can become everyone's issue, and hence no one's.

The degree to which the problem of underlap matters depends on the complexity of the policy problem. Highly complex policy issues depend on orchestrated action in policy areas that are administered separately. Hood (1974) uses the example of urban deprivation to illustrate: stopping the decline of cities or neighbourhoods depends on joint action in many fields including housing, schooling, crime and justice, health care, etc. Effective policies in one area, e.g. schooling, would be offset if complementary policies are not adopted and implemented in the others areas, e.g. housing. What makes these coordination problems so difficult to deal with is that the separate institutionalisation of these issues is not necessarily the better option given the demand for specialised competencies and expertise to handle them. For example, creating a new ministry for a cross-cutting issue such as migration/integration is not without risks since such a ministry would still have to rely on the expertise, power, and budget of the stronger traditional ministries to get something done—at least initially it would work with limited programme autonomy. Hence the German federal government, like many others, has created the position of a commissioner (or 'czar') for migrants and refugees (in the position of a parliamentary state secretary) to act as an advocate for these issues and to facilitate coordination. Coordinating the diverse organisations that are involved in a complex field such as migration/integration policy is extremely challenging since it involves constantly stepping on the 'turf' of many departments. Still, keeping policy-making in the hands of few organisations is neither feasible nor desirable—since the knowledge and capacity of the full range of organisations are required when dealing with 'wicked' policy issues.

In contrast with underlap, the problem of 'overlap' results from the opposite relation between different organisations. In this case, a particular policy issue is of similar key relevance for the different organisations, with the result that they both/all want to be involved in policy-making. However, these organisations approach the same issue from different perspectives and follow—to some extent—different objectives. Again at a more street level, this is the case when different agencies are involved in decisions about urban planning, but the environment agency has a different interest than the economic development unit. At the central government level, overlap problems materialise in interdepartmental conflicts related to issues that affect different constituencies. Classic candidates for such conflicts are business versus labour or industry versus environmental interests.

Energy policy in general and the reform programme of the German government, the so-called *Energiewende* (energy turnaround), are cases of such coordination problems. The decision (taken in 2011) to increase the share of renewable energy to 35 per cent and to phase out nuclear energy by 2020 amplified pre-existing coordination problems between the two main ministries involved at the time, the Ministry for Economic Affairs (BMWi) and the Ministry for Environment, Nature Conservation, and Nuclear Safety (BMU). The problem was not only that jurisdiction in the field of energy policy was divided between these two ministries, but also that the ministries represented conflicting societal interests. Further complications include the key role of the energy-producing industry and the *Länder* that need to be involved in the coordination process. In mid 2012, the *Energiewende* was perceived as being in crisis. Conflicts between the two key ministries, the BMWi and BMU, appeared to hamper efficient coordination within the federal government. Decisions were said to be delayed, and there seemed to be no effective positioning of the federal government in negotiations with powerful provider companies, transmission grid operators, governments, and at the EU level (Neller 2012). Whether the rearrangement of ministerial responsibilities after the 2013 federal elections that brought energy squarely into the remit of the renamed Ministry for Economic Affairs and Energy resolves these problems remains to be seen.

Since the problem in the energy domain is less one of orchestrating a high number of activities but more of agreeing on particular policy designs—in particular the incentive system for renewable energy production (feed-in subsidies)—the coordination problem is one of negotiation and bargaining between actors with at least partially contradictory objectives. Strategies of bargaining and turf wars include strategic use of the media, in particular when it comes to the framing of the problem (related to consumer prices of energy, for example) and the uncoordinated launch of policy initiatives in the public. The key challenge in coordinating problems of 'overlap' is not only to overcome deadlock, but to do so while still motivating those parties that need to 'give in' to provide input to policy design and implementation. A too strong-handed hierarchical enforcement of 'coordinated' solutions comes with the risk of losing the intelligence of motivated input from decentralised units, as will be further discussed below.

In sum, coordination in executive government has to deal with rather different problems. While the problem of overlap is mainly one of solving conflicts and searching for solutions that allow maximising overall welfare but also offering some benefit for the involved parties, the problem of underlap is one of initiating and orchestrating diverse policy activities which collectively matter for policy outcomes. Against this background, the following section moves to generic ways to deal with such coordination problems, in order to discuss how they 'fit' with these two types.

Modes of coordination

In order to explore the capacity of executives to deal with these coordination problems, we need some analytical guidance concerning the potential 'solutions'. The literature on coordination usually distinguishes between markets, states/organisations, and networks as generic forms of coordination. The logic of that classification is transposed to governmental coordination when hierarchical coordination is distinguished from (variants of) self-coordination. The following discusses these and two further modes of coordination, namely incentive-based modes and 'spontaneous coordination' to show their inherent logics and limitations.

Coordination has long been seen as synonymous with hierarchical coordination, if only implicitly. Hierarchical coordination, i.e. decisions made either by executives in their position as leaders or by majoritarian vote, come with the potential to maximise the collective welfare irrespective of the individual distribution of costs and benefits of this decision: for example, with respect to the policy positions of individual ministries or different affected parties. But as Scharpf (1994, 1997) has shown, the achievement of this welfare-maximising potential is not a given. Scharpf identifies two recurring problems of hierarchical coordination: motivation and information.

The motivation problem relates to the importance of the self-interest of those in positions to make hierarchical decisions and the risk that hierarchical power will be abused (Scharpf 1994: 33). However, institutional design to limit this risk of abuse also constrains the scope for hierarchical coordination. For example, the 'cabinet principle' as one of the constitutional doctrines of executive coordination in Germany limits the capacity of the Chancellor to hierarchically coordinate policies.

The second problem of hierarchical coordination lies in the limited capacity of the centre to process information. In the course of transferring information from lower to higher levels, some distortion will happen, and key traits of 'local knowledge' get lost, resulting in ill-informed decisions. Moreover, central decision-makers can only engage in a limited number of issues at the same time, so that hierarchical coordination always has to be selective in order to avoid an overload of the capacity of the central level.

With respect to problems of overlap in particular, the disposition of executive leaders to intervene hierarchically is also shaped by a political calculus: since the different objectives and positions taken by subunits—ministerial departments in the case of executive government—reflect different societal interests, executive leaders have to take into account the salience of these voices in the evolving public debate. The executive leader needs to avoid making a decision that turns out to be unpopular and for which he/she is publicly blamed. Such blame-management calculations put additional limits on the capacity of hierarchical coordination.

Given these limits to hierarchical coordination, horizontal self-coordination is a ubiquitous practice in executive government. Scharpf (1972) has distinguished two types of self-coordination, positive and negative, both of which are derived from empirical observations of policy-making in the German federal system (Mayntz and Scharpf 1975). The pattern of negative coordination is characterised by sequential involvement of organisational units that starts with the development of a draft policy/legislation by the section with the main responsibility (*Federführung*) for the issue. This draft is vetted first within the department and next across all departments within federal governments. This vetting is limited to checking whether the draft violates the turf of other units or contradicts their policy positions. Negative coordination implies that drafts are developed from the narrow perspective of highly specialised working units in ministries. Concerns of others are only accounted for with respect to avoiding violation of jurisdiction. While negative coordination allows the parallel processing of a range of policy issues and reduces the complexity of executive government, this results in a status quo and specialist bias. Lowest common denominator—rather than innovative—solutions are the typical outcome of negative coordination processes.

Positive coordination, on the other hand, allows addressing more complex policy issues by pooling the policy proposals of diverse units in order to develop a draft. Task forces and inter-ministerial working groups are typical real-world examples from which Scharpf developed the notion of positive coordination. The limitation of this mode of coordination is its high complexity—the number of proposals to be discussed is multiplied, as are the opportunities for outmanoeuvring other departments/units. Positive coordination can only realise its potential for developing welfare-maximising proposals when there is an open exchange of ideas, following the mode of joint problem-solving and arguing rather than position-oriented bargaining—a rare phenomenon in particular between ministries representing opposing societal interests. However, displaying a too cooperative, open behaviour comes with the risk that other participants exploit such behaviour. In other words, it is questionable whether the high aims of positive coordination can be achieved in practice.

While hierarchy and variants of horizontal self-coordination are considered to be the main modes of coordination in executive government, two additional modes can be identified (see Hood et al. 2004), namely, incentives/competition and spontaneous coordination. The first relates to market forms of societal coordination that convert incentives and competition into modes of coordination. Such modes have gained in popularity with the rise of the New Public Management since the 1980s, but mainly with respect to vertical coordination. Variations of performance and contract management, quasi-markets, and league-table-type rivalry have been used not only to govern the delivery of public service, but also to recalibrate the relation between ministries and (executive) agencies. Within the executive, such forms of incentives and competition are less well known, at least not as intentional modes of coordination. More recently, however, cross-departmental league tables and benchmarking activities have been used to control the activities of different departments in a given field, and in particular in cross-cutting policy areas, such as cutting red tape or other areas of administrative reform.

As a final mode, spontaneous coordination relies on opportunistic initiatives of individual actors that trigger responses by others. Such patterns are well known under the rubric of 'garbage-can'-type decision-making (Cohen, March, and Olsen 1972), in which problems, actors, and solutions are generally coupled in an opportunistic way—if a particular decision situation allows the preferred solution to be 'thrown in', any actor will do so. The garbage-can model was developed to describe organisational choice and later inspired models of agenda-setting dynamics. Understood as a mode of coordination, such dynamics link to Lindblom's (1965) notion of 'mutual adjustment', i.e. actors responding to initiatives by adjusting their expectations and strategies. While Scharpf (1994; Scharpf and Mohr 1994) discusses partisan mutual adjustment in the context of variants of self-coordination relying on various forms of negotiation, Lindblom stresses the element of adjustment without interaction. Other scholars have stressed the informal nature of non-hierarchical coordination. Chisholm (1989), for example, argues that informal ties in multi-organisational systems are activated when there is a need for coordination. Referring to horizontal coordination between German federal states, Benz, Scharpf, and Zintl (1992) argue that such informal ties can help overcome coordination problems and that they can be facilitated by institutional design.

How do these modes of coordination relate to the two types of coordination problem (overlap and underlap) introduced in the previous section (see Table 3.1)? Hierarchy seeks to address problems of overlap by assigning responsibilities and imposing priorities and of underlap by installing procedural requirements for joint work. In the mode of self-coordination, problems of both over- and underlap would be resolved by developing joint identities—to avoid deadlock in policy conflicts in the case of overlap and to raise common awareness for problems of underlap. To solve problems of overlap, typical incentives include package deals and side payments, while competition could be employed in the form of 'policy markets' or bidding processes. In

Table 3.1. Modes of coordination (with responses to over- and underlap)

Spontaneous	Hierarchy
Overlap: informal coordination Underlap: increase encounters	Overlap: assignment of responsibilities; imposition of priorities Underlap: procedural requirements to work together
Incentives & competition	**Self-coordination**
Overlap: side payments and package deals (incentives); policy markets (competition) Underlap: incentives to contribute	Overlap: development of joint identities (problem-solving mindset) Underlap: development of joint identities (joint problem awareness)

terms of underlap, incentives can be offered to encourage contributions. Finally, those considering spontaneous coordination as the way forward expect informal coordination to emerge in the absence of central intervention to resolve overlap. Problems of underlap pose a particularly tricky challenge to the spontaneous mode of coordination. However, increasing the number of chance encounters would be one way to facilitate spontaneous coordination.

What can be said about the significance of these modes of coordination in practice? As mentioned above, the data from the COCOPS executive survey only allow exploration of the hierarchical mode and self-coordination. Aggregated to a country level, our survey data support a rather conventional view of the role of different modes of coordination in executive government.[3] First, as shown in Figure 3.1, the classic response to solving coordination problems between organisations is to refer them upwards in the hierarchy (consistently across all three hierarchical levels included in the survey). Note that these findings do not suggest that hierarchical coordination takes precedence over horizontal coordination, but rather that coordination problems are—in the end—usually solved by referring issues up the hierarchy. It should be noted that in all but three countries—i.e. Norway, Netherlands, and Ireland—respondents indicated that hierarchical coordination was more common, with the differences being statistically significant at 5 per cent. This finding supports conventional views about administrative culture in Europe, since those three 'outlier' countries would be considered as more individualist and less hierarchical in their administrative culture than the other countries in the sample.

Looking at horizontal coordination approaches, we find that the set-up of some sort of inter-organisational working group is a standard response to an

[3] The empirical findings presented in this chapter are meant to illustrate differences in coordination approaches, trends, and outcome evaluations on a country level. For this purpose we look at the country average evaluation or score for each variable of interest. Much of the nuance is lost via this aggregation, and while the data lend themselves to much more thorough analysis, this is beyond the scope of this chapter.

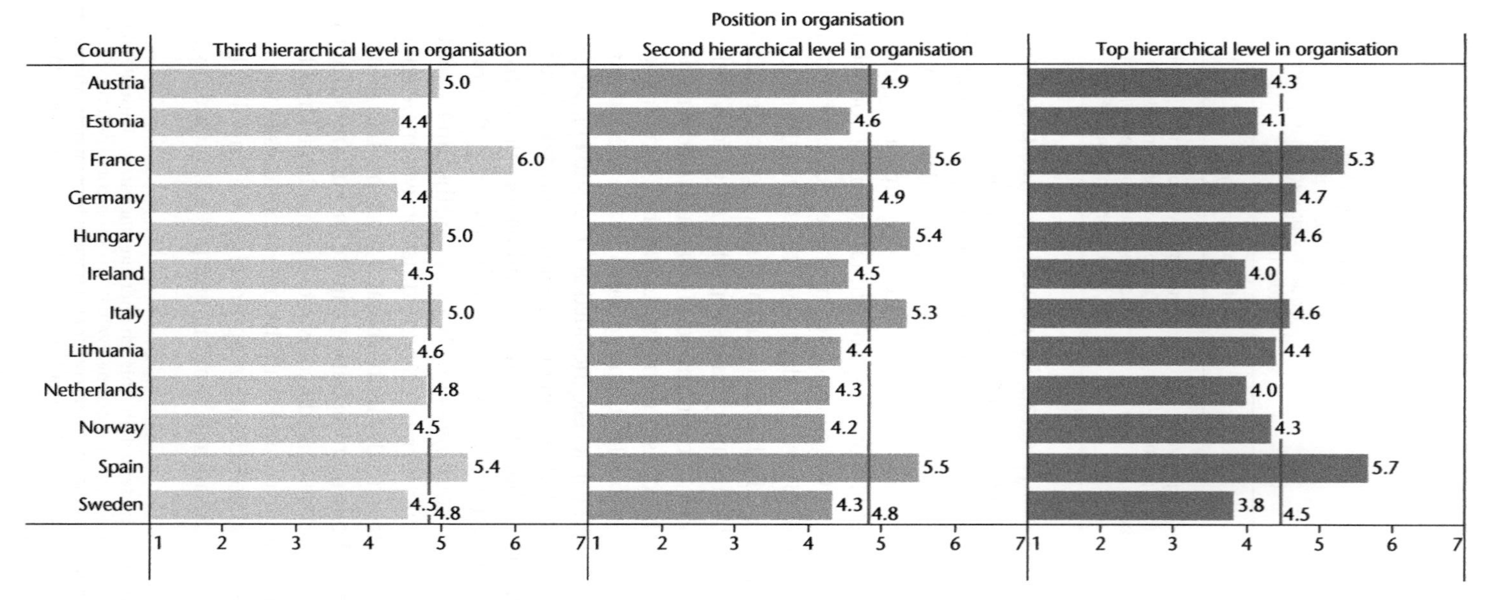

Figure 3.1. Hierarchical coordination: Referring the issue up the hierarchy, according to position in organisation. Question: *To resolve coordination problems when working with other organisations, we typically refer the issue up the hierarchy*

Source: Hammerschmid, Oprisor, and Štimac (2013)

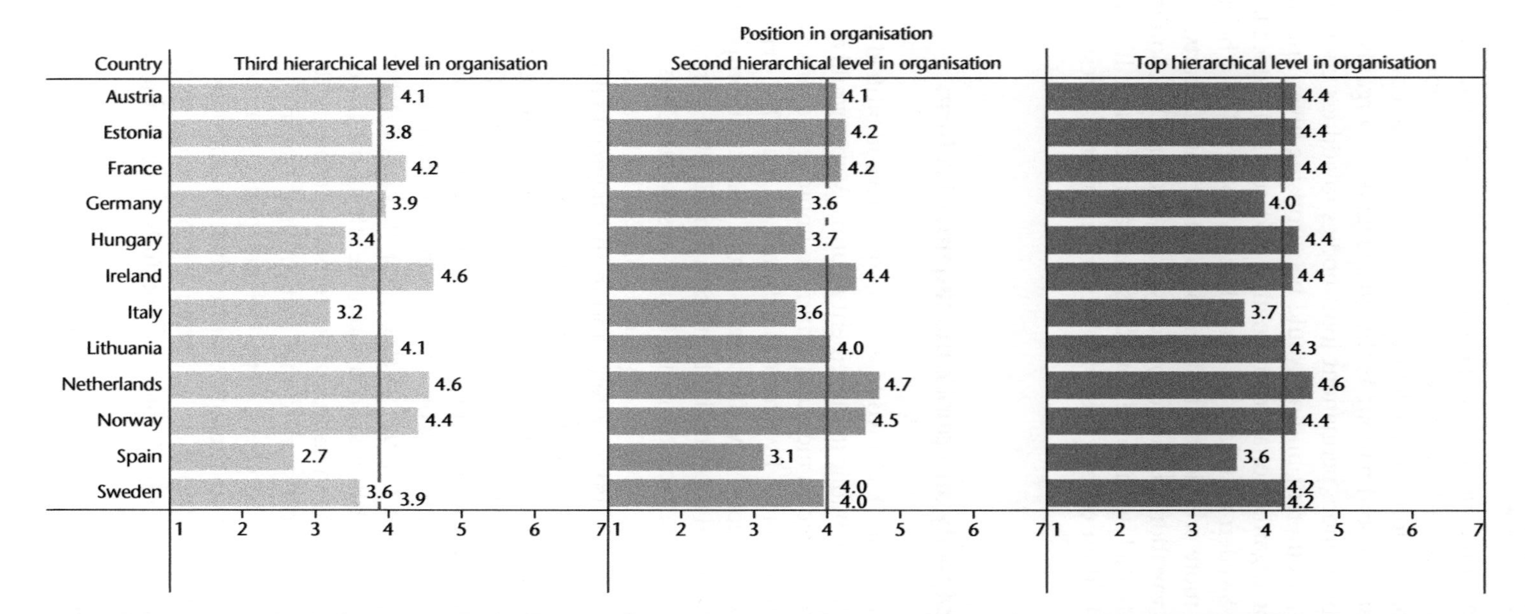

Figure 3.2. Horizontal coordination: Use of ad hoc working groups, according to position in organisation. Question: *To resolve coordination problems when working with other organisations, we typically set up a cross-cutting work/project group (ad hoc, temporary)*

Source: Hammerschmid, Oprisor, and Štimac (2013)

emergent coordination issue across organisational boundaries (see Figure 3.2). Although the set-up of such ad hoc coordination devices cannot be equated with positive coordination, such a device might be considered as a necessary condition for positive coordination. As shown in Figure 3.3, organisations are reluctant to establish more permanent joint bodies to address coordination problems—again, a different finding would be surprising given the importance of 'turf' for organisational maintenance and survival. Indeed, in all countries except Sweden and Italy we find that ad hoc modes of horizontal coordination are more prevalent than their permanent counterparts.[4]

Note that the variation in the reported typical response to coordination problems is substantial, with some countries displaying a more hierarchical coordination style than others. We will further explore these results in the next section.

Coordination capacity and public management reform

Governments across the OECD world and beyond have identified 'coordination' as an objective of public management reforms. Many would argue that the need to introduce reform measures aiming to improve executive coordination has been precipitated by previous reforms of the NPM type. These reforms, the argument goes, have favoured single- over multi-purpose agencies and have introduced accountability mechanisms for the performance of individual organisations. According to many observers (Christensen and Lægreid 2007; cf. Wegrich 2010; Lodge and Gill 2011), these reforms have created a fragmented executive system, and in this fragmented system, performance management has spurred organisational egocentrism.

Responding to these perceived unintended effects of a strong reliance on NPM type of reforms, many OECD governments have made the improvement of coordination a reform theme in its own right. Significant reform trends include the strengthening of central coordination units, the formulation of joint targets, and the use of strategic policy approaches for cross-cutting issues. However, little is known about the effects and the effectiveness of such reforms. Available measures of coordination capacity (Bertelsmann Stiftung 2011) mainly focus on formal institutional features, such as the existence of procedures to check departmental policy drafts. Case study evidence focuses mainly on the fate of individual reform policies (Lægreid et al. 2013) but have difficulties in attributing outcomes to (innovative) coordination practices. This chapter cannot fully address the limitations

[4] The differences are statistically significant at 5 per cent in all instances except in Sweden and Italy.

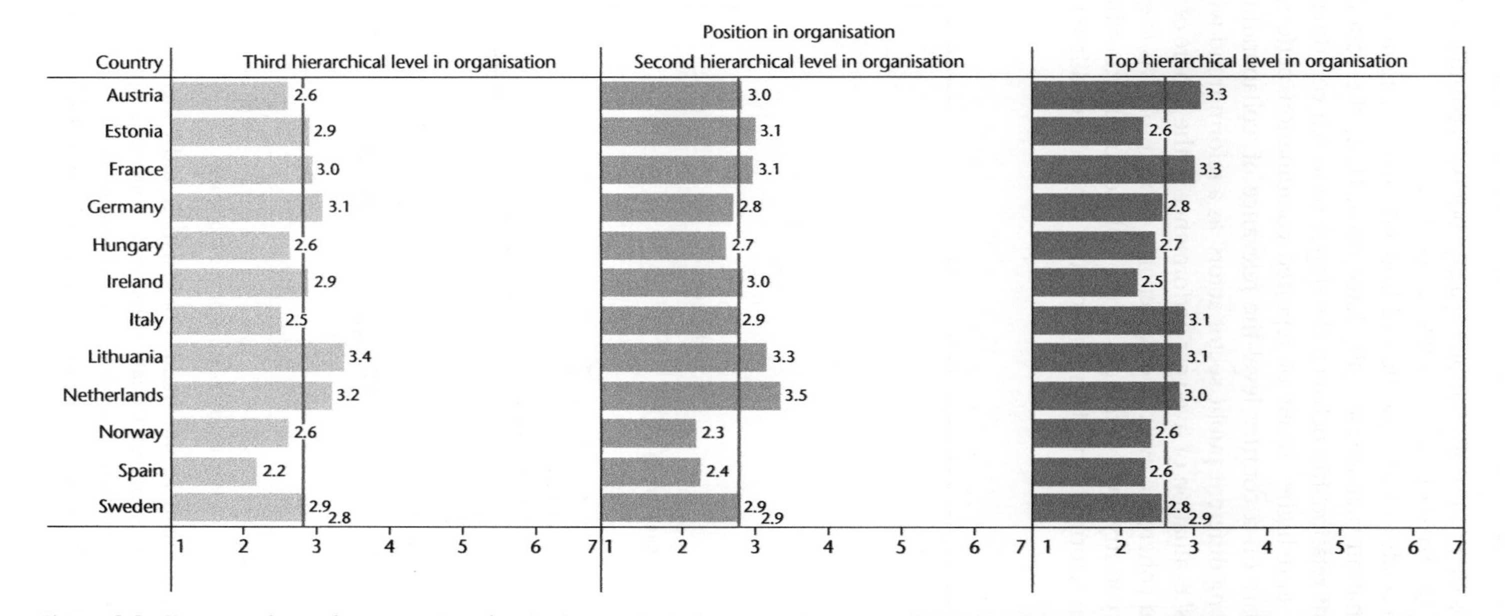

Figure 3.3. Horizontal coordination: Use of special purpose bodies, according to position in organisation. Question: *To resolve coordination problems when working with other organisations, we typically set up special purpose bodies (more permanent)*

Source: Hammerschmid, Oprisor, and Štimac (2013)

of the existing research on coordination capacity, but two central claims can be developed on the basis of the COCOPS survey data.

The first claim relates to the question of how effective the reform efforts targeting coordination practices actually have been. Here, the data do not show a significant relationship between the degree to which coordination is a reform theme and higher levels of reported coordination performance. When we compare on a country level the relevance of 'collaboration and cooperation among different public sector actors' as a reform trend with the senior executives' evaluation of five-year performance in the sphere of policy coordination and coherence, we can only report a 'non-result'. As is evident from Figure 3.4, country-level variation in the salience of the coordination and collaboration reform theme does not account for country differences in

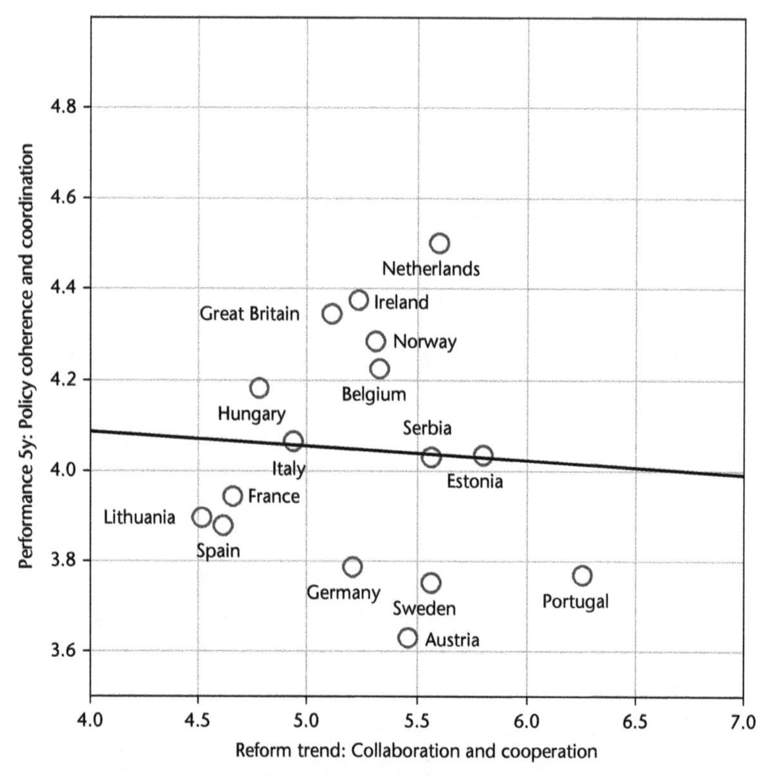

Figure 3.4. Performance and reform trend: Coordination and coherence performance in relation to the relevance of 'Collaboration and cooperation among different public sector actors' reform trend. Question: *How do you think public administration has performed in your policy area over the last five years in terms of policy coherence and coordination?*

reported coordination performance. In short, these reforms do not seem to have a strong impact on levels of reported coordination performance.

However, another look at the data reveals an interesting pattern that leads us to the second claim. We investigated to what extent the most relevant variations in hierarchical[5] and horizontal[6] coordination approaches identified in Figures 3.1 and 3.2 are related to the reform trend 'Collaboration and cooperation among different public sector actors'. The findings presented in Figure 3.5 suggest that hierarchical coordination does not seem to be identified with collaboration and cooperation reforms. On the other hand, horizontal coordination approaches do tend to be associated with this reform trend. In other words, those countries where horizontal coordination is more common are also those that engage in coordination reforms.

These findings could be interpreted as a direct response to the widely discussed problems of horizontal coordination (see above). Coordination problems are often considered to be the result of power dispersion and the prevalence of 'veto players'. However, the COCOPS data suggest otherwise when we relate the same measure of coordination performance over five years shown on the vertical axis in Figure 3.4 to the salience of the two methods of coordination. As shown in Figure 3.6, we find an ostensibly negative, but not statistically significant, relationship between policy coordination performance and hierarchical coordination. However, horizontal coordination does seem to coincide with greater improvement in policy coordination and coherence (significant at 10 per cent). In short, according to the survey results, a horizontal coordination style correlates with higher levels of coordination performance.

While we have to be careful not to stretch the interpretation of survey results—in particular because we compare perceptions across different countries with very different contexts and hence baselines and expectations of performance—we can at least offer some evidence that suggests that those countries that follow a less hierarchical approach to coordination also seem to be doing better in achieving outcomes in terms of coordination performance. What that implies for debates on coordination capacity is that the bias towards formal institutional structures and provisions might be unjustified. Our country-level analysis suggests that it is the 'right' culture that matters for coordination capacity, much more than some procedural or structural coordination device.

[5] Question: To resolve coordination problems when working with other organisations, we typically refer the issue up the hierarchy.

[6] Question: To resolve coordination problems when working with other organisations, we typically set up a cross-cutting work/project group (ad hoc, temporary).

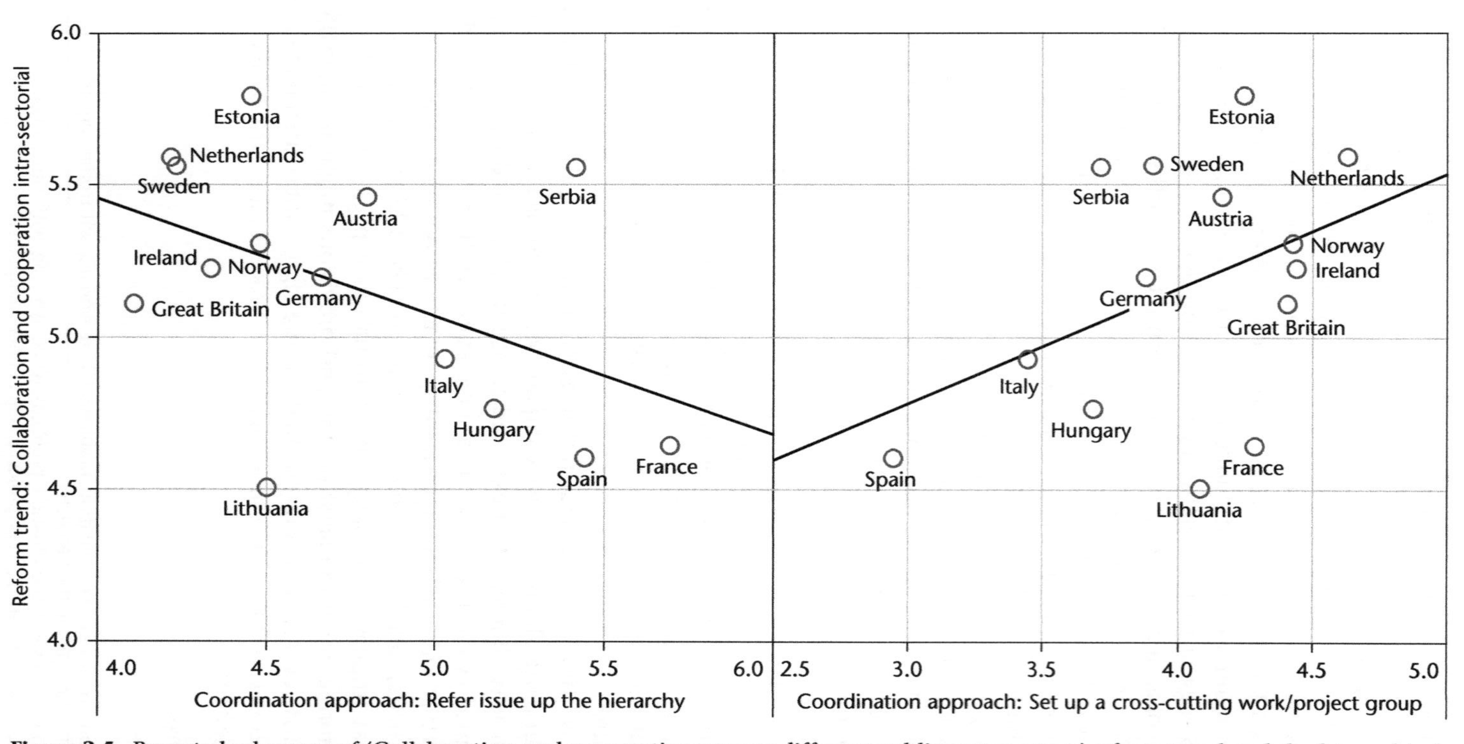

Figure 3.5. Reported relevance of 'Collaboration and cooperation among different public sector actors' reform trend and the hierarchical and horizontal coordination approaches

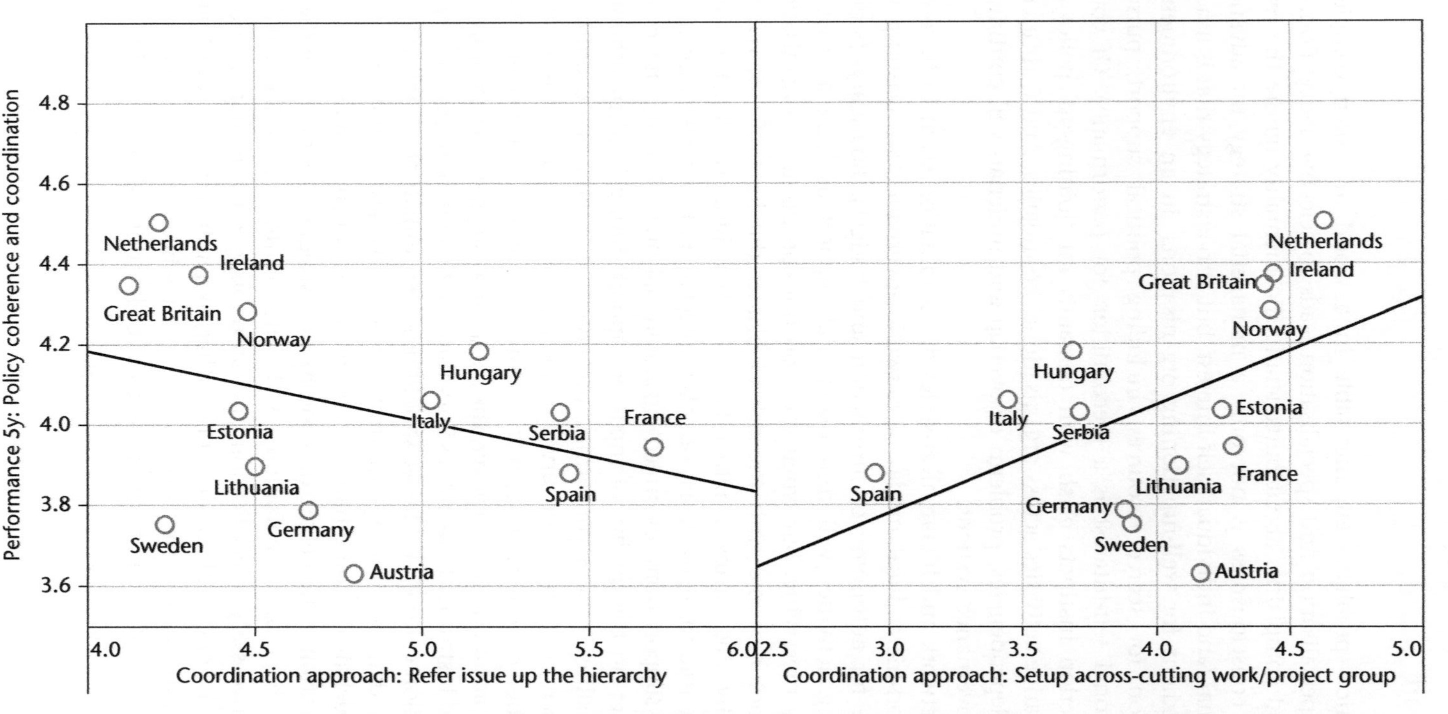

Figure 3.6. Reported policy coherence and coordination performance and the hierarchical and horizontal coordination approaches

Conclusion

Coordination problems are inevitable in a world in which complexity requires specialisation and specialisation leads to selective perception. The widespread complaints about bureaucratic silo mentality ignore the reality that turf consciousness is not only a managerial strategy for advancing institutional (and individual) self-interest, but also a strategy that is a necessary ingredient for well-functioning organisations. In an environment of competition for scarce resources, including political support, pursuing organisational self-interest is a precondition for performance. Of course, turf-protection instincts clash with demands for 'joining-up' policy and administrative activities across organisational boundaries. And with increasing interdependencies, problems of overlap and underlap will continue to trouble governance systems.

Both network and hierarchical styles of coordination seem to have their limits. Non-hierarchical modes of network governance are clashing with the desire for autonomy of jurisdiction and budgets. Boundary-spanning networking activities will find managerial support as long as they are autonomy preserving, but when these do not contribute to organisational maintenance or come with the risk of blame, the level of 'coordination' achieved by this means is rather limited. Hierarchical coordination might potentially lead to higher levels of policy integration, but comes with the risk of lack of support from 'overruled' organisational units that may have negative impact on the quality of input or support during implementation.

Such disillusionment concerning the potential to enhance coordination capacity is reinforced by our survey results that suggest that all reform efforts to strengthen coordination seem to have limited effects on the perceived level of coordination quality. However, the survey also suggests that coordination modes and instruments are not as important as the underlying organisational 'coordination culture'. While we should not overestimate the implications of the survey data, the findings are strong enough to question the focus of the scholarly debate on coordination focusing on instruments, modes, solutions, and innovations. The debate on coordination should rather explore the factors that shape an organisational style and culture that strike a balance between necessary specialisation and autonomy, on one hand, and the requirements of coordination, on the other. When it comes to coordination modes or instruments, the two modes that have been widely under-studied, namely competition and spontaneous coordination, should receive more attention.

References

Ansell, C., and Gash, A. (2008). 'Collaborative Governance in Theory and Practice', *Journal of Public Administration Research and Theory*, 18(4): 543–71.

Benz, A., Scharpf, F. W., and Zintl, R. (1992). *Horizontale Politikverflechtung. Zur Theorie von Verhandlungssystemen*. Frankfurt, New York: Campus.

Bertelsmann Stiftung (2009). *Sustainable Governance Indicators 2009: Policy Performance and Executive Capacity in the OECD*. Gütersloh: Bertelsmann Stiftung.

Bertelsmann Stiftung (2011). *Soziale Gerechtigkeit in der OECD—Wo steht Deutschland? Sustainable Governance Indicators*. Gütersloh: Bertelsmann Stiftung.

Chisholm, D. W. (1989). *Coordination without Hierarchy: Informal Structures in Multi-organizational Systems*. Berkeley: University of California Press.

Christensen, T., and Lægreid, P. (2007). 'The Whole-of-Government Approach to Public Sector Reform', *Public Administration Review*, 67(6): 1059–66.

Cohen, M. D., March, J. G., and Olsen, J. P. (1972). 'A Garbage Can Model of Organizational Choice', *Administrative Science Quarterly*, 17(1): 1–25.

Dearborn, D. C., and Simon, H. A. (1958). 'Selective Perception: A Note on the Departmental Identifications of Executives', *Sociometry*, 21: 140–4.

Hammerschmid, G., Oprisor, A., and Štimac, V. (2013). COCOPS Executive Survey on Public Sector Reform in Europe. Berlin.

Hood, C. (1974). 'Administrative Diseases: Some Types of Dysfunctionality in Administration', *Public Administration*, 52(4): 439–54.

Hood, C., James, O., Peters, B. G., and Scott, C. (2004). *Controlling Modern Government: Variety, Commonality, and Change*. Cheltenham, Northampton: Edward Elgar.

Jann, W., and Wegrich, K. (2008). 'Wie bürokratisch ist Deutschland? Und warum? Gernalisten und Spezialisten im Entbürokratisierungsspiel', *Der Moderne Staat*, 1(1): 49–72.

Lægreid, P., Randma-Liiv, T., Rykkja, L. H., and Sarapuu, K. (2013). The Governance of Social Cohesion: Innovative Coordination in Public Managment. COCOPS Work Package 5.

Lindblom, C. E. (1965). *The Intelligence of Democracy: Decision Making through Mutual Adjustment*. New York: Free Press.

Lodge, M. (2013). 'Co-ordinating and Controlling Dispersed Systems of Governing'. Unpublished Manuscript.

Lodge, M., and Gill, D. (2011). 'Toward a New Era of Administrative Reform? The Myth of Post-NPM in New Zealand', *Governance*, 24(1): 141–66.

Matthews, F. (2012). 'Governance, Governing, and the Capacity of Executives in Times of Crisis', in M. Lodge, and K. Wegrich (eds), *Executive Politics in Times of Crisis*. Basingstoke: Palgrave Macmillan.

Mayntz, R., and Scharpf, F. W. (1975). *Policy-Making in the German Federal Bureaucracy*. Amsterdam: Elsevier.

McGuire, M., and Agranoff, R. (2011). 'The Limitations of Public Management Networks', *Public Administration*, 89(2): 265–84.

Neller, M. (2012). *Der alltägliche Irrsinn der deutschen Energiewende*. Retrieved from <http://www.welt.de/wirtschaft/article111755829/Der-alltaegliche-Irrsinn-der-deutschen-Energiewende.html> (accessed 16 January 2014).

Rhodes, R. A. W. (1997). *Understanding Governance: Policy Networks, Governance, Reflexivity, and Accountability*. Buckingham: Open University Press.

Rittel, H. W. J., and Webber, M. M. (1973). 'Dilemmas in a General Theory of Planning', *Policy Sciences*, 4(2): 155–69.

Scharpf, F. W. (1972). 'Komplexität als Schranke der politischen Planung', in E. Faul (ed.), *Gesellschaftlicher Wandel und politische Innovation*. Wiesbaden: VS Verlag für Sozialwissenschaften, 168–92.

Scharpf, F. W. (1994). 'Games Real Actors Could Play: Positive and Negative Coordination in Embedded Negotiations', *Journal of Theoretical Politics*, 6(1): 27–53.

Scharpf, F. W. (1997). *Games Real Actors Play: Actor-Centered Institutionalism in Policy Research*. Boulder: Westview Press.

Scharpf, F. W., and Mohr, M. (1994). 'Efficient Self-Coordination in Policy-Networks. A Simulation Study', MPIFG Discussion Paper 94/1. Cologne: Max-Planck-Insitut für Gesellschaftsforschung.

Simon, H. A. (1962). 'The Architecture of Complexity', *Proceedings of the American Philosophical Society*, 106(6): 467–82.

Simon, H. A. (2000). 'Public Administration in Today's World of Organizations and Markets', *Political Science and Politics*, 33(4): 749–56.

Thompson, J. D. (1967). *Organizations in Action: Social Science Bases of Administrative Theory*. New York: McGraw-Hill.

Wegrich, K. (2010). 'Post-New Public Management', in B. Blanke, F. Nullmeier, C. Reichard, and G. Wewer (eds), *Handbuch zur Verwaltungsreform*. 4th edn. Wiesbaden: VS Verlag, 90–7.

Wilson, J. Q. (1989). *Bureaucracy: What Government Agencies do and why They do it*. New York: Basic Books.

4

Regulatory Capacity

Martin Lodge

> *You have transparency, and monitoring and coloured diagrams, peer pressure and prayer—and that's it... that is not going to be good enough in a world where there will be multiple significant capital markets all potentially interpreting and applying the rules in different or slightly different ways.*
>
> *David Wright, Secretary-General, International Organisation of Securities Commissions*
>
> (as quoted in Fleming 2013)

The 'regulation' word has enjoyed considerable currency in recent years. Contemporary regulation is linked to a number of developments: ideationally, regulation, at least in the period covering the past 30 years, has been associated with a shift in emphasis from fairness to efficiency (Majone 1997). In terms of organisational arrangements, regulation is mostly associated with separate, if not autonomous, agencies that have been specialising in oversight activity (see Levi-Faur 2005). More recently, it has been associated with risk-based instruments that also seek to shift responsibility for regulatory compliance to (private) organisations. More than ever, regulatory activities are said to be shared between public and private sectors and between actors at trans-national, national, regional, and local level.

As a governance strategy, a reliance on regulation—as a rhetorical device and as a set of instruments—appeals to a number of audiences. For some, the 'regulation' word offers the comforting reassurance of predictability and reliability. Similar to the regulator in the mechanical world, a device that keeps other processes in check, regulation offers the promise of a predictable and regular process, far removed from the turbulence of political life. It is a world that seems to safeguard administrative values of fairness as a result of due process, impartiality, and credibility. It is this understanding of regulation that is at the heart of the contemporary attraction: it offers an image of discipline and control (Roberts 2010).

The reliance on regulation as a governance strategy has become particularly prominent in an age of constrained public finances, public scepticism regarding 'big government', and growing internationalisation and complexity of economic life. Regulation is said to offer the functionally superior or seemingly successful (i.e. appropriate) solution to the time-inconsistency problems affecting governments. That is, the world of economic activity places an increased premium on predictable regulation where the likelihood of change due to fluctuating governmental preferences is seen as threatening private financial returns. In addition, growing complexity also means that an increased premium has been placed on expertise which cannot be provided within ministerial bureaucracies where 'generalist' civil servants climb the career ladder by swapping portfolios.

Regulatory capacity, therefore, has been associated, at the turn of the 21st century at least, with an institutional arrangement where privately operated public services are contractually procured and where oversight is conducted through specialist, often autonomous, units that are separate from traditional ministerial bureaucracies. Regulatory capacity has been about the exercise of predictable, expertise-rich judgement.

It is therefore not surprising that the focus of contemporary criticism about regulation focuses primarily on issues of capacity. For one, failure in regulatory oversight is seen as one of the reasons for the financial crisis of the late 2000s, whether it is because of organisational hubris or industry 'capture' (see Carpenter and Moss 2014). More generally, regulatory practice has been accused of being toothless, ill-informed, and poorly resourced. For others, regulatory activities represent an image of government overreach that seeks to spread its controlling tentacles into ever more niches of private, social, and economic life. Others regard regulatory activities as inherently about the dominance of corporate power (or 'capture') or of markets that undermine social solidarity. A further criticism suggests that regulators have become all-powerful and unaccountable branches of government that are 'out of control'.

Further critical views focus on the inconsistencies in regulatory standards (Breyer 1993), the 'unreasonable' application of enforcement strategies (Bardach and Kagan 1982), and costly information gathering (Wegrich 2011). The dispersed nature of regulatory activity is seen as problematic as it generates inconsistent approaches and problems of over- and underlap (Koop and Lodge 2013), as the epigraph to this chapter suggests. Attempts at facilitating consistency through centralising devices conflict with the goal of ensuring autonomy (Black 2007). Discussions regarding regulatory capacity, therefore, relate to the capacity of regimes consisting of dispersed actors with shared authority, as well as the capacity of individual organisations.

Regulatory capacity involves the informed exercise of regulatory discretion as well as constraints that check on regulatory discretion. Such procedural constraints are provided for by, for example, ex ante cost–benefit analysis and sunset clauses. In addition, discretion is checked by training and the development of distinct expertise. Given the competing logics that drive such attempts at placing constraints on administrative discretion, it is not surprising that these initiatives have generated major disagreements, among practitioners and researchers alike (Lodge and Wegrich 2009).

Therefore, regulatory capacity itself can be defined as the ways in which resources are allocated to ensure that systems of control maintain their well-functioning in often uncertain environments. Capacity is about the exercise of discretion and putting into practice of formal provisions. It involves trade-offs between competing values, such as fairness, efficiency, and redundancy (Hood 1991). Well-functioning is defined here in the sense of having a reputation for being competent. This involves 'a set of beliefs about the unique and separable capacities, roles and obligations of [a regulatory regime], where these beliefs are embedded in audience networks' (Carpenter 2010: 45). Defining capacity in this way highlights a number of key problems that are at the heart of this chapter: reputation is about the acceptance by others, it is a result of interdependent activities among a set of often organisationally fragmented actors, and it is about the interaction between these informal understandings and formal–legal institutional arrangements.

Regulation is, as noted in the introductory chapter of this volume, inherent to government activities. Accordingly, approaches as to how to organise regulatory capacity (and what its central purpose is) have gone through a series of phases. These range from the pro-regulatory responses that were triggered by scandals and crises in, for example, meat and financial markets in the early 20th century (see, for example, Upton Sinclair's (1906) classic *The Jungle*), to the more critical views of the 1970s that were informed by 'capture' theory, but which were accompanied at broadly the same time by the rise of social and environmental regulation. At the turn of the 21st century, the discussion moved to the 'better regulation' agenda that sought to supersede 'deregulation'-type arguments. The financial crisis and the subsequent sovereign debt crises offered the latest instalment of such debates where calls for tougher oversight and less trust in the self-regulatory activities of private organisations were accompanied by the cutting of public budgets with immediate implications for regulatory enforcement activities. Over the past decade and a half, regulatory capacity and quality have been at the heart of the OECD's interest in developing standards for good regulation and in conducting 'regulatory reviews' of national experiences in economic regulation. A similar concern has also driven the World Bank to create a handbook to evaluate infrastructure regulators (Stern 2010). More generally, an interest in formal standards and the exercise of official discretion has been a long-standing concern in political science and public administration.

In sum, challenges to regulatory capacity in the contemporary age range from the transnational consequences of national regulatory activity (i.e. national regulatory decisions are likely to have an effect on markets in other jurisdictions), the need to be accountable and transparent, to have expert judgement, and to deal with the coordination of dispersed nature of regulatory activities, to questions as to how actual oversight activities are being organised and conducted.

What is regulatory capacity?

Regulatory capacity is, as suggested above, about reputation. The exercise of authority requires not just the existence of formal powers to do something, but also the acceptance by other actors that one has the legitimacy to do so. Rejection of such a role by the targets of regulatory activity is likely to lead to resource-consuming disputes, whereas rejection by the wider political environment is likely to lead to elimination or at least modification. Such a context is widely seen to hinder regulatory activity, especially enforcement. For example, McAllister (2008) noted, in the context of environmental enforcement activities in Brazilian states, how lack of political support encouraged a high degree of formalism, so as to avoid putting careers at risk by shuffling responsibility upwards through protocolisation. It was also characterised by a lack of acceptance by regulated firms as they could rely on their superior resources and myriad legal review provisions to frustrate any form of enforcement action.

Actors tasked with regulatory activity will strive towards autonomy in order to protect their 'turf' (Wilson 1989). They do so by paying particular attention to issues that may affect their reputation rather than those that they regard as less significant, they will pay close attention to the relational aspects of their activities, and their activities will seek to display 'competence' in a number of ways (see Gilad 2012). For Carpenter (2010), such activities can be separated in a number of dimensions, ranging from technical and procedural appropriateness to concerns about performance and the moral implications of one's decisions.

This definition of capacity in the sense of reputation for competence across different dimensions points to the varied activities that are inherent in regulation, namely standard setting, information gathering, and behaviour modification. These activities are conducted, jointly or separately, within ministerial departments, or separate units or dispersed sets of organisations. The notion of 'audience networks' highlights that regulatory activities are performed in front of and, sometimes in collaboration with, varied 'stakeholders', whether this includes politicians, industry, specialists, or other interested parties. Furthermore, as regulatory capacity relies on often fragmented actors performing their roles, having a reputation for competence depends on the performance of others, in whatever organisational configuration (be they, for example, industry parties, ministries, or regulatory offices). Good regulation is about due process, fairness, and efficiency in arriving at decisions—however, how efficiency and fairness are assessed, weighted, and evaluated is a matter for interpretation. Good regulation, therefore, is about the use of discretionary powers in the context of interdependent and fragmented organisations, and their reception by various audiences in terms of their procedural, technical, performative, and moral implications.

A number of implications arise from such a perspective. One is that regulatory capacity links to issues about regulatory instruments in at least two ways. On the one hand, a lack of capacity has implications for the choice of regulatory techniques. The less the reputation for capacity, the more there has been a call for the use of non-discretionary regulatory techniques so as to reduce the temptation for politicians and others to interfere. On the other hand, it also has implications for the design of regulatory instruments as it highlights that their operation is not just a matter of formal institutional prerequisites, but also the presence of particular informal understandings about the way in which regulation is being practised.

Another implication is that reputation is based on the views of 'audience networks', as defined by Carpenter (2010: 45). This suggests that a reputation-based view on capacity is closely related to earlier work on autonomy and development. As noted by Peter Evans (1995; Lodge and Stirton 2002), developmental outcomes (in South-East Asia) could be explained by a state of 'embeddedness' of social ties (as defined by Granovetter). Accordingly, autonomy was achieved when organisations were not too closely tied to other social networks so as to be able to operate with a degree of autonomy. They were also not too loosely tied so as to be ignored or be in a position of ignorance, thereby avoiding ill-adjusted regulatory interventions.

It is difficult to define 'embeddedness' in any precise way as it is not clear whether it is a binary or a continuous state of affairs, and because the diagnosis of a particular degree of thickness of ties may be interpreted as 'too close' by some and 'too loose' by others. However, it highlights that capacity to govern in general, and regulatory capacity in particular, is about perception by others and strategic behaviours of individuals to enhance, or at least maintain, their reputation.

The recent interest in reputation as an explanatory device to account for the behaviours of regulatory organisations refers back to the seminal work by Goffman on *The Presentation of Self in Everyday Life* (Goffman 1959). According to Goffman, individuals seek the approval of their audiences, just like actors seek to present a credible impersonation of the role that their audiences expect, while at the same time being able to shape, to some extent at least, the audience's reception. A concern about reputation also leads to a bias towards consistent behaviour. Individuals suffer when they sense that their sense of self is not shared by their audience. A similar argument has been made in the early socio-legal literature on the role of regulatory enforcement officers (Hawkins 1984). Here it was argued that inspectors developed their own 'model' of how to act and build relationships with their wider 'audience'. They, therefore, exercised sanctioning in discretionary ways so as to maintain their status. The use of draconian sanctions, for example, was therefore a rare occasion as it might imply the failure to detect wrongdoing on previous occasions. Similarly, understanding regulatory capacity on an organisational level can explain why certain regulatory activities will be conducted in certain ways rather than in others as they might be seen as a direct threat to organisational survival.

On another level, understanding regulatory capacity through the lens of reputation and the perception of audience networks also highlights that regulatory regimes are usually not concentrated in any one organisation, but are fragmented across organisations at the same or at different levels of government. Thus, enforcement activities are likely to be organisationally separate from standard setting and information gathering (see Hood, Rothstein, and Baldwin 2001). In other words, regulation takes place under conditions of interdependence where reputations can be made and broken by actions outside the immediate control of any one organisation.

In order to consider the implications for the study of regulatory capacity, the rest of this chapter first looks at the ways in which criticisms about capacity have been formulated. It then explores whether supposedly 'better regulation' instruments succeed in advancing regulatory capacity, as defined here. Finally, the chapter considers measurements of regulatory quality in the context of regulatory capacity.

Challenges for regulatory capacity

How then can we start thinking about regulatory capacity in a contemporary setting without falling back on stating the banal, such as pointing to 'appropriate institutional governance arrangements', 'great people', or 'well-designed rules and processes' (OECD 2013)? It is unlikely that poorly designed rules and processes, ill-equipped individuals, and inappropriate institutional arrangements will lead to capacity-rich regulation. At the same time, such instructions might be well-meaning, but it is not clear what their actual meaning is. So rather than developing some generic perspective on 'good' things that might lead to capacity-rich regulatory practice, this section looks at diagnosed capacity deficits. After all, if regulation is reputed to be failing in particular ways rather than others, then one can already draw some conclusions about capacity.

The specific context of the early 21st century has proven problematic in terms of the challenges to regulatory capacity. One critical background condition is the internationalised nature of contemporary regulation that involves dispersion of regulatory authority within and across countries, as well as between public and private sectors. The exercise of regulatory authority is said to have immediate international repercussions: one 'incapable' regulatory unit in one jurisdiction may cause other regulatory units to suffer reputational crises and is likely to have implications across markets. For example, 'light' oversight in one jurisdiction may trigger failure in that particular jurisdiction, but this failure might also destabilise companies' other operations in other (more tightly regulated) markets. Similarly, a regulatory decision in one jurisdiction may lead banks to refocus their commercial activities across jurisdictions, or customers may stop eating particular types of foods due to a diagnosed shortcoming in a different jurisdiction.

These illustrations highlight the problematic nature of regulating highly internationalised markets where production chains are tricky to identify and where product complexity makes straightforward detection of risks problematic. Furthermore, after a period during which it was fashionable to suggest that 'command-and-control' regulation (i.e. regulation that involved formal statements of direction backed by legal sanction) was mostly ineffective, so-called 'alternatives to (traditional) regulation' have also come under criticism. Given overall uncertainty about effective regulatory strategies, it is therefore also not clear what kind of regulatory capacities the state should have. This has given rise to a number of responses, such as organisational rearrangements in financial regulation, accompanied by an insistence on tougher sanction regimes, whereas elsewhere budgetary cutbacks have brought about a reduction in enforcement activities.

Furthermore, debates about effective regulatory capacity have gone hand in hand with a growing concern about accountability and responsibility. With regard to the latter, contemporary challenges such as demography, climate change, and public finances have triggered debates about the appropriate distribution of functions between elected and non-elected parts of government. For example, pricing rules have distinct implications on the type of energy generation and infrastructure capacity that is going to emerge. Such challenges blur the appropriate boundary line between regulatory and wider policy objectives, making discussions about lines of responsibility more acute. These kinds of boundary conflicts have triggered demands for enhanced accountability, as non-elected bodies were seen to take on more and more decision-making functions traditionally allocated within ministerial bureaucracies. This has given rise to an interest in the ways accountability has moved beyond formally prescribed methods towards 'voluntary accountability' and more customer-facing activities to explain agency actions and to support customer choice (Koop forthcoming).

But what about perceptions of regulatory capacity? The following presents an overview of criticisms regarding regulatory capacity that were found in select UK broadsheets (*Financial Times, Guardian, The Times*) over a five-year time period (26 February 2008 – 26 February 2013). Of course, debates about regulation as found in newspaper articles may only reflect the views of a limited set of audiences, and the overview focuses on regulatory agencies rather than regulation as an activity at large. However, it nevertheless offers one way in which to explore what various audiences think of 'their' regulatory regime.

Stories were downloaded from Nexis UK that featured the search words 'regulator' and 'criticism'. The sole jurisdiction under consideration was the UK. Rather than offer a comprehensive overview, this search was intended to chart concerns about lack of capacity over time. The sample included financial, health care, utility, and airport domains. The search generated 373 stories, and a total of 363 claims were extracted for the period covered. Figure 4.1 illustrates the observed patterns, with the curves representing the claims aggregated in six-month periods. The most prominent stories covered include the meltdown of the British banking sector and subsequent criticism of the regulatory regime that applied to the world of UK finance, problems in healthcare oversight, and criticism of the regulatory approach taken by the airport regulator, the Civil Aviation Authority (in 2008). However, the vast majority of claims related to criticism of the financial regulator, peaking in 2010. As Figure 4.1 illustrates, 'lack of hierarchy'-type criticisms dominate overall. This criticism refers to the lack of 'tough action' and the absence of 'strict rules' to prevent future occurrences of particular crises. In the particular case of the UK, this criticism was voiced in the context of the Financial Services Authority and, to a lesser extent, various health regulators due to problems in hospitals. There was a notable decline in critical stories following the second half of 2012.

However, despite the potential bias of a search that includes 'criticism' and 'regulator' (that are likely to accentuate the demand for 'more rules and oversight'), criticism is not only directed at the lack of 'rules', 'tough' enforcement, and hierarchy. There are three other types of criticism. One points to the perverse and uncertain effects that accompany regulatory intervention (often voiced by businesses that oppose particular proposals), another to the need for regulators to understand markets better so as to encourage business

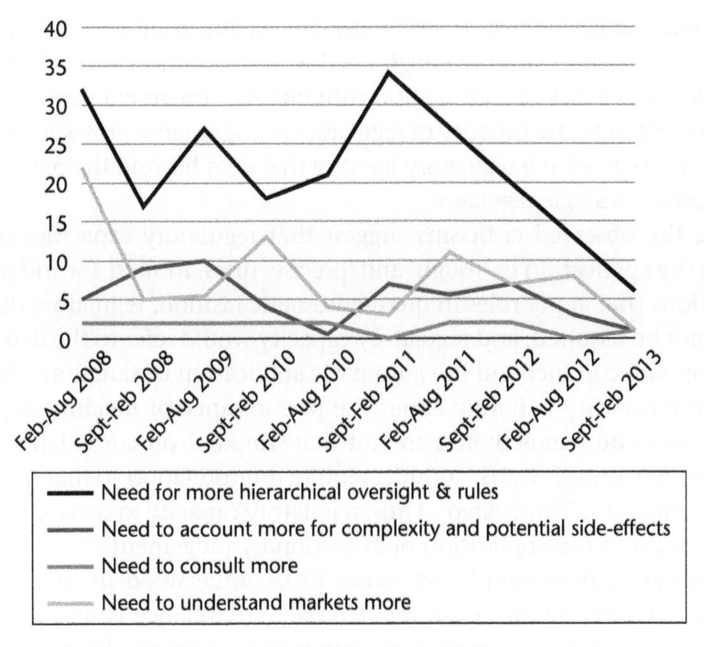

Figure 4.1. Trends in criticisms of regulatory capacity

activity which otherwise was impeded by regulatory intervention (this criticism was voiced by airlines in the context of the airport charging regime), and a further one to the lack of consultation and a lack of a 'professional' conversation within and between regulatory bodies. It is surprising that despite the academic interest in 'regulatory conversations' (Black 2002), this 'lack of consultation' type of criticism does not feature as prominently among the extracted claims. In addition, and maybe due to the type of search that was conducted, criticism was largely directed at particular regulators and not the interaction between different (levels of) regulatory bodies.

These four broad types of criticism highlight the kind of 'deficits' that are associated with regulatory capacity; they also highlight that the perception of regulatory activity (as presented in the print media at least) is not about the mechanical application of rules, but rather about a dynamic setting that involves negotiation about rules, their application, and the adaptation to their effects. One broad type of criticism, related to the most frequently voiced claim of a lack of 'tough' rules, refers to the capacity to formulate informed rules and to establish predictability and credibility. A second, related to the criticism that regulation generates unpredictable and perverse outcomes, refers to the capacity to avoid regimes that reduce overconfidence in regulatory methodologies and encourage active consideration of competing problem definitions and solutions. Third, the criticism that regulatory interventions undermine market rationality and entrepreneurship relates to the capacity of regulators to engage with the enlightened self-interest of market actors. Finally, the criticism of a lack of consultation with different interested parties and other regulators refers to the capacity of regulators to engage in a professional conversation and to develop a regulatory identity that goes beyond the organisational boundaries of a single regulator.

Thus, the observed criticisms suggest that regulatory capacities not only refer to the application of 'tough' and 'precise' rules. In such a world of formal institutions that apply rules in quasi-automatic fashion, regulatory discretion would not be required, and regulatory capacity would refer to the detection of inappropriate conduct and the automatic application of sanctions. However, regulatory capacity is hardly about the performance of machine-type activities, as most human activities are not that simple. Non-compliance and the underlying reasons for such conduct require interpretation so that they can be categorised and 'administered'. Thus, regulatory capacity to detect, assess, and enforce is about the application of discretionary judgement.

Furthermore, non-compliance needs to be understood in the context of regulatee motivation and capacity. After all, compliance is usually a matter of being informed, and having the resources to comply. Therefore compliance is not merely about the probabilities of detection and sanctioning but about understanding other parties' motivations and capacities, as the regulatory enforcement literature has noted (Ayres and Braithwaite 1992; Gunningham 2010). This again highlights how regulatory activity is shaped by the interaction between those regulating and the regulated and, thus, also by the ways in which the different parties seek to present themselves to the other.

In sum, therefore, debates about contemporary regulatory capacity could be said to be about the utilisation of oversight strategies in a context where various audiences are said to be increasingly sceptical about the possibility of effective regulation by state (and non-state) actors. If capacity is related to reputation in terms of legal-procedural, technical, performative, and moral dimensions, then the contemporary challenges are considerable. Technical expertise is disputed, and performance in terms of achieving intended results requires co-production under conditions of (transboundary) interdependence. Furthermore, procedural aspects are challenged by the continued blurring of responsibilities and by reduced resources, while the moral dimension in decision-making signals that regulation is far from a technocratic exercise, whether it involves life-or-death choices in medical regulation, redistributive choices in utility regulation, or the protection of vulnerable individuals in the regulation of institutions such as prisons, old people's homes, or schools.

Regulatory capacity innovations

If therefore regulatory capacity is at a premium, then what kind of capacity-enhancing strategies have been put forward? This section mostly concentrates on different regulatory strategies, considering system-design approaches applicable to both standard setting and behaviour modification, and 'better regulation' approaches in turn. It is noticeable that the literature is largely about (often functional) accounts of regulatory strategies while an interest in the ways in which actual regulators seek to enhance their capacity to pursue such strategies is lacking. Furthermore, while the literature highlights the importance of acknowledging the limits of authority and hierarchy, it is noticeable how little emphasis has been placed on understanding the underlying institutional (and behavioural) prerequisites for certain regulatory techniques to perform as officially intended.

Innovation in system-design approaches refers to attempts at developing regimes that rely primarily on the regulated to develop self-regulatory systems (so-called 'meta-regulation'; see Gilad 2010). The role of the regulator turns into one that checks self-compliance (Coglianese and Lazer 2003; Coglianese and Mendelson 2010). It is argued that such an approach allows for greater flexibility, encourages 'good citizenship' among regulated parties, and reduces the costs of inspection. In this respect, such approaches have the potential to address a number of criticisms, noted above. It allows for a focusing of regulatory attention, it encourages flexibility and discretion, and it also, arguably, encourages professional conversations among regulators and regulatees about goals and means.

One example of system-design-type innovation is so-called management-based standards. This approach relies on the development of regulatory compliance plans among firms (according to their self-diagnosed risk profile), the regulatory task being then to assess whether such plans are credible and reliable (Coglianese and Lazer 2003; Coglianese and Mendelson 2010). Exercising such a capacity is far from unproblematic: it requires an ability to assess whether firms are capable and motivated to comply, especially in highly distributed businesses. Problems of compliance are more likely to occur as a result of communication difficulties between corporate headquarters and subsidiary activities (Gunningham and Sinclair 2009), and detecting such problems requires a high degree of regulatory capacity. In other words, management-based standards assume that the regulated organisation is concerned about its reputation and is therefore motivated to (self-)comply. However, such reputational concerns may not be shared all across the firm (or its supply chain). At the same time, such approaches have also considerable reputational implications for those who are doing the regulating.

As management-based regulation is about verification, one key pressure is to deal with the tension between assuming that the self-regulatory activities of regulated entities are credible and the risk that such documents are mere facades.

Similarly, performance-based standards require considerable regulatory capacities (May 2003). Performance-based standards allow regulatees considerable flexibility in determining the way they produce their services or goods, as long as they remain within particular output or outcome targets. First, and most fundamentally, they require a capacity to measure outputs and outcomes. Second, such regimes require certainty that the observed performance standards are robust indicators of the kind of regulatory goal whose achievement is sought. Third, such regimes require detection mechanisms that minimise the risk of gaming by regulatees. The key threat to regulatory actors is therefore that outputs and outcomes will be seen as failures, as was the case in the New Zealand 'leaky building' episode (May 2003). In that case, a change in building code towards a performance-based regime was accompanied by changes in building materials and styles. These were only later shown to be incompatible with the New Zealand climate (i.e. this indicates a lack of technical capacity), leading to a large number of homes having to be condemned and homeowners facing financial ruin.

The well-known 'responsive regulation' framework advocates that regulatory enforcement should be responsive along the lines of a 'tit-for-tat' model of cooperation (Ayres and Braithwaite 1992; Parker 2013). This implies that regulatees are capable and motived to fix the diagnosed problems, and only face formal sanctions should they be seen to be non-cooperative (the 'benign big gun', according to Ayres and Braithwaite 1992). In turn, regulators concentrate their resources on those cases where formal enforcement action is really essential. The outcome is a regulatory order that grants discretion to regulators and delegated responsibility to regulatees. Again, however, this innovation is highly demanding in terms of its prerequisites. First, apart from assuming that the regulatory relationship is not 'disturbed' by the existence of other regulators and approaches, it requires continued interaction. Second, it requires an interest in cooperation. Third, it requires a good understanding among regulators and regulatees of the goals of 'responsive regulation', although both parties may, at the same time, be interested in reducing the scope for discretionary decision-making (the regulators seek to reduce their responsibility and thus 'blame-ability'; the regulatee seeks to reduce uncertainty as to how to comply). This may especially be the case as any blame may be interpreted as an attack on one's reputation. Fourth, it requires a highly capable regulator too, in the sense that any attempt at a 'mixed' enforcement strategy will challenge regulatory staff. Seeking to create a reputation with the local regulatee population in terms of 'cooperation' leads to a reluctance to turn on the 'big gun'. In other words, 'responsive regulation' may be seen as a model of enforcement that not only makes sense of the diverse enforcement actions that can be empirically observed, but also seeks to develop a model of regulation that assumes cooperation. However, for such a relationship to emerge, it requires considerable capacities that may be viewed as near unobtainable when seen through the perspective of reputation.

A less discretionary approach, with somewhat different reputational implications, is the so-called risk-based approach towards enforcement. Here the emphasis is on reducing the risk of regulatory 'overstretch'. A risk-based approach also supposedly signals that regulatory activity will always face resource limitations. Accordingly, a risk-based approach is assumed to offer a methodology through which regulators can identify which areas they should focus their attention on (namely systemic risks). Thus, regulators are able to focus on the important rather than the trivial. However, again, such a methodology places considerable demands on regulators. First of all, it requires an understanding as to what constitutes systemic risks. Second, it also requires a continued awareness of potential risks that might be emerging 'below the radar'. Third, it also requires that regulated firms are willing and capable of responding to identified risks. Fourth, it requires a capability to detect risks in the first place. Again, a focus on reputational concerns points to further problems. One is that the identification of problems may already be seen as an admittance of regulatory failure ('Why was this not identified before?'). Second, the identification of systemic risks will be biased on dominant worldviews and, thus, will reflect reputational concerns. Again, therefore, at first sight the 'risk-based' enforcement approach seems to make 'perfect' sense. However, once one considers the reputational and institutional prerequisites for such an approach to function, such an approach appears far more limited in terms of enhancing actual capacity.

While these strategies are mostly interested in the way in which regulators deal with their target population, 'better regulation' approaches seek to develop more consistency in regulatory decision-making across different bodies. Measures such as cost–benefit analysis, regulatory impact assessments, and administrative simplification exercises via standard cost models can therefore be seen as a response from the centre to the concern that dispersed regulatory activities will be captured, develop inconsistent approaches, and become non-steerable. Joint methodologies allow for comparison and a degree of oversight. Again, however, such innovations in controlling discretionary decision-making have their implications in terms of regulatory capacity. First of all, such ex ante tools require considerable resources, they delay decision-making and reduce flexibility, and they may have their inbuilt biases that facilitate certain approaches as opposed to others without actually taking the regulatory problem into account. Second, they create conflict between regulators and those ('meta-regulators' or central oversight units) that are assessing their compliance with guidelines. As the wider literature has shown, oversight units usually lack the political clout to challenge departmental or agency decision-making successfully. Measures that were supposed to 'rationalise' decision-making therefore advance bureaucratic politics. The same applies to ex post tools, such as sunsetting. Here, the innovation is to establish review mechanisms that allow for the updating and discarding of regulatory provisions after fixed time periods. However, given the lack of impartiality that accompanies any issue, sunsetting has had the perverse result of encouraging concentrated interests to lobby on particular provisions, leading to more captured regulation than before. Again, to bias against this kind of capture requires considerable regulatory capacity.

In short, innovations in regulatory capacity are highly demanding. They have emerged in the context of dissatisfaction with traditional 'command and control', but far from developing a regulation-'light' regime, they placed additional and more challenging capacity demands on those making regulatory decisions. These innovations have also introduced their own side effects and trade-offs—and how they can be utilised in a context of depleted resources requires further investigation. While there is an extensive literature on innovative strategies and (less so) their limitations, less is known in terms of how regulators themselves have sought to enhance their own capacity. In addition, there has been very little attention on the reputational consequences of these supposedly innovative strategies. In particular, in terms of performative and technical dimensions, the innovations discussed in this section raise challenges in that they require more rather than less technical expertise of regulators and regulatees alike, the performance has been questioned (as being both too interventionist and too light-handed) by various audiences, and the increased emphasis on discretion and responsibility fits badly with expectations regarding procedural capacity as all parties will wish to avoid blame by codifying their activities. Finally, in terms of moral implications, any attempt at 'rationalising' costs and benefits, systematising enforcement activities, or discussing how much discretion regulatees should be given to control their own operations involves moral choices. In terms of behaviours, reputation-centred accounts can explain a reluctance to verify or condemn in public, and they help account for the fact that 'better regulation' is exercised in a way so as to facilitate political will at any given time. Most of all, none of the 'innovations' fully addresses the dispersed nature of contemporary regulation, apart from, at most, noting the potential resources of third parties.

Measuring regulatory capacity

If strategies to advance regulatory capacity raise considerable challenges, how can regulatory capacity be identified? In contrast to other administrative capacities covered in this volume, the area of regulation has arguably attracted considerable interest in terms of measurement (see Stern 2010). This interest can be separated into two lines of investigation. One seeks to understand the extent of regulatory capacity so as to develop regulatory tools. Much has been made of the trade-off between discretion and capacity (thereby representing a precursor to Fukuyama's claim about the trade-off between autonomy and capacity; Fukuyama 2013). In other words, the argument has been made that the more capable regulation is said to be (i.e. the more technocratic decision-making can take place without the unchecked involvement of political interests or the threat of legislative reversal), the more discretion can be granted to those making regulatory decisions. In other words, it is argued that regulatory capacity can either be based on discretionary and resourceful decisions by regulators, or on non-discretionary contractual devices. The other interest is in 'measuring' formal independence of regulatory agencies and the perception of their quality. In general, the interest in measurement has involved a variety of methodologies and approaches.

The institutional design literature has linked regulatory capacity with the way in which different jurisdictions should go about institutionalising regulatory regimes (Levy and Spiller 1994). For example, a context in which there are limited expertise and financial resources, and where political systems' decision-making rules allow for quick reversal, is a context in which a reliance on regulatory agencies and their discretionary decision-making is unlikely to generate a high degree of capacity. Rather, contractual devices, such as licences, should be drawn up that minimise discretionary decision-making; a low degree of system capacity therefore determines the extent to which regulatory capacity (in the sense of resourceful discretionary decision-making) is desirable or not. Alternatively, regulatory capacity may require the building of outside support among regulated constituencies that make political opposition to its decisions too costly. Thus, regulatory capacity has to be seen not just as the presence of particular resources among those involved in the immediate oversight activities, but also in the wider context of politics that may, under certain conditions, be able to overturn regulators' decision-making competencies. Measuring regulatory capacity therefore requires an acknowledgement of the political institutional context and the likelihood that regulators and regulatory decisions can be reversed by alternative actors (put more formally, this indicator reflects the extent to which particular political systems are vulnerable to the time-inconsistency problem) (for criticism, see Perry-Kessaris 2003).

A second way of measuring regulatory capacity relates to the various ways in which observers have sought to measure formal and de facto independence (see Gilardi 2002, 2008). Accordingly, particular features drawn from those accounts that emphasise 'deckstacking' via procedural and structural devices are being highlighted (McCubbins, Noll, and Weingast 1987). For example, this involves methods of appointment, governance structures, tenure, financing, and decision-making procedures. For Stern (2010: 231), 'genuinely independent regulators' are those that are not funded from general budget revenues and are equipped with security of tenure for regulatory staff. Such measurements assume that particular institutional remedies can be placed along a continuum from 'low' to 'high' independence. These measurements of formal regulatory independence allow for an assessment as to whether higher degrees of formal independence are related to features of the political system, testing the hypothesis that a higher likelihood of governments being tempted to reverse regulatory decisions should be reflected in higher degrees of formal independence. It also allows for cross-sector comparison. Gilardi and Maggetti (2011), for example, find that telecommunications regulators are generally more independent than food regulators, with the latter also displaying a much larger range in terms of degree of formal independence. German and Austrian regulators are interpreted as much less independent than their counterparts in the Netherlands, Greece, or France, with Ireland, Italy, and the UK having the formally most independent regulatory authority.

The problem with measuring independence is not only that it places too much emphasis on the importance of formal provisions at the expense of informal norms and conventions (for a different critique, see Hanretty and Koop 2012). In addition, the idea of independence implies that regulatory activities are set free from their political context and that therefore reputation does not matter. At best, 'independence' can be seen in the way in which particular decisions do not require the signature of a particular political minister, but instead that of an appointed regulatory chairperson and director-general. Similarly, being cut off from the general budget may not enhance regulatory capacity much if this then leads to a resource-starved regulator whose financing is solely dependent on the (reluctant) funding from industry sources. Furthermore, individuals and organisations operate within a political context, their reputation is based on their reception by their various audiences (politicians, the media, industry, consumers, and so on), and relational ties further link regulators to their context. In other words, the idea of 'independence' and measuring it as an indicator for capacity are not particularly helpful. Statutory provisions do not offer much of an insight in terms of the reputational basis on which regulatory authority is being exercised.

Those concerned with the way in which governments seek to address 'better regulation' are largely interested in the existence of particular procedural devices, such as the mandatory requirement that regulatory impact assessments should accompany all decision-making, and how such procedural requirements are overseen. While relatively easy to assess from the comforts of the academic armchair or the consultant's clipboard, such measures of regulatory capacity are more about formal artifices than the actual processes involving 'better regulation'. Furthermore, such measurements are based on specific interpretations as to why particular instruments have been introduced and what their effect is going to be.

Alternative ways to think about regulatory capacity in different jurisdictions would be to look at a variety of output and outcome measures that are associated with specific domains. Such measures could include prices/charges of regulated services, quality indicators, and the extent to which regulatory decisions have been reversed by courts on the basis of procedural or substantive error. Similarly, regulators may be measured in terms of their capacity to process claims, or by their ability to settle acts of rule breaking. In addition, private investment in regulated services and the 'risk surcharge' on financial markets for such regulated activities may also be seen as a way to measure regulatory capacity. However, such output measures are always problematic. For example, how should the extent of regulatory fines be measured, especially in a cross-national perspective? Should a 'heavy-handed' approach with high fines be associated with a higher degree of capacity than a regulator that settles quickly and informally, but without imposing large fines?

Two further ways of measuring regulatory capacity rely on biographical and on perception-based work. Biographical work usually seeks to explore to what extent a 'revolving door' exists between the worlds of regulators and regulated. This indicator is not directly a measure of capacity, but might be seen as an indicator of 'closeness'. 'Closeness' could also be assessed in the context of sanctioning; we should expect that those domains where we observe a high degree of closeness between regulators and regulated attest to a reliance on informal and less draconian sanctions (Lodge and Hood 2010).

In contrast, perception-based work relies on surveys of interested parties. While such surveys of business or of so-called experts (email addresses copied from various academic conferences on regulation) might offer insights into perceptions of regulatory regimes, it is questionable whether such surveys offer much insight into cross-national and cross-sectoral experiences. Such a perception-based index, reflecting an aggregation of a number of surveys, is provided by the World Bank as part of the Worldwide Governance Indicators project it supports. In terms of 'regulatory quality' (defined as 'perceptions of the ability of the government to formulate and implement sound policies and regulations that permit and promote private sector development') and on a scale of +2.5 to –2.5, countries such as Ireland (+1.65), the Netherlands (+1.84), UK (+1.62), Germany (+1.51), and the USA (+1.49) score higher than Romania (+0.72), Serbia (+/–0.01), Brazil (+0.17), Trinidad and Tobago (+0.40), Greece (+0.51), or, indeed, China (–0.20), Argentina (–0.74), Indonesia (–0.33), or the Russian Federation (–0.35).[1] It is questionable whether this is an indicator of 'regulatory capacity' per se or of wider highly contingent views about particular countries. Furthermore, it is also debatable what the meaning of such scores are, and how to interpret change in scores over time.

The key problem with such indicators is that they are unable to distinguish between the capacity of individual regulatory bodies, the capacities of regulatory regimes, or of all regulation in a country setting. As noted, regulatory capacity emerges in the context of the interplay between different units, often allocated at different levels of government *and* across different national systems. Furthermore, those accounts that emphasise the importance of reputation in accounting for regulatory behaviour rather than formal independence per se suggest that regulatory capacity is something that evolves over time and has to do with agency leadership and strategies that seek to enhance the autonomy of the agency (Carpenter 2010; Gilad 2012). Thus, regulators may have equal formal authority to take certain decisions, but their actual capability to do so (especially when such decisions fly in the face of wider governmental preferences) depends on the willingness of other actors to contest such decisions. Regulators with a high degree of reputation will therefore attract less contestation than those with a low degree of reputation. A reputation-based view also suggests that regulatory capacity is hardly static but evolves over time. This makes the study of formal provisions as an indicator of capacity even more problematic.

Establishing indicators of regulatory capacity is further limited by the contested rationales that justify regulation. For example, the presence of resource-strong regulatory bodies can clearly be only one indicator of regulatory capacity. After all, authority requires not just the presence of statutory and other powers but also a willingness to comply on the part of the target population. However, the degree to which regulatory activity is perceived as legitimate varies and thus any indicator of regulatory capacity will similarly reflect the views of particular constituencies rather than others.

In other words, measuring regulatory capacity through a reputation-related perspective faces a number of challenges. Existing indicators that reflect some aspects of regulation may offer some first-level approximation, but are limited. They are usually based on assessing and judging formal legal provisions, or they rely on surveys. Neither of these methods offers a reliable indicator of what regulatory capacity is when seen from a reputation perspective. For such a perspective, one would need a measurement to investigate a) how regulatory

[1] <http://info.worldbank.org/governance/wgi/index.aspx#home> (last accessed 29 August 2013).

activities 'proceed' in terms of resource allocation, b) on what kind of technical expertise decisions across all parts of a regulatory regime are made, c) how regulatory regimes and particular interventions 'perform' (and this requires an agreement as to the different bases on which performance can be assessed), and d) what the moral implications of regulatory decisions are. None of these is easily obtainable through using box-ticking of formal legal provisions or the use of output and outcome measures. They would, however, allow for a more comprehensive and transparent view on how regulatory capacity is exercised.

Conclusion

In his managerialist book *The Regulatory Craft*, Malcolm Sparrow (2000: 17) noted how regulators have to deal with contradictory demands, such as calls for effectiveness, less intrusiveness, quicker processing, more informed decision-making, higher responsiveness to particular circumstances, and consistency. Thinking about regulatory capacity needs to go beyond formal provisions and towards an understanding that focuses on reputation. Approaches that concentrate on formal independence measures and demand more accountability and transparency, while also calling for 'role clarity' are misleading as they fail to understand the context of executive politics: roles are never clearly defined, formal independence is at best an argumentative resource in the battle for turf, and calls for more accountability usually do not acknowledge the variety of ways in which accountability and transparency can be incorporated and what kind of side effects such measures might incur. Furthermore, it hardly accounts for the dispersed nature of regulatory activities. This does not imply that we should not seek to develop indicators to measure 'independence' or 'accountability', but we should not conflate them with capacity. We should be conscious of the time-limited and contingent character of regulatory capacity: regulatory capacity is based on evolving mutual understandings between those doing the regulating, their interdependent co-regulators, and different interested audiences.

Such a conclusion may be seen as highly fatalist. It suggests that oversight will always be incomplete and that formal provisions will always be compromised when the going gets tough. It also suggests that conversations about enhancing regulatory capacity should focus on extrapolation (Bardach 2004), limitations, prerequisites, and trade-offs rather than on formal artefacts that have little to do with actual practices (see Sahlin-Andersson 2001). Such discussions are rather demanding and cannot take place in the glare of transparency in front of a mostly critical audience. Such conversations are also problematic as they take place in view of competing and contradictory demands for more central consistency (as demanded by central government, regulators, and business actors) and calls for greater sectoral flexibility (as demanded by the very same central government actors, regulators, and regulated firms).

Innovation in regulatory capacity is about the ability to deal with uncertainty and conflicting principles. It is also about avoiding over-zealous endorsements of specific regulatory approaches and the superficial discussion of content-free regulatory ideas. Regulatory capacity therefore deals with multiple demands and affects multiple levels. At the individual level, it requires a capacity to consider multiple problem definitions and potential solutions, a capacity in terms of technical expertise, a capability to communicate with different audiences, a capability to 'read' the wider political context, and, finally, a capacity to understand the interface between regulatory intervention and regulated target. No one individual is likely to be equally capable across these four areas. The demand for regulatory capacity at the organisational level, therefore, is to recognise the need for ensuring that these various capacities are present.

At the system-wide level, regulatory capacity is about recognising the inherent limitations of regulation and understanding the reputational basis of much of regulatory activity. As noted in the epigraph, regulatory effects are not just a matter of the direct interaction between a regulator and a regulatee in one jurisdiction, but a consequence of other regulatory strategies in different jurisdictions. This interdependence can be addressed in different ways, such as international mediation and enforcement bodies or professionalised networks among regulators. As one key 'audience' of regulatory activity, politics is about understanding the inherent tension between, on the one hand, granting discretion and autonomy to various fields to enhance specialisation (and possibly blame shifting), and, on the other hand, the wish to maintain control through centralising means. Any informed debate about this tension needs to understand that regulatory activities are not only about 'capture' or self-interested empire building, but about enhancing the reputation for capable regulation. In other words, if one is thinking of enhancing regulatory capacity, then one needs an understanding of the reputational basis of individual and organisational behaviour. Any attempt to impose systems that fly in the face of such reputation-driven behaviours is unlikely to generate much lasting support.

In sum, regulatory capacity is about multiple demands: it is about preventing too much corporate or other concentrated interest influence (if one assumes that regulation in the 'public interest' is not a misnomer), it is about developing expertise and robust processes, and it is about developing processes for fair and informed decision-making. In such a setting, uncontroversial and error-free regulatory decision-making is unlikely to exist. Regulatory capacity is fundamentally about acknowledging the inherent limits to oversight.

References

Ayres, I., and Braithwaite, J. (1992). *Responsive Regulation: Transcending the Deregulation Debate*. New York: Oxford University Press.

Bardach, E. (2004). 'The Extrapolation Problem: How Can We Learn from the Experience of Others?' *Journal of Policy Analysis and Management*, 23(3): 205–20.

Bardach, E., and Kagan, R. A. (1982). *Going by the Book: The Problem of Regulatory Unreasonableness*. Philadelphia: Temple University Press.

Black, J. (2002). 'Regulatory Conversations', *Journal of Law and Society*, 29(1): 163–96.

Black, J. (2007). 'Tensions in the Regulatory State', *Public Law* (Spring): 58–73.

Breyer, S. G. (1993). *Breaking the Vicious Circle: Toward Effective Risk Regulation*. Cambridge: Harvard University Press.

Carpenter, D. P. (2010). *Reputation and Power: Organizational Image and Pharmaceutical Regulation at the FDA*. Princeton: Princeton University Press.

Carpenter, D. P., and Moss, D. A. (2014). 'Introduction', in D. P. Carpenter, and D. A. Moss (eds), *Preventing Regulatory Capture: Special Interest Influence and How to Limit It*. New York: Cambridge University Press, 1–21.

Coglianese, C., and Lazer, D. (2003). 'Management-Based Regulation: Prescribing Private Management to Achieve Public Goals', *Law and Society Review*, 37(4): 691–730.

Coglianese, C., and Mendelson, E. (2010). 'Meta-Regulation and Self-Regulation', in R. Baldwin, M. Cave, and M. Lodge (eds), *The Oxford Handbook of Regulation*. Oxford, New York: Oxford University Press, 146–68.

Evans, P. B. (1995). *Embedded Autonomy: States and Industrial Transformation*. Princeton, NJ: Princeton University Press.

Fleming, S. (2013). 'Regulator Warns of Cross-Border Risk to Markets', *Financial Times* (London Edition), 25 November 2013: 20.

Fukuyama, F. (2013). 'What Is Governance?' *Governance*, 26(3): 347–68.

Gilad, S. (2010). 'It Runs in the Family: Meta-Regulation and Its Siblings', *Regulation and Governance*, 4(4): 485–506.

Gilad, S. (2012). 'Attention and Reputation: Linking Regulators' Internal and External Worlds', in M. Lodge, and K. Wegrich (eds), *Executive Politics in Times of Crisis*. Basingstoke: Palgrave Macmillan, 157–75.

Gilardi, F. (2002). 'Policy Credibility and Delegation to Independent Regulatory Agencies: A Comparative Empirical Analysis', *Journal of European Public Policy*, 9(6): 873–93.

Gilardi, F. (2008). *Delegation in the Regulatory State: Independent Regulatory Agencies in Western Europe*. Cheltenham, Northampton: Edward Elgar.

Gilardi, F., and Maggetti, M. (2011). 'The Independence of Regulatory Authorities', in D. Levi-Faur (ed.), *Handbook on the Politics of Regulation*. Northampton: Elgar, 201–14.

Goffman, E. (1959). *The Presentation of Self in Everyday Life*. Garden City: Doubleday.

Gunningham, N. (2010). 'Enforcement and Compliance Strategies', in R. Baldwin, M. Cave, and M. Lodge (eds), *The Oxford Handbook of Regulation*. Oxford, New York: Oxford University Press, 120–45.

Gunningham, N., and Sinclair, D. (2009). 'Organizational Trust and the Limits of Management-Based Regulation', *Law and Society Review*, 43(4): 865–900.

Hanretty, C., and Koop, C. (2012). 'Measuring the Formal Independence of Regulatory Agencies', *Journal of European Public Policy*, 19(2): 198–216.

Hawkins, K. (1984). *Environment and Enforcement: Regulation and the Social Definition of Pollution*. Oxford: Clarendon Press.

Hood, C. (1991). 'A Public Management for All Seasons?' *Public Administration*, 69(1): 3–19.

Hood, C., Rothstein, H., and Baldwin, R. (2001). *The Government of Risk: Understanding Risk Regulation Regimes*. Oxford, New York: Oxford University Press.

Koop, C. (forthcoming). 'Theorizing and Explaining Voluntary Accountability', *Public Administration*.

Koop, C., and Lodge, M. (2013). 'Memorandums of (Mis-)Understanding? Assessing Regulatory Cooperation'. Paper presented to PSA Annual Conference, Cardiff, March 2013.

Levi-Faur, D. (2005). 'The Global Diffusion of Regulatory Capitalism', *The Annals of the American Academy of Political and Social Science*, 598(1): 12–32.

Levy, B., and Spiller, P. T. (1994). 'The Institutional Foundations of Regulatory Commitment: A Comparative Analysis of Telecommunications Regulation', *Journal of Law, Economics and Organization*, 10(2): 201–46.

Lodge, M., and Hood, C. (2010). 'Regulation inside Government', in R. Baldwin, M. Cave, and M. Lodge (eds), *The Oxford Handbook of Regulation*. Oxford, New York: Oxford University Press, 591–609.

Lodge, M., and Stirton, L. (2002). 'Embedding Regulatory Autonomy in Caribbean Telecommunications', *Annals of Public and Cooperative Economics*, 73(4): 667–93.

Lodge, M., and Wegrich, K. (2009). 'High-Quality Regulation: Its Popularity, Its Tools and Its Future', *Public Money & Management*, 29(3): 145–52.

Majone, G. (1997). 'From the Positive to the Regulatory State: Causes and Consequences of Changes in the Mode of Governance', *Journal of Public Policy*, 17(2): 139–67.

May, P. J. (2003). 'Performance-Based Regulation and Regulatory Regimes: The Saga of Leaky Buildings', *Law and Policy*, 25(4): 381–401.

McAllister, L. K. (2008). *Making Law Matter: Environmental Protection and Legal Institutions in Brazil*. Stanford: Stanford Law Books.

McCubbins, M. D., Noll, R. D., and Weingast, B. R. (1987). 'Administrative Procedures as Instruments of Political Control', *Journal of Law, Economics and Organization*, 3(2): 243–77.

OECD (Organisation for Economic Co-operation and Development) (2013). 'Principles for the Governance of Regulators'. Public Consultation Draft, 21 June. Paris: OECD.

Parker, C. (2013). 'Twenty Years of Responsive Regulation: An Appreciation and Appraisal', *Regulation and Governance*, 7(1): 2–13.

Perry-Kessaris, A. (2003). 'Finding and Facing Facts about Legal Systems and Foreign Direct Investment in South Asia', *Legal Studies*, 23(4): 649–89.

Roberts, A. (2010). *The Logic of Discipline: Global Capitalism and the Architecture of Government*. Oxford, New York: Oxford University Press.

Sahlin-Andersson, K. (2001). 'National, International and Transnational Construction of New Public Management', in T. Christensen, and P. Lægreid (eds), *New Public Management: The Transformation of Ideas and Practice*. Aldershot, Burlington: Ashgate, 42–72.

Sinclair, U. (1906). *The Jungle*. New York: Doubleday.

Sparrow, M. K. (2000). *The Regulatory Craft: Controlling Risks, Solving Problems, and Managing Compliance*. Washington, DC: Brookings Institution Press.

Stern, J. (2010). 'The Evaluation of Regulatory Agencies', in R. Baldwin, M. Cave, and M. Lodge (eds), *The Oxford Handbook of Regulation*. Oxford, New York: Oxford University Press, 223–58.

Wegrich, K. (2011). *Das Leitbild 'Better Regulation'. Ziele, Instrumente, Wirkungsweise*. Berlin: Edition Sigma.

Wilson, J. Q. (1989). *Bureaucracy: What Government Agencies do and why They do it*. New York: Basic Books.

5

Analytical Capacity

Salvador Parrado

Introduction

Knowledge in and of the policy process is one of the key interests that lie at the heart of the field of policy analysis. This interest, as set out by Lasswell (1951), was inherently democratic. In an age in which, he argued, technocrats were in possession of superior knowledge in terms of substance, as well as in terms of forms of communication, the field of policy analysis was created to 'open up' the process and make it more transparent. At the same time, this field highlighted the importance of how governments seek to establish and maintain analytical capacity.

In practice, the importance placed on analytical capacity has varied over time. Furthermore, a noticeable shift in the kind of analytical competencies demanded by politics and the policy process has occurred. Three different trends related to interest in the analytical capacity of executive government can be distinguished over the past 50 years: first, growing demands for evidence-based research and data for planning in the 1960s and 1970s; then, disillusionment with such ambitious social policies, leading to waning interest in the late 1970s, 1980s, and much of the 1990s; and finally, a resurgence since the late 1990s.

The initial interest in analytical capacity coincided with the expansion of the welfare state during the 1960s and 1970s, especially in Europe. The growth of social expenditure triggered social experimentation (especially in the field of education in Germany—see Wollmann 1989) and an interest in so-called evidence-based research. It was believed at the time that the state was capable of 'planning' society and the economy. Analytical capacities were deployed to monitor the impact of social policies. The normative justification for strengthening analytical capacity was to focus on citizenship and the well-being of the entire population, not on the creation of markets or the constraints on consumers. Government interest in evaluating social policies led not only to the growth of research units within government, but also to the rise of government-sponsored research institutes, agencies, advisory bodies, and expert commissions. The development of quasi- or extra-governmental capacity reflected, in part, criticism suggesting that, in terms of both structure and attitude, existing ministerial bureaucracies were not well-placed to deal with the challenges of the expanded welfare state of the 1970s (Mayntz and Scharpf 1975).

In the United States and Canada, by contrast, the expansion of policy analysis during this period stemmed from large-scale social and economic planning processes that were taking place in defence and urban redevelopment. Dobuzinskis, Laycock, and Howlett (2007), however, argue that the rise of policy analysis in the area of defence was already well established by the time the Second World War had ended, as evidenced by the creation of organisations such as RAND.

By the mid 1970s, disillusionment with ambitious social policy programmes came along with doubts about the capacity of governments to systematically use knowledge to inform a more forward-looking and society-changing style of policy-making. These two factors led to reduced interest in government's analytical capacity. Still, the organisational capacities of government to produce and commission knowledge have largely remained in place.

Analytical capacity in terms of an interest in 'what works' re-emerged in the late 1990s, in part because the extensive public sector reforms and the attempt to restructure welfare states required a more 'solid' evidence base. 'Evidence-based' policy reflected in particular centre-left governmental interests, as had been the case in the 1970s (Head 2008). Yet the earlier interest in advancing 'democracy' or the 'welfare state' had been replaced by a focus on the individual user of the service. Accordingly, attention was directed at the study of specific services and programmes in order to find out what works and what options would deliver more effective (if not more efficient) results (Davies, Nutley, and Smith 2000). This trend led to some 'thickening' of analytical capacity-related units at the top of public administration. Broadly speaking, this particular set of analytical capacities consists primarily of evaluation and research that target individual policy interventions (and not so much wider governmental planning and policy development).

At the same time, analytical capacity was further affected by changes in the organisation of government. Once created through the process of 'agencification', sector-specific agencies established their own demands for analytical capacity, if only to justify their existence. For example, the adoption of a more US-style competition law across the European Union led to the development of different regulation technologies, such as impact assessment and risk-based policy tools, each of which required its own analytical (or technocratic) support. Indeed, the growing concern about 'risk' as a central theme in policy-making led to demands for quantification in order to justify action (or non-action) (see Baldwin and Black 2007; Black and Baldwin 2010). This concern carried over into central banking, resulting in what some have called the 'econocratisation' of analytical capacity in executive government.

The late 1990s also witnessed the growing prominence of a different set of analytical capacities, namely those associated with the 'spin doctor'. Policy advice in terms of enhancing the electoral profile of one's minister or one's overall government has always been part and parcel of the analytical capacities of government. However, it could be argued that the growing prominence of these 'masters of spin' (Jones 1999) reflected a strengthening of these analytical capacities, especially when it came to the way in which governments communicated with the media and the way in which electoral and other campaigns were being conducted. In other words, this analytical capacity reflects those of the 'spin doctor' who is able to read the runes of the political game and those of trends in public opinion.

Finally, there was also increased demand for more 'coordination' within government. The argument that government agencies operated in a segmented way so that social and other problems fell between the cracks of different departmental jurisdictions was hardly new. The late 1990s saw a growing emphasis on introducing 'czars' and 'commissioners' who were to understand the different demands of stakeholders within a domain, bring these together, and mediate among them. Such a position of policy coordinator requires an analytical capacity to be able to move between social systems and different knowledge communities, thereby reflecting a certain degree of 'boundary-spanning'.

In sum, analytical capacity has usually been associated with think tanks or other kinds of 'eggheads' within government that seek to explore trends, evaluate policy impacts, and conduct pilot studies. However, upon closer look, it becomes apparent that other types of tasks, such as spin doctoring, 'econocracy', and boundary-spanning, also place demands on analytical capacity. In the rest of this chapter, a particular focus will be paid to 'policy analytical capacity', namely the capacity that is widely associated with policy evaluation and analysis.

Policy analytical capacity and its challenges

Policy analytical capacity has been defined as the generation of knowledge (organised or sponsored by government) to be used in policy-making (Wollmann 1989; MacRae 1991; Leeuw 1991; Adams 2004). In the context of this chapter, policy analytical capacity refers to the research that executive governments produce or access (from non-governmental organisations) in order to understand, forecast, and anticipate public opinion, users' needs, potential actions on the part of businesses, and policy impacts. Policy analytical capacity is therefore an essential prerequisite for evidence-based policy-making (Howlett 2009: 161).

Some authors (Lindquist 2010; Tiernan 2011) distinguish policy analytical capacity from policy advice. Whereas analytical capacity focuses on medium- to long-term agenda setting, policy advice refers to the provision of analysis and information from the short to the long term at all stages of the policy process including policy implementation and service delivery. Policy advice entails analytical skills, the coordination of advice from several sources (governmental and non-governmental), as well as accountability between the advisor and the decision-maker (Lindquist 2010). As noted, this chapter focuses on the narrower concept of policy analytical capacity.

In order to make sense of the way in which analytical capacity is organised within the policy-making process, a number of classification schemes have been developed. For example, according to Lindquist (1990), there are three 'communities' that demand, supply, or repackage knowledge: decision-makers, knowledge creators, and knowledge brokers. 'Decision-makers' work on the demand side of knowledge generation: they have the authority to make choices and are normally the recipients of policy analysis. 'Knowledge generators' provide research data upon which analysis is made and are typically based at universities, research institutes, and private contractors. 'Knowledge brokers' analyse primary data and package them for the use of decision makers and can be found among policy advisers, government research staff, members of commissions and advisory bodies, and think-tank experts. Policy analysis is effective when the evidence needed to make decisions is transferred from the knowledge-generation phase to decision-making. Such a stylised account of how knowledge is transferred and generated between different communities will necessarily become blurred in the real world of policy-making, especially as some knowledge 'generators' may also be involved in brokering and some 'brokers' may also generate analysis.

Head (2010) identifies three enabling factors for evidence-based policy readiness: professionals with skills in data processing, high-quality information databases on relevant topic areas, and incentives for using evidence-based analysis in the policy process. According to Howlett (2009), additional features include the ability to institutionally coordinate between different organisations and stakeholders producing information and knowledge; the 'boundary-spanning' links between public sector, private sector, and non-governmental organisations; and finally, a vibrant policy community made up of well-resourced think tanks and media outlets that can offer a critical view of the analysis advanced by government.

Such accounts offer useful summaries of various factors that may, or may not, matter. They point to the highly demanding conditions that are required for policy analytical capacity to play a role (Mayntz and Scharpf 1975; Wollmann 1989; Edwards and Evans 2011; OECD 2012). However, a number of challenges to analytical capacity can be identified.

First, policy-making is not a value-free exercise. In an era in which populations are said to be highly demanding, but also display contradictory attitudes to issues such as economic growth, environmental sustainability, social integration, fiscal consolidation, and job creation, it is not always clear what kind of evidence will be required to justify or dismiss some initiative rather than another. Politicians may not want to know of findings that suggest that their pet topic is not having the desired impact as long as these initiatives are popular among voters. Politicians may not be interested in 'evidence' in itself, but rather in the processes of bargaining and interaction between the values and interests of different stakeholders (Head 2008, 2010). Furthermore, evidence is also not value-neutral: it matters what kind of methodologies are used, how experiments and pilots are set up, and how information is presented. More generally, the existence of competing value claims suggests that policy analytical capacity can only be one aspect of policy-making and will never (and should never) play a dominant role.

Second, there are also institutional constraints that affect the exercise of analytical capacity. One constraint is the presence of electoral cycles. Policy analysis that was produced for one government may not be of interest once a different party has entered government. Priorities change and therefore analytical concerns vary, leading to the abandonment of some key studies. Some governments may not prefer evidence that flies in the face of their own ideological concerns. Authoritarian and over-centralised governments are often said to be less interested in encouraging research that may challenge their own worldviews. A different type of institutional constraint is generated by different types of understandings about the role of bureaucracy. In a highly legalist system, certain evidence will play a more important role than in one that is staffed by a more 'generalist' civil service population. Similarly, bureaucratic career structures that allow for the bringing together of civil servants from across different departments will lead to a different kind of policy analytical thinking than bureaucratic structures where such cross-domain mobility is not present. Furthermore, the linkages between bureaucracy and select areas of society also constrain analytical capacity. Where there is a strong connection between bureaucrats and, say, trade unions and social welfare organisations, there will be a different way of reflecting on evidence about the evolution of the welfare state than those systems in which bureaucracy is said to stand apart from such societal organisations. In short, the nature of politics and bureaucracy influences what kind of evidence is seen as legitimate and establishes the time horizons for much analytical work.

The nature of the evidence itself can act as a third constraint. In an ideal world, policy analysis is based on high-quality data collection and storage that are carried out consistently by leading experts in the field. Yet such conditions are rarely present. In spite of the growth of social science research institutions since the 1970s, the financing of social science research is meagre compared to other scientific areas. One reason for this may be that governments do not wish to support evidence-based research that contradicts current policy-making. For example, when studies suggested that austerity measures negatively impact the most vulnerable in society, the British government discontinued government-based legal research in 2013. Another reason may be that the choice of research questions does not necessarily coincide with the kind of questions about which government actors would like to be informed (see LSE GV314 Group 2013). Finally, the demand for 'hard data' may reduce interest in generating qualitative research, or bias interest towards more economics-based analysis rather than interdisciplinary approaches. Indeed, it may be argued that the interest in creating statistical significance will encourage (some) researchers to eliminate important differences in social phenomena. In other words, the interaction between demand and supply of analysis creates its own problems.

A fourth constraint to analytical capacity relates to communication, especially between the research community (including research institutes and think tanks) and government (Mayntz and Scharpf 1975). Outside well-established channels (such as among veterinarians meeting in working groups and consultative fora), decision-makers and researchers do not meet with regularity. In the absence of this regular interaction, research institutes may develop their own agendas far removed from the needs of government. Such conflicts arise from the self-definition of researchers who may not be willing to conduct 'applied' research or to explore themes that are of interest to those that distribute taxpayers' money. According to Mayntz and Scharpf (1975), the relationship between ministries and research institutes in Germany (although this conclusion can be expanded to include other governments) is problematic because research institutes try to establish independence and autonomy in their work. This autonomy has two potential consequences: either the research priorities of the institutes are irrelevant to government decision-making processes, or they are too dependent on the needs of government. Though rarer, this dependency may jeopardise the legitimacy of the advice given. While frequent interaction between researchers and government is certainly likely to generate a consensus about problems and potential methodologies as to how to study particular problems, such institutional settings are also associated with risks related to the inclusion or exclusion of certain scientific opinions over others. Who decides what kind of expertise should be represented in these interactive fora therefore matters.

Fifth, in an ideal world, there would be sufficient time for analysts to conduct their research. However, many policy issues in executive government do not allow for long-term research, even where potential data may be available. In crisis situations in particular, or those processes which Mayntz and Scharpf (1975) called reactive policy-making, there is limited time to go through the large amounts of data, often held at different levels of government and across different units.

Finally, policy analysis, and therefore analytical capacity in government, is challenged by the way in which knowledge is understood. Local knowledge, usually held by lay people, front-line staff, and users, is too often neglected.

These inherent constraints on policy analytical capacity apply to executive government in general. The next section considers some specific cases.

The analytical capacity of governments

What shapes the quality of policy analytical capacity? While available literature is mainly limited to single-case studies, several works do address these issues.

In the United Kingdom, Hallsworth and Rutter (2011) and a report by the Cabinet Office (2000), *Adding It Up*, suggest that civil servants and ministers alike were not satisfied with the policy-making process during the Labour government, even though Prime Minister Blair tried to develop a systematic approach to evidence-based policy-making from the outset of his first term (Head 2010). Problems of policy analysis in the United Kingdom were identified as stemming from both the demand and the supply sides (HM Government Cabinet Office 2000), although these problems are familiar in other polities (for example, New Zealand; see Review of Expenditure on Policy Advice 2010).

On the demand side, the key issues are numerous. For example, international constraints or targets (for instance, from the European Union) on the policy process led to an emphasis on meeting targets rather than reflecting on policy substance (for instance, reducing carbon emissions). Similarly, manifesto commitments made during the electoral campaign triggered new initiatives regardless of (and prior to) any analysis. Furthermore, lack of interest in cross-cutting questions emerged from the departmentalism that generally characterises any government department primarily concerned with its own turf (Wilson 1989). In some cases, departments whose analysis has to be published have no incentive to conduct an analysis that may yield negative results. In others, tight deadlines associated with policy-making do not allow for proper policy analysis.

On the supply side, the key elements include shortcomings in planning long-term analytical efforts, especially across departmental jurisdictions. Problems were also detected in terms of the joined-up working between policy analysts (considered to be number crunchers) and policy-makers and in terms of recruiting and retaining staff. This long list of concerns that emerged during a period in British government in which 'evidence-based policy-making' was supposedly at the heart of government shows how prominent the constraints affecting analytical capacity are.

Somewhat different findings have emerged in the context of Canada. On the basis of a survey of 1,229 researchers, Landry et al. (2001) found that nearly half of the research results were used by practitioners (contrast with LSE GV314 Group 2013). Two key factors explain this degree of knowledge utilisation. First, the results suggested that research findings were used considerably more in the areas of social work and industrial relations than in other areas of social science, such as economics, sociology, anthropology, and political science. Second, knowledge utilisation was largely a result of the interaction between researchers and government users rather than the attributes of the research products themselves. While this particular study suggested a relatively high degree of knowledge utilisation (a finding backed by the Hertie School Governance Report's Administrative Capacity Dashboard; see Stanig 2014), other accounts suggest that policy analytical capacity is low in Canada, which then feeds into the (low) quality of the evidence bases in policy-making (Colebatch and Radin 2006; Dobuzinskis, Laycock, and Howlett 2007).

In the case of Australia, Tiernan and Wanna (2006) note how the declining quality of policy advisory capacity from Australian governmental departments reflects a 'discourse of declining policy capacity' (see also Lindquist 2010). In 2009, a report from KPMG stated that Australia benchmarked poorly against other countries as regards the way in which the views from external experts and citizens were integrated in the policy process. Less than half of the agencies providing advice to ministers collected formal feedback. Another report (Edwards and Evans 2011) denounced the low capability of the Australian public service in providing quality policy advice. These assessments were based on the interaction between policy-makers and analysts (either individuals or organisations).

Reading across these studies, several features stand out. One key feature is that the actual way in which policy-makers interact with policy analysts reflects attitudes and interaction patterns rather than the extent to which it is possible to systematically collect data, especially as the computing capabilities across governments have increased over time (Dobuzinskis, Laycock, and Howlett 2007; Banks 2009; Head 2010).

As noted, these brief assessments of different national experiences are rather limited because no cross-country systematic studies are available and because those studies that exist analyse the quality of analytical capacity of civil servants and think tanks separately. With the exception of one study, none has assessed users, citizens, and external stakeholders as an active and passive source of knowledge and their integration in policy analysis. The next section discusses how analytical capacity might be measured and assessed in a more systematic way.

Assessing analytical capacity

Assessing and measuring analytical capacity are difficult tasks that have as yet not been performed in a systematic way. Several dimensions, clustered in three groups, can be used to assess the analytical capacity of government: skills of policy analysts to analyse data, organisation and financing of policy analysis, and the context in which evidence-based research is carried out. For most of these dimensions, some proxies can be found, as shown in *The Governance Report* (<http://www.governancereport.org>; see especially Stanig 2014). However, those proxies are imperfect measures of the policy analytical capacity of governments. This section considers a range of proxies that have been used to assess analytical capacity in executive government.

Skills for policy analysis

For Riddell (2007), several skills that can be grouped into two sets are needed to carry out policy analysis. One set of 'hard' analytical skills comprises environmental scanning, trends analysis, forecasting methods, statistics, applied research, modelling, theoretical research, and the evaluation of the means of meeting targets. Another set of 'soft' skills refers to consultation and managing relations, programme design, implementation monitoring and evaluation, the capacity to articulate medium- and long-term priorities, and the skills to outsource policy analysis to consulting firms or to research institutes (see Boston 1994). In their empirical study of the Canadian civil service, Howlett and Wellstead (2009) found that the most widely used techniques were social network analysis, survey and problem-mapping techniques, consultative techniques, and mathematical modelling tools.

The presence of 'hard' analytical skills at the disposal of government can only be measured indirectly. One way to do so would be to identify the number of persons that work in government with a background to carry out analysis and the number of research institutes and think tanks in a country. Policy analysts can be found in government either as political advisers or civil servants. However, the information related to them is very scarce (Waller 1992; Bakvis 1997). If one looks at job classifications, it is difficult to identify who the professional policy analysts in Canada and the United States are (Colebatch and Radin 2006). Further, organisational charts are hardly reliable indicators to know whether they have the skills mentioned above.

A report from the UK Cabinet Office (HM Government Cabinet Office 2000: 161) identified 1,804 researchers working for government, including economists, operational researchers, social researchers, and statisticians. One can assume that these people would qualify as indicators for analytical capacity in government. *The Governance Report* counts the number of social science researchers as a proxy (see Stanig 2014). However, it not only assumes that social science has something to add to analytical capacity, but it also does not tell us much beyond perceptions when it comes to whether knowledge is actually utilised. It is here where the key questions arise: namely how is knowledge procured, under what conditions, and how it is eventually utilised?

Organising and financing policy analysis

ANALYTICAL AND RESEARCH UNITS

The number of research units devoted to analysis is also a good proxy to assess the potential capacity of government. As mentioned above, diverse organisational units are involved in analytical activities: governmental departments, units close to the prime minister or head of government, advisory commissions, research institutes, private contractors, and think tanks.

Counting the number of departmental units devoted to analysis is not an easy task. Wollmann (1989) made a preliminary assessment of the analytical capacity of Germany's ministries on the basis of the presence of planning units. However, these newly established units did not replace other units (*Referate*) in their analytical work. Again, the presence of a unit does not tell us much about the actual utilisation of the resulting information.

External contractors like consultancy firms have increased their analytical leverage in the last decades, although there is not enough empirical research to properly assess their impact on the tasks of government. In Canada, Howlett and Migone (2013) found out that a number of departments were particularly prominent in terms of procuring analysis from external contractors. Five per cent of the companies (even considering small budgeted contracts) controlled more than 80 per cent of management consulting funding in the federal government. Such a level of market concentration raises a further concern (Speers 2007): to what extent is analytical capacity procured in an open marketplace or has the world of consulting become a world of a few international public service consultants that outgun the resources of any national government and that are therefore in an ideal cartel-like position to sell their templates across the world (with governments at least benefiting from the possibility to sell reform packages as 'verified' by international 'best practice')? Another concern is that some companies have received very large multi-year contracts, which reduces the pool of potential bidders and diminishes the capacity of government to reap the benefits of competition (Kim and Brown 2012).

A further popular proxy for analytical capacity is to measure the number of think tanks. In 2010, there were 1,815 think tanks in the United States, 428 in China, 285 in the UK, 261 in India, and 190 in Germany (McGann 2010). Abelson (2002) gives several reasons for the prominent role of think tanks in the United States: political parties are weak and do not always align with the views of the executive or the representatives in the two legislative chambers; power is distributed among legislative and executive; and there is a revolving door between the senior levels of government and the policy research community.

The Hertie School *Governance Report* (Stanig 2014) counts and ranks the number of economic departments and think tanks (also adjusted by country population) and counts the number of policy schools. Furthermore, the report offers a measure of the funding devoted to research in general and to social science research in particular. All in all, one must assume that the number of research institutes and think tanks adjusted by population would give an idea of the amount of externally produced analysis. However, this is a partial view on the matter. The number of think tanks is an imperfect proxy, as some authors indicate that think tanks are relatively weak in many jurisdictions in terms of their impact on policy-making. After all, many think tanks play more of an advocacy than an analytical role (Stone and Denham 2004; Abelson 2007).

FINANCING POLICY ANALYSIS

Policy analysis commissioned by government is usually financed through public budgets. Measuring the proportion of public money invested in policy analysis might give an idea of its relative importance in policy-making. However, it is difficult to find out how much public expenditure is actually devoted to in-house research or to the procurement of external advice. Most budgets do not indicate expenditures according to types of analytical capacity, apart from a few countries where such information might be available due to their specific regimes regarding the disclosure of information.

Some information does, however, exist for the cases of Australia and Canada. In Australia, managers in charge of units producing policy analysis face difficulties in maintaining their budgetary allocations once ministers lose interest in their advice or where there is no wider governmental interest in their research. More generally, it is often argued that such cycles of initial interest and subsequent neglect have an overall harmful effect on the analytical capacities within government (Lindquist 2010). In Canada, unlike many other jurisdictions, it is compulsory to publish contracts that have been awarded to private consultancy firms. The published information suggests a growth in the extent to which external firms are utilised for policy analysis (Perl and White 2002). However, Howlett and Migone (2013) note that there was actually a reduction in expenditure after 2007.

In conclusion, it is difficult to come to a robust view as to how well different executive governments do in terms of mobilising policy analytical capacity. Different proxies exist that might tell us something about the universe in which such capacity might exist, but it tells us little about the actual way in which analytical activities are encouraged, conducted, and ultimately utilised.

The context

It is also important to point to another constraint on understanding analytical capacity, namely, the context in which executive politics takes place. Accordingly, it is important to underline those specific challenges, although it should be noted that these are not necessarily seen as 'bad' for analytical capacity. This section seeks to highlight how different logics within executive government do not necessarily reinforce each other, but are often in competition with one other.

THE IMPACT OF GOVERNMENT CHANGE

Every change of government is likely to entail a mismatch between newly incoming ministers and the existing policy expert community, which is, at times, considered as 'dependent' on the previous government. There are several examples of this mismatch or mistrust even in governments that are supposedly keen on evidence-based policy-making. For instance, in Australia new incumbents in 1996 and 2007 complained after each change of government of the slow pace of the Australian public service to adapt to the new party's priorities in terms of policy analysis (Lindquist 2010). Aucoin (2008) has argued that political executives increasingly distrust the public service because former governments have tried to use it in a partisan fashion so that the permanent policy experts have lost independence, reliability, and credibility as a source of expertise. Therefore, repeated turnover in government may hinder the capacity to build up a permanent source of policy analysis.

SHORT- VERSUS LONG-TERM ANALYTICAL CAPACITY NEEDS

Governments need both long- and short-term analytical capacity. Long-term perspectives are required especially for issues that require large-scale investment, such as infrastructure, demographic change, or the environment. Short-term analysis is needed to deal with the day-to-day world of crises. However, as noted, crises are a highly problematic area when it comes to the utilisation of analytical capacity. On the one hand, studies of decision-making in crisis situations have suggested that decision-makers are unlikely to reach out for evidence, but will rather 'bunker down' and centralise decision-making. On the other hand, crises are contexts in which politicians quickly feel the media heat and therefore demand 'definite' statements that might be difficult to produce. In some cases, 'Pavlovian' responses that economise on rationality (i.e. policy responses may be devised without costly research and consultation processes) may be sufficient (Hood and Lodge 2005), but in other cases, such as responses to E. coli outbreaks, the need to justify decisions with science may lead to a conflict between the political urge for definite statements and the scientific need to establish somewhat robust results.

More generally, analytical capacity within government is said to be geared towards the short term. Howlett and Wellstead's survey (2009) of the perceptions of analysts regarding their job and the future of government shows how responses are mostly related to a short-term perspective that seeks to satisfy political demands in response to external events. Other responses suggested that there was a lack of overall top-down direction in terms of evidence-based policy-making, whilst others emphasised more their boundary-spanning activities in terms of managing networks of analytical activities. In sum, government-based analysts see themselves and their work as reactive and not as anticipating future challenges and developing blueprints.

Further, in his empirical study on Canada, Howlett (2009) found that analysts in government were clustered primarily in short-to-medium-term areas of interest, while long-term interest in policy analysis was neglected. He established that analysts were engaged in five areas: environment and resources, social services, business and economics, culture, sports and tourism, and police and security. This concentration did not correlate with the size of overall budgetary expenditure. It seemed that the focus had to do more with post-9/11 security issues and the response to the post-2007–8 financial and economic crisis. The trade-off between requiring analytical efforts to deal with high-profile headline issues and analysing the effects of long-established and less prominent programmes seems to be usually resolved in favour of the former.

Examples of units dealing with long-term policy challenges over time are rare. The 'blue sky thinking' unit under Tony Blair was quickly abandoned as soon as Gordon Brown became prime minister. In New Zealand, the Treasury is widely held as responsible for developing the blueprint for the extensive public sector reforms that commenced in the 1980s. Here it was the actual neglect by the previous prime minister that led officials in the Treasury to establish a unit to encourage 'radical thinking'. However, the Treasury's close association with the various initiatives that came to characterise New Zealand's public sector also meant that the incoming Labour government in the late 1990s was highly sceptical of its advice (Lodge and Gill 2011). In other words, creating the conditions for long-term analytical capacity to exist within government requires support from prime ministers or other senior ministers (Lindquist 2010).

As noted already, it is also difficult to maintain analytical priorities over time. For example, priorities for analysis in the Australian federal government shifted from strategic advice to issues of implementation and delivery during the economic and financial crisis of the late 2000s (Lindquist 2010).

It is therefore not surprising that long-term analysis is conducted among think tanks and government-backed research institutes rather than within government itself. However, it is also noticeable, as Abelson (2002) suggests, that think tanks have become increasingly more engaged in and concerned with the short-term needs of policy-makers at the expense of a focus on long-term analytical capacity.

In sum, it is therefore difficult to come to a view as to how to measure analytical capacity and how to assess whether some governments are 'more informed' than others in terms of organising and utilising knowledge. Political priorities change, funding changes, and intellectual fashions change—all of which make measurement of one proxy over time highly problematic.

Innovation in analytical capacity

Innovation in analytical capacity can be identified in at least three areas: expanding the actors who provide analysis, establishing strategies to increase the number of long-term studies, and enhancing the capacity for short-term analysis for governmental crisis management.

One innovation that has extended the number of actors that deliberate over policy has been an increased reliance on open data and online deliberation via social networks and crowdsourcing. Such initiatives are wide ranging, including for example, websites that allow citizens to report problems (thereby enhancing the information basis for governments), or websites that allow for online deliberation as to how to address particular challenges. Examples include ideas in the UK government that allowed interested parties to suggest areas in which spending was to be cut, or where 'red tape' was hindering business activities (HM Treasury). The record of such initiatives is, at best, mixed. Similarly, in the area of health, networks of patients with chronic illnesses and disabilities are used to enhance the interaction between patients and doctors (Griffiths et al. 2012). Such information flows are good at adding to the information basis on which governments may make decisions, but they rarely involve including citizens in analysing the data.

The 'open data' movement suggests that such analytical tasks could increasingly be taken on by concerned citizens or some other third parties. After all, the release of data is reducing the information asymmetry that government has held over its subjects. However, again, it is not clear whether the enhanced ability of third parties to analyse government data leads to more knowledge utilisation by government of these additional sources of analysis. In a recent comparative research of five countries, Huijboom and Van den Broek (2011) showed that there was no clear evidence on the impact of open data.

Another set of innovative practices has to do with the development of capacity for long-term analysis. Some governments have established government-financed research organisations with a focus on future developments that are equipped with considerable budgets to commission research. For instance, the Scientific Council for Government Policy (WRR) in the Netherlands began as an advisory committee in 1972. Since the early 1980s, its work has focused on broader and forward-looking social issues. The Institute for Future Studies in Stockholm also started its activities in the early 1970s and became an independent research foundation in 1987. In France, the Centre d'analyse stratégique was in charge of research into future challenges until it was replaced in 2013 by the Commissariat général à la stratégie et à la prospective that reports to the prime minister and the president. Other countries have similar institutions, but most countries seem to lack an institute devoted to the analysis of trajectories and future trends.

A final set of innovative practices relates to the more short-term analytical capacities available to executive governments, particularly to deal with crises. How to develop analytical capacities that enable governments to respond to shocks and crises, especially of an environmental kind, was the object of several intergovernmental seminars organised by the Public Governance Direction of the OECD, prompted by the economic and financial crisis (OECD 2012).

These concerns also gave rise to the notion of 'strategic agility', which was initially applied by the Finnish government in the late 2000s. The concept of strategic agility, which originated from the private sector, is based on the argument that big corporations evolve in a context characterised by rapid change, requiring flexible cooperation across departments and networking approaches towards problem-solving. Three factors supposedly enable organisations to be strategically agile: 1) sensitivity to identify and frame emerging issues, which is fostered through an open strategy process that encourages dialogue internally as well as with customers; 2) mobilisation of resources to where they are needed; and 3) leadership unity to meet tough collective decisions. In terms of policy analytical capacity, then, strategic agility requires an open system of knowledge acquisition as well as an entrenched culture of taking advantage of expertise from different sources (OECD 2012).

It is too early to tell whether ideas regarding 'strategic agility' will have much currency in the future. Nevertheless, the concept highlights that analytical capacity is not just about staff in ministries or the presence of research institutes. Instead, it is about bringing together different sources of knowledge and identifying potential challenges not only to existing policy paths, but also to scientific orthodoxies.

Conclusion

This chapter has focused on policy analytical capacities as a subset of a much broader set of analytical capacities that are required by governments to contribute to problem-solving. In many ways, however, this focus has pointed to the inherent constraints that exist in terms of organising knowledge for government. The notion of 'evidence-based' policy-making offered a vision of a technocracy developing policy options that would not just be 'best in the world', but also sufficiently bespoke to respond to particular contexts. However, as noted, the context of executive government and the inherent contestations as to what knowledge constitutes pose considerable challenges for analytical capacity. Such challenges range from questions about how to tap into information about existing trends in a reliable way to questions about how to analyse such information and by whom. This chapter has also highlighted the extensive nature of 'outsourcing' that characterises analytical capacity today. Again, this raises issues about the appropriate boundaries between the type of analytical capacity we expect to exist within ministerial bureaucracies, regulatory, or executive agencies on the one hand, and the world of private sector consultancies, firms, other societal organisations, research institutes, and even universities on the other.

References

Abelson, D. E. (2002). *Do Think Tanks Matter? Assessing the Impact of Public Policy Institutes*. Montreal, Ithaca: McGill-Queen's University Press.

Abelson, D. E. (2007). 'Any Ideas? Think Tanks and Policy Analysis in Canada', in L. Dobuzinskis, D. H. Laycock, and M. Howlett (eds), *Policy Analysis in Canada: The State of the Art*. Toronto, Buffalo: University of Toronto Press, 298–310.

Adams, D. (2004). 'Usable Knowledge in Public Policy', *Australian Journal of Public Administration*, 63(1): 29–42.

Aucoin, P. (2008). 'New Public Management and the Quality of Government: Coping with the New Political Governance in Canada'. Paper presented at Conference New Public Management and the Quality of Government SOG and the Quality of Government Institute, University of Gothenburg, 13–15 November.

Bakvis, H. (1997). 'Advising the Executive: Think Tanks, Consultants, Political Staff and Kitchen Cabinets', in P. M. Weller, H. Bakvis, and Rhodes, R. A. W (eds), *The Hollow Crown: Countervailing Trends in Core Executives*. New York: St. Martin's Press, 84–125.

Baldwin, R., and Black, J. (2007). 'Really Responsive Regulation'. LSE Law, Society and Economy Working Papers 15/2007. London: London School of Economics.

Banks, G. (2009). *Evidence-Based Policy Making: What is it? How do we get it?* Melbourne: Productivity Commission.

Black, J., and Baldwin, R. (2010). 'Really Responsive Risk-Based Regulation', *Law and Policy*, 32(2): 181–213.

Boston, J. (1994). 'Purchasing Policy Advice: The Limits to Contracting Out', *Governance*, 7(1): 1–30.

Colebatch, H. K., and Radin, B. A. (2006). 'Mapping the Work of Policy', in H. K. Colebatch (ed.), *The Work of Policy: An International Survey*. Lanham: Rowman & Littlefield, 217–26.

Davies, H. T. O., Nutley, S. M., and Smith, P. C. (2000). *What Works? Evidence-Based Policy and Practice in Public Services*. Bristol: The Policy Press.

Dobuzinskis, L., Laycock, D. H. and Howlett, M. (eds) (2007). *Policy Analysis in Canada: The State of the Art.* Toronto, Buffalo: University of Toronto Press.

Edwards, M., and Evans, M. (2011). *Getting Evidence into Policy-Making: ANZSIG Insights*. Canberra: ANZOG Institute for Governance.

Griffiths, F., Cave, J., Boardman, F., Ren, J., Pawlikowska, T., Ball, R., Clarke, A., and Cohen, A. (2012). 'Social Networks—The Future for Health Care Delivery', *Social Science and Medicine*, 75(12): 2233–41.

Hallsworth, M., and Rutter, J. (2011). *Making Policy Better: Improving Whitehall's Core Business*. London: Institute for Government.

Head, B. W. (2008). 'Three Lenses of Evidence-Based Policy', *Australian Journal of Public Administration*, 67(1): 1–11.

Head, B. W. (2010). 'Evidence-Based Policy: Principles and Requirements', in Australian Government (ed.), *Strengthening Evidence-Based Policy in the Australian Federation: Roundtable Proceedings: Canberra, 17–18 August 2009, Volume 1*. Melbourne: Productivity Commission, 13–26.

HM Government Cabinet Office (2000). *Adding It Up: Improving Analysis and Modelling in Central Government*. London: The Stationery Office.

HM Treasury [website]. *Spending Challenge: Ideas Being Taken Forward at Spending Review*. Retrieved from <http://webarchive.nationalarchives.gov.uk/20130405170223/>; <http://www.hm-treasury.gov.uk/spend_spendingchallenge_ideas_taken_fwd.htm> (accessed 14 January 2014).

Hood, C., and Lodge, M. (2005). 'Aesop with Variations: Civil Service Competency as a Case of German Tortoise and British Hare?', *Public Administration*, 83(4): 805–22.

Howlett, M. (2009). 'Policy Analytical Capacity and Evidence-Based Policy-Making: Lessons from Canada', *Canadian Public Administration*, 52(2): 153–75.

Howlett, M. P., and Migone, A. (2013). 'The Supply of Policy and Management Consultancies to Canadian Federal Departments: New Evidence on Contract Size, Type and Structure'. Lee Kuan Yew School of Public Policy Research Paper No. 13-03. Singapore: Lee Kuan Yew School of Public Policy.

Howlett, M. P., and Wellstead, A. M. (2009). 'Re-Visiting Meltsner: Policy Advice Systems and the Multi-Dimensional Nature of Professional Policy Analysis'. Paper Prepared for the Australian Public Policy Network Conference University of Tasmania Hobart, Tasmania.

Huijboom, N., and Van den Broek, T. (2011). 'Open Data: An International Comparison of Strategies', *European Journal of ePractice*, 12: 1–13.

Jones, N. (1999). *Sultans of Spin*. London: Gollancz.

Kim, Y. W., and Brown, T. L. (2012). 'The Importance of Contract Design', *Public Administration Review*, 72(5): 687–96.

KPMG (2009). *Benchmarking Australian Government Administration Performance*. Canberra: KPMG.

Landry, R., Amara, N., and Lamari, M. (2001). 'Utilization of social science research knowledge in Canada', *Research Policy* 30: 333–49.

Lasswell, H., and Lerner, D. D. (1951). *The Policy Sciences: Recent Developments in Scope and Method*. Stanford: Stanford University Press.

Leeuw, F. L. (1991). 'Policy Theories, Knowledge Utilization, and Evaluation', *Knowledge and Policy*, 4(3): 73–91.

Lindquist, E. (2010). 'From Rhetoric to Blueprint: The Moran Review as a Concerted, Comprehensive and Emergent Strategy for Public Service Reform', *Australian Journal of Public Administration*, 69(2): 115–51.

Lindquist, E. A. (1990). 'The Third Community, Policy Inquiry, and Social Scientists', in S. Brooks, and A. Gagnon (eds), *Social Scientists, Policy, and the State*. New York: Praeger, 21–52.

Lodge, M. and Gill, D. (2011). 'Toward a New Era of Administrative Reform? The Myth of Post-NPM in New Zealand' *Governance* 24(1): 141–66.

LSE GV314 Group (2013). 'Evaluation Under Contract: Government Pressure and the Production of Policy Research', *Public Administration*: 1–16 (early view: DOI: 10.1111/padm.12055).

MacRae, D. (1991). 'Policy Analysis and Knowledge Use', *Knowledge and Policy*, 4(3): 27–40.

Mayntz, R. and Scharpf, F. W. (1975). *Policy-making in the German Federal Bureaucracy*, Amsterdam: Elsevier.

McGann, J. (2010). *2010 Global Go-To Think Tanks Index Report*. Philadelphia: University of Pennsylvania.

OECD (Organisation for Economic Co-operation and Development) (2012). 'Strategic Agility for Strong Societies and Economies'. Summary and Issues for further Debate. International Workshop Paris: OECD.

Perl, A., and White, D. J. (2002). 'The Changing Role of Consultants in Canadian Policy Analysis', *Policy and Society*, 21(1): 49–73.

Review of Expenditure on Policy Advice (2010). *Improving the Quality and Value of Policy Advice: Findings of the Committee Appointed by the Government to Review Expenditure on Policy Advice*. Wellington: The Treasury.

Riddell, N. (2007). *Policy Research Capacity in the Federal Government*. Ottawa: Policy Research Initiative.

Speers, K. (2007). 'The Invisible Private Service: Consultations and Public Policy in Canada', in L. Dobuzinskis, D. H. Laycock, and M. Howlett (eds), *Policy Analysis in Canada: The State of the Art*. Toronto, Buffalo: University of Toronto Press, 339–421.

Stanig, P. (2014). 'Governance Indicators', in Hertie School of Governance (ed.), *The Governance Report 2014*. Oxford: Oxford University Press, 111–50.

Stone, D. and Denham, A. (eds) (2004). *Think Tank Traditions: Policy Research and the Politics of Ideas*. Manchester, New York: Manchester University Press.

Tiernan, A. (2011). 'Advising Australian Federal Governments: Assessing the Evolving Capacity and Role of the Australian Public Service', *Australian Journal of Public Administration*, 70(4): 335–46.

Tiernan, A., and Wanna, J. (2006). 'Competence, Capacity, Capability: Towards Conceptual Clarity in the Discourse of Declining Policy Skills: Presentation to an ICPA Forum Workshop'. Canberra: The Australian National University.

Waller, M. (1992). 'Evaluating Policy Advice', *Australian Journal of Public Administration*, 51(4): 440–6.

Wilson, J. Q. (1989). *Bureaucracy: What Government Agencies Do and Why They Do It*. New York: Basic Books.

Wollmann, H. (1989). 'Policy Analysis in West Germany's Federal Government: A Case of Unfinished Governmental and Administrative Modernization?' *Governance*, 2 (3): 233–66.

6

Management Capacity and Performance in European Public Administrations[1]

Gerhard Hammerschmid, Vid Štimac, and Kai Wegrich

Introduction: increasing popularity and limitations of measuring government capacity

While administrative capacity is generally said to be a key precondition for effective policy-making and hence an ingredient of good governance, the state of administrative capacity is problematic both at a practical level and in terms of scholarly analysis of capacities. On a practical level, the financial crisis has stretched state (financial) capacities and is said to have left a 'depleted state' with little muscle to deliver key services, at least in some countries. A key challenge then is determining how to develop capacities in times of scarce resources and increasing demands in terms of policy-making and service delivery. On a scholarly level, the last two decades have witnessed a 'boom' or 'explosion' of quantitative governance and government-related indicator sets. The question is how valuable these indicators are for exploring not only the broad forces that shape (good) governance, but also the role that management tools, instruments, and institutional reform play and how they can be designed to improve government performance.

Many existing indicator studies rank countries in dimensions that fall outside the scope of these issues. For example, the Worldwide Governance Indicators, sponsored by the World Bank, draw on many data sources to compile a set of six aggregate indicators on broad aspects such as 'rule of law', 'government effectiveness', 'regulatory quality', and the openness of

[1] The research leading to these results has received funding from the European Union's Seventh Framework Programme under grant agreement No. 266887 (Project COCOPS), Socio-economic Sciences and Humanities.

the democratic political process. The World Bank's Doing Business Project develops indicators for topics ranging from starting a business to enforcing contracts to compare business regulation environments across economies. These indicators introduce regulatory choices that might be the result of political priorities (for example, the 'flexibility' in the regulation of employment) and contested political variables. While these indicators have received much attention and criticism (Arndt and Oman 2006; Buduru and Pal 2010; Pollitt 2011), they tend to focus more strongly on the market-enabling capacities of the state rather than administrative capacities more specifically.

From those studies that do target public administration, the 'bureaucratic professionalism' index (Dahlström, Lapuente, and Teorell 2012) stands out. The index is part of a large-scale effort to collect and develop a quality of government indicators set that covers a range of aspects of government activity, effects, and outcomes and draws from a variety of sources. The index related to bureaucratic professionalism is based on primary data from an expert survey conducted in order to measure the extent to which the personnel policy of governments is in line with criteria of Weberian bureaucracy. Countries rank high on the bureaucratic professionalism index when their recruitment and promotion decisions are based on merit criteria rather than on political considerations. The limitation of this approach is that it does not specify which dimensions of merit are considered, and it has a rather narrow focus on personnel policies. For example, the whole shift of competency requirements from subject matter-related competencies to more managerial or analytical competencies is not reflected in the indicator set (see also the discussion in Lodge and Wegrich 2014).

In a sense, existing indicator studies are either too broad, often not offering any practical recommendations for public sector managers mostly operating at an organisational level, or too narrow, with a focus on specific aspects of bureaucracies. They also follow very different understandings of administrative capacity or quality of government. Overall, the debates around these indicator studies remain surprisingly detached from more recent research on organisational performance—especially the impact of management and management instruments, such as performance management on government effectiveness—or public management more generally (Rainey and Steinberger 1999; Ingraham, Joyce, and Donahue 2003; Christensen and Gazley 2008; Andrews and Boyne 2010; Walker, Boyne, and Brewer 2010; Pollitt and Bouckaert 2011). Key questions concerning the impact of management capacity within public administration on public sector performance have not entered this debate about measuring and ranking the quality and effectiveness of governments. In terms of data sources, existing large-scale indicator sets also rely heavily on the assessment of external experts, and seldom directly involve executives who can be seen as central knowledge carriers and play a crucial role in shaping government capacity and reform processes (Enticott 2004).

Addressing some of the shortcomings in the world of governance indicators, this chapter seeks to introduce a public management perspective and an organisational focus into debates on quality of government and government capacity. It draws on the COCOPS (Coordinating for Cohesion in the Public Sector of the Future) survey of European public executives in order to develop an index of Administrative Management Capacity (AMC). Based on the growing literature that links administrative capacity and public management with performance (Rainey and Steinberger 1999; Andrews and Boyne 2010; Ashworth, Boyne, and Entwistle 2010), the AMC index groups the relevant items from the survey data into six capacity dimensions—coordination, strategic capacity, human resources, organisational culture, performance measurement, and leadership—that capture key public management aspects with an impact on government performance. This allows us not only to measure and rank countries, but also to highlight differences across size and type of public administration within and across countries. In addition, our operationalisation enables us to systematically test the relationships between key AMC dimensions and respondents' evaluations of public sector performance.

In developing the index, the chapter seeks to explore the relation between management capacity in public administration and public sector performance and contributes to the field of measuring government capacity based on a unique set of data. While our data come with limitations usually associated with perception-based surveys, they also offer the advantage of surveying respondents from government organisations rather than external experts. By focusing on public managers and their perceptions of organisational-level phenomena, we avoid attributing features of the (national) political and economic context, in which the public executive is embedded, to the management capacities of the administration itself. At the same time—by including perceptions with regard to a series of both managerial but also more governance-related factors—we hope to ensure that the resulting measure has bearing on the whole, rather than only a subsection, of the public management sphere.

The following section briefly situates our chapter in the increasing stream of research on public management and its effect on performance, and outlines the theoretical framework on which the proposed index rests. We then introduce the data and our method of index construction and validation. Subsequently we present the findings with a specific focus on country variations of administrative management capacity, its impact on performance, and the relevance of organisation type and size on administrative management capacity.

The impact of administrative management factors on government performance

In order to strike a balance between too general and overly specific, and to operationalise administrative capacity in a more management-relevant form, we develop a preliminary index of Administrative Management Capacity (AMC). Strengthening management capacity has been described as one of the most pressing issues facing public administrations (Ingraham, Joyce, and Donahue 2003) and as a crucial component for achieving service delivery improvement in public service organisations (Andrews and Boyne 2010). In broad terms, management capacity can be defined as 'the ability to perform appropriate tasks, effectively, efficiently and sustainably' (Grindle and Hilderbrand 1995: 455) or 'the ability of an organisation to act effectively on a sustained basis in pursuit of its objectives' (Polidano 2000: 808). In light of the increasingly widespread argumentation on 'management matters', we see renewed attempts to better understand the linkage of capacity and performance as central concepts of public management. Although governments across the globe have tackled this issue by initiating a broad range of reforms to improve management systems (Pollitt and Bouckaert 2011), evidence of its impact on government performance is still rather limited.

Important contributions come from first empirical studies exploring management capacity, its determinants, and its effects on performance (e.g. Hou, Moynihan, and Ingraham 2003; Ingraham, Joyce, and Donahue 2003; Ingraham 2007; Andrews and Boyne 2010). Intending to dissect the 'black box models of public management', this research suggests that the combined effect of managerial leadership and different components of a management system such as financial management, human resource management, IT, and managing for results—as well as the alignment and integration of these components—is crucial for high-performing organisations. In spite of some initial progress, the relationship between management capacity, leadership, and government performance can be described as an 'unexplored area of public administration research' (Andrews and Boyne 2010: 443), where empirical evidence stems mostly from the USA and the UK. In terms of theoretical contributions, Rainey and Steinberger (1999) developed a theory of effective government organisations, which proposes a broad set of factors such as agency autonomy, a strong mission-oriented culture, development of human resources, or certain leadership behaviours as conditions indicating when public agencies are more likely to perform effectively.

A key question of capacity and performance management research and practice is which capacity factors can be considered key drivers of government performance. Our selection of dimensions and items for the construction of the index builds on those factors, i.e. management instruments and organisation characteristics that have been identified to contribute to high management capacity (discussed in the literature under the headline of 'criteria-based approaches'; see Hou, Moynihan, and Ingraham 2003). Our preliminary choice of administrative management factors is based on known drivers of government performance identified in the literature and empirical research (for an overview, see Ashworth, Boyne, and Entwistle 2010) and constraints dictated by the availability of relevant indicators coming from the COCOPS executive survey. This leads to a six-dimensional conceptualisation of capacity: strategic capacity, human resource management, organisational culture, the degree to which performance measurement is practised within the organisation, leadership, and coordination with other organisations. The dimensions we choose clearly resemble the Common Assessment Framework, a Total Quality Management system promoted by an initiative of European member state governments.

As noted above, each of these factors has been argued in public management research to be positively related to government performance:

- **Strategic capacity**, defined as the ability of an organisation to develop formal strategic plans that allow it to clarify and communicate its goals and set the future direction, is a recurring theme in public management literature (Boyne 2010), and research has confirmed this positive impact on performance (e.g. Ingraham, Joyce, and Donahue 2003; Chun and Rainey 2005; Boyne and Chen 2007).
- **Human resources** are a key component of an effective management system and are included as a core dimension in most operationalisations of management capacity (for an overview, see Christensen and Gazley 2008). Previous research illustrates that higher-capacity governments are able to achieve better human resources outcomes, such as increased staff motivation, trust, and satisfaction, that lead to higher organisational performance (e.g. Tzafrir 2005; for an overview, see Gould-Williams 2010).
- **Organisational culture** has been commonly argued and theorised as a condition for an effective government organisation (Rainey and Steinberger 1999; Ashworth 2010), and evidence shows that a mission-driven organisational culture is a powerful predictor of government performance (e.g. Brewer and Selden 2000; Moynihan and Pandey 2005).

- Another key aspect of public management reform, the extent and use of **performance measurement** and information (Pollitt and Bouckaert 2011), is also included in our conceptualisation. The extent to which government organisations 'manage for results' is regarded as a key element of management capacity (e.g. Ingraham, Joyce, and Donahue 2003), but its effect on performance is still a highly debated issue.
- Improving **leadership** has been at the heart of many public management reforms (i.e. 'letting managers manage'), and empirical evidence from public management research confirms a positive effect of leadership capacity on performance (e.g. Ingraham, Joyce, and Donahue 2003; Andrews and Boyne 2010).
- Whereas in the public management literature, capacity is often defined as a purely internal organisational quality comprising management resources (e.g. Ingraham, Joyce, and Donahue 2003), we also include **coordination** capacity as a more external dimension in our index. Understood as the overall ability to mediate between and bring together dispersed actors to achieve joint action (Lodge and Wegrich 2014; Wegrich and Štimac in this volume), the coordination capacity dimension allows us to link with broader debates on administrative capacity and governance capability. Along these lines, Hou, Moynihan, and Ingraham (2003) have argued that a too narrow managerial approach can be overcome by incorporating the influence of wider political and institutional structures. Networked governance, for which the capacity to coordinate and collaborate is a prerequisite, is thought to improve performance by reducing transaction costs (Jones, Hesterly, and Borgatti 1997) and buffering the organisation from external shocks (O'Toole 1997).

We acknowledge that none of these factors' relationships to organisational performance is without controversy and that our choice of items to represent them is by no means exhaustive. We do however believe that the dimensions we selected capture at least some key facets of management capacity of government organisations. What remains to be dealt with is the question of which dimensions of government performance should be used to evaluate the impact of our AMC construct. Government performance is complex and multidimensional and can be judged from different perspectives and by multiple constituencies (Boyne 2003). Andrews, Boyne, and Walker (2011) list a number of measures of government agency performance usually employed in the public performance management literature. Of these we select the three most general ones: cost and efficiency, service quality, and policy effectiveness. We also add staff motivation and attitudes towards work, and citizens' trust in government.

Data and method

COCOPS Executive Survey and dataset

As one of the largest comparative public management research projects in Europe, Coordinating for Cohesion in the Public Sector of the Future (COCOPS) aims to provide a comprehensive picture of the current developments and challenges within European public administrations, and more specifically to explore the impact of New Public Management (NPM)-style reforms in Europe in a comparative and systematic manner. As a cornerstone of the project, the COCOPS Executive Survey on Public Sector Reform in Europe intends to offer an insight into the beliefs, attitudes, and opinions of top civil servants in Europe in relation to these public sector developments. The resulting dataset is currently the largest of its kind in Europe.

The survey, jointly developed by a team of researchers from 11 European universities,[2] explores the executives' perceptions regarding their work context and experiences with administrative reforms, as well as the impact of these reforms on public sector performance more generally. It is based on a full census of central government ministries and agencies, and the sample covers all top and higher-level public sector executives who are most likely involved in the public administration reform processes as well as likely to be affected by them. In all central government ministries and the most relevant subordinate agencies, the two administrative top levels are addressed, with the third level being included in some cases. Local government and service delivery levels are excluded from the sample.

The survey was launched in May 2012 and implemented in two rounds (May–July 2012 and September–November 2012) and later extended to also cover Lithuania, Portugal, Serbia (February–June 2013), and Sweden (October–November 2013). All together, invitations were sent to over 29,536 high-ranking civil servants in the participating countries. By December 2013, there were 8,117 valid answers available, equivalent to a 27.5 per cent response rate. As shown in Table 6.1, we experienced great disparity in response rates, which can by and large be explained by country-specific factors. In particular, we find that smaller countries—and especially those such as Serbia, Sweden, and Austria where the local teams secured high-level inside support for the survey—tended to perform better in this regard.

[2] Erasmus University (Rotterdam), Hertie School of Governance (Berlin), University of Bergen, Bocconi University (Milan), University of Cantabria, Cardiff University, Centre national de la recherche scientifique (CNRS) (Paris), Corvinus University (Budapest), University of Exeter, Katholieke Universiteit (KU) Leuven, Tallinn University of Technology. For more information on the COCOPS survey, see <http://www.cocops.eu/work-packages/work-package-3>.

Table 6.1. Invitations, responses, and response rates by country for the COCOPS survey

Country	Invitations sent	Responses	Response rate
Austria	1,745	637	36.5%
Estonia	913	321	35.2%
France	5,297	1,193	22.5%
Germany	2,295	566	24.7%
Hungary	1,200	351	29.3%
Ireland	2,330	529	22.7%
Italy	1,703	343	20.1%
Lithuania	1,850	500	27.0%
Netherlands	977	293	30.0%
Norway	1,299	436	33.6%
Portugal	1,234	371	30.1%
Serbia	2,522	1,367	54.2%
Spain	1,778	321	18.1%
Sweden	1,293	536	41.5%
United Kingdom	3,100	353	11.4%
Total	**29,536**	**8,117**	**27.5%**

Constructing an Administrative Management Capacity index

We operationalise our index by assigning various items from the COCOPS questionnaire to each of the dimensions laid out above. An overview of the items used, together with the associated questions and the COCOPS database variable names, is given in Table 6.2. All items were measured on 7-point Likert scales, e.g. 'Q: In my work I use performance indicators to . . . ' was measured on a 1 'Not at all' to 7 'To a large extent' scale; 'Q: People in my organisation . . . ' on a 1 'Strongly disagree' to 7 'Strongly agree' scale. As noted previously, the sets of items for the six dimensions were picked so as to best capture factors we believe exemplify the selected administrative management capacity dimensions and which have been argued by previous research and theories as relevant for improving government performance. In the following we briefly outline the relevance of these items used for the operationalisation of our six capacity dimensions.

- **Strategic capacity**: Following Boyne (2010), we operationalise strategic capacity as the extent to which formalised business and strategic planning are practised within the respondent's organisation, as well as the degree of goal clarity and communication of goals to staff within the respondent's organisation. For a further specification we also include items to capture the organisation members' commitment to task and mission accomplishment, which has been theorised by Rainey and Steinberger (1999) as a condition of effective government organisation.
- **Human resources management**: Following current debates (e.g. Gould-Williams 2010), we operationalise human resources through the extent of human resources management (HRM) tool implementation, the (lack of)

politicisation of senior appointments—similar to the conceptualisation of meritocratisation by Dahlström, Lapuente, and Teorell (2012)—and the respondent's job satisfaction as an individual-level performance outcome (Gould-Williams 2010: 129). We also include a further item: the relevance of flexibilisation of employment towards more individualised and decentralised arrangements, which has become a major reform trend in the field of HRM over the last decades (Pollitt and Bouckaert 2011: 87ff.).

- **Organisational culture**: Organisational culture is operationalised as a set of items measuring organisational social capital as proposed by Nahapiet and Ghoshal (1998), which has a great influence in management studies. In addition we use items measuring the respondent's self-assessed organisational commitment as suggested by Allen and Meyer (1990).
- **Performance measurement**: The performance measurement sub-index is comprised of items measuring the use of tools such as customer surveys, benchmarking, or Management by Ojectives (MbO), and the self-reported use of performance information for internal management purposes.
- **Leadership**: In line with Rainey and Steinberger's (1999) theory of effective government, we measure leadership through the executives' commitment to achieving results as well as the respondent's degree of management autonomy and the lack of political interference.
- **Coordination**: Finally, the coordination dimension has been operationalised through a set of items measuring the quality of inter-organisational and multi-level collaboration, and the existence of different arrangements to resolve inter-organisational coordination problems.

We calculate the country score on each dimension by first averaging up all the item values for each respondent. This gives us the dimension score for each respondent. For each of the dimensions, we then average out these scores per country to obtain the score per country. The AMC index is then calculated by taking the average country score of all six dimensions.

Each of the six dimensions is given equal weight in the AMC index. We calculated Cronbach's alpha measures to test the extent of internal consistency of the various sub-dimensions (see also Table 6.2). In general, the values are larger than 0.7 and fall well into the acceptable range (performance management 0.85, organisational culture 0.85, strategic capacity 0.82, and coordination 0.73). The exceptions are the human resource management (0.54) and leadership (0.65) indices, which is to be expected, since capacity in these two dimensions is not easy to define unambiguously. Our sub-indices should therefore not be interpreted as scales measuring a latent construct, but rather as composite indices that define the concept, much akin to measures of, for example, socio-economic status. In such instances, internal consistency is not a necessary condition for the overall validity of the index itself (see e.g. Streiner 2003).

Table 6.2. Overview of AMC index component items (COCOPS comparative database variable listed in italics before item)

COORDINATION (Cronbach's alpha: 0.73)	
Q: In my work I use performance indicators to	
q9_8	Engage with external stakeholders (e.g. interest groups)
Q: How would you characterise collaboration in your own policy field between:	
q11_1	National government bodies within the same policy area
q11_3	National and local/regional government bodies
q11_4	National and supra-national bodies/international organisations
q11_5	Government bodies and private and voluntary sector stakeholders
Q: To resolve coordination problems when working with other organisations, we typically	
q13_4	Set up a cross-cutting work/project group (ad hoc, temporary)
q13_5	Set up a cross-cutting policy arrangement or program
q13_6	Decide on one lead organisation
q13_7	Consult civil society organisations or interest groups
STRATEGIC CAPACITY (Cronbach's alpha: 0.82)	
Q: To what extent are the following instruments used in your organisation?	
q7_1	Business/strategic planning
Q: To what extent do the following statements apply to your organisation?	
q8_1	Our goals are clearly stated
q8_2	Our goals are communicated to all staff
q8_3 (R)	We have a high number of goals
Q: People in my organisation	
q14_7	Share the same ambitions and vision for the organisation
q14_8	Enthusiastically pursue collective goals and mission
q14_9	View themselves as partners in charting the organisation's direction
ORGANISATIONAL CULTURE (Cronbach's alpha: 0.85)	
Q: People in my organisation	
q14_1	Engage in open and honest communication with one another
q14_2	Share and accept constructive criticisms without making it personal
q14_3	Willingly share information with one another
q14_4	Have confidence in one another
q14_5	Have a strong team spirit
q14_6	Are trustworthy
Q: When thinking about my work and the organisation I work for	
q15_5	I really feel as if this organisation's problems are my own
q15_6	I would be very happy to spend the rest of my career with this organisation
HUMAN RESOURCE MANAGEMENT (Cronbach's alpha: 0.54)	
Q: To what extent are the following instruments used in your organisation?	
q7_5	Codes of conduct
q7_13	Staff appraisal talks / performance appraisal
Q: What is your view on the following statements	
q12_2 (R)	Politicians regularly influence senior-level appointments in my organisation
Q: When thinking about my work and the organisation I work for	
q15_4	I would recommend it as a good place to work
Q: How important are the following reform trends in your policy area?	
q17_10	Flexible employment
LEADERSHIP (Cronbach's alpha: 0.65)	
Q: I mainly understand my role as public sector executive as	
q5_3	Achieving results
Q: In my position, I have the following degree of autonomy with regard to	
q6_1	Budget allocations
q6_6	Changes in the structure of my organisation
q6_7	Policy choice and design
q6_8	Policy implementation
Q: What is your view on the following statements	
q12_1	Politicians respect the technical expertise of senior executives
q12_3 (R)	In my organisation politicians interfere in routine activities
PERFORMANCE MEASUREMENT (Cronbach's alpha: 0.85)	
Q: To what extent are the following instruments used in your organisation?	
q7_2	Customer/ user surveys
q7_4	Quality management systems
q7_6	Internal steering by contract
q7_7	Management by objectives and results
q7_8	Benchmarking
q7_9	Cost accounting systems
q7_14	Risk management
Q: In my work I use performance indicators to	
q9_1	Assess whether I reach my targets
q9_3	Identify problems that need attention
q9_4	Foster learning and improvement

In addition to computing the sub-indices and the aggregate AMC index, we investigate some properties of the indices with regard to their impact on public sector performance. First, we look at how both the AMC index and its various dimensions relate to different dimensions of performance. As noted earlier, the dimensions of government performance we examine are cost and efficiency, service quality, policy effectiveness, staff motivation and attitudes towards work, and citizens' trust in government. In contrast to previous management capacity research, we measure not organisational performance, but rather broader government performance at the level of the policy field. The relationship between these five dimensions of government performance and the six dimensions of the AMC index is investigated through an ordered probit specification (see e.g. Greene 2003) in which we take a respondent's evaluation of each dimension of performance as the dependent variable and put the six sub-indices as independent variables. We explicitly do not control for country effects as this would (inappropriately) change the interpretation of our results.

Second, we investigate how the type and size of the public administrations relate to our index scores. In this instance, we perform a regular regression analysis in which we take the AMC index and its sub-dimensions as the dependent variables, and set the organisational variables as the independent variables. In this case, we control for country effects because otherwise differences in the distribution of organisation types or size over countries would translate into our estimates.

Findings: comparing administrative management capacity in Europe and its impact on performance

The country-level results (see Table 6.3) confirm some of the received wisdom of comparative public administration. For example, the top ranking of the Netherlands and Sweden in the composite index supports the view that these two countries combine a public administration that values professionalism and public service ethos with a substantial effort to introduce managerial tools into the governance of public sector organisations. The UK's third rank is also in line with a range of other indicator studies of good governance, although academic public administration research is more sceptical concerning the impact of the waves of managerial reforms that have been introduced in the UK since the 1980s (Wegrich 2009). It might be considered a surprise that Norway is not ranked higher than the UK. Less surprising is the ranking of other countries, such as Mediterranean countries at the lower end of the rankings and continental European countries somewhere in the middle. It is also interesting to see rather high variation within the central and eastern

Table 6.3. The overall AMC scores for each country, and the country scores for each AMC dimension

	AMC	Coordination	Strategic capacity	Organisational culture	Human resources	Leadership	Performance measurement
Netherlands	4.91	4.08	5.04	4.84	5.65	5.17	4.69
Sweden	4.87	4.28	5.14	4.92	5.32	4.63	4.96
UK	4.81	4.36	5.15	5.05	4.63	4.54	5.11
Norway	4.80	4.17	4.98	5.14	5.10	4.81	4.60
Estonia	4.71	4.29	4.87	5.08	4.99	4.46	4.58
Lithuania	4.68	4.46	5.04	5.10	4.42	4.10	4.95
Italy	4.50	4.40	4.55	4.71	3.74	4.59	4.99
Ireland	4.48	4.14	4.92	4.93	3.61	4.69	4.58
Germany	4.45	3.79	4.50	4.74	4.64	4.71	4.33
Serbia	4.32	4.49	4.42	4.88	3.94	3.71	4.48
Austria	4.29	3.90	4.80	4.89	3.64	4.26	4.24
Portugal	4.20	3.98	4.77	4.86	3.16	3.56	4.89
Hungary	4.18	4.04	4.48	5.08	3.52	4.15	3.79
France	4.13	3.44	4.30	4.72	3.78	4.49	4.05
Spain	3.74	3.44	4.29	4.77	2.61	3.91	3.44
COCOPS mean	4.47	4.08	4.75	4.91	4.18	4.39	4.51
COCOPS max	4.91	4.49	5.15	5.14	5.65	5.17	5.11
Observations	2,441	4,266	6,727	7,262	5,454	5,958	5,211

European countries indicating different paths of development all coming from a similar starting point as transition countries. Whereas Estonia, as might be expected, scores rather high, the similarly high score of Lithuania and the relatively high score of the non-EU member Serbia—and especially the top rank with regard to coordination—come as more of a surprise and beg further investigation. Overall, we see the high position of countries such as Norway and Sweden, as well as the Netherlands and UK, similar to that in other existing rankings.

Looking at some of the sub-indicator results, we also observe the general trend to be in line with conventional wisdom. For example, coordination capacity is higher in smaller countries such as Estonia, Lithuania, Serbia, and the Netherlands, but more problematic in Napoleonic (France, Portugal, Spain) and federal continental European systems (Austria, Germany). That Germany's complex federal system makes coordination difficult is hardly news. France's low score in the coordination index is perhaps more surprising.

One can also easily agree with the results for strategic capacity, ranking the UK first and showing high values for Sweden and the Netherlands, as well as Lithuania. With regard to the below-mean score for Germany, the literature has frequently highlighted differences in policy styles, with Germany being characterised by 'disjointed incrementalism' and the UK by strong central initiative and steering and a strong prevalence of business-style strategic planning. Similarly intuitive are the results for performance measurement: countries such as the UK, Sweden, Lithuania, and Italy, which have undertaken a more prolific performance measurement reform agenda over the last decades, rank high in this dimension, whereas the scores for Austria, France, Germany, Hungary, and Spain confirm the reputation of these countries as public management laggards or maintainers (Pollitt and Bouckaert 2011). A clear contrast can also be observed with regard to human resources, where Scandinavian countries score rather high—similar to the results of Dahlström, Lapuente, and Teorell (2012)—and Mediterranean countries especially low.

There are also, however, some counterintuitive results. For example, Hungary's high score on the organisational culture dimension is not only a surprise as such, but even more so when one considers its consistently below-mean scores in the other capacity dimensions. Germany's above-mean score for leadership is also unexpected, not only because of the historically loaded notion of leadership in this country, but also because the checks and balances of the institutionally fragmented 'semi-sovereign state' (Katzenstein 1987) do not offer a breeding ground for strong leadership styles. This result might be an effect of the strong representation of labour administration officials in the survey, since it is in this area and in particular in the federal labour agency where administrative leadership has played a crucial role in the past.

Finally, comparing the results of the sub-indices, the result for coordination and HRM capacity stands out: the mean of these two dimensions—especially of coordination—is substantially lower than that of the other sub-indices. According to our interpretation, coordination remains the most problematic aspect of administrative capacity in today's world of governance. We also observe that, while the cross-country variation is considerably lower with regard to organisational culture, strategic capacity, and leadership, the variations with regard to HRM are particularly high, confirming the persistence of rather heterogeneous national systems in this area.

Our data also allow more in-depth analyses of certain countries and especially a visualisation of country-specific particularities in the form of radar charts, as shown in Figure 6.1 for Germany. By comparing the country results to the COCOPS mean and max, we can easily see the relatively weak position of German public administration with regard to coordination, strategic capacity, and performance measurement. However, with regard to leadership and human resources, Germany scores well above most other countries included in our analyses.

In a second step we tested the impact of our AMC construct by evaluating the Spearman's rank correlation coefficient as well as the Kendall's tau measure of correlation between the AMC index and the respondents' evaluations of

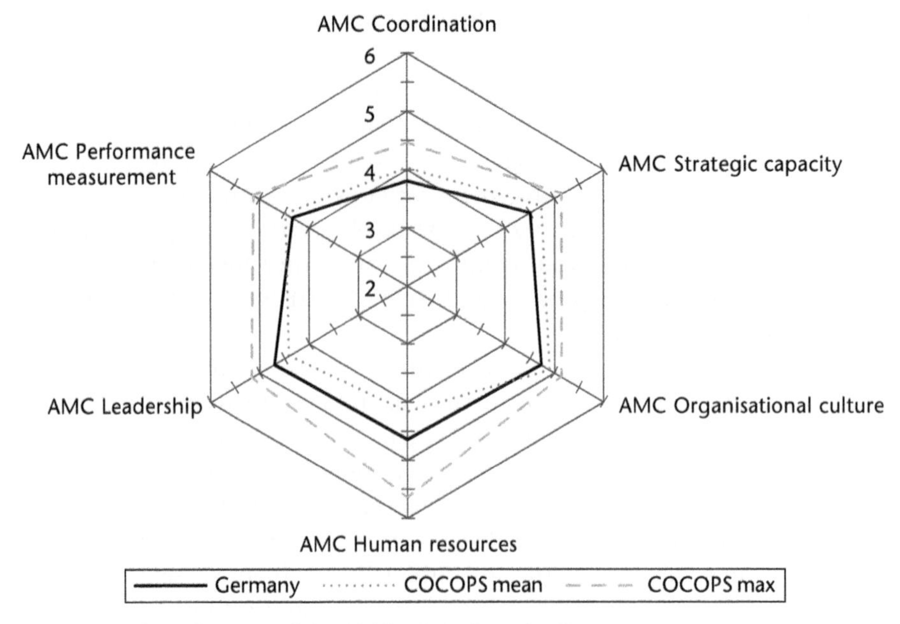

Figure 6.1. Visualisation of the AMC sub-indices for Germany

government performance.[3] We find that in all instances the AMC index shows a strong positive and statistically significant correlation with these assessments of performance.

The ordered probit estimates elaborated upon earlier are shown in Table 6.4. Overall, we find a clear positive relationship between our administrative management capacity measure and the performance dimensions analysed, albeit with different dimensions of the AMC index impacting different dimensions of performance. Coordination shows a strong and statistically significant (at 1 per cent) relationship with all five dimensions of performance, but particularly so with staff motivation, service quality, and policy effectiveness. In general, coordination comes out as the most important capacity dimension to improve government performance.

As expected, strategic capacity is most strongly related to citizens' trust in government and policy effectiveness, as well as to staff motivation and attitudes towards work; it also exhibits a statistically significant relationship (at 1 per cent) to service quality. The finding that organisational culture appears to be especially related to staff motivation and attitudes towards work is plausible since organisational culture and staff motivation are both related to the

[3] Note that these measures of association were chosen because the performance evaluation measures are ordinal rather than interval. Kendall's tau estimates range from 0.25 to 0.34, while the Spearman's rank correlation coefficients range from 0.37 to 0.50.

Table 6.4. Ordered probit estimates for five dimensions of performance

	Dimension of performance				
AMC index dimension	Cost and efficiency	Service quality	Policy effectiveness	Staff motivation and attitudes towards work	Citizens' trust in government
Coordination	0.203	0.216	0.209	0.217	0.145
	[0.036]***	[0.036]***	[0.036]***	[0.036]***	[0.036]***
Strategic capacity	0.017	0.088	0.148	0.141	0.198
	[0.022]	[0.023]***	[0.023]***	[0.023]***	[0.023]***
Organisational culture	0.032	0.083	0.08	0.211	0.088
	[0.028]	[0.028]***	[0.028]***	[0.028]***	[0.028]***
Human resources	−0.016	0.032	−0.076	0.14	0.106
	[0.020]	[0.020]	[0.020]***	[0.020]***	[0.020]***
Leadership	0.205	0.086	0.212	0.064	0.03
	[0.026]***	[0.026]***	[0.026]***	[0.026]**	[0.026]
Performance Measurement	0.131	0.115	0.068	0.005	0.004
	[0.022]***	[0.022]***	[0.022]***	[0.022]	[0.022]
Observations	2,528	2,528	2,519	2,518	2,514

* $p < 0.1$; ** $p < 0.05$; *** $p < 0.01$

internal working conditions of public sector organisations. Organisational culture also displays a significant relationship with service quality, policy effectiveness, and citizens' trust in government, but the estimated impact is not very strong in any of these cases. The human resources dimension can be related to staff motivation and citizens' trust in government; however, we find a puzzling negative relationship with policy effectiveness. Leadership is (statistically) significantly related to each dimension of performance except citizens' trust in government, perhaps reflecting the more internal nature of this dimension. In particular, leadership is associated with improved cost and efficiency as well as policy effectiveness, implying that 'letting managers manage' can indeed deliver results. While the other two 'softer' dimensions of performance exhibit a statistically significant relationship with the leadership sub-index, the strength of this relationship is somewhat weaker. Finally, performance measurement shows a strong, and statistically significant, relationship with cost and efficiency, service quality, and policy effectiveness, but exhibits no relationship with the other two dimensions of performance.

Starting instead from the dimensions of performance, our results indicate that the most relevant factors to improve cost and efficiency are coordination, leadership, and performance measurement. For service quality, good coordination and performance measurement matter, whereas policy effectiveness seems to be mostly affected by coordination, leadership, and strategic capacity. The major factors leading to improved staff motivation and attitudes towards work are coordination and organisational culture and—to a lesser degree—strategic capacity and human resources. Finally citizens' trust in

Table 6.5. Organisational variables and the AMC index estimation results

Organisational variables	AMC index	Strategic capacity	Coordination	Organisational culture	Human resources	Leadership	Performance measurement
Agency†	0.221 [0.037]***	0.101 [0.027]***	0.095 [0.038]**	0.029 [0.031]	0.253 [0.034]***	0.209 [0.030]***	0.316 [0.040]***
50–99‡	–0.028 [0.068]	–0.228 [0.047]***	–0.082 [0.066]	–0.279 [0.053]***	–0.001 [0.060]	0.119 [0.053]**	0.1 [0.073]
100–499‡	–0.058 [0.054]	–0.292 [0.038]***	–0.028 [0.054]	–0.411 [0.042]***	0.016 [0.048]	0.031 [0.042]	0.113 [0.059]*
500–999‡	–0.036 [0.061]	–0.316 [0.044]***	0.029 [0.063]	–0.457 [0.050]***	–0.011 [0.056]	–0.019 [0.049]	0.157 [0.068]**
1,000–5,000‡	0.07 [0.061]	–0.252 [0.043]***	–0.057 [0.061]	–0.372 [0.048]***	0.204 [0.055]***	0.051 [0.049]	0.356 [0.066]***
over 5,000‡	0.048 [0.064]	–0.209 [0.045]***	–0.008 [0.065]	–0.416 [0.050]***	0.171 [0.056]***	–0.187 [0.050]***	0.795 [0.068]***
Observations	2539	6613	4768	7120	6692	5472	5150
R^2	0.13	0.11	0.08	0.03	0.30	0.18	0.15

* $p < 0.1$; ** $p<0.05$; *** $p < 0.01$; country effect estimates omitted
† Estimate indicates index score difference between agencies and ministries
‡ Estimates indicate index score difference between listed size category and the category 'less than 50'

government is most strongly linked to strategic capacity and coordination capacity.

Table 6.5 shows the regression results where the AMC index and its sub-dimensions are in turn set as the dependent variables, and organisation type—agency or ministry—and size are set as the independent variables. Country differences have been controlled for, but the estimates themselves have been omitted.

In terms of organisational type, we find that agencies have a significantly higher overall management capacity than ministries. By taking a closer look at the various sub-dimensions we can see that this difference stems from agencies' significantly higher scores in the human resources, leadership, and performance measurement dimensions. Both strategic capacity and coordination scores do not differ significantly between agencies and ministries.

In terms of organisation size, we find that for the overall AMC index, size does not seem to matter. This can also be confirmed for coordination, whereas the results for leadership are somewhat ambiguous. In the case of strategic capacity, we find that small organisations (<50 employees) seem to score significantly better than larger organisations. The scores for organisational culture also tend to decrease with the size of the organisation, whereas the performance measurement score increases steadily with organisation size. Finally we find that the human resource score is significantly higher for organisations with over 1,000 employees.

In general, however, we do not find that organisation size and type of organisation, nor country effects, account for a very large share of index variance (the R^2 for the full index regression equals only 13 per cent), which implies that there is considerable room left for improving these first models.

Conclusion and outlook

The AMC index developed in this chapter seeks to address the shortcoming of existing indicators that do not explore the role that management and organisational-level factors play in determining administrative capacity. By linking the public management literature with the debate about governance capacity, the chapter draws from the COCOPS Executive Survey to develop an administrative capacity management index. It allows for not only a cross-national ranking of capacity, but also an exploration of the role of both internal, managerial factors and more external, institutional, and governance-related factors. Of course, both the construction of the index and the analysis presented here come with several limitations—ranging from general limitations of perception-based surveys to the rather broad-brush analysis of a range of management capacity dimensions. Moreover, our analysis of the data is preliminary and shows only the potential of such an index.

Nevertheless, many of the findings are suggestive, in particular the result that those countries that perform higher in terms of government effectiveness dimensions also display higher (perceived) management capacities. The analysis also shows some interesting variations in terms of which management dimensions matter more than others for government effectiveness. And finally, a factor that is usually not associated with classical management concepts, coordination capacity, turned out to be the most important factor for performance.

A more fine-grained analysis of specific results remains wanting (see Wegrich and Stimac in this volume on coordination). Still, this chapter has fulfilled its purpose of demonstrating the potential of an index that combines organisational and management factors with country-level capacity data. This approach is surely open for criticism, but a combination of the COCOPS data with objective data is on our own to-do list to address the index's most important limitation.

References

Allen, N. J., and Meyer, J. P. (1990). 'The Measurement and Antecedents of Affective, Continuance and Normative Commitment to the Organization', *Journal of Occupational Psychology*, 63(1): 1–18.

Andrews, R., and Boyne, G. A. (2010). 'Capacity, Leadership, and Organizational Performance: Testing the Black Box Model of Public Management', *Public Administration Review*, 70(3): 443–54.

Andrews, R., Boyne, G., and Walker, R. M. (2011). 'The Impact of Management on Administrative and Survey Measures of Organizational Performance', *Public Management Review*, 13(2): 227–55.

Arndt, C., and Oman, C. (2006). *Uses and Abuses of Governance Indicators*. Paris: OECD Publishing.

Ashworth, R. (2010). 'Organizational Culture', in R. Ashworth, G. A. Boyne, and T. Entwistle (eds), *Public Service Improvement: Theories and Evidence*. Oxford, New York: Oxford University Press, 98–119.

Ashworth, R., Boyne, G. A. and Entwistle, T. (eds) (2010). *Public Service Improvement: Theories and Evidence*. Oxford, New York: Oxford University Press.

Boyne, G. A. (2003). 'Sources of Public Service Improvement: A Critical Review and Research Agenda', *Journal of Public Administration Research and Theory*, 13(3): 367–94.

Boyne, G. A. (2010). 'Strategic Planning', in R. Ashworth, G. A. Boyne, and T. Entwistle (eds), *Public Service Improvement: Theories and Evidence*. Oxford, New York: Oxford University Press, 60–77.

Boyne, G. A., and Chen, A. A. (2007). 'Performance Targets and Public Service Improvement', *Journal of Public Administration Research and Theory*, 17(3): 455–77.

Brewer, G., and Selden, S. C. (2000). 'Why Elephants Gallop: Assessing and Predicting Organizational Performance in Federal Agencies', *Journal of Public Administration Research and Theory*, 10(4): 685–711.

Buduru, B., and Pal, L. A. (2010). 'The Globalized State: Measuring and Monitoring Governance', *European Journal of Cultural Studies*, 13(4): 511–30.

Christensen, R. K., and Gazley, B. (2008). 'Capacity for Public Administration: Analysis of Meaning and Measurement', *Public Administration and Development*, 28(4): 265–79.

Chun, Y. H., and Rainey, H. G. (2005). 'Goal Ambiguity and Organizational Performance in U.S. Federal Agencies', *Journal of Public Administration Research and Theory*, 15(4): 529–57.

Dahlström, C., Lapuente, V., and Teorell, J. (2012). 'The Merit of Meritocratization: Politics, Bureaucracy, and the Institutional Deterrents of Corruption', *Political Research Quarterly*, 65(3): 656–68.

Enticott, G. (2004). 'Multiple Voices of Modernization: Some Methodological Implications', *Public Administration*, 82(3): 743–56.

Gould-Williams, J. (2010). 'Human Resource Management', in R. Ashworth, G. A. Boyne, and T. Entwistle (eds), *Public Service Improvement: Theories and Evidence*. Oxford, New York: Oxford University Press, 120–42.

Greene, W. H. (2003). *Econometric Analysis*. 5th edn. Upper Saddle River: Prentice Hall.

Grindle, M. S., and Hilderbrand, M. E. (1995). 'Building Sustainable Capacity in the Public Sector: What Can Be Done?', *Public Administration and Development*, 15(5): 441–63.

Hou, Y., Moynihan, D. P., and Ingraham, P. W. (2003). 'Capacity, Management, and Performance: Exploring the Links', *The American Review of Public Administration*, 33(3): 295–315.

Ingraham, P. W. (2007). *In Pursuit of Performance: Management Systems in State and Local Government*. Baltimore: Johns Hopkins University Press.

Ingraham, P. W., Joyce, P. G., and Donahue, A. K. (2003). *Government Performance: Why Management Matters*. Baltimore: Johns Hopkins University Press.

Jones, C., Hesterly, W. S., and Borgatti, S. P. (1997). 'A General Theory of Network Governance: Exchange Conditions and Social Mechanisms', *The Academy of Management Review*, 22(4): 911–45.

Katzenstein, P. J. (1987). *Policy and Politics in West Germany: The Growth of a Semi-Sovereign State*. Philadelphia: Temple University Press.

Lodge, M., and Wegrich, K. (2014). 'Administrative Capacities', in Hertie School of Governance (ed.), *The Governance Report 2014*. Oxford: Oxford University Press, 27–48.

Moynihan, D. P., and Pandey, S. K. (2005). 'Testing How Management Matters in an Era of Government by Performance Management', *Journal of Public Administration Research and Theory*, 15(3): 421–39.

Nahapiet, J., and Ghoshal, S. (1998). 'Social Capital, Intellectual Capital, and the Organizational Advantage', *The Academy of Management Review*, 23(2): 242–66.

O'Toole, L. J. (1997). 'Treating Networks Seriously: Practical and Research-Based Agendas in Public Administration', *Public Administration Review*, 57(1): 45–52.

Polidano, C. (2000). 'Measuring Public Sector Capacity', *World Development*, 28(5): 805–22.

Pollitt, C. (2011). '"Moderation in all Things": International Comparisons of Governance Quality', *Financial Accountability and Management*, 27(4): 437–57.

Pollitt, C., and Bouckaert, G. (2011). *Public Management Reform: A Comparative Analysis*. Oxford, New York: Oxford University Press.

Rainey, H. G., and Steinberger, P. (1999). 'Galloping Elephants: Developing Elements of a Theory of Effective Government Organizations', *Journal of Public Administration Research and Theory*, 9(1): 1–32.

Streiner, D. L. (2003). 'Being Inconsistent About Consistency: When Coefficient Alpha Does and Doesn't Matter', *Journal of Personality Assessment*, 80(3): 217–22.

Tzafrir, S. S. (2005). 'The Relationship Between Trust, HRM Practices and Firm Performance', *The International Journal of Human Resource Management*, 16(9): 1600–22.

Walker, R. M., Boyne, G. A., and Brewer, G. A. (2010). *Public Management and Performance: Research Directions*. Cambridge, New York: Cambridge University Press.

Wegrich, K. (2009). 'Public Management Reform in the United Kingdom: Great Leaps, Small Steps, and Policies as Their Own Cause', in S. Goldfinch, and J. Wallis (eds), *International Handbook of Public Management Reform*. Cheltenham, Northampton: Edward Elgar, 137–54.

Part II

Challenges and Capacities in Key Policy Areas

7

Demographic Change and Welfare State Restructuring

Michaela Kreyenfeld and Anika Rasner

Nowadays people in the majority of industrialised countries live longer and healthier lives than previous generations (European Commission 2010). At the same time, period fertility rates have declined and the share of people who remain childless has increased in many European countries. This unprecedented increase in life expectancy, combined with the seemingly irreversible downward trend in fertility, means that most European countries are undergoing a profound demographic transition characterised by the ageing of the population. These demographic changes are widely expected to have repercussions for the functioning, productivity, capacity to innovate, and future sustainability of modern welfare states (Demeny 2003; Macura, MacDonald, and Haug 2005; European Commission 2006, 2012; Barr and Diamond 2008).

In most European countries, policy-makers have enacted policy measures to address these challenges related to population ageing and low fertility (Majer et al. 2013). Although most European nations face similar demographic challenges, the policy responses vary greatly across these countries. The differences in the speeds and the degrees of the responses can be attributed not only to differences in levels of awareness of the population challenges, but also to the economic means countries have available to address population issues; some countries have a greater capacity than others to enact social policy reforms. Moreover, countries vary considerably in their traditions in approaching population issues.

In this chapter, we focus on the responses to demographic change in the areas of family and pension policies. We do not address migration policies nor attempt to cover the whole range of welfare regimes in Europe in this limited space. We will, however, discuss landmark reforms in typical welfare state regimes and explore the question of whether population concerns have played a decisive role in recent policy reforms. Furthermore, we will focus on the capacities of countries to formulate and implement effective policies for increasing fertility and sustaining the pension system. Finally, we will attempt to determine which of the innovative policy measures (such as a better integration of pension, employment, and tax policies or the establishment of an automatic, progressive link between retirement age and life expectancy) implemented so far have been effective in tackling population-related challenges.

Demographic facts

Fertility

When we look at the hard demographic facts, we can see that there is substantial variation across time and space. With respect to fertility dynamics, we must conclude that low and declining fertility is hardly a recent phenomenon. Most of the northern and western European countries experienced a rapid decline in their period fertility rates starting in the 1970s, with a similar decrease beginning in southern Europe in the 1980s and in the central and eastern European countries after the collapse of the communist systems at the beginning of the 1990s. Most of this decline in period fertility rates was related to the so-called 'tempo effect', i.e. the annual birth rates fell because women were postponing having children to later ages.

A more accurate measure of the level of fertility is the cohort fertility rate, which is the number of children born to each birth cohort of women. In many European countries, the cohort fertility rates have fallen below the replacement level. Germany currently has the lowest cohort fertility rate in Europe. A German woman who was born in 1965 had about 1.5–1.6 children on average. By comparison, an average French or Swedish woman of the same cohort had about two children.

Recent predictions suggest that the average number of children per woman will increase (Myrskylä, Goldstein, and Cheng 2013), with Germany being among the countries for which a reversal of the current trend has been predicted (Goldstein and Kreyenfeld 2011). While fertility will likely remain below replacement level in many countries of Europe in the years to come, it is important to note that population projections that are based on period fertility rates are most likely too low.

Life expectancy

Gains in life expectancy are the second major contributor to population ageing. In recent decades, life expectancy has been steadily rising across all of the industrialised countries, albeit at very different speeds. For more than 25 years, Japanese women were the world record holders in life expectancy at birth (Oeppen and Vaupel 2002): between 1961 and 2010, their average lifespan increased by more than 12 years (OECD 2012). Since 2011, women in Hong Kong have had the highest life expectancy worldwide. A girl born in Hong Kong today is likely to live to age 87. In Europe, Spanish women have the highest life expectancy, at over 85 years. They have gained more than 13 years over the past five decades. However, the most striking advances in longevity seen in Europe in recent years have been in the former East Germany, where life expectancy at birth has increased by more than six years since reunification (Vogt 2013).

Most of the reductions in mortality occurred among people aged 70 and older. Because of progress in medical care and the effects of public health campaigns that aim at improving people's health behaviour, life expectancy will likely continue to increase (Hashimoto et al. 2012; Majer et al. 2013). At this point, there is no evidence to suggest that the ultimate limit to human life expectancy will be reached any time soon (Oeppen and Vaupel 2002).

Population ageing and the old-age dependency ratio

The low birth rates and the rise in life expectancy have resulted in a substantial ageing of the European population. The median age of the population is now over 40 in most European countries, and since the 1980s, Germany has had one of the oldest populations in Europe. In 2012, the median age of the German population was 45. The neighbouring countries of Denmark and France—which share many major demographic characteristics with Germany, but which have much higher birth rates—have median ages that are about five years younger than Germany's. Population projections tell us that these ageing trends will continue in the coming years.

The old-age dependency ratio (the ratio of persons aged 65 and older to persons aged 20 to 64), which is a more policy-relevant measure of the expansion of the elderly population, shows a similar development. Compared to other geographic regions, many European countries, like Germany and Italy, face record-high old-age dependency ratios; exceeded only by that of Japan (European Commission 2012).

These populations will age rapidly over the next 40 years due to low fertility, continuous gains in life expectancy, and the ageing of the baby boomer cohorts, who are currently approaching retirement (Westermeier, Rasner, and Grabka 2012). For the year 2050, the medium-fertility variant of the *World Population Prospects* of the United Nations projects that, in Japan, there will be 76 elderly people for every 100 people of working age—a doubling of today's ratio. In Europe, the old-age dependency ratio will grow fastest for Spain and Italy, from 28 in 2010 to 68 in 2050 in Spain, and from 34 in 2010 to 67 in 2050 in Italy (United Nations 2011). The post-socialist countries will also experience rapid ageing in the years to come, due to the steep declines in the period fertility rates and the significant gains in life expectancy they experienced after the collapse of the communist regimes. As longer lives and low fertility are expected to result in increasing old-age dependency ratios, there have been calls for sustained policy responses at the national (and the supra-national) level, especially in the areas of pension and long-term care policies. However, population concerns have also influenced reforms in the realm of family policies.

Family policies and population concerns

The European Union has, in principle, no formal authority with respect to family policies (Hantrais 2004). Nevertheless, as low fertility rates and population decline have become increasingly important topics of discussion, the European Union has started to address family-related issues. At least since 2000, the European Commission has expressed concerns over low fertility rates, and has formulated clear statements in which it urged national governments to take steps to counteract low fertility. The European Commission has shown particularly strong support for policies that help couples combine work and family life, arguing that these policies promote higher fertility. It based its endorsement of work–family reconciliation policies on results from comparative research indicating that, since the 1980s, fertility has been higher in countries that intensified their efforts to integrate mothers into the labour market (Esping-Andersen 1999; Neyer 2003). The alternative suggestion that policies that support 'home-centred women' (Demeny 2003: 268) could increase fertility was never seriously considered in the realm of EU policies. Thus, the EU has been advocating work–family reconciliation policies in order to stimulate higher fertility and higher labour market productivity (European Commission 2005: 2ff.). The major regulations in this context have been the recommendation of the EU summit in Barcelona in 2002 that obliged national governments to increase the provision of childcare for children under age three to a level of 33 per cent (European Council 2002: paragraph 32). The goal formulated in the 2000 Lisbon Strategy and Europe 2020 of increasing female labour market participation can also be seen as part of this larger strategy (Daly 2010).

The responses of national governments to the EU policy recommendations have, however, varied greatly. Countries also differ in their traditions regarding the use of work–family reconciliation policies to counteract low fertility. The western European forerunners in this area have been the Nordic countries, which reformed their family policies in the 1970s, soon after fertility rates started to decline across western Europe. Population concerns have clearly contributed to welfare state reforms in countries like Sweden. However, in the absence of significant migration flows, the mobilisation of the female workforce was probably the more immediate reason why work–family reconciliation policies were intensified (Chesnais 1996: 732). Mätzke and Ostner (2011: 388ff.) argued that the Swedish tradition 'in "engineering" family formation and the care and socialisation of children' can still be seen in Swedish social policies today. This description might fit family policies like the 'speed premium', which encourages a close spacing of children. Nevertheless, it does not sufficiently acknowledge the extent to which gender equality has become an important goal in its own right in the agendas of the Nordic governments.

In the conservative welfare state regimes, work–family reconciliation policies were not seen as a means of alleviating low fertility before 2000. Most western European governments have been rather reluctant to formulate any explicit population goals. The misuse of population policies during the fascist era is one reason why many western governments shied away from dealing with population issues in the post-war period. An exception is France, where government officials never hesitated to openly express their concerns about the declining population size or low fertility (Bras 1997; Martin 2011). In a 1982 report on the European Population Conference, which included summaries of the demographic objectives of the national governments, the French representatives celebrated the 'excellent' increase in their country's fertility rate to about 1.9 (Council of Europe 1982: 2). Meanwhile, the West German government did not express any concerns about the country's low fertility. At that time, Germany had already recorded period fertility rates of only 1.4 for almost a full decade, and a decline in the size of the German population was projected by the end of the 1980s (Bretz 2001). Nevertheless, demographic issues were not yet on the political agenda, and 'a limited reduction of the total population' was tolerated at that time (Bretz 2001: 2).

Since 2000, however, population issues have been on the agenda of the German government. The conservative Christian Democratic Party (CDU/CSU) has always been more open to population concerns than the left-wing Social Democrats. However, it was a great surprise to most observers when the conservative party, who in the past favoured 'home-based' family policies, was the party that adopted work–family reconciliation policies with the goal of reversing fertility trends (Henninger, Wimbauer, and Dombrowski 2008; Fleckenstein 2011). Although the previous 'Red–Green' government (the coalition of the Social Democrats and the Green Party) had set the stage for this reform, it was the 'Grand Coalition' (of the CDU/CSU and the Social Democrats) under the leadership of the conservative family minister, Ursula von der Leyen, who eventually pushed this reform through. Fleckenstein (2011: 545) attributed this decision to the conservative party's need to mobilise the votes of young women, 'which are perceived as imperative for electoral success'. However, it seems unlikely that this consideration alone could have had the power to trigger a reform of this magnitude, which shattered the basic principles of the conservative family model. Population arguments certainly contributed to the enactment of this reform. In the parental leave benefit reform bill, low fertility is explicitly mentioned in the statement that 'the challenge of family policies is to facilitate family formation' (Deutscher Bundestag 2006: 2). 'Home-based' family policies, which would have been more in line with conservative principles, probably were not seriously considered given the overwhelming empirical evidence showing that conservative family policies, which had been strictly followed for decades, had resulted in record-low levels of fertility.

While western European countries have usually discussed low fertility issues in conjunction with work–family reconciliation policies and gender equality, central and eastern European countries have followed a different track. Most post-socialist countries have a long tradition of pro-natalistic policies. The most extreme example is the well-known Romanian case, in which the Ceauşescu government boosted fertility from 1.9 in 1966 to 3.7 in 1967 by prohibiting abortion. Other countries used less coercive measures to increase fertility, but nevertheless pursued unmistakably pro-natalistic goals. The East German government liberalised abortion and started providing free access to contraceptives in 1972. To prevent a (further) decline in fertility, a wide range of policy measures was enacted over the course of the 1970s. As in other socialist countries, these measures included the expansion of public childcare and various forms of assistance to women in combining work and family life. However, promoting gender equality was never seen as an obvious means of increasing fertility. Instead, the universal employment of mothers was taken for granted, and the goal of pro-natalism was to encourage women to have three or more children. The role of gender issues has remained ambiguous in most of the former socialist countries (Pascall and Manning 2000; Saxonberg and Sirovátka 2006; Schmitt and Trappe 2010). Mothers were pushed into full-time employment by socialist regimes, but the behaviour of fathers and the traditional division of housework were never really seriously questioned, resulting in the famous 'double burden' for women in these countries.

When fertility rates fell sharply after the demise of the socialist systems, central and eastern European governments were not hesitant to voice pro-natalistic views. The developments in the Russian Federation have been especially striking. Alarmed by low fertility rates and projections that showed a decline in the size of the population, the Putin government enacted policies that included substantial increases in child benefits, particularly for second and higher-order children (PDR 2006; Vishnevsky and Bobylev 2008: 31). The pro-natalistic orientation of these policies was clearly discernable, as they were expressly designed to increase higher-order birth rates. Although the policy package also included an extension of maternity leave and the coverage of childcare costs, the cornerstone of these measures had not been work–family reconciliation policies, but rather substantial cash benefits for higher-order births. Home-care allowances and extended unpaid or low-paid parental leave periods have also been introduced in many other former socialist countries over the last decade (Saxonberg and Sirovátka 2006; Thévenon 2011). The Swedish-type parental leave system, which would have been more in line with the family policies of the previous socialist systems, was mostly not considered as an immediate option. The high cost of such programmes is certainly among the main reasons why many central and eastern European governments did not follow 'the Swedish path', and instead reduced parental leave benefit payments (Saxonberg and Sirovátka 2006). It is also likely that the reluctance of these governments to consider gender equality as a relevant policy goal in its own right contributed to this development. Many central and eastern European countries seem to have reverted to a 're-familisation' of their family policies, even though their female employment rates have remained high relative to those of most western European countries, and despite the fact that women's earnings are an essential source of household income for most families in these countries.

Just as budgetary constraints are generally seen as a barrier to the implementation of work–life reconciliation policies in eastern European countries, they are also regarded as among the reasons for the 'rudimentary', 'fragmented', and 'underdeveloped' family policies in southern Europe (Bianculli and Jacint 2013). Many southern European countries like Greece, Portugal, and Spain enjoyed relatively high fertility rates until the early 1980s, but experienced a rapid decline to below replacement level fertility since then. The government of Greece was probably the first of these countries to openly express population concerns in light of declining fertility rates. Recently, other southern European countries, like Italy, voiced similar concerns. However, public spending in southern European countries on family-related initiatives remained far below the European average (Bianculli and Jacint 2013). Although efforts to expand family policies have been intensified since 2000 (Naldini and Saraceno 2008; Bianculli and Jacint 2013), the current global financial crisis has put the southern European welfare states under severe economic pressure, making any further reforms in this area unlikely. In fact, Spain has already withdrawn some recent family policy reforms in response to the crisis. The 'baby cheque', a birth grant of 1,500 euros, was introduced in 2007, but was withdrawn in 2010. Similarly, a national plan established in

2008 to create public day care for children under age three was eliminated in 2012 (Bianculli and Jacint 2013).

Ageing/pensions and policy responses

With respect to pensions, the European Union has no legislative power to directly influence policy-making at the national level. Instead, the EU uses a soft approach based on the so-called 'open method of coordination' (OMC).[1] The Maastricht Treaty first introduced this new governance strategy (Articles 98–104) to coordinate national economic policies at the EU level (Scharpf 2002). At the Lisbon summit, European member states agreed to extend the OMC to the issue of pensions. The goal of this governance strategy is to provide a framework for strategic developments at the national level and to coordinate policies between EU countries. The member states have thus formulated some common objectives, but have retained the freedom to decide whether to enact certain policies to achieve these goals (Natali 2008). The European Union regularly monitors the progress made and assesses whether national policies are in line with the common objectives.

In its most recent *Joint Report on Pensions*, the European Commission acknowledged that there is considerable variation in the major demographic challenges each EU member state faces. Despite these differences, the Commission has emphasised that all of the member states need to take action to ensure 'sustainable, accessible, and adequate retirement incomes now and in the future' (European Commission 2010). These efforts should strike a balance between adequate replacement levels and the sustainability of the pension scheme. However, demographic pressures do not directly translate into policy-making. Although these matters are pressing, the severity of the problem is not the best predictor of whether a national government will successfully take action and reform its country's public pension system. These reforms are risky political undertakings, as they might incur considerable political costs that pose a threat to re-election. The success or failure of reforms, as well as their timing, instead depend on the political system (Lijphart 1999), the electoral rules, the cycles and the majorities (Bonoli 2001), the executive regime, and the potential veto points and veto players (Tsebelis 2002; Immergut, Anderson, and Schulze 2007).

The fiscal impact of population ageing on national budgets is undisputed (European Commission 2012). The fundamental demographic shifts imply

[1] The EU exerts more direct powers over the budgetary policies of the member states with binding policy objectives that indirectly affect retirement programmes at the national level (Natali 2008).

that a decreasing number of people of working age will have to support a growing number of retirees, which will result in a gradual increase in the old-age dependency ratio. Increasing the statutory retirement age is the most obvious—but also the most contested—policy response to increasing longevity. Without corresponding changes to the retirement age, longer lifespans will result in extended periods during which people will be entitled to receive pension payments. Moreover, the decline in mortality rates contributes to an increase in the number of individuals who are living past retirement age. Both factors threaten the long-term financial sustainability of national pension schemes. Ideally, policy-makers should establish an automatic link between life expectancy and the statutory retirement age, but in reality, hikes in the retirement age provoke fierce political opposition. Because of the unpopularity of raising the retirement age, the mean statutory retirement age was increased by less than half a year between 1965 and 2005, even though the average male life expectancy rose by almost nine years over the same period (Bloom, Canning, and Fink 2011).

Despite ongoing opposition, national governments have started to increase the statutory retirement age, although significant variations across countries remain (Eichhorst 2011). In 2010, the age at which men could start collecting a pension was 57 in Greece, but it had already risen to 67 in Norway and Iceland. Other countries, including Germany and the United Kingdom, are expected to follow these vanguard countries within the next few years.[2] Of the 34 countries of the OECD, 19 have increased the retirement age for men and 23 have raised the retirement age for women (OECD 2012). Denmark, the Czech Republic, Italy, and Greece went one step further by automatically linking the retirement age to improvements in life expectancy with no upper limit, although with long transitional periods (OECD 2011).

Increases in the retirement age should be accompanied by activation policies for older employees, especially since most countries have eliminated generous early retirement options.[3] Without an effective employment strategy for older people, hikes in the retirement age will harm older workers who fail to find or stay in a job. These individuals will be forced into unemployment or early retirement, which implies a reduction in their pension benefits. To boost the labour market integration of older workers, national governments can enact active labour market policies (ALMP) or set tax incentives.

[2] The most recent German pension reform proposal allows for a small subgroup of future retirees to retire at age 63 if they have at least 45 years of contributory periods. In 2012, fewer than 4 per cent of first-time pensioners would have qualified for this early retirement provision. For all others, the enacted hikes in retirement age will continue to apply.

[3] The elimination of early retirement incentives is one of the reasons for the recent increase in the labour force participation of older workers (ages 55 to 64) after a decade-long decline (O'Brien 2010; OECD 2011).

Sweden has been a forerunner in promoting the labour market participation of people above the retirement age (aged 65+) through targeted tax incentives. As part of a larger tax reform, the government has gradually introduced an earned income tax credit (*Jobbskatteavdraget*) that is much larger for older employees. In addition, older workers have been granted a payroll tax reduction of about 16 percentage points (Laun 2012). The Netherlands has also implemented a work-continuation tax credit targeted at older employees (aged 62+), even as the country has eliminated early retirement options.

Activation policies for individuals with health impairments are intended to prevent workers from exiting the labour market early. Austria, for example, has replaced its fixed-term disability benefit with active labour market measures, including professional reintegration and occupational retraining measures combined with an extension of the eligibility for sickness allowances. Germany has introduced work subsidies (*Kombilohn*) targeted at older employees, as well as subsidies for employers that hire older long-term unemployed workers.

As ageing populations are putting a strain on state pension budgets, governments are increasingly reducing the generosity of their earnings-related second-tier pensions, and most are moving to multi-tier pension systems (Bettio, Tinios, and Betti 2013).[4] The purpose of promoting additional occupational or private pensions is to offset cuts in the public pension scheme. Unlike second-tier pensions that are mandatory, coverage in third-tier pensions is not. To ensure that these occupational and private schemes function as effective supplements to the public pension system, governments have a strong interest in promoting membership in these schemes. While countries vary greatly in terms of how they aim to increase coverage, the move toward multi-tier systems brings new actors into the area of pension politics, and changes the rules of the game. These new actors are responsible for the design of pension schemes, but are bound by the regulatory framework in which they operate. With the dispersion of functions and competencies in the provision of pensions, governments have to reinterpret their regulatory and coordination capacities.

We observe large cross-country differences in the maturation of multi-tier pension schemes. For example, in the 1980s, the Netherlands was late in making the transition because it lacked a universal pay-as-you-go pension system (Myles and Pierson 2001). Here, the circumstances were favourable for introducing a quasi-mandatory occupational pension scheme that today covers more than 95 per cent of the Dutch workforce (Anderson 2008). The

[4] According to the OECD pension typology, 'first-tier, redistributive pensions' aim at preventing poverty among the elderly by providing some kind of means-tested minimum pension. The 'second-tier, mandatory insurance pensions' refer to earnings-related schemes that provide benefits roughly equivalent to the previous income. 'Third-tier pensions' refer to private, employer-provided or occupational pensions that are voluntary (OECD 2005).

government mandated that unions extend the bargained benefits to non-unionised workers, which explains the high degree of coverage. In contrast, Germany had a mature public pension system in the 1980s. As public pensions were designed to guarantee the standard of living achieved during an individual's working life, most employees relied exclusively on benefits from the second tier (Rasner 2006). Hence, a systematic expansion of coverage in the third tier did not start until 2002, when a fully funded but voluntary private pension was introduced. To encourage participation, the government grants tax breaks and pays subsidies.

Based on its distinct level of maturation, each country needs to address the various issues surrounding the new pension mix in its own way. These issues may, for example, include market failure, a lack of coverage, or an uneven distribution of benefits (Antolin 2009). Governments face the dilemma of no longer bearing direct responsibility for the delivery of future pension obligations in these supplemental schemes, but of having to oversee occupational pension structures (Anderson 2008). For example, in 2007 the Dutch government passed a law to protect the equity of occupational pension funds and to help prevent underfunding. The law requires pension fund managers to immediately report to the supervisor of the Dutch Central Bank if the market value of pension assets no longer covers the liabilities of the respective pension fund. Furthermore, the law strengthens the individual's right to obtain regular information about the occupational pension rights accrued (Bertelsmann Stiftung 2010).

A number of countries have strengthened the right of individuals to access information, as the multi-tier pension systems make effective retirement planning more complex. Moreover, research in a number of countries has demonstrated a lack of pension awareness and a high degree of financial illiteracy among citizens when it comes to retirement preparedness (Lusardi and Mitchell 2008). To bridge this information gap, a growing number of countries are trying to find ways to provide regular information on individual pension levels, even if there is no legal obligation to do so. Denmark is a vanguard in providing comprehensive information to its citizens on their pension levels (Block 2010). First, the pension statement is not mailed once a year, but is accessible on the Web at any time. Second, information on pension levels is not limited to the second tier, but is available for all types of retirement benefits, including survivor's benefits and disability pensions. Third, the website provides detailed information on different scenarios, including retirement benefits for different retirement ages and for different forms of taxation. Similarly, the 'orange envelopes' distributed by the Swedish government include projections of retirement income from both public and private pensions, as well as a number of scenarios with varying rates of growth for average salaries, individual salaries, and pension funds. Poland's Social

Insurance Institution provides an online tool that allows beneficiaries to forecast their future retirement income under different assumptions.

Conclusion and outlook

Longer lifespans and persistently low fertility rates represent a challenge for pension systems throughout the world. In terms of both pension and family policies, activation measures that aim to bring older workers and women with children into the labour market have been among the prime measures used to address population issues. However, national policy responses to demographic pressures vary, not only in terms of content, but also with respect to timing.

In the realm of family policies, most western European governments and most EU politicians appear to agree that work–family reconciliation policies can help to counteract low fertility. Pro-natalistic policy goals have not been overtly pursued in western European countries. Instead, labour market and gender role issues are generally mentioned in conjunction with concerns about low fertility. Central and eastern European governments have, however, been less hesitant to express their worries about low fertility and to formulate explicitly pro-natalistic policy goals, independent of any gender role considerations. While southern European countries have gradually expanded their previously fragmented and underdeveloped family policies since 2000, the recent financial crisis will most likely block any further reforms in this area.

Path dependency has played a critical role in recent family policy reforms. For the governments of southern European countries, which have traditionally shown little interest in implementing family policies, financial limitations currently represent the greatest barrier to reform. In conservative welfare states, the idea that work–family reconciliation policies could increase fertility has been slow to take hold. While increasing fertility has never been alien to conservative thinking, the suggestion that fertility can only be boosted by integrating women into the labour market has created a dilemma for conservative family policy-makers. This was probably most apparent in the case of Germany, where the Grand Coalition, under the leadership of a conservative family minister, pushed through a parental leave benefits reform in 2007 that was modelled on the Swedish system. A move to expand public day care, another cornerstone of the national government's reconciliation policies, exposed the limitations in the government's administrative capacities to implement reforms. Because public day care is mainly the responsibility of the local communities in Germany, the expansion of public day care depended to a large extent on the priorities of local community leaders, who did not necessarily see integrating mothers into the labour market as a high priority. Likewise, as education is under the control of the individual states, the expansion of full-time schooling (*Ganztagsschule*) was and is contingent on the family model that each state adheres to, regardless of the ambitions of the national government.

In the realm of pension policies as well, differences in reform patterns are the result of the path dependencies of existing welfare state structures (Starke 2006). Hence, policy-makers face constraints that arise because of institutional and programmatic choices made in the past. This path dependence implies that despite facing similar pressures, countries will not converge in the design of their pension systems, and that radical departures from past practice are rather unlikely (Myles and Pierson 2001). For this reason, mature systems, such as the German pay-as-you-go pension system, will never become a fully funded scheme, but will instead add a capital-funded component to its pension mix. Moreover, as long as the European Union has no legislative power and continues to adopt a soft approach with the open method of coordination, cross-country differences in pension policies are likely to prevail.

Nevertheless, an assessment of two decades of pension reform policies in the European countries reveals some broader trends. First, even though most countries legislated increases in the statutory retirement age and discontinued early retirement options in response to the continuous increases in life expectancy, only a few countries have established an automatic link between the statutory retirement age and future increases in life expectancy. Second, in light of increasing retirement ages, governments will have to increase their coordination capacities to reconcile employment and pension policies. Without adequate employment opportunities up to the point of retirement, older workers have to exit the labour market prematurely. Third, the majority of countries have shifted to multi-tier schemes for retirement provision, mainly in order to take some of the pressure off public pension budgets and to offset cuts in the second tier with pensions from supplemental schemes. Despite this move to multi-tier schemes, large cross-country variations remain with respect to the timing, the degree of compulsion, and the public-to-private mix in pension provision. The use of multi-tier schemes brings new actors with different regulatory bodies and objectives into the provision of retirement benefits. In this context, retirement planning becomes more complex and requires governments to redefine their regulatory capacities in retirement provision.

References

Anderson, K. M. (2008). 'The Politics of Multipillar Pension Restructuring in Denmark, the Netherlands and Switzerland'. WZB Discussion Paper SP I 2008–205, Berlin: WZB.

Antolin, P. (2009). 'Private Pensions and the Financial Crisis: How to Ensure Adequate Retirement Income from DC Pension Plans', *Financial Market Trends* (2): 1–21.

Barr, N. A., and Diamond, P. A. (2008). *Reforming Pensions: Principles and Policy Choices*. Oxford, New York: Oxford University Press.

Bertelsmann Stiftung (2010). *International Reform Monitor Issue 14: A Cross-National Comparison of Social Policies, Labor Market Policies and Industrial Relations*. Gütersloh: Bertelsmann Stiftung.

Bettio, F., Tinios, P., and Betti, G. (2013). *The Gender Gap in Pensions in the EU*. Luxembourg: European Commission.

Bianculli, A., and Jacint, J. (2013). 'The Unattainable Politics of Child Benefits Policy in Spain', *Journal of European Social Policy*, 23(5): 504–20.

Block, M. de (2010). European Colloquium: Communication on Pension Rights in Europe. Brussels: General National Pensions Office.

Bloom, D. E., Canning, D., and Fink, G. (2011). 'Implications of Population Ageing for Economic Growth', *Oxford Review of Economic Policy*, 26(4): 583–612.

Bonoli, G. (2001). 'Political Institutions, Veto Points, and the Process of Welfare State Adaptation', in P. Pierson (ed.), *The New Politics of the Welfare State*. Oxford, New York: Oxford University Press, 238–64.

Bras, H. L. (1997). 'The Demographic Argument in France: Coherence, Reference and Metaphors', in M. Cross, and S. Perry (eds), *Population and Social Policy in France*. London, Washington: Pinter, 21–33.

Bretz, M. (2001). 'Zur Treffsicherheit von Bevölkerungsvorausberechnungen', *Wirtschaft und Statistik*, 1(11): 906–21.

Chesnais, J.-C. (1996). 'Fertility, Family, and Social Policy in Contemporary Western Europe', *Population and Development Review*, 22(4): 729.

Council of Europe (1982). *European Population Conference 1982: Demographic Trends and Policy Responses*. Strasbourg: Council of Europe.

Daly, M. (2010). 'Assessing the EU Approach to Combating Poverty and Social Exclusion in the Last Decade', in E. Marlier, and D. Natali (eds), *Europe 2020: Towards a More Social EU?* Bruxelles: Peter Lang, 143–61.

Demeny, P. (2003). 'Population Policy Dilemmas in Europe at the Dawn of the Twenty-First Century', *Population and Development Review*, 29(1): 1–28.

Deutscher Bundestag (2006). 'Gesetzentwurf der Fraktionen der CDU/CSU und SPD: Entwurf eines Gesetzes zur Einführung des Elterngeldes'. Drucksache 16/1889. Berlin: Deutscher Bundestag.

Eichhorst, W. (2011). 'The Transition from Work to Retirement', *German Policy Studies*, 7(1): 107–33.

Esping-Andersen, G. (1999). *Social Foundations of Postindustrial Economies*. Oxford, New York: Oxford University Press.

European Commission (2005). 'Confronting Demographic Change: A New Solidarity Between the Generations'. Green Paper. COM(2005) 94 final. Brussels: European Commission.

European Commission (2006). *The Demographic Future of Europe: From Challenge to Opportunity*. Luxembourg: Office for Official Publications of the European Communities.

European Commission (2010). 'Joint Report on Pensions: Progress and Key Challenges in the Delivery of Adequate and Sustainable Pensions in Europe'. European Economy Occasional Papers 71, Luxembourg: European Commission.

European Commission (2012). 'The 2012 Ageing Report: Economic and Budgetary Projections for the 27 EU Member States (2010–2060)'. European Economy 2/2012, Luxembourg: European Commission.

European Council (2002). *Presidency Conclusion: Barcelona European Council 15 and 16 March 2002*. Barcelona: European Council.

Fleckenstein, T. (2011). 'The Politics of Ideas in Welfare State Transformation: Christian Democracy and the Reform of Family Policy in Germany', *Social Politics*, 18(4): 543–71.

Goldstein, J. R., and Kreyenfeld, M. (2011). 'Has East Germany Overtaken West Germany? Recent Trends in Order-Specific Fertility', *Population and Development Review*, 37(3): 453–72.

Hantrais, L. (2004). *Family Policy Matters: Responding to Family Change in Europe*. Bristol: Policy.

Hashimoto, S., Kawado, M., Yamada, H., Seko, R., Murakami, Y., Hayashi, M., Kato, M., Noda, T., Ojima, T., Nagai, M., and Tsuji, I. (2012). 'Gains in Disability-Free Life Expectancy From Elimination of Diseases and Injuries in Japan', *Journal of Epidemiology*, 22(3): 199–204.

Henninger, A., Wimbauer, C., and Dombrowski, R. (2008). 'Demography as a Push toward Gender Equality? Current Reforms of German Family Policy', *Social Politics: International Studies in Gender, State & Society*, 15(3): 287–314.

Immergut, E. M., Anderson, K. M., and Schulze, I. (2007). *The Handbook of West European Pension Politics*. Oxford, New York: Oxford University Press.

Laun, L. (2012). 'The Effect of Age-Targeted Tax Credits on Retirement Behavior'. Working Paper 18. Stockholm: Institute for Evaluation of Labour Market and Education Policy.

Lijphart, A. (1999). *Patterns of Democracy: Government Forms and Performance in Thirty-Six Countries*. New Haven: Yale University Press.

Lusardi, A., and Mitchell, O. S. (2008). 'Planning and Financial Literacy: How Do Women Fare?' *American Economic Review*, 98(2): 413–17.

Macura, M., MacDonald, A. L., and Haug, W. (eds) (2005). *The New Demographic Regime: Population Challenges and Policy Responses*. New York, Geneva: United Nations.

Majer, I. M., Stevens, R., Nusselder, W. J., Mackenbach, J. P., and Baal, Pieter H. M. (2013). 'Modelling and Forecasting Health Expectancy: Theoretical Framework and Application', *Demography*, 50(2): 673–97.

Martin, C. (2011). 'The Reframing of Family Policies in France: Processes and Actors', *Journal of European Social Policy*, 20(5): 410–21.

Mätzke, M., and Ostner, I. (2011). 'Introduction: Change and Continuity in Recent Family Policies', *Journal of European Social Policy*, 20(5): 387–98.

Myles, J., and Pierson, P. (2001). 'The Political Economy of Pension Reform', in P. Pierson (ed.), *The New Politics of the Welfare State*. Oxford, New York: Oxford University Press, 305–33.

Myrskylä, M., Goldstein, J. R., and Cheng, Y. A. (2013). 'New Cohort Fertility Forecasts for the Developed World', *Population and Development Review*, 39(1): 31–56.

Naldini, M., and Saraceno, C. (2008). 'Social and Family Policies in Italy: Not Totally Frozen but Far from Structural Reforms', *Social Policy and Administration*, 42(7): 733–48.

Natali, D. (2008). *Pensions in Europe, European Pensions: The Evolution of Pension Policy at National and Supranational Level.* Brussels: Peter Lang.

Neyer, G. (2003). 'Family Policies and Low Fertility in Western Europe', *Journal of Population and Social Security*, 1(Supplement): 63–93.

O'Brien, M. (2010). 'Older Male Labour Force Participation in OECD Countries: Pension Reform and "the Reserve Army of Labour"', *International Labour Review*, 149(3): 239–59.

OECD (Organisation for Economic Co-operation and Development) (2005). *OECD Pensions at a Glance 2005: Public Policies Across OECD Countries.* Paris: OECD.

OECD (Organisation for Economic Co-operation and Development) (2011). *Pensions at a Glance 2011: Retirement-Income Systems in OECD and G20 countries.* Paris: OECD.

OECD (Organisation for Economic Co-operation and Development) (2012). *OECD Pensions Outlook 2012.* Paris: OECD.

Oeppen, J., and Vaupel, J. W. (2002). 'Broken Limits to Life Expectancy', *Science*, 296(5570): 1029–31.

Pascall, G., and Manning, N. (2000). 'Gender and Social Policy: Comparing Welfare States in Central and Eastern Europe and the Former Soviet Union', *Journal of European Social Policy*, 10(3): 240–66.

PDR (2006). 'Vladimir Putin on Raising Russia's Birth Rate', *Population and Development Review*, 32(2): 385–9.

Rasner, A. (2006). 'Mind the gap! Einbeziehung internationaler Benchmarks bei der Beurteilung der geschlechtsspezifischen Rentenlücke in Deutschland', *Deutsche Rentenversicherung*, 61(11–12): 737–54.

Saxonberg, S., and Sirovátka, T. (2006). 'Failing Family Policy in Post-Communist Central Europe', *Journal of Comparative Policy Analysis: Research and Practice*, 8(2): 185–202.

Scharpf, F. W. (2002). 'The European Social Model', *Journal of Common Market Studies*, 40(4): 645–70.

Schmitt, C. and Trappe, H. (eds) (2010). *Gender Relations in Central and Eastern Europe: Change or Conitnuity?*, Zeitschrift für Familienforschung, 22(3). Opladen, Berlin: Budrich.

Starke, P. (2006). 'The Politics of Welfare State Retrenchment: A Literature Review', *Social Policy and Administration*, 40(1): 104–20.

Thévenon, O. (2011). 'Family Policies in OECD Countries: A Comparative Analysis', *Population and Development Review*, 37(1): 57–87.

Tsebelis, G. (2002). *Veto Players: How Political Institutions Work.* Princeton, NJ: Princeton University Press.

United Nations (2011). *World Population Prospects: The 2010 Revision.* New York: Department of Economic and Social Affairs, Population Division.

Vishnevsky, A. G., and Bobylev, S. N. (2008). *National Human Development Report Russian Federation 2008: Russia Facing Demographic Challenges.* Moscow: UNDP.

Vogt, T. C. (2013). 'How many Years did the Fall of the German Wall Add? A Projection of East German Life Expectancy', *Gerontology*, 59(3): 85–92.

Westermeier, C., Rasner, A., and Grabka, M. M. (2012). 'The Prospects of the Baby Boomers: Methodological Challenges in Projecting the Lives of an Aging Cohort'. SOEP Paper 440-2012, Berlin: Deutsches Institut für Wirtschaftsforschung.

8

Sustainability

Innovations through Sector Integration and New Instruments

Andrea Lenschow

Introduction

Sustainability is a broad, ambiguous term, but this is not the place to enter into a conceptual debate. At its core is the notion of keeping a balance between resource consumption and resource renewal in order to maintain the carrying capacity of our planet and meet the long-term needs of humankind. The Brundtland Report (WCED 1987) popularised the term sustainable development (SD) and broke it down into three constituent parts—economic, social, and ecological sustainability—emphasising their mutual interdependence. This landmark publication also highlighted the governance dimension in achieving SD:

> The major central economic and sectoral agencies of government should now be made directly responsible and fully accountable for ensuring that their policies, programmes, and budgets support development that is ecologically as well as economically sustainable.
>
> (WCED 1987: 314)

> The real world of interlocked economic and ecological systems will not change; the policies and institutions concerned must.
>
> (WCED 1987: 9)

The first part of this chapter focuses on the intersectoral dimension of sustainability and discusses governance innovations and their limitations, as observed in the past efforts of OECD countries and the European Union (EU) to integrate the environment into sectoral policies as a key element in the transition to sustainability (Jordan 2008; Jordan and Lenschow 2008). This study will highlight environmental policy integration (EPI) and assume that, in the OECD world, long-term innovation impulses stem from economic decision-making responding to environmental pressures resulting from actions already taken (e.g. climate change); the social pillar of the sustainability concept will be ignored in this chapter as its innovative potential lies primarily in the non-OECD world. This focus is further justified by the numerous initiatives and innovations we have witnessed both in the area of EPI and in environmental policy. This part will also survey the effectiveness of some of these innovations.

The second part of this chapter discusses governance innovation within the specific field of environmental policy—addressing deficits in the performance of traditional policy tools. The Fifth Environmental Action Programme of the EU, entitled 'Towards Sustainability', built on the Brundtland Report by broadening the governance debate to also encompass the choice of policy instruments and actor networks. It thus makes explicit the need to address behavioural change in support of sustainability with innovative, non-coercive means:

> The basic strategy therefore is to achieve full integration of environmental and other relevant policies through the active participation of all the main actors in society (administration, enterprises, general public) through a broadening and deepening of the instruments for control and behavioural change including, in particular, greater use of market forces.
>
> (CEC 1992: 49)

This announcement echoed a wider discussion in national and international governmental and expert organisations (e.g. OECD 1991, 1994, 1999; Öko-Institut e. V. 1998; SRU 1998), triggering policy reforms in environmental protection and climate change mitigation. I will reflect on the state of the art on 'new' environmental policy instruments and their contribution to delivering sustainability.

Thirdly, this chapter elaborates on the problem of governing in multi-level systems and related administrative capacity issues that arise. It builds on both the public administration literature that focuses on effective coordination across vertical levels of government in decision-making and implementation, and the observation of environmental scientists who point out that ecosystems rarely match political and administrative boundaries, thus resulting in inefficiencies, spatial externalities, and spillovers (Moss and Newig 2010). Drawing on the example of EU ambient air policy, I will discuss how the new paradigm of environmental planning in EU environmental policy continues to run into problems of delivery at the local level.

The chapter concludes by arguing that we see no shortage of governance innovation and the transboundary diffusion of innovative ideas in the field of sustainability. It is unclear, however, whether this has brought us any closer to effective problem-solving. To some extent this can be explained by a lack of necessary administrative capacities or capacity mixes for making the novel tools work. At the same time, we may ask how realistic it is to plan for these capacities to be built up—not only in times of financial crises, but also in an ever more complex world. 'Muddling through' is likely to remain at the core of administrative evolution.

Sustainability as an issue of coordinative governance and 'environmental policy integration' (EPI)

Sustainability measures explicitly aimed at the integration of economic, social, and ecological dimensions, and thus addressing the horizontal problems of policy incongruences, highlight the coordination capacity of government as a prerequisite for delivering sustainable policy results (see Wegrich and Štimac, this volume, for more on coordination capacity). Coordination for sustainability not only involves an effective exchange of information and overcoming of bureaucratic turf battles, but may also depend on setting policy principles and priorities. Thus, apart from organisational approaches to facilitating coordination, in practice we see multiple tools employed, ranging from information generation and exchange to the provision of financial incentives and the imposition of procedural provisions.

In our previous work, Jordan and I identified a number of policy 'tools' for achieving (environmental) policy integration (Jordan and Lenschow 2008). Table 8.1, which surveys the OECD world with regard to the adoption of these tools, distinguishes between general framing and information instruments, which have enjoyed the largest uptake in the observed countries. While constitutional provisions frame the SD discourse and convey political commitment in a top-down manner, strategies and plans target the policy-programming phase and give direction to this process. Authoritative instruments refer to binding procedural steps in the policy-making process that ensure assessment of the impact of policy measures on sustainable development. The financial instrument of 'green budgeting' reflects public revenues and spending on the basis of the criterion of environmental protection in order to raise awareness and support. Finally, organisational instruments aim at the horizontal diffusion of environmental concerns at cabinet, departmental, and working levels of government.

Although many of the instruments listed look back at a longer history, e.g. the United States introduced environmental impact assessments already in 1969 (Hoornbeek 2008), states and international polities like the EU continue experimenting with these tools in order to improve their effectiveness.

Table 8.1. Policy strategies in the pursuit of environmental policy integration (EPI) in OECD countries

	General framing and informational instruments					Authoritative instruments			Financial instrument	Organisational instruments		
	Constitutional provision	NEP	NSSD	Sectoral strategies	Reporting obligations	Independent evaluation*	SEA (data until 2007)	Impact assessment	Green budgeting	Amalgamation of departments	Green cabinet	Interdepartmental networking groups
Australia		•	•			•	•					
Austria	•	•	•		•	•	•			•		•
Belgium	•		•		•	•	•	•				•
Canada		•	•	•	•	•	•					•
Czech Republic	•	•	•			•	•					
Denmark		•	•	•			•		• (dismissed in 2002)	• (dismissed in 2002)		
Finland	•	•	•	•		•	•					
France		•	•			•	•					•
Germany	•		•		•	•	•				•	•
Greece	•		•				•					•
Hungary	•	•	•		•	•	•				•	•
Iceland		•					•					
Ireland			•			•	•					•
Italy			•		•	•	•					
Japan		•	•		•	•	•					•
Korea	•	•	•			•						•
Luxembourg			•									
Mexico		•	•	•	•	•						•
Netherlands	•	•	•		•	•	•	•	• (experimental)			
New Zealand		•					•					•
Norway	•		•	•	•	•	•		•		•	•
Poland	•	•	•	•	•	•	•					
Portugal	•	•	•			•	•					•
Slovak Republic	•	•				•	•					
Spain	•		•				•					
Sweden	•	•	•			•	•			• (dismissed in 2006)		•
Switzerland	•		•			•						
Turkey	•	•										
United Kingdom		•	•	•	•	•	•	•	•		•	•
United States					•	•	•	•		•		•
Count	17	20	26	7	14	23	25	4	4	4	4	18

* Independent evaluation could be considered either an informational instrument or an authoritative instrument

Since the mid 1990s, we have witnessed a period of innovation towards EPI in several countries. Such EPI innovations have combined decentralised measures that encourage sectoral policy departments to adopt strategies and take initiatives to incorporate environmental objectives, and centralised instruments such as national plans and strategies, which have in practice ranged from mere rhetorical commitments to the formulation of clear objectives and authoritative monitoring benchmarks (OECD 2002: Jacob and Volkery 2007; Jacob, Volkery, and Lenschow 2008).

In the 2000s, a time of economic downturn, the general commitment to sustainable development has lost momentum and entered a period of critical review (cf. also Jordan and Schout 2006). Furthermore, the emphasis is now shifting towards 'climate policy integration' (CPI) and a 'low carbon' and 'green growth' narrative, as this framing appears more responsive to issues of economic sustainability and a political agenda of economic growth (Jordan and Lorenzoni 2007; Adelle and Russel 2013; Kurze and Lenschow under review). CPI and associated 'roadmaps' to 'smart, sustainable and inclusive growth' or towards a 'competitive low carbon economy' (European Commission 2010, 2011b) effectively combine the objectives of climate change mitigation and adaptation with pressing concerns for economic growth through technological innovation. The German Expert Council on the Environment identified this as a 'megatrend' in environmental policy (SRU 2008), analogous to older strategies of 'ecological modernisation' (Jänicke and Jacob 2006).

Before turning to the strategies of CPI below, let us briefly look at the uptake and effectiveness of several EPI instruments, i.e. instruments that tend to prioritise environmental sustainability. Notably, informational tools are the most widely used in OECD countries. First, this has to do with global diffusion channels and mechanisms, e.g. provisions of Agenda 21 (United Nations 1992) calling on signatory states to develop national plans and strategies with appropriate institutional anchors (e.g. SD commissions). Secondly, it reflects general and widely visible 'mission statements' of front-runner states in the form of constitutional provisions and national environmental plans. Independent institutions are more often established in the form of advisory bodies than as evaluation and controlling bodies; true auditing of EPI in sectoral departments (i.e. an authoritative rather than mere informational measure) is the exception (but see Canada, New Zealand, and the UK: Jacob, Volkery, and Lenschow 2008).

Relatively little empirical material exists allowing us to judge the effectiveness of these informational tools in moving towards SD. Steurer (2008) noted the high coordinative potential of SD strategies considering their (potentially) systematic and orchestrated approach to integrating policies, timescales, jurisdictions, and stakeholders into governance processes, as a way of conveying a common sense of direction and of inviting iterative learning processes. Nonetheless, he also pointed to likely 'disharmony' between politicians and administrators in utilising these strategies: '[W]hile administrators regard sustainable development strategies as important guidelines for policy-making, politicians will probably not care much about the strategy documents as a guidance-providing instrument, but consider them a form of political communication' (Steurer 2008: 105f).

In more recent work Steurer and colleagues present a disillusioned view on the performance of SD strategies. While these may have contributed to awareness raising and also facilitated analytical capacity-building in the public sectors, the strategies have failed in their coordinative function and have not offered as much 'reflexivity' as hoped (Casado and Steurer forthcoming; Nordbeck and Steurer under review). Without the necessary political backing, they have been unable to set priorities and benchmarks. The adoption of vague 'win–win' rhetoric introduced in the Brundtland Report has helped the SD concept gain wide acceptance and has thus served political communication purposes. However, the SD rhetoric has also concealed rather than resolved sectoral turf battles. Steurer and co-authors suggest SD strategies be 'recalibrated' into thematically more focused environmental or climate policy integration strategies. Indeed, the EU, which in the 1990s was still a big advocate of comprehensive strategies (e.g. its own 'Cardiff process'), has already abandoned the all-encompassing SD strategy in favour of thematic strategies in the more recent 6th and 7th Environmental Action Programmes (European Parliament and the Council 2002; European Commission 2012) and EU 'roadmaps' to greening the economy, climate change mitigation and adaptation, and biodiversity (European Commission 2011a, 2011b, 2011c). Roadmaps have the potential for 'recalibration' as long as they develop sectorally specific scenarios and milestones, and identify concrete measures. However, the climate roadmaps are still judged as too broad and vague, and thus unlikely to resolve cross-sectoral conflicts (Steurer, personal communication in November 2013).

Organisational attempts to improve the delivery of EPI have typically followed a networking approach to establishing bureaucratic procedures for the exchange, coordination, and set-up of networking fora at different levels of government (interdepartmental groups, expert groups, green cabinets, or joined-up ministries). Few of these organisational measures are innovative, and the success of different organisational arrangements seems highly contingent upon a favourable political environment.

The administrative and organisational studies literature has not identified 'blueprint' solutions for coordinating for SD. According to the bureaucratic politics view of informal bargaining, competition and turf battles within bureaucracy may set creative potential for SD free. However, this creativity may come at the risk of dominant economic sectors winning out over environmental interests. Thus, advocacy for either 'mega' or strong environmental departments capable of authoritative control aims to compensate for such competitive disadvantages. Such proposals match organisational perspectives looking for ways to build up coordination capacities. Here, Jordan and Schout (2006) offer one of the most authoritative comparative accounts and suggest that no single organisational measure suffices. Instead, something resembling a ladder of coordination (cf. Metcalfe scale), ranging from the bottom to the top echelon of government, is needed for handling potentially stark value differences interfering with SD and EPI and for counteracting the typical volatility of political commitment. Similar to Steurer and colleagues (Casado and Steurer forthcoming; Nordbeck and Steurer under review), Jordan and Schout (2006) suggest that 'super-structures' like the EU Cardiff process, national SD strategies, and highly visible governmental reforms (e.g. the restructuring of ministries) will be insufficient. While none of the scholars argues that administrative reforms are conducted merely to pretend responsiveness to an international SD agenda, they do suggest that mimicry may be as much of a driver of such reforms as a clear problem-solving orientation, which may explain some naïveté of grand administrative designs (see also Schout and Jordan 2008: 54ff., 66).

Financial signals and incentives might be an alternative tool for encouraging EPI measures. At the general governmental level, the use of 'green budgeting' has been rare and fitful. Typically, green budgeting implies that all spending is evaluated in depth in terms of its environmental effects and any possible alternatives. Effective green budgeting depends on the sanctioning power of parliaments to insist on environmentally friendly spending choices when adopting the budget. At EU level, sanctioning may extend into the implementation phase of spending policies, since projects may be stopped, and payment withheld, if environmental 'cross-compliance' rules are violated (Wilkinson, Benson, and Jordan 2008).

With the forthcoming EU multi-annual financial framework (2014–20) we are now witnessing an interesting turn towards 'climate budgeting'. The framework goal is to spend 20 per cent of the overall budget on policies related to climate adaptation and mitigation (European Commission 2013a). Spending will be mainstreamed into all major EU spending programmes, in particular the regional development, energy, transport, and research and innovation programmes, as well as the Common Agricultural Policy. Based on existing OECD methodology, the EU is conducting 'climate tracking' in order to identify climate-related spending. In 2014, 12.7 per cent of the annual budget has been given a climate 'marker', and spending in this category is projected to increase in subsequent years (European Commission 2013b: Annex V). The Commission has announced that it will continue to fine-tune the methodology and thus build analytical capacities for climate budgeting.

Finally, policy appraisals and assessments have a long history in policy-making and involve a range of specific instruments that differ in scope (ranging from policies, projects, and programmes to plans and strategies) and focus (overall regulatory impact or environmental impact). In practice, these 'meta-instruments' (cf. Lodge and Wegrich's introduction to this volume) combine a range of strategies to ensure effective governance. They aim at improving the evidence base used in policy decisions, and thus serve an informational function. In doing so, they may require the involvement of certain participants in decision-making (e.g. consultation rights) and hence contribute to the organisation of decision-making. Finally, these instruments exercise oversight powers and may ensure that certain substantive benchmarks are met.

Environmental impact assessments (EIAs) and strategic environmental assessments (SEAs) are firmly established tools in governmental repertoires—particularly due to binding EU directives. They also appear prominently in EU reports on the national implementation of EU law, signalling problems in legal and practical application. Recent reforms have focused on administrative streamlining (hinting at problems with regard to coordination capacity); they also aim at widening the scope of the assessments to climate change, biodiversity, and natural disasters. With regard to scope, the limited administrative coordination and analytical capacities are highlighted in Commission communications (e.g. European Commission 2009b, 2009a) and in the literature on the implementation of regulatory impact assessments (e.g. De Francesco, Radaelli, and Troeger 2012). Once more, reform pressure is judged to be higher with respect to the more general strategic assessment instruments that require a holistic perspective. Not only are they more analytically demanding, but they also suffer from the emergence of new(er) tools such as sustainability appraisals, sustainability impact assessments, and climate appraisals, which contribute to a process of losing sight of the regulatory goal of avoiding further environmental deterioration (Bina 2008).

In summary, this section highlighted the numerous tools that are available to support coordinative governance towards sustainability. Informational, organisational, financial, and authoritative instruments can be identified in the repertoire of OECD countries and the European Union. Indeed, the rhetoric of sustainable development and the operational strategy of environmental policy integration clearly emphasise that building up capacity to overcome fragmented governmental structures and turf conflicts through coordination is crucial for effective SD and EPI. However, a close look at the instruments and their past performance indicates that analytical and regulatory capacities must complement these efforts. They may be the true bottleneck in the pursuit of grand designs. More generally, the failure of the EU Cardiff process to establish EPI as a normative principle in EU policy-making and the dead end of many multi-sectoral strategies point to capacity deficits as well as the limits of the guiding optimism behind these ideas. These limits have long been acknowledged in the state of the art in bureaucratic and organisational science and curiously have been a main trigger of the governance debate.

Sustainability as an issue of policy instruments and the use of 'new environmental policy instruments' (NEPIs)

In this section we turn our attention from the discussion of tools aiming toward integrated (and coordinated) governance to instruments addressing the effective delivery of environmental goals. To some extent, the larger discussion of SD—and the issue of prioritising environmental goals—reflects disillusionment with traditional regulatory instruments in environment policy and the recognition that sectoral policies need to take responsibility for reducing pressures on the long-term carrying capacity of the planet (see above). Within the field of environmental policy-making, we have witnessed policy innovation and a diversification of instruments, which mirror a wider debate on modes of governance in highly developed states (for an early discussion, see Mayntz 1993). 'New' modes of government aim at modifying the relations of political actors in decision-making and implementation for improved policy outcomes.

First, I will provide an overview of the uptake of so-called 'new environmental policy instruments' (NEPIs) at EU level and in some pioneering states. As shown in Table 8.2, I have adapted existing data to the classification of governance tools (i.e. authority, finance, organisation, and information) suggested in Lodge and Wegrich's introductory chapter to this volume. Although there has been a shift towards NEPIs pursuing non-authoritative strategies, rhetoric exceeds numbers. More importantly, the adoption of NEPIs has not necessarily resulted in better implementation. I suggest that implementation problems are partly linked to the publicly underestimated but considerable implications that the adoption of NEPIs has for administrative structures and capacities. This section will elaborate on this point in a discussion of the emission trading scheme (ETS) to reduce greenhouse gases.

By and large, existing typologies (cf. Wurzel, Zito, and Jordan 2013) and categories used to classify environmental policy instruments correspond to the policy strategies identified by Lodge and Wegrich in this volume's introductory chapter. The authoritative strategy relies on the exercise of regulatory power and primarily covers standard-setting policy instruments, prohibitions, and procedural obligations. There has been some innovation in the instruments belonging to this field, namely a shift toward 'framework regulations', which tend to combine authoritative with organisational features. In

Table 8.2. Uptake of 'new environmental policy instruments' (NEPIs) at the EU level

Policy strategy	Total # in 2000	%	Total # in 2005	%
Authority[1] (predominantly 'old' environmental instruments)	221	84.7	256	79.5
Finance (economic instruments)	11	4.2	17	5.3
Information[2]	15	5.7	21	6.5
Organisation (governmental and private actor networks; excluding administrative reforms[3])	14	5.4	28	8.7
Sum	*261*	*100.0*	*322*	*100.0*

Table adapted from Holzinger, Knill, and Lenschow (2009) to incorporate the categories of instruments outlined in Lodge and Wegrich's introductory chapter in this volume

[1] This field includes all items linked to the 'hierarchical mode' in the original table as well as liability rules and licenses, which were originally included in the competition—now finance—mode

[2] The informational strategy overlaps largely with the 'cooperative mode' in the original table. The item 'coordination of member state policies' has been moved to the organisation field

[3] The organisational box is likely to underestimate true numbers, as it consists of member state coordination and voluntary environmental instruments involving industrial actors, but ignores intra-governmental measures as discussed in the previous section on EPI

the next section, I will return to this category to review their implications for multi-level governance. The finance strategy builds on the behavioural effects of positive and negative financial incentives; apart from financial funding, it includes the important ETS (see below). The information category groups non-binding target setting, informational tools like labelling, and environmental campaigns and appeals, all aiming to change individual behaviour. Finally, the organisation strategy refers to the EU level's facilitation of the contribution of public and private actors to achieving higher levels of environmental protection; it includes the controversial instrument of voluntary agreements between actors in industry (substituting hierarchical standard setting with industrial self-regulation).

The moderate (though rising) uptake of new instruments (at EU level) has to do with a combination of factors. On the one hand, the substitutability of regulatory instruments based on political authority is limited (e.g. for setting harmonised and binding standards in order to level the playing field in a common market or to protect citizens from certain dangers). On the other hand, political support is minimal due to traditional styles of policy-making (Holzinger, Knill, and Lenschow 2009). We lack precise statistics on the uptake of different environmental policy instruments at the member state level,[1] although the literature concurs that traditional command-and-control

[1] Data collection is confronted with demarcation issues given the cross-cutting nature of environmental policy and problems of isolating subnational from national, and national (EU member state) from supranational law. In addition, the complex legal structures of framework regulations depend on technical instructions and administrative law, which may not be listed as environmental legislation.

regulatory instruments have been and remain the standard instrument in environmental policy (Jordan et al. 2012; Wurzel, Zito, and Jordan 2013). Converging patterns of adoption largely reflect the authoritative power of the EU, pushing procedural rules for greater transparency, stakeholder consultation, and administrative coordination as well as (potentially) greater discretionary powers for street-level bureaucrats in countries such as Germany and Austria, while imposing old-style regulatory instruments in the UK. At the same time, 'different jurisdictions [adopt] distinctive policy instrument mixes' (Wurzel, Zito, and Jordan 2013: 207ff.). Germany pioneered eco-labels (an information tool), voluntary agreements (an organisation tool), and eco-taxes (a financial tool); the UK has been an innovative force in the adoption of environmental management (information tool) and emission trading (financial tool) schemes; and the Netherlands has led the way with regard to voluntary agreements, eco-taxes, and emission trading.

However, early adoption does not necessarily correspond to good implementation results—pointing to some unresolved capacity problems. Generally, and contrary to early hopes for the removal of administrative burdens, NEPIs have not been a panacea from the implementation perspective (Knill and Lenschow 2000) and have proved challenging from the perspective of all capacity dimensions discussed in this volume. Depending on the existing institutional structures and regulatory styles, countries may encounter deficits in delivery capacity. Such deficits may arise from administrations being delegated previously unknown discretionary powers or asked to adapt their traditional understanding of state–society relations. One 'classic' example is Germany's initial failure to comply with the EU Environmental Information Directive, as the directive implied a novel service relationship between regulatory public authorities and the public (Knill and Lenschow 2000: 262ff.).

Problems may also arise due to insufficient regulatory capacity, e.g. where authoritative structures to supervise certification, trading, or 'voluntary' schemes are missing. Market and voluntary environmental instruments generally have been underestimated with respect to the degree of public administration and state control they require for proper functioning; this has been one of the main lessons to be learned in the implementation of the ETS in Europe.

The challenge of developing coordination capacities takes us back to the previous section's discussion of EPI, which depends on successfully managing new structures of horizontal and vertical intra-governmental integration. Apart from federal states, this tends to demand reforms in highly fragmented bureaucratic structures. Finally, analytical capacity, e.g. to produce the data and analyses required for both control and informational purposes, tends to be an issue in southern and eastern Europe where resources are not available and where public demand for the build-up of capacities is insufficient.

Analytical capacities are also required in order to fine-tune the new instruments in such a way that financial and reputational incentives or the information provided actually trigger the desired behavioural reaction. The diverse mix of policy instruments seems to call for institutional and procedural changes, as well as a wider mix of professional backgrounds within the administration.

Notably, some policy problems are particularly targeted by NEPIs. Climate and energy-related measures seem to be at the forefront of introducing innovative tools. For example, financial tools include CO_2 and energy taxes, financial support schemes for renewable energies, and the ETS. In addition, binding energy efficiency labels and climate change appraisals constitute hybrids of informational and authoritative instruments.[2] In the European context, the functioning of the ETS, the 'newest' kid on the NEPI bloc, will ultimately determine the success in meeting national and European greenhouse gas reduction targets. Interestingly, the 'innovation journey' of the ETS (cf. Voß 2007: 330ff.) goes all the way back to the 1960s, with economists and later the Environmental Protection Agency in the USA developing basic concepts and designs. In the 1990s, prototypes were launched in the USA and UK, which eventually informed debates at the turn of the century amongst both UN and corporate actors in the oil industry. In the 2000s, the journey is leading to Europe, with experimentation in some front-runner states (UK, Denmark, Netherlands) and the EU's construction of a European ETS system with increasingly centralised legislative and administrative competences.

The result has been a supranational emission trading system, covering most of the big industrial emitters across Europe and accounting for approximately half of the EU's total CO_2 emissions. It works as a 'cap and trade' instrument, i.e. there are set limits for national emissions and companies buy and sell allowances for their emissions within these limits. In the first phase, the ETS was organised in a decentralised fashion; member states were responsible for deciding on the amount and allocation of allowances in the context of National Allocation Plans (NAPs) (European Parliament and the Council 2003). Allowances were handed out free of charge,[3] and the total amount was based on a 'grandfathering system' (i.e. past emissions). Participation in the Joint Implementation (JI) and Clean Development Mechanisms (CDM) introduced by the Kyoto Protocol offers credits that count towards the targets of European installations—an option which critics identified early as a loophole for fraudulent behaviour. Not unexpectedly, the original ETS led to a number of implementation problems linked to the overall management of the

[2] For useful overviews and analysis of a fuller range of instruments adopted, see Oberthür and Pallemaerts (2010) and Berkhout et al. (2010).

[3] A gradual transition towards an auctioning mechanism is now under way.

scheme, and general over-allocation of allowances and exploitation of JI and CDM. In the post-pilot phase, the EU Commission adopted a stronger watchdog role, and more sophisticated 'banking' mechanisms for industry were introduced. Continuing concerns about compliance and requests from industry for harmonised rules were major triggers for the revised, more centralised system introduced in 2009. The new system provided for a single EU-wide cap and reduction timeline until 2020, harmonised allocation rules, auctioning procedures, more restrictive rules on JI and CDM, and transition and redistribution arrangements to account for effects of international competition on participating sectors (European Parliament and the Council 2009). The Commission proposes the installation of a 'market stability reserve' for the next trading period starting in 2021 in order to be able to more flexibly respond to economic volatilities and related overallocation of allowances. This tool would replace the controversial postponement of the auctioning of emission allowances (or: 'back loading') introduced in 2013 (see <http://ec.europa.eu/clima/policies/ets/reform/index_en.htm>).

This brief description of the scheme indicates the enormous administrative burdens that were first placed on the member states (typically environmental agencies), and are now placed on the European Commission to set up, run, and control the emissions trade. Wurzel et al. cite a British official reporting that 'it is an astonishingly common misperception that market-based instruments will lead to significantly less bureaucracy and legislation. They can work only because of regulatory back up. The market needs government protection' (2013: 185). Indeed, Voß argues that the ETS has resulted in the formation of a transnational policy regime with its specific social constituency:

> Various parts of the working configuration (such as public agencies, trading departments in companies, auditors for emissions) plus elements of the multi-level infrastructure of policy development (newly created departments in public administration, think tanks, consultancy and law firms) and the carbon industry (project developers, traders, banks, exchanges) rely on, and mutually reinforce, each other.
>
> (Voß 2007: 339)

While his main objective is to point to the stabilising forces required in such a regime, which can potentially run out of (democratic) control, my more limited aim is to highlight the scope of the administrative challenges as well as ongoing administrative adjustments that are increasingly connecting national, European, and international levels of governance and involving public and private actors.[4]

[4] The most recent 'addition' is the International Aviation Agency, which seeks to resolve the international dispute that has emerged due to the extension of the ETS to the aviation sector (and thus international airlines entering the European air space).

The example of the ETS suggests that it may be too easy to point to institutional inertia as a dominant characteristic in the take-up and implementation of new environmental instruments. Due to international institutional diffusion channels (Jörgens, Lenschow, and Liefferink 2013) as well as the recognition of regulatory gaps, the evolution of national and EU policy repertoires has been quite dynamic. It is doubtful that administrative capacity-building has kept up in this dynamic process because the need for such capacity-building was—at least politically—underestimated due to the rhetoric of 'slimming' and 'rationalising' the state. Capacity gaps are specific to individual member states, reflecting the unique nature of administrative traditions. The extent to which EU-led capacity-building (e.g. the Network for the Implementation of Environmental Law, known as IMPEL, or the EU implementation pilot) contributes to learning and administrative convergence is a question for future research.

Governance for sustainable development in a multi-level perspective: the case of ambient air quality policy in the European Union

In this final section, I will turn to a core issue in the sustainability discourse, namely the 'empowerment' of actors at the local level (cf. the Local Agenda 21 signed 1992 in Rio and the Aarhus Convention of 1998). The involvement of actors at the local level in shaping policies was expected to produce a sense of 'ownership' of the policy outputs and thus improve the implementation record and generate innovative, context-sensitive policy ideas. This agenda overlaps with the new instruments agenda, which also aims at being more context sensitive.[5] In the environmental field, local involvement should contribute to generating policy instruments that are well matched to the respective biophysical system, i.e. that are responsive to water pollution or flooding issues at the 'river basins' in question, or to traffic noise or air ambient pollution concentrated in 'urban hotspots'. In the European Union we see a trend to address those levels of governance that are most congruent with the geographical scope of the environmental problem in question. Durner and Ludwig (2008) speak of a new paradigm in EU environmental policy that combines an authoritative strategy of setting binding protection standards (i.e. old style of regulation) with a more discretionary (NEPI-like) planning approach that aims to link up local, regional, and national levels of governance and facilitate effective governance through organisational means.

[5] Market instruments, while emphasising individual choice, typically operate most successfully at a larger scale.

The EU air quality policy adopted between 1996 and 2008 is a good example of this new trend in environmental policy.[6] While responsibility for the transposition of EU directives lies (as usual) in the hands of the member states, the 2008 EU Ambient Air Quality Directive (European Parliament and the Council 2008) explicitly calls for the selection of the most 'appropriate' level and bodies of governance to effectively conduct the various tasks implied (Art. 3). Notwithstanding the fact that local concentrations of pollutants are caused by emissions from many different sources and activities at local, regional, national, and transboundary levels, 'zones and agglomerations' that take account 'of the size of populations and ecosystems exposed to pollution' (prelim 5) are prioritised. Air quality plans are to be developed for those zones and agglomerations where concentrations of pollutants exceed the set limits. It is up to the member states to decide on specific institutional arrangements and make sure that the managing institutions possess the required legal, financial, and analytical competences. Case study research (Becker, Lenschow, and Mehl focus on Germany, the Netherlands and Poland; Haus and Zimmermann 2007 analyse German cities) shows that the down-scaling implied in the concept of zones and agglomerations has indeed resulted in a shift of responsibility to the local level. The corresponding challenges are worth highlighting.

In meeting the requirements of the European air quality policy, local and regional administrations carry much of the burden in fulfilling the inherent planning obligations (Haus and Zimmermann 2007: 256ff; Durner and Ludwig 2008: 464). Their input is essential to collecting, interpreting, and preparing data for the air quality plans and making them accessible to the general public. Due to their formal jurisdiction over local hotspots, local governments (and city councils) are expected to develop actual measures for reducing pollution levels to reach compliance with EU standards, although arguably the local level has very limited legal and administrative competence to tackle the problem. Neither do local authorities set technical standards for vehicles (e.g. the EU does or should), nor do they plan and finance many of the most problem-relevant road networks[7] or rail infrastructure. Even for measures like local speed limits, road pricing, congestion charges, low emission zones, or investments in cycling paths or public transport, local governments are often heavily constrained by their (inferior) jurisdictional status and limited financial capacities. Thus neither in the Netherlands nor in Poland may local governments formally decide on emission zones—a tool that is widely used in Germany. German cities, in turn, may have to implement

[6] For another, well-known, example, please compare the literature on the EU Water Framework Directive, e.g. Moss and Newig (2010), for the analytical perspective on 'scalar dynamics'.

[7] Local traffic hotspots are typically nodal points in the system of regional and national roads.

measures decided at higher federal levels without the adequate resources. Federal systems like Germany also encounter particular problems in cross-sectoral coordination. Land-use, housing, and transport responsibilities may be allocated to different levels of government, thus requiring complex horizontal and vertical 'networking' at the same time. Spatial 'misfit' is not limited to intra-governmental relations, but extends to the European level. Apart from a temporal imbalance between planning rhetoric and tight deadlines in the directive, insufficient European norms for vehicles largely explain why cities in the Netherlands, which are embedded in a vertically and horizontally well-coordinated National Air Quality Programme and benefit from secure financing, hardly perform better than German and Polish cities.

Reflecting on the development of capacities, we first note that—similar to the case of NEPIs—'old' regulations that were reformed in the name of subsidiarity and local ownership have produced unexpected demands for and gaps in administrative capacities. Depending on the complexities of multi-level structures, the development of delivery and regulatory capacities proves most challenging when financial resources and legal competences are locked at higher levels and inaccessible to local actors. With regard to coordination and analytical capacities, some countries benefit from centralised support (the Netherlands). Elsewhere, administrative networking and learning strongly depend on administrative entrepreneurs, the relative wealth of the municipality, and the authoritative force of European Court rulings for overcoming formidable formal barriers. On the whole, EU environmental framework legislation has placed more weight on (local) administrations. Due to pressures for multi-level output, we now see administrative decision-making strengthened instead of the empowerment of the local public.

Conclusions

This chapter reflected on the highly dynamic and quite innovative policy area of sustainability, or more specifically the environment–economy nexus in OECD countries. This nexus has been widely acknowledged as crucial for the long-term survival of our planet, and more immediately for sustaining the high quality of life of the industrialised world. The issue of climate change has served to place governance challenges associated with SD on the top of the political agenda. However, it is not the only challenge that deserves attention, as biodiversity, survival of the oceans, and public health problems linked to local environmental pollution are formidable crises equally in need of problem-solving at different levels and across different sectors of governance. This chapter has therefore pointed to a wide variety of problem areas and identified three major governance themes—horizontal policy integration, vertical coordination in multi-level settings, and choice of policy instruments—to discuss the performance of innovations in these areas.

Although the dynamism in SD policy can be characterised as impressive—despite some SD fatigue in rhetoric and policy since the global debt crisis—the results have been highly ambiguous. While the literature on SD administrative capacity tends to be discussed largely as a 'problem of the south' (or more precisely: the global south and the European south-east), the framework presented in Lodge and Wegrich's introductory chapter has helped to define the concept of administrative capacity and detect capacity problems across all three thematic dimensions throughout the OECD world. Interestingly, while innovations in the SD field have frequently targeted the analytical, delivery, and even regulatory capacity of civil society and business in contributing to SD, the administrative capacity of public bodies has received surprisingly little attention. Governance innovations that explicitly target administrative structures and procedures tend to be oriented along universal designs, overestimating the capabilities available for planning complex systems and underestimating the challenge of developing coordinative administrative capacities under politically volatile circumstances. On the basis of this diagnosis, it would be risky to propose a problem-solving perspective that does not at least balance the administrative capacity dimension with political commitment and leadership—commitment that is also required to build the necessary capacities.

References

Adelle, C., and Russel, D. (2013). 'Climate Policy Integration: A Case of Déjà Vu?', *Environmental Policy and Governance*, 23(1): 1–12.

Becker, S. T., Lenschow, A., and Mehl, C. (forthcoming). 'Scalar Dynamics and Legitimacy Implications of Ambient Air Quality Management in the EU', *Journal of Environmental Policy and Planning.*

Berkhout, F., Haug, C., Rayner, T., van Asselt, H., Hildingsson, R., Huitema, D., Jordan, A., Monni, S., and Stripple, J. (2010). 'How do Climate Policies Work? Confronting Governance Dilemmas in the European Union', in M. Hulme, and H. Neufeldt (eds), *Making Climate Change Work for Us: European Perspectives on Adaptation and Mitigation Strategies*. Cambridge: Cambridge University Press, 137–64.

Bina, O. (2008). 'Strategic Environmental Assessment', in A. Jordan, and A. Lenschow (eds), *Innovation in Environmental Policy? Integrating the Environment for Sustainability.* Cheltenham: Edward Elgar, 134–56.

Casado, J., and Steurer, R. (forthcoming). 'Integrated Strategies on Sustainable Development, Climate Change Mitigation and Adaptation in Western Europe: Communication rather than Coordination', *Journal of Public Policy.*

Commission of the European Communities (CEC) (1992). *Towards Sustainability. A European Community Programme of Policy and Action in Relation to the Environment and Sustainable Development*, COM (92) 23/fin, Brussels.

De Francesco, F., Radaelli, C. M., and Troeger, V. E. (2012). 'Implementing Regulatory Innovations in Europe: The Case of Impact Assessment', *Journal of European Public Policy*, 19(4): 491–511.

Durner, W., and Ludwig, R. (2008). 'Paradigmenwechsel in der europäischen Umweltrechtsetzung?', *Natur und Recht*, 30(7): 457–67.

European Commission (2009a). 'Report from the Commission to the Council, the European Parliament, the European Economic and Social Committee and the Committee of the Regions on the application and effectiveness of the EIA Directive'. COM (2009) 378 final. Brussels: European Commission.

European Commission (2009b). 'Report from the Commission to the Council, the European Parliament, the European Economic and Social Committee and the Committee of the Regions on the Application and Effectiveness of the Directive on Strategic Environmental Assessment'. COM (2009) 469 final. Brussels: European Commission.

European Commission (2010). 'Communication from the Commission. Europe 2020. A Strategy for Smart, Sustainable and Inclusive Growth'. COM (2010) 2020 final. Brussels: European Commission.

European Commission (2011a). 'Roadmap to a Resource Efficient Europe'. COM (2011) 571 final. Brussels: European Commission.

European Commission (2011b). 'A Roadmap for Moving to a Competitive Low Carbon Economy in 2050'. COM (2011) 112 final. Brussels: European Commission.

European Commission (2011c). 'Our Life Insurance, Our Natural Capital: An EU Biodiversity Strategy to 2020'. COM(2011) 244 final. Brussels: European Commission.

European Commission (2012). 'Proposal for a Decision of the European Parliament and of the Council on a General Union Environment Action Programme to 2020 "Living well, within the Limits of our Planet"'. COM(2012) 710 final. Brussels: European Commission.

European Commission (2013a) [website]. *Commissioner Hedegaard: Summit Deal on EU Budget is 'Major Step Forward to Climate Action'*. Retrieved from <http://ec.europa.eu/clima/news/articles/news_2013020801_en.htm> (accessed 7 March 2014).

European Commission (2013b). 'Statement of Estimates of the Commission for 2014'. (Preparation of the 2014 Draft Budget). SEC (2013) 370 final. Brussels: European Commission.

European Parliament and the Council (2002). 'Decision No 1600/2002/EC of the European Parliament and of the Council of 22 July 2002 laying down the Sixth Community Environment Action Programme'. Official Journal, L 242, 10. Brussels.

European Parliament and the Council (2003). 'Directive 2003/87/EC of the European Parliament and of the Council of 13 October 2003 Establishing a Scheme for Greenhouse Gas Emission Allowance Trading within the Community and Amending Council Directive 96/61/EC'. Official Journal, L 275/32, 25. Brussels.

European Parliament and the Council (2008). 'Directive 2008/50/EC of the European Parliament and of the Council of 21 May 2008 on Ambient Air Quality and Cleaner Air for Europe'. Official Journal, L 152/1, 21. Brussels.

European Parliament and the Council (2009). 'Directive 2009/29/EC of the European Parliament and of the Council of 23 April 2009 Amending Directive 2003/87/EC so as to Improve and Extend the Greenhouse Gas Emission Allowance Trading Scheme of the Community'. Official Journal, L 140/16. Brussels.

Haus, M., and Zimmermann, K. (2007). 'Die Feinstaubproblematik als Governance-Herausforderung für die lokale Umweltpolitik', in K. Jacob, F. Biermann, P.-O. Busch, and P. H. Feindt (eds), *Politik und Umwelt*. 1. Aufl. Wiesbaden: VS Verlag für Sozialwissenschaften, 243–61.

Holzinger, K., Knill, C., and Lenschow, A. (2009). 'Governance in EU Environmental Policy', in I. Tömmel, and A. Verdun (eds), *Innovative Governance in the European Union: The Politics of Multilevel Policymaking*. Boulder: Lynne Rienner Publishers, 45–61.

Hoornbeek, J. (2008). 'The United States of America', in A. Jordan, and A. Lenschow (eds), *Innovation in Environmental Policy? Integrating the Environment for Sustainability*. Cheltenham: Edward Elgar, 268–88.

Jacob, K., and Volkery, A. (2007). 'Umweltpolitikintegration und Selbstregulierung: Ein Vergleich von Instrumenten der Umweltpolitikintegration in den OECD Ländern', in K. Jacob, F. Biermann, P.-O. Busch, and P. H. Feindt (eds), *Politik und Umwelt*. 1. Aufl. Wiesbaden: VS Verlag für Sozialwissenschaften, 360–81.

Jacob, K., Volkery, A., and Lenschow, A. (2008). 'Instrument for Environmental Policy Integration in 30 OECD Countries', in A. Jordan, and A. Lenschow (eds), *Innovation in Environmental Policy? Integrating the Environment for Sustainability*. Cheltenham: Edward Elgar, 24–45.

Jänicke, M. and Jacob, K. (eds) (2006). *Environmental Governance in Global Perspective: New Approaches to Ecological Modernisation*. FFU Report 01-2006. Berlin: Freie Universität Berlin.

Jordan, A. (2008). 'The Governance of Sustainable Development: Taking Stock and Looking Forwards', *Environment and Planning C: Government and Policy*, 26(1): 17–33.

Jordan, A. and Lenschow, A. (eds) (2008). *Innovation in Environmental Policy? Integrating the Environment for Sustainability*. Cheltenham: Edward Elgar.

Jordan, A., and Lorenzoni, I. (2007). 'Is There Now a Political Climate for Policy Change? Policy and Politics after the Stern Review', *The Political Quarterly*, 78(2): 310–9.

Jordan, A., and Schout, A. (2006). *The Coordination of the European Union: Exploring the Capacities of Networked Governance*. Oxford, New York: Oxford University Press.

Jordan, A., Benson, D., Wurzel, R., and Zito, A. (2012). 'Environmental Policy: Governing by Multiple Instruments?', in J. J. Richardson (ed.), *Constructing a Policy-Making State? Policy Dynamics in the EU*. Oxford: Oxford University Press, 104–24.

Jörgens, H., Lenschow, A. and Liefferink, D. (eds) (2013). *Understanding Environmental Policy Convergence: The Power of Words, Rules and Money*. Cambridge: Cambridge University Press.

Knill, C., and Lenschow, A. (2000). 'Do New Brooms Really Sweep Cleaner? Implementation of New Instruments in EU Environmental Policy', in C. Knill, and A. Lenschow (eds), *Implementing EU Environmental Policy: New Directions and Old Problems*. Manchester, New York: Manchester University Press, 251–86.

Kurze, K., and Lenschow, A. (under review). *Towards a New 'Principled Priority': A Discourse Analysis of the EU's Integrated Climate and Energy Policy*.

Mayntz, R. (1993). 'Governing Failures and the Problem of Governability: Some Comments on a Theoretical Paradigm', in J. Kooiman (ed.), *Modern Governance: New Government-Society Interactions*. London, Newbury Park: Sage, 9–20.

Moss, T., and Newig, J. (2010). 'Multilevel Water Governance and Problems of Scale: Setting the Stage for a Broader Debate', *Environmental Management*, 46(1): 1–6.

Nordbeck, R., and Steurer, R. (under review). *Multi-Sectoral Strategies as Dead Ends of Policy Coordination: Lessons to be Learned from Sustainable Development.*

Oberthür, S. and Pallemaerts, M. (eds) (2010). *The New Climate Policies of the European Union: Internal Legislation and Climate Diplomacy*. Brussels: VUB Press.

OECD (Organisation for Economic Co-operation and Development) (1991). *Envrionmental Labelling in the OECD Countries*. Paris: OECD.

OECD (Organisation for Economic Co-operation and Development) (1994). *Managing the Environment: The Role of Economic Instruments*. Paris: OECD.

OECD (Organisation for Economic Co-operation and Development) (1999). *Environmental Taxes and Green Reform*. Paris: OECD.

OECD (Organisation for Economic Co-operation and Development) (2002). *Policies to Enhance Sustainable Development: Critical Issues*. Paris: OECD.

Öko-Institut e. V. (1998). *New Instruments for Sustainability: The New contribution of Voluntary Agreements to Environmental Policy*. Freiburg: Öko-Institut e. V.

Schout, A., and Jordan, A. (2008). 'Administrative Instruments', in A. Jordan, and A. Lenschow (eds), *Innovation in Environmental Policy? Integrating the Environment for Sustainability*. Cheltenham: Edward Elgar, 49–69.

SRU (Sachverständigenrat für Umweltfragen) (1998). *Umweltgutachten 1998. Umweltschutz. Erreichtes sichern, neue Wege gehen.* Stuttgart: Metzler-Poeschel.

SRU (Sachverständigenrat für Umweltfragen) (2008). *Umweltgutachten 2008. Umweltschutz im Zeichen des Klimawandels*. Berlin: Schmidt.

Steurer, R. (2008). 'Sustainable Development Strategies', in A. Jordan, and A. Lenschow (eds), *Innovation in Environmental Policy? Integrating the Environment for Sustainability*. Cheltenham: Edward Elgar, 93–113.

United Nations (1992). 'Agenda 21'. United Nations Conference on Environment & Development, Rio de Janeiro, Brazil, 3 to 14 June 1992. Rio de Janeiro: United Nations.

Voß, J.-P. (2007). 'Innovation Processes in Governance: The Development of "Emissions Trading" as a New Policy Instrument', *Science and Public Policy*, 34(5): 329–43.

WCED (World Commission on Environment and Development) (1987). *Our Common Future*. New York: Oxford University Press.

Wilkinson, D., Benson, D., and Jordan, A. (2008). 'Green Budgeting', in A. Jordan, and A. Lenschow (eds), *Innovation in Environmental Policy? Integrating the Environment for Sustainability*. Cheltenham: Edward Elgar, 70–92.

Wurzel, R. K., Zito, A. R., and Jordan, A. J. (2013). *Environmental Governance in Europe: A Comparative Analysis of New Environmental Policy instruments*. Cheltenham: Edward Elgar.

9

Governance Dilemmas of the Contemporary State

The Politics of Infrastructure Policy

Jacint Jordana

Infrastructure is required for economic development and social communication, and represents an essential aspect of statehood. In this era of governance, the study of how states develop and invest in infrastructure helps to illustrate whether, and if so how, regulatory policies and instruments are able to resolve certain inherent policy challenges at the heart of infrastructure policy and politics. For both developed and developing countries, the appropriate use of regulatory instruments promised to offer more resources for (mainly private) infrastructure investment, more stable regulatory oversight—due to a greater involvement of experts and scientists in the decision-making processes—and more efficiently designed and long-term infrastructure policies. Innovative regulatory techniques were supposed to address the traditional market failures inherent in infrastructure industries. However, after decades of reform, the doubts about whether these promises have been fulfilled are great. Natural monopoly characteristics, for example, remain critical in the governance of infrastructure industries.

This chapter identifies three main challenges to the governance of infrastructure, focusing primarily on developed countries, in particular OECD countries. Developing world issues are somewhat different, especially as infrastructure provision is largely about supply shortages (Bourguignon and Pleskovic 2008). Nevertheless, some of the policy innovations in the governance of infrastructures that we analyse—particularly novel regulatory schemes and public–private initiatives—have been widely implemented in the developing world (Estache 2007), although policy options used to be different

(Klein 2012). As a consequence, some of the arguments developed in this chapter are applicable for both developed and developing world contexts.

The first challenge is to identify what combination of public and private involvement is likely to be most appropriate for the provision and maintenance of different types of public infrastructure. What kinds of factors have been used to justify the choices governments have made in different countries and sectors? What are the benefits and risks of adopting particular strategies that involve private participation?

Identifying the appropriate level of infrastructure provision is a second challenge. Mega-projects, such as infrastructure projects, are often associated with problems of over- and under-provision, delays, and cost overruns, partly because of inherent decision-making biases involved in their planning, partly because of the unintended and uncertain consequences associated with highly interdependent and tightly coupled projects (Jennings and Lodge 2012). The governance challenges of mega-projects are defined by both political decision-making processes and administrative capacities, ranging from delivery ('project management'), to regulatory oversight, to boundary-spanning capacities. Administrative capacities are required when it comes to issues such as whether infrastructure capacities should be demand or supply driven, what particular technologies should be adopted, and how much 'slack' or spare capacity should be provided so as to accommodate peak demand or future demand patterns.

The third challenge is to establish policy-making processes that provide for democratic legitimacy. One tension is said to exist between long-term planning and shorter electoral cycles. A second tension is how to combine societal participation and expert opinion when making decisions regarding large-scale infrastructure projects. Furthermore, decision-making over infrastructure provision involves questions as to the appropriate level of decision-making, in particular whether such decisions should be made in a decentralised or centralised manner, and at what level of government.

This chapter has three main sections. The first section explores some of the governance challenges in the area of infrastructure that have been encountered in the developed world over the past few decades. The next section considers the kind of administrative capacities required, especially those involving regulatory strategies. The third section concentrates on the institutional and organisational resources employed by states to strengthen governance performance.

The transformation of infrastructure policies

Defining the field of infrastructure policy is not easy. There is no common or agreed definition of public infrastructure. Its definition tends to be 'vague and imprecise' (Button 2006: 325). Roads, ports, communication networks, airports, channels, and railways, among other structures, all are usually identified as infrastructure. These are physical facilities for communication and transportation. The provision of physical support for health services, education, or public administration more generally might also be considered infrastructure. Furthermore, irrigation systems, flood protection defences, energy networks, parks, and other public spaces would usually count as infrastructure. In addition to these physical infrastructures, there are also those of a more virtual nature. Examples include information technology systems that support transportation and communication systems.

Alternative ways of defining infrastructure are similarly faced with blurred boundaries. For example, infrastructures are said to be characterised by natural monopoly characteristics and as having 'network externalities' in that their provision usually generates benefits that go beyond those accruing to those that use the service directly. Natural monopoly characteristics, however, are not necessarily fixed but depend, to at least some extent, on technical developments. Others argue that infrastructures are defined by their 'fixed asset' characteristics in that upfront initial investment is critical for the provision of services. In addition, these high fixed asset costs also mean that decisions are difficult to reverse.

It is also difficult to identify which criteria should guide decision-making. For example, it is not clear what the appropriate time horizon is (long vs short term). Infrastructures are not necessarily public goods in the sense of being characterised by the non-excludable and non-rival nature of their provision. Crowding does occur, and individuals can be excluded from consuming particular benefits. Thus, consumption of infrastructure can be 'charged', and price mechanisms can apply to such 'club goods'. The challenge is to establish the appropriate level of consumption (not too 'empty' but not too 'crowded').

Furthermore, it is problematic to identify the value of the (positive) network externalities; for example, the value of the exponential growth of nodes between users that emerges from adding individual members to a network is hard to 'price'. Other non-economic factors also come into play, such as the idea that infrastructures should facilitate economic and social development and therefore should not necessarily be profit making. Thus, the provision of infrastructure is associated not only with economic, but also with social solidarity rationales.

This chapter focuses on the most conventional understanding of infrastructure, namely that associated with transport, communication, energy, and water. The following concentrates on infrastructures for public use or those providing public goods, irrespective of whether they have been designed, produced, or provided by private or public actors. Therefore, this chapter does not deal with private firm- or club-type infrastructures that may only be available to employees of particular firms or members of particular organisations.

The objectives of infrastructure policy are similarly difficult to identify because they usually encompass a multiplicity of aims. For one, infrastructure policy often comes as part of a wider set of policies, such as regional development, military capacity, or political and/or territorial integration. These objectives have been central to infrastructure policy throughout time. At the same time, infrastructure policy is about addressing economic and social concerns regarding the provision of transportation and communication. However, identifying the level and intensity of demand is far from easy, especially as policy environments continue to change.

Policy priorities also change and have a direct impact on the way in which societies communicate with each other, consume energy, or move around. Questions about sustainability and climate change have a direct impact on the way in which energy and transport networks are being developed today. For example, questions arise as to the desired portfolio of energy sources, the development of future technologies that may change the cost profile of different energy sources, and thus also the way in which energy networks have to be developed. Sustainability-related questions also raise issues as to how to influence individual behaviours in the short term (Chapman 2007).

The financial crisis of 2007–8 and the subsequent sovereign debt crises have triggered debates about how to generate sufficient financial resources to secure investment in infrastructure. At the same time, infrastructure policies are also often seen as one way to stimulate economic growth, both directly in the sense of generating employment and activity, and indirectly, by providing for enhanced connections between centres and (former) peripheries. Moreover, demographic trends create uncertainties about where and how much infrastructure capacity will be required. Ageing societies, processes of urbanisation, changes in family structures, and the like affect infrastructure needs and transform demands for land use and travel (Button and Nijkamp 1997). Other problems, such as stagnation or reduced economic growth, might also affect the definition of goals in infrastructure policy.

Given these contextual changes, it is not surprising that the governance of infrastructure policy has been transformed across countries. A few decades ago, most infrastructure industries were owned and managed within the public sector (at various levels of government and in different forms of public ownership). Privately provided infrastructure remained the exception (outside the United States). Depleted public budgets, reluctance among voters to support tax increases, changing ideas about the role and instruments of the state, changes in technologies, and rising demands for investment in infrastructure modernisation forced states to explore new forms of infrastructure provision. The end result has been a growing reliance on the private sector.

The most noticeable changes have occurred in the telecommunications sector. Over the course of the past three decades, countries moved towards competitive markets. State-owned providers turned into international operators, and new providers emerged (Levi-Faur 2003). This major change has to be understood as a result of the extensive technological changes that occurred in the communications sector. In other areas, such as electricity, gas, and water, some movement towards more private and liberalised markets also occurred. However, these changes were far less extensive than in telecommunications. In transport, developments largely affected the way in which provision was contractualised in terms of organising the maintenance, management, and modernisation of infrastructure and services.

In other words, private involvement in the provision of infrastructure is an international phenomenon. This private involvement varies from public–private partnerships to other forms of collaboration between private and state-owned enterprises to fully privatised markets. This shift has also led to adjustments in the wider governance arrangements, especially in terms of the way in which thinking about regulation has evolved. A global diffusion of new ideas and regulatory tools occurred (Henisz, Zelner, and Guillen 2005). These ideas have circulated through specific channels in different sectors, with a central role being played by international organisations, such as the OECD (Jordana, Levi-Faur, and Fernandez-Marin 2011). As a consequence, many countries adopted these innovations during the 1990s and 2000s, culminating in a very successful expansion of regulatory instruments, and finally sanctioning a major change.

The expected benefits that are to be derived from infrastructure investments constitute another major issue for infrastructure governance. It has been argued that investment in infrastructure industries is characterised by diminishing returns, once a ceiling is reached. Despite considerable investment requirements due to technological change, contemporary investment in infrastructure capacity has not had the same impact on enhancing economic growth as did investments in earlier decades. In addition, regardless of its impact on economic growth, any decision about infrastructure investments has a considerable impact on distributional patterns and questions of access (Button 2006). In some cases, indeed, infrastructure investments have produced little else but 'white elephants' that are said to have diverted essential resources away from other areas and/or whose costs have proven to be considerably higher than the benefits they have generated.

In sum, questions about infrastructure investment arise across the OECD world and beyond. Debates about sustainability and climate change have added to debates about levels of investment and what kinds of technologies should be preferred over others. Such choices affect, for example, decisions about energy sources or about modes of transport. Furthermore, such choices ultimately have an impact on the way in which burdens are to be shared across consumers (private and business).

Infrastructure industries are also affected by their particular politics. In other words, they offer a good example of policies that have their own politics. One reason for this situation is that particular technological choices have 'lock-in' effects, meaning that infrastructure decisions have long-lasting effects in terms of generating supportive constituencies (among universities, research institutes, and industry alike) and spillovers into other economic and social areas that make any decision difficult to reverse.

Furthermore, infrastructure policies generate their own 'bandwagon' effects (Dunleavy 1986). One example is the massive expansion of a high-speed railway network in Spain during the 2000s. By the 2010s, it is argued that the network's capacity is far above requirements, especially when comparing the size of the Spanish railway network with those much smaller ones in more densely populated European states (Albalate and Bel 2012). Such policy bandwagons cannot be explained simply in terms of rational cost–benefit calculations. Rather, they emerge in the context of the interplay between political and economic interests. These economic interests include construction firms, powerful users, producers, and engineers, which form coalitions with government departments whose portfolio and professional ties create close linkages to these concentrated economic interests. Policy bandwagons are further accelerated through territorial competition: different regions and cities compete over having high-speed railway connections, art installations, water treatment plants, or airport capacity. Over time, such short-term boosts to local or regional economies is 'competed away' as other regions and cities establish similar infrastructures.

In the light of these political pressures, it is difficult to create governance structures that hold up against such policy bandwagons. Competing pressures may exist and, at least temporarily, delay the building of new infrastructure capacity. For example, pressure groups may mobilise in opposition to the creation of new infrastructures, because of either wider environmental concerns, political opposition to particular technologies, or the immediate impact on their area (e.g. noise).

Apart from the governance challenge of balancing competing values and interests, infrastructure policies are embedded in wider multi-level politics that involve intergovernmental resource allocation issues. Decisions on planning, financing, and technological options are not necessarily made in one department, let alone at one level of government. Such settings give rise to coordination problems, as different levels of government and different departments will seek to protect their turf, shuffle the cost to other administrative units, and seek to impose their preferred policy option. Road systems, for example, are usually an area in which separate levels of government have different degrees of responsibility. Such problems are further accentuated in the case of cross-national infrastructure planning. For example, the European Union has played an important role in the coordination (and financing) of cross-national infrastructure provision in some areas, and multiple difficulties have arisen in coordinating these policies. Key issues here concern the development of joint (minimum) technical standards to ensure interoperability.

In other words, infrastructure policy involves a long-term time horizon, but takes place within the context of the short-term cycle of electoral politics. The governance challenge is to establish institutional settings that balance these competing interests, that reduce particular decision-making biases, and that allow for sufficient openness to civic participation. Furthermore, the lock-in effects of earlier decisions mean that infrastructure policies are difficult to reverse, creating tensions when earlier choices conflict with changing political or societal preferences, or with changing demands due to economic trends. Not surprisingly, all these considerations usually interact, making long-term planning very uncertain and a source of severe governance problems. However, and in spite of these challenges, long-term planning is essential in infrastructure policy-making because it facilitates the emergence of coordination among actors and reduces the prevailing uncertainty to a great extent, particularly for many private and public agents who develop their own investment plans.

Administrative capacities and the governance of infrastructure

Globalisation has had a direct effect on the way in which national infrastructure policies are made and implemented. International diffusion of 'best practice' guidance has been extensive, whether because of the presence of international organisations, the prominence of international private providers of infrastructure services, or the tendency of national public servants to seek legitimacy by referring to international benchmarks. Indeed, this setting is said to have sharpened the potential consequences of 'bad' regulation because public finances are depleted and a premium is therefore placed on attracting private finance. It has been argued that private finance will only invest in national infrastructure policies if the regulatory regime offers a 'credible commitment' about its stability and reliability, avoiding risks of unexpected changes in the policy framework (Spiller and Tommasi 2005).

Thus, the governance of infrastructure is not just globalised in the sense of a trafficking of ideas; it is also globalised in the sense that the potential 'penalty' for 'poor' regulatory design is said to have increased (Lodge and Stirton 2006). Globalisation of policies is therefore both about emulation and copying, and about locational competition.

In the context of administrative capacities, as discussed in this volume, one can diagnose some changes, not just in terms of 'more' or 'less', but also in terms of whether there has been a shift in terms of where capacities reside, i.e. whether they reside in government and bureaucracy or predominantly in the private sector. The rest of this section considers primarily demands on regulatory capacity, but will also, less extensively, consider the three other administrative capacities outlined in the introductory chapter by Lodge and Wegrich.

Demands on regulatory capacities have altered considerably over the past decades. One key challenge, arguably, is that regulatory capacities have been in stronger demand not just in the area of government, but also among transnational private companies. This is not to deny that state-owned monopolies were always in a powerful position vis-à-vis public administration and politics, but the age of international private public service providers has thrown this imbalance in capacities into sharper relief. Furthermore, the growing prominence of regulatory agencies illustrates how institutions and methodologies of regulation have become increasingly important in the oversight over national (and transnational) infrastructure.

It is therefore not surprising that the 'regulation' word is omnipresent in the production and delivery of infrastructure-related policies. Direct public involvement, for example, through public ownership, has not completely gone away. However, the dominant concerns have involved the design of regulatory institutions and instruments, as well as different contracting techniques. Different ways of designing incentive regimes, such as the 'price cap', were established so as to counter the diagnosed shortcomings of previous regulatory techniques and to encourage private providers to seek efficiency and innovation. Liberalisation linked to structural measures to encourage competition is used in some jurisdictions to overcome the limitations of seeking to control a private monopoly. Another example of innovative regulatory strategies is the linkage of regulation of utility services with commitments of private firms to extend networks and advance service quality. So-called asymmetric regulation has been used to impose obligations on incumbent firms or dominant providers so as to enable new entrants to compete on the market.

Regulatory capacity is not merely about oversight relating to economic and social objectives. Increasingly, additional objectives have been imposed on regulators and regulatory regimes. These include network expansion (in coverage and capacity), the use of particular technologies or mixes of technologies (e.g. renewables), or other environmental objectives. Rather than direct financial subsidies, interventions have taken the form of regulatory instruments, such as through the manipulation of the price mechanism. Furthermore, regulatory instruments have also been used to prevent that purely commercial considerations apply to particularly vulnerable parts of the population. In other words, regulatory instruments often are intended to provide for internal cross-subsidisation as a way to avoid direct public support to particular policy goals.

In some countries, such as the United Kingdom, privatisation of public infrastructure has gone beyond telecoms and energy to include airports and railways, for example. The construction of new roads, railways, or water systems has often been undertaken through public–private partnerships. In these cases, new regulatory schemes have been put in place. Infrastructure maintenance has also progressively been privatised in many countries under regulatory supervision. Long-term concessions to privately operated public infrastructures have been another regulatory instrument.

The shift towards more private sector involvement in infrastructure provision did not occur simultaneously in every type of infrastructure in developed countries. New toll roads were common in countries such as France, Spain and Italy even in the 1970s, meaning that private investment or public–private partnerships were already in operation. In many other sectors, private ownership and involvement only started during the 1990s. Public ownership of telecommunications infrastructure has declined in importance since the late 1990s. The same became increasingly true for gas and electricity in the late 2000s and to a limited extent in rail systems during the 2000s (Sutherland et al. 2011). However, highway networks and water infrastructure remain more stable, in some countries with well-established models of private participation under public regulation that have remained unaltered for many decades.

In the new policy framework, it is assumed that public authorities are responsible for planning the characteristics of new infrastructures while establishing regulatory mechanisms to allow for private provision at the minimum possible cost to the public. However, policy change using regulatory instruments has also been introduced without abandoning public ownership. For example, on occasion, although no privatisation or private involvement has occurred, the authorities have dictated prices for the use of public infrastructure as a way of focusing on sustainability and limiting demand. The many different modes of combining private and public involvement in infrastructure delivery vary according to the specific sector and to the policy options each country has adopted.

As a consequence, a large number of regulatory instruments have been developed during the last decades to create or sustain markets and to enhance competition in general (OECD 2009). It is unclear to what extent regulation of market competition should drive long-term infrastructure developments. In the context described above this is a critical choice that might cause conflict in different administrative areas. How the use of regulatory instruments could be coordinated with planning and other strategic policies presents a fundamental governance problem in infrastructure policy. There is no single answer; it depends very much on the sector. In some cases, as in telecommunications, planning almost disappeared, and coordination has become largely a private activity. In other cases, for example transport systems, public coordination maintains a dominant role, often hierarchically structured.

To better understand the initial success of regulatory instruments during the 1990s, it is necessary to remember that this was a period of vast technological change in different utilities sectors, especially telecommunications. The introduction of digital technologies allowed a significant reduction in the costs of monitoring multiple market segments, which facilitated regulatory guidance. Also, production costs in infrastructure experienced a gradual decline because of the intensive use of digital technology in many sectors. As costs were decreasing because of technological advances, the main regulatory strategy was focused on stimulating price cuts. Even when implemented, this conceptual framework for regulation has not brought success to all sectors or locations. Not all infrastructures have experienced a sustained decline in prices: in fact, only the telecommunications sector has shown a clear downward trend in the last 20 years. Furthermore, the modest price reduction that did occur in other sectors, such as energy, was probably due to already amortised infrastructures and considerable extra capacity. In other sectors, regulation-induced competitive pressures eventually reduced costs, but often at the expense of lower investment in modernising infrastructures.

All in all, it appears that regulation as an administrative technique for managing infrastructure policy has shown some limitations despite its growing prominence in recent times. With great variations across sectors, the introduction of regulatory instruments allowed private involvement in public infrastructure investment and its management. Privatisation reduced the need to spend public funds and had the potential to produce additional income. These innovations noticeably alleviated the fiscal pressures most developed countries experienced to sustain their welfare states since the 1980s. However, connections between regulation and other administrative procedures were not always suitable for steering the policy over the long run, and the potential for relying on such regulatory instruments as the dominant tools in infrastructure policy was probably overestimated.

It is not just in the area of regulation that administrative capacities matter. In terms of analytical capacities, there has arguably been less of a shift from public to private actors. However, the demands on analytical capacities have changed, as noted above, because the diversity of inputs and worldviews has increased. Analytical capacities involve questions about what kind of infrastructure is desired in terms of quality, coverage, and affordability. Quality means that infrastructure has to be 'fit for purpose': users should feel confident that they will not face volatile levels of services or even interruptions. Coverage, referring to the reach of particular infrastructure services and their financing, has been the subject of questions relating to industrial policy (i.e. infrastructure subsidies to stimulate industrial activity in remote areas) and national integration (i.e. signalling that the 'same' service levels are available throughout the country and not just in privileged metropolitan areas). Affordability raises issues about 'universal service' obligations and fairness. The analytical questions here are about what kind of service (level) is required in order to ensure that citizens and businesses can fully participate in social and economic life, while, at the same time, ensuring that infrastructure providers are sufficiently compensated for the provision of such (often loss-making) services.

Like analytical capacities, coordination capacities have witnessed mainly a shift towards growing complexification, rather than a shift from public to private actors. In the face of growing opposition to particular forms of energy provision (e.g. nuclear energy), more coordination capacities have become necessary in order to achieve some degree of mutual recognition of policy positions among different actors in the energy policy community. Similarly, infrastructure planning at the local, national, and transnational levels has involved a growing emphasis on aligning stakeholders, seeking compromise, and spanning boundaries between different constituencies.

In terms of delivery capacities, the main change is less substantive, but mostly about the prominent move from public to private sector employment. Elsewhere, too, public service provision is in the hands of private providers, either because of outright privatisation of services, or because of other public–private 'partnership' models, such as franchising. The use of franchising, for example, suggests that there has been a move within the public sector from delivery toward regulatory capacities, as the main function of the state has become oversight of service delivery rather than delivery of the service itself. At the same time, delivery capacity is still required when private providers fail or abandon services and continuity of supply is required. In other words, given that public services always involve a risk to government, regardless of whether they are provided by public, third-party or private sector providers, public administrations will always require keeping some delivery capacity available.

The particular capacity challenges vary across domains and countries. As noted, different domains are faced with different challenges: there are obviously differences when contrasting the provision of high-speed broadband 'superhighways' with water sewage facilities or the franchising of rail or bus services.

What has been absent from the discussion so far, however, is the role of politics. As noted, 'regulation' is seen as a way to avoid politics and discretion. At the same time, the absence of politics in considering infrastructure policy seems rather problematic. Indeed, is it actually possible to disentangle technical challenges from substantive political differences in the various areas of infrastructure provision? Does the political role in infrastructure policy come into play only in terms of policy preferences?

Obviously, territorial interests are very salient in policy-making related to infrastructure and require some delicate political bargaining. Bargaining, as noted, also includes non-territorial issues such as, for example, deliberations over different providers and technological options. Given the long-term effects of such choices and the high degree of technical uncertainty that is often associated with them, it is important to highlight that politics matters. More generally, regulation—and any other administrative capacity for that matter—will always be faced by a triple tension, namely between providing policy stability to investors, dealing with the implications of technological changes at the right moment, and ensuring the representation of political and societal preferences.

Institutional resources for the governance of infrastructure

The design of institutions and their performance are highly relevant for defining the interactions between different administrative capabilities and the connections between politicians and the administrative state. For this reason, the institutional design of infrastructure governance requires careful examination; as noted, there are numerous instruments and many goals involved in policy-making, and devising a single 'all-purpose' institution is unlikely to constitute the best option.

Over recent decades, one of the most prominent features has been the creation of free-standing regulatory agencies for most sectors. These agencies mushroomed worldwide during the 1990s at the national level (Jordana, Levi-Faur, and Fernandez-Marin 2011). This was seen as a critical administrative restructuring in order to separate out politics from policy in these areas. In a nutshell, the rationale behind this move was that regulatory agencies should govern markets in the infrastructure sector. Market regulation was considered largely a technical (and economic) task, to be performed by independent administrative units nurtured by professionals applying scientific tools: economic models were to simulate and stimulate market competition, and sophisticated instruments were to be applied to obtain accurate information about the market (OECD 2009).

This ideal-type regulatory agency was expected to concentrate on competition-related matters and not make decisions that could be seen as 'political'. Infrastructure markets were to be developed by the application of sophisticated regulatory instruments so that they would provide as much welfare as possible. Politics was only involved when it came to the decision to delegate regulatory authority to a free-standing agency and (usually) in the matter of leadership appointments. Even in the area of appointments, there was a premium on recruiting individuals with a reputation for competence. With regard to the danger of regulatory policy being exposed to political interference or being vulnerable to economic capture, regulatory agencies were usually designed in order to be decoupled from political oversight and the immediate interests of ministerial bureaucracies. Such decoupling and granting of independence were to allow for 'credible commitment' and therefore put a check on short-term government interference, particularly of a 'malicious' nature which could disrupt markets that require long-term investments to work optimally. Independence and strong professionalism were seen as highly important to achieve market guidance and control. An emphasis on the ethos of the public servant, although different from that of normal bureaucrats, was also intended to ward off political capture. Agencies were to select personnel with professional standards, while also maintaining strong links with relevant scientific communities.

The boundary between political and regulatory decisions was not seriously considered. It was suggested that regulatory agencies were to consider 'economic regulation' in the light of their statutory remit. However, statutory remits were never that straightforward and political instincts led to a growing number of (not necessarily compatible) objectives being piled onto regulatory agencies. Furthermore, it proved difficult (at least in jurisdictions such as the UK) to retain professional regulatory staff when they were often poached by regulated firms.

The key animating idea, however, was to achieve independence by separating out regulatory oversight functions from the more general business of ministerial departments. The case of regulatory agencies in infrastructure areas clearly exemplifies the problem of relying on 'independence'. Initially 'independence' was considered as a solution to the problems of governance in these sectors. In response, regulatory agencies were separated as much as possible from conventional policy processes, but this often rendered them too weak to pursue their objectives. Also, because of their isolation, regulatory agencies faced problems in terms of coordinating with other governmental units.

This is not to deny that regulatory agencies continue to be regarded as useful devices to deal with various aspects of infrastructure policy. However, it has also become clear that regulatory agencies, even with their 'independence', are unable to address many problems involving the governance of infrastructure. The governance of infrastructure policy requires more administrative capacities than those of regulatory oversight. It requires coordination capacities in bringing together different constituencies; analytical capacities in order to deal with complex political economy problems in their regulated markets; and delivery capacity in terms of being able to manage complex projects and processes. In other words, regulation is not always the primary policy tool in the field of infrastructure governance, and other administrative skills are important.

Furthermore, there are also key differences when it comes to type of regulatory intervention. In some sectors, such as telecommunications or energy, regulatory instruments have become a central tool to define the sector's development and manage the markets created. However, not all sectors show a distinct form of successful regulatory intervention. For example, in the water sector, pro-market regulation has been strongly contested, and in power supply, regulation success is limited to rare cases. It appears that governing infrastructure provision only by means of market forces has proved to be a limited strategy when applied as a general formula.

Moreover, 'independence' has not proven to be an all-encompassing recipe for success. The accountability ties to politics, ministerial departments, other agencies, regulated industries, and other stakeholders clearly matter. The boundaries between what is an appropriate 'regulatory' issue and what is a 'political' decision have become ever more blurred. It is increasingly difficult to identify issues which are clearly within the remit of political decisions and therefore should be handled at the level of the ministerial department, and those areas which should be 'contained' within the remit of 'independent' regulatory authorities. Such concerns suggest that 'independence' is not necessarily the most relevant dimension when considering key governance challenges such as sustainability or demographic change.

At the same time, questioning the relationship between regulatory agencies and ministerial bureaucracies and politics more generally also has implications for the study of 'traditional' bureaucracy. It raises issues about what sort of competencies should, in turn, reside in the ministerial bureaucracies in order to deal with long-term planning issues that involve uncertainty and considerable political risk. In other words, however governance is organised, it is difficult to escape the basic tension between insulated 'expertise' and wider participation that provides for flexibility and (democratic) legitimacy, the reality of dealing with different time horizons, and the pressures of dealing with often multiple levels of government and dispersed authority.

Concluding remarks

At the outset, three key challenges affecting infrastructure industries were identified. The first concerns how to develop administrative capacities to deal with complex financing arrangements and risk management issues involving both public and private actors. A second challenge relates to decisions regarding a range of infrastructure provision questions. The third involves the design of decision-making processes that both provide private investors with certainty and ensure sufficient flexibility to accommodate democratic preferences.

In conclusion, one may wish to consider what the long-term implications would be if there were no governmental involvement in infrastructure policy. For one, under-provision might occur in some areas, given the presence of positive externalities that can only be captured through the public authority of the state, or the problem of non-excludability, which would require state intervention, too. Similarly, infrastructures would develop unevenly, depending on economic development and other factors, considering that many industries benefit from natural monopolies. Infrastructure 'bubbles' may also emerge as investors rush into certain industries only to realise that the predicted returns are unlikely to be forthcoming (as happened in the 19th century with railways in many countries, or the global dot-com crisis of 2000). Furthermore, as markets tend to be myopic, whether markets in infrastructure will allow for the competitive selection of the 'best' technology is questionable, given the path-dependent nature of infrastructure industries (not meaning that public monopolies would perform better in this respect).

The justification for public policies in infrastructure industries emerges from the problems summarised here. However, administrative capacities and policy instruments should be combined wisely to avoid the risk of government failures. For example, intrusive public policies designed to correct regulatory failures might lean towards specific technologies or sources of energy in favour of non-market principles, such as long-term sustainability. Yet, to be cost effective, active policy intervention in these sectors cannot disregard market-making instruments entirely. Furthermore, infrastructure `bubbles' occur not only in the private realm. As noted above, policy bandwagons often emerge that combine different powerful constituencies. What is more, political prestige projects may fly in the face of economic cost–benefit calculations. In other words, bringing markets into infrastructure policy can indeed address some of the limitations of administrative and political behaviour.

How then can one think of strengthening governance in infrastructure policy? One key ingredient is a changing conception of risk to political decision-makers. Risk aversion and optimism bias, whether because of behavioural biases, political needs (pork-barrel and log-rolling politics), or demands of powerful interests, mean that decision-making can never be 'rational'. A strengthening of 'regulatory capacities' was supposed to enhance the likelihood of rational decision-making. Similarly, insulation in independent regulatory agencies was intended to remove decision-making from the hustle and bustle of political decision-making. However, while such insulation might be convenient for some, it does not provide for the kind of decision-making that allows for the transparent consideration of different options and the incorporation of different political preferences, as expressed through democratic processes.

Over the past three decades, the importance of insulated regulation in the provision of infrastructure policies was emphasised in infrastructure governance regimes. This placed a premium on the study of formal mechanisms that were supposed to ensure agency independence. By contrast, too little emphasis was paid to the actual capacities that were required of those doing the regulating. At the same time, isolating infrastructure policies from politics has proven to be unable to effectively address problem-solving capacity bottlenecks in infrastructure policies. Choices involving technologies have long-term implications and cost implications that affect different constituencies (and future generations). They also require democratic legitimisation that goes beyond that provided by economic cost–benefit analysis. In the short term, regulatory decisions made by independent agencies in infrastructure industries address, to some extent at least, policy problems inherent in the governance of these sectors. However, these decisions may increasingly demonstrate a limited ability to deal with risks, technological uncertainties, and their long-term implications.

Acknowledgements

I am grateful for comments by the editors. I acknowledge Martin Lodge for his essential contribution in carefully reviewing the chapter, helping to better elaborate some of the main arguments. Support from the Spanish Ministry of Economy and Competitiveness (research project CSO2012-39693) is also acknowledged.

References

Albalate, D., and Bel, G. (2012). *The Economics and Politics of High-Speed Rail: Lessons from Experiences Abroad*. Lanham: Lexington Books.

Bourguignon, F., and Pleskovic, B. (eds) (2008). *Rethinking Infrastructure for Development: Annual World Bank Conference on Development Economics—Global 2007*. Washington, DC: The World Bank.

Button, K. (2006). 'Transportation and Infrastructure', in B. G. Peters, and J. Pierre (eds), *Handbook of Public Policy*. London: Sage, 323–38.

Button, K., and Nijkamp, P. (1997). 'Social Change and Sustainable Transport', *Journal of Transport Geography*, 5(3): 215–18.

Chapman, L. (2007). 'Transport and Climate Change: A Review', *Journal of Transport Geography*, 15(5): 354–67.

Dunleavy, P. (1986). 'Explaining the Privatization Boom: Public Choice versus Radical Approaches', *Public Administration*, 64(1): 13–34.

Estache, A. (2007). 'Infrastructures et développement. Une revue des débats récents et à venir', *Revue d'économie du développement*, 21(4): 5.

Henisz, W. J., Zelner, B. A., and Guillen, M. F. (2005). 'The Worldwide Diffusion of Market-Oriented Infrastructure Reform, 1977–1999', *American Sociological Review*, 70(6): 871–97.

Jennings, W., and Lodge, M. (2012). 'Critical Infrastructures, Resilience and Organisation of Mega-Projects: The Olympic Games', in B. M. Hutter (ed.), *Anticipating Risks and Organising Risk Regulation*. Cambridge, New York: Cambridge University Press, 161–84.

Jordana, J., Levi-Faur, D., and Fernandez-Marin, X. (2011). 'The Global Diffusion of Regulatory Agencies: Channels of Transfer and Stages of Diffusion', *Comparative Political Studies*, 44(10): 1343–69.

Klein, M. (2012). 'Infrastructure Policy: Basic Design Options'. Policy Research Working Paper 6274. Washington, DC: The World Bank.

Levi-Faur, D. (2003). 'The Politics of Liberalisation: Privatisation and Regulation-for-Competition in Europe's and Latin America's Telecoms and Electricity Industries', *European Journal of Political Research*, 42(5): 705–40.

Lodge, M., and Stirton, L. (2006). 'Withering in the Heat? In Search of the Regulatory State in the Commonwealth Caribbean', *Governance*, 19(3): 465–95.

OECD (Organisation for Economic Co-operation and Development) (2009). *Economic Policy Reforms 2009: Going for Growth*. Paris: OECD.

Spiller, P. T., and Tommasi, M. (2005). 'The Institutions of Regulation: An Application to Public Utilities', in C. Menard, and M. M. Shirley (eds), *Handbook of New Institutional Economics*. Boston: Springer, 515–43.

Sutherland, D., Araújo, S., Égert, B., and Kozluk, T. (2011). 'Public Policies and Investment in Network Infrastructure', *Economic Studies* (OECD Journal), 2011(1): 161–83.

Part III
Capacities and Innovations beyond the State

10

Wicked Problems, Clumsy Solutions, and Messy Institutions in Transnational Governance

Marco Verweij

Wicked transboundary problems

In this chapter, I argue that decision-makers often fail to reach their goals, and wreak additional havoc, by trying to solve 'wicked' transboundary problems as if they were 'tame'. In addition, I sketch the types of solutions with which decision-makers can address wicked transboundary issues, as well as the modes of decision-making processes in which such solutions may emerge. I conclude by spelling out the capacities that (inter)governmental actors need to acquire so as to help generate these types of solutions and modes of decision-making.

The distinction between wicked and tame problems was introduced by Horst Rittel and Melvin Webber in 1973. They argued that contemporary societies had become skilled at resolving tame issues. These issues are characterised by widespread consensus among stakeholders as to the causes and possible solutions of the problems at hand. Such problems lend themselves to a standard, linear decision-making process, in which the problem is first unambiguously defined, after which relevant data are collected and analysed, and an optimal decision is taken.

An example of a tame transboundary problem is the thinning of the ozone layer. Since the late 1980s, it has been widely accepted that the depletion of the ozone layer has been caused by the release of chlorofluorocarbons (CFCs) and related halocarbons into the atmosphere. At the time, only 17 companies, operating in 16 countries, were involved in producing CFCs and halocarbons. Moreover, affordable substitutes were readily available. This relatively simple nature of the problem helps explain why the 1987 Montréal Protocol on Substances that Deplete the Ozone Layer has been a success (Rayner 2004).

Wicked problems are far harder to resolve because they share the following traits: (1) each wicked problem is unique and incomparable; (2) many people, organisations, as well as social and natural domains, are involved; (3) the range of their causes is large and uncertain; (4) the set of solutions is equally large and uncertain; (5) each of these solutions involves vast amounts of time, energy, and money that will result in large-scale changes in human behaviour, ecosystems, infrastructure, and technology; (6) implementing any solution will create new problems; and (7) as wicked problems are hard to define, multifaceted, and enduring, it is not appropriate to speak of 'right' solutions in an absolute sense—it is preferable to use relative terms, such as 'better', 'more helpful', and 'more widely acceptable'.

Rittel and Webber (1973) argued that much harm has come from attempts to resolve the wicked problems that abound in today's complex societies with methods that are only appropriate for tame issues. An example is the failure of the governmental efforts to combat the highly wicked threat of climate change. The success of the Montréal Protocol induced the belief among decision-makers that climate change could also be tackled with a formal accord between all states of the world (Benedick 1998: 306). The failure to implement and renew the 1997 Kyoto Protocol has shown that climate change is too complex to be resolved with just the traditional tools of diplomacy (Rayner 2010). Yet this is precisely what governments have done by centring their climate change policies on the Kyoto Protocol.

The international climate change regime is far from the only wicked transboundary issue area in need of improved governance. Others, for instance, include the financial sector (with its euro, banking, and debt crises) and official development assistance (where the UN Millennium Development Goals will not be met come 2015). Hence, a pressing challenge for transnational governance is how to identify processes, tools, and approaches with which to address wicked transboundary problems.

Clumsy solutions

It is vital to first address the question: which type of solution can successfully resolve wicked problems? An answer can be derived from the cultural theory (or theory of plural rationality) developed by anthropologists Mary Douglas, Michael Thompson, and Steve Rayner as well as political scientists Aaron Wildavsky, Richard Ellis, and Christopher Hood, among others.[1]

[1] Some of the main theoretical contributions are Thompson, Ellis, and Wildavsky (1990); Douglas and Ney (1998); Hood (1998); and Thompson (2008).

According to this approach, whenever stakeholders begin to resolve or discuss a wicked problem, four opposing points of view will emerge on how to define and solve it. These four perspectives represent different ways of organising, perceiving, and justifying social relations. Labelled individualism, egalitarianism, hierarchy, and fatalism, these four 'ways of life' are derived from assigning high and low values to two underlying dimensions of social life: stratification (the extent to which people's choices are circumscribed by status and power differentiation) and collectivity (the degree to which people feel part of a larger community). Individualism represents a way of life in which people are neither constrained by a lot of stratification nor feel part of a larger community. Hierarchy stands for a way of life in which status and power differences, as well as feelings of solidarity and community, abound. Egalitarianism captures a manner of interacting and thinking characterised by a strong sense of community combined with a relative absence of ranking and role differentiation. Fatalism is a pattern of organising and perceiving social life marked by an unequal status and power distribution as well as low levels of community and solidarity.

Cultural theory also states that collective efforts to tackle a wicked social problem will fail when not based on ample consideration, and flexible combination, of all these ways of life. This is the case as each of these: (1) captures a particular aspect of the problem at hand; (2) is in accordance with the wishes of at least some stakeholders (whose consent and cooperation are needed); and (3) represents a way of organising that cannot exist in isolation (i.e. has to be supported by the other ways of organising). Efforts to resolve a wicked problem that are not based on all four ways of defining and resolving the issue therefore eventually fail, not just according to the excluded ways of life, but also in terms of the included ones. By contrast, more effective, efficient, and equitable efforts to resolve wicked problems creatively and flexibly combine all four opposing perspectives. Such efforts tend to be endorsed by a clear majority of stakeholders, albeit for very different reasons (cf. Sunstein 1995). To flag that such policy responses are based on contradictory viewpoints, theorists of plural rationality have labelled these efforts 'clumsy' solutions—but the term 'polyrational' (Davy 2012) has been used as well.

Human-made climate change again provides an illustration. Using cultural theory, both Steve Rayner (Rayner and Malone 1997) and I (Verweij 2003) predicted early on that the Kyoto Protocol would not work—as it predominantly relies on a single perspective (a hierarchical one) on what the problem was and how it should be addressed. Since it recently became well-nigh undeniable that the Protocol had not dented greenhouse gas emissions (Helm 2012), an alternative set of policies advocated by cultural theorists has gained influence. Instead of centring the efforts to curb climate change on a global, binding treaty, this alternative emphasises domestic governmental support to make renewable energy competitive, further exploration of adaptation strategies, and more R&D for geoengineering, biochar, and carbon capture (Verweij et al. 2006; Prins et al. 2010; Shackley and Dütschke 2012). These policies combine a hierarchical call for wise, top-down regulation, an individualistic preference for competitive processes, an egalitarian emphasis on local production and consumption (as renewable energy is more localised than fossil energy), and a fatalistic belief that all we can do is adapt. As such, it satisfies, to a greater extent, proponents of a variety of policy perspectives. This not only emerged from stakeholder workshops in Britain (Mander et al. 2008), but also from the successful implementation of some of these policies in the energy sector of Nepal (Gyawali, Thompson, and Verweij forthcoming).

By now, cultural theory's hypotheses regarding governance failure and success have been confirmed in case studies of more than 20 other wicked issues. These range from the reconstruction of Birmingham's traffic infrastructure after the Second World War, to anti-discrimination measures in the Netherlands, to flood protection in eastern Hungary (Hendriks 1999; Verweij and Thompson 2006; Verweij 2011).

Missing in transnational action

What is striking about the empirical examples that have been collected so far is that it is harder to find clumsiness at the transnational level than at the domestic or local plane, at least within democratic polities. This stands to reason. Clumsy solutions thrive in institutional settings in which stakeholders representing all four different points of view (and any combinations thereof) are able to influence, but not dominate or endlessly stall, the ways in which issues are resolved. In well-functioning liberal democracies—with their independent courts, rule of law, competitive elections, relatively corruption-free civil service, freedom of press, speech, and association, etc.—chances are that such conditions prevail, at least from time to time. In dictatorships and tyrannies, these chances will be slimmer, and this may be one important reason why liberal democracies do better on a variety of fronts: economic growth, income distribution, environmental protection, care for the poor, longevity, literacy, fight against corruption, and so on (Przeworski et al. 2000; Siegle, Weinstein, and Halperin 2004; Farzin and Bond 2006).

Something similar applies to the transnational level. Within transboundary arenas, issues also tend to be less intensely debated, scrutinised, and contested than are domestic issues within liberal democracies. For a number of reasons, the decision-making processes to do with pressing transnational problems are usually dominated by the views of those who work for the relevant international organisations and/or the governments involved. First, national media tend to spend less attention on the intricacies of transboundary issues than on domestic political affairs, and even then tend to gravitate to developments within the United States (Wu 2000; Harcup and O'Neill 2001). To give an example, not many Finnish press reports will have been filed in the mid 1990s on how a project of the Finnish development ministry, developed in tandem with a Finnish logging company, threatened the livelihood of the Nepali living in the Tarai district by privatising the Bara forest on which they depended (Gyawali and Koponen 2004). If such a hare-brained (and highly individualistic) scheme had been implemented in a Finnish province, surely the local press would have reported it. Nepali newspapers did report it (e.g. Shrestha and Britt 1996; Pradhan 1997), but presumably not many Finnish voters read the Nepali press. Plus, the states involved in transnational decision-making are often themselves not democracies (e.g. China), and are therefore less influenced by non-state actors from within (or beyond) their borders. Furthermore, as former World Bank chief economist Joseph Stiglitz (2003) has experienced, the national ministries that have been charged with the oversight of international organisations seldom do so. In addition, the politicians, diplomats, and civil servants involved in transnational decision-making often do not live in the places affected by their decisions, or only do so for a relatively short period of time. They will therefore seldom be around to see (never mind suffer) the consequences of their decisions.

The decisions of multilateral organisations can also seldom be challenged in any courts of law. As a result, there is usually no legal redress available for those who feel unfairly treated by international organisations. Moreover, although a 'global civil society' has arisen in recent decades, and could one day play a vital role in truly pluralised debates on global issues, it is currently still too embryonic and thinly spread to be able to make a sustained impact on global governance (Keane 2003). Lastly, the representatives of (global, national, and local) civil society are presently still too often shunned by international organisations, despite the beginnings of greater openness in the last ten years.

All this means that the citizens and businesses directly affected by transnational policies typically cannot reach and influence those responsible for these measures, and that decision-making about many a transnational or global issue still remains the prerogative of a small circle of sheltered, often like-minded decision-makers. Given that even within liberal democracies clumsy solutions do not always appear thick on the ground, it should therefore not come as a surprise that even fewer such solutions appear to exist in the international realm. This is all the more reason to highlight the decision-making processes that tend to generate clumsy solutions.

Messy institutions

Cultural theory also offers insight into how the interactions between stakeholders should be arranged so as to facilitate the emergence of clumsy solutions (Hendriks 2010; Verweij and Ney 2012). The theory posits that there are four (ideal-typical) ways of generating clumsy solutions, each with its own strengths and weaknesses. The most useful institutional set-ups are flexible and creative mixes of all these modes.

The egalitarian model for generating clumsy solutions consists of an open, honest deliberation among all those who could be affected by the final outcomes. Participants should only argue in terms of the public good, and not openly or covertly push for private interests. They should participate of their own volition, and be willing to listen emphatically and patiently to each other's life stories and concerns. Differences of rank, status, or power of any kind among the participants should be eliminated as much as possible, for instance by wearing non-conspicuous clothing and using simple, clear language. Deliberations should be held in a public space, organised in the form of a round table. Only technology should be used that is cheap and simple, and that can be collectively operated. Decisions have to be reached on the basis of a full consensus. As much time needs to be taken as is necessary for consensus, if not a collective will, to emerge.

The hierarchical path to clumsiness presumes that the emergence of clumsy solutions is too important to be left to the free interplay of social forces. Instead, the interaction between stakeholders with different perspectives and interests needs to be mediated, steered, and formalised by the relevant experts and authorities. The topics that need to be discussed, the ways in which this has to be done, when and where meetings need to take place, and who can participate need to be regulated by experienced and trained mediators. Once the designated stakeholders have had their say on what the issues are and how they should be resolved, the appropriate authorities face the task of synthesising all these views into a clumsy policy, which then needs to be imposed on the organisation or public involved.

The individualist path to clumsiness is the one least travelled in the fields of policy and organisational studies. It involves the setting up of a competitive process in which stakeholders with different views on the problem and its solution are given the freedom to implement their ideas. Thus, stakeholders can demonstrate, through actions rather than words, that their plans are superior to those of others. The most persuasive stakeholders can keep a part (or all) of the rewards of their labour—be it in terms of prestige or material resources gained. Here, time is money and should not be wasted. By setting up a competitive process driven by self-interest, speediness and efficiency are assured. If it is not possible to create competition, then bargaining between, or majority voting by, stakeholders with different perspectives is acceptable as well.

The fatalistic manner of generating clumsy solutions is to chance upon them. This is the argument that clumsy solutions cannot be willed or planned for, but only longed for and occasionally stumbled upon. According to the fatalistic perspective, we are living in a dog-eat-dog world in which people are too busy with increasing their relative power positions by hook or by crook to strive after any lofty ideals. Polyrationality can therefore only come about in a haphazard, random manner.

Hence, four alternative views on the types of institutions in which clumsy solutions will emerge can be derived from cultural theory. Each of these has its drawbacks. The egalitarian approach is weakened by its insistence on the emergence of a collective will, which may be slow in coming (if it ever arrives). The hierarchical approach may leave stakeholders with a feeling that their views and opinions have not been seriously considered at all, and that instead they have been manipulated into endorsing what the authorities and experts had already decided upon. The competitive processes on which the individualistic approach relies seem to go against the spirit of community and tolerance often needed to collectively resolve wicked problems, and may in any case not always be feasible. Finally, the fatalistic strategy is in essence a counsel of despair.

The shortcomings of each alternative way of generating clumsy solutions can only be compensated for by the other three ways. Egalitarianism's sluggishness can be at least partly overcome through hierarchical steering, individualistic competitiveness and bargaining, and fatalism's arbitrariness. The centrifugal forces sparked by the individualistic approach to polyrationality can be brought under control by hierarchical planning and mediation, and be tempered by an egalitarian sense of community and belonging. The risks of alienating stakeholders that are run by the hierarchical approach can be lessened by the more inclusive processes preferred by egalitarianism, as well as by the independent initiatives prescribed by individualism. Hence, decision-making procedures that do not comprise elements of all four ways of enabling clumsy solutions will be less successful than those that do. Procedures for decision-making that creatively and flexibly combine all four alternative modes of generating clumsy solutions are called 'messy institutions' because, unlike the sleek organigrams commonly found on websites, they embrace and engage messy pluralism (cf. Ackoff 1974).

Messy institutions come in a wide variety of forms. Some of these make use of blueprints for decision-making structures that have been formulated by organisational theorists. In an overview of the literature, Steven Ney and I (Verweij and Ney 2012) found no fewer than 20 proposals for how to organise decision-making regarding wicked issues. Only six of these—namely, deliberative polling, planning cells, citizens' juries, design thinking, future searches, and 21st-century town meetings—turned out to be truly messy.

Planning cells, for instance, have been developed by German sociologist Peter Dienel (1997). Their hierarchical elements include the selection of topics by a commissioning body, the circulation of background material, the presence of process stewards, the testimony of experts and interest groups, the division of the process into three distinct phases (consisting of information gathering, deliberation, and voting in small breakout groups, and the ranking of the various proposals made in the small groups by the entire assembly), as well as the fact that the outcomes of the deliberations are written up by a moderator in a citizens' report, which serves to inform and advise the authorities. Individualistic components encompass the payment of participants, the short duration of the whole process (four to seven days), the voting on options within the breakout groups, and the insistence that consensus does not need to be attained. Egalitarianism is brought in through intense deliberations among equals within the breakout groups consisting of five people. Fatalism is represented by the random selection of participants, and the frequent random redistribution of participation across the small groups. Thus, planning cells creatively combine all four types of decision-making, and have made constructive and creative contributions to a wide range of policy issues (Dienel 2009).

Which of these six messy decision-making procedures is most appropriate for a specific situation will depend on practical considerations. One such consideration is the number of participants that is deemed appropriate.[2] Planning cells, citizens' juries (Crosby, Kelly, and Schaefer 1986), future searches (Weisbord and Janoff 2010), deliberative polling (Fishkin 2009), and 21st-century town meetings (Lukensmeyer and Brigham 2002) resemble one another, and can all be used for taking major, strategic decisions about the solutions to a specific wicked problem. However, due to variations in the selection of participants and the aggregation of opinions, they allow for different numbers of participants. A citizens' jury typically consists of 12 to 16 people, even though a single process may include several juries. Planning cells comprise 25 to 40 participants. Future searches usually involve 60 to 80 individuals. Even more can be accommodated by deliberative polling, which brings together about 130 to 450 people. Due to the use of technological gadgets, 21st-century town meetings allow for the greatest number of participants, and involvement has ranged from 500 to 5,000 people. Design thinking (Brown 2009) is a bit different, as it requires a final customer to act as the

[2] Another practicality is the amount of funds that is available; these decision-making procedures come with different price tags.

ultimate arbiter of the outcomes. Moreover, it is mostly used for wicked problems that require physical solutions that can be designed, prototyped, and presented.

As a result of the time, energy, and money that these six messy procedures require, they can usually only be employed when making overall, strategic decisions about the collective efforts that will be undertaken to resolve a wicked problem. This leaves the organisation of ordinary, day-to-day activities, interactions, and decisions unaccounted for. To generate clumsy solutions, these everyday processes also have to consist of inventive combinations of coordination, collaboration, competition, and randomness. The current efforts to battle malaria illustrate that when an international regime is thus organised, it may not always be necessary to employ any of the six academic blueprints mentioned above.

Battling (over) malaria

A comparison between the transboundary regime to reduce malaria as it existed in the 1970s and 1980s, and as it has functioned since 2008, brings out the importance of clumsy solutions and messy institutions. People become malarious after having been bitten by a female *Anopheles* mosquito that carries parasites of the genera *Plasmodium (P.) malariae, P. vivax, P. ovale, P. knowlesi* or *P. falciparum*. In the 1970s, after a long period of decline, malaria numbers started to rise again, especially in sub-Saharan Africa.

One of the factors behind this resurgence of malaria was the radically egalitarian 'Health for All by the Year 2000' strategy advocated by the World Health Organization (WHO) from 1973 to 1988. This strategy asserted that the widespread attainment of health required the wholesale levelling of the world's economic, social, and political structures. The idea was to create small-scale, self-sustaining communities whose members would collectively decide on, finance, and implement locally acceptable ways in which to improve their health, protect the environment, defend women's rights, etc. all over the globe. Attempts were made to restructure the WHO itself on similarly horizontal lines. By giving the responsibility for undertaking highly complicated health tasks (including the prevention and treatment of malaria) to local people hardly trained to undertake such obligations, and by then recommending that they should do so on the basis of the most difficult procedures for reaching decisions, namely consensus, the WHO's Health for All strategy greatly hampered the fight against malaria. The organisation admitted this in 2000 (WHO 2000: 13). By accusing medicine schools, the pharmaceutical industry, philanthropic organisations, UNICEF, the World Bank, physicians' professional associations, health ministries, and hospitals of being—in the words of WHO Director Kenneth Newell—'counter revolutionaries' (Newell 1988: 903), the strategy ensured that little funding became available for campaigns against malaria and other diseases (Litsios 2002: 730f.).

This egalitarian policy perspective (which nowadays is still propagated by the WHO Commission on the Social Determinants of Health) differs from those that have been adhered to by other stakeholders in the international anti-malaria regime. According to an oft-advocated, hierarchical viewpoint of 'integrated malaria control', malaria is such a multifaceted disease that it can only be tackled with a wide arsenal of governmental tools, including the administration of medicine to the ill, the provision of bed nets in endemic regions, the construction of houses that keep mosquitoes out, landscape corrections to restrict breeding grounds, general improvement of nutrition, public information campaigns, early-warning systems to nip potential epidemics in the bud, and so on. All this requires long-term planning and coordination by appropriate authorities. An individualistic viewpoint has frequently been expressed as well. This perspective insists that the creativity of the private sector needs to be harnessed to defeat malaria. This can be done by priming local markets in bed nets, or by relying on the private supply of anti-malaria medicine. If such 'social marketing' is not possible, and public programmes are unavoidable, then these have to concentrate fully on those few measures (such as DDT spraying, the invention of vaccines, or the use of genetically modified mosquitoes) that give the biggest bang for the buck. A fatalistic perspective has not been absent either. It cautions against ambitious plans to reduce malaria, as these inevitably fail, and then leave once partially resistant people defenceless.

These four policy perspectives, and combinations thereof, have resurfaced in the anti-malaria regime time and again. The Health for All strategy that dominated the regime in the 1970s and 1980s made use of only one of these (the egalitarian one) and thus failed to reach its goals. In sharp contrast stands the 2008 Global Malaria Action Plan decided upon by the Roll Back Malaria Partnership (which is the initiative that, since 1998, has brought together all the relevant stakeholders from government, industry, academia, philanthropy, and civil society). This plan has provided much-needed coordination of the activities of the hundreds of organisations involved by spelling out the various ways in which the governments of malaria-ridden countries can reduce the disease (and the precise steps involved in taking these paths), by identifying which public and private organisations could best assist in making these steps, and by coordinating the available public and private sources of funding. With the adoption of the Global Malaria Action Plan, the anti-malaria regime has become highly polyrational in terms of the actors included in decision-making, the procedures according to which these actors take decisions, and the ensuing policies and strategies.

Representatives of all possible perspectives are now involved in the effort to reduce malaria. These include outfits that tend to advocate more egalitarian policies (such as Health Gap), those that veer more towards individualistic solutions (such as USAID and GlaxoSmithKline), those that are more drawn to hierarchical plans (e.g. the World Bank and the European Commission)—and all the other organisations that find themselves in between these positions.

The current transboundary regime against malaria also makes productive use of the different organisational principles that are spelled out in cultural theory—and is therefore highly messy. Competition—individualism's allocation mechanism—takes place among the various research teams that are vying to discover the first effective vaccine. It is part and parcel of the way in which the Gates Foundation (a major player in this field) allocates its vast budget over grant seekers. Solidarity and the inversion of established authority patterns—stressed in egalitarianism—is assured by the large sums of money that are flowing from northern governments, companies, and foundations to the poorest in the south, and by the fact that the malaria-endemic countries have by far the largest single bloc of votes on the Board of the Roll Back Malaria Partnership. An essential (though not overbearing) amount of central planning and coordination—hierarchy's allocation mechanism—has recently been restored with the adoption of the Global Malaria Action Plan.

What is also remarkable is the relative accountability, openness to criticism, and willingness to change that are becoming characteristic of the Roll Back Malaria Partnership. Most of the relevant documents are easily available online. Furthermore, when in the mid 2000s the Partnership became increasingly criticised for not being coordinated enough, it did not ignore this dissent and close ranks. Instead, it publicly acknowledged its shortcomings and undertook (together with NGO Malaria No More and McKinsey consultancy) a comprehensive but swift review of its operations, which led to the Global Malaria Action Plan. Such accountability and openness are features of global governance that are favoured by the low-grid perspectives of individualism and egalitarianism, and are far too rare in the international arena.

Last, as a result of the inclusive and messy nature of the present anti-malaria regime, today's policies also represent mixes of the different perspectives. Long-term efforts at integrated control go hand in hand with attempts to swiftly eradicate malaria once and for all with the help of vaccines. The empowerment of community health workers coincides with targeted DDT spraying. The drive to distribute subsidised bed nets is coordinated with the build-up of local bed nets industries. This clumsy set of policies has also met with considerable success. Between 2003 and 2008, the funding available increased 30-fold from less than 100 million US$ to around 3 billion

US$ (Snow et al. 2008). Currently about 20 vaccines are in clinical trials, some of which appear highly promising (Morelle 2013). Finally, malaria mortality rates have fallen by more than 25 per cent globally since 2000, and by 33 per cent in Africa (WHO). This is a remarkable feat after more than three decades of spiking malaria rates.

Conclusion: administrative capacities needed for international organisations

Governance successes with resolving wicked issues, such as the Global Malaria Action Plan or the restoration of the Rhine river (Verweij 2000), as well as governance failures, point to the need to make several straightforward, but potentially far-reaching, changes to the administrative capacities of international organisations. The following administrative adaptations will help these bodies address wicked problems more effectively (cf. Wildavsky 1994):

- International organisations need to acquire the ability to distinguish between tame problems (which can be fruitfully resolved with traditional diplomatic means and textbook policy tools such as cost–benefit analysis) and wicked ones (which require the use of novel governance tools).
- When confronted with wicked issues, these organisations also need to master the ability to map the policy perspectives (including underlying views of nature, human nature, time, space, economising, technology, risk, etc.) that stakeholders (including the international organisations themselves) have adhered to.
- As perceiving and organising social relations go hand in hand (Douglas 1987), mastering this ability will also necessitate some lessening of the classic bureaucratic principles on which too many international organisations themselves are still largely run.
- International organisations will need to make sure that no single perspective is systematically excluded from the processes of problem definition and selection of solutions.
- Moreover, they have to monitor that the policies and strategies decided upon and implemented are inventive combinations of all available perspectives on what the problem is and how it should be resolved—and are therefore acceptable to the large majority of stakeholders.
- In order to facilitate the emergence of such polyrationality, international bodies will have to avoid attempts to remake transboundary regimes along the lines of a single way of organising.

- Lastly, they will have to gain the ability to deliberately promote polyrationality by engaging stakeholders through such creative decision-making procedures as planning cells, deliberative polling, design thinking, 21st-century town meetings, future searches, citizens' juries, and similar techniques.

These changes to the administrative capacities of international organisations are feasible. Still, they have considerable consequences for their hiring policies, internal structure, and external relations. With regard to recruitment: these adaptations require employing more people who are trained in a wider variety of social science disciplines than just economics. Political scientists, organisational scholars, anthropologists, and sociologists have to be brought in as well. Moreover, the internal structures of international organisations have to become somewhat flatter, and their external boundaries more porous. This will take effort. But such is the price to be paid for more effectively addressing wicked transboundary problems.

References

Ackoff, R. L. (1974). *Redesigning the Future: A Systems Approach to Societal Problems*. New York: Wiley.

Benedick, R. E. (1998). *Ozone Diplomacy: New Directions in Safeguarding the Planet.* Enlarged edn. Cambridge, MA: Harvard University Press.

Brown, T. (2009). *Change by Design: How Design Thinking Can Transform Organizations and Inspire Innovation.* New York: HarperCollins Publishers.

Crosby, N., Kelly, J. M., and Schaefer, P. (1986). 'Citizens Panels: A New Approach to Citizen Participation', *Public Administration Review*, 46(2): 170–8.

Davy, B. (2012). *Land Policy: Planning and the Spatial Consequences of Property*. Burlington: Ashgate.

Dienel, P. C. (1997). *Die Planungszelle: Der Bürger plant seine Umwelt.* 4th edn. Opladen: Westdteutscher Verlag.

Dienel, P. C. (2009). *Demokratisch—praktisch—gut. Merkmale, Wirkungen und Perspektiven der Planungzelle*. Bonn: Dietz.

Douglas, M. (1987). *How Institutions Think*. London: Routledge and Kegan Paul.

Douglas, M., and Ney, S. (1998). *Missing Persons: A Critique of the Social Sciences*. New York: Russell Sage Foundation.

Farzin, Y. H., and Bond, C. A. (2006). 'Democracy and Environmental Quality', *Journal of Development Economics*, 81(1): 213–35.

Fishkin, J. S. (2009). *When the People Speak: Deliberative Democracy and Public Consultation*. Oxford, New York: Oxford University Press.

Gyawali, D., and Koponen, J. (2004). 'Missionary Zeal on Retreat', in S. Sharma, J. Koponen, D. Gyawali, and A. Dixit (eds), *Aid Under Stress: Water, Forests, and Finnish*

Support in Nepal. Lalitpur: Published by Himal Books for Institute of Development Studies, University of Helsinki and Interdisciplinary Analysts, Kathmandu, 115–62.

Gyawali, D., Thompson, M. and Verweij, M. (eds) (forthcoming). *Development, Climate Change and Clumsiness: The Lessons from Nepal*. London: Earthscan.

Harcup, T., and O'Neill, D. (2001). 'What Is News? Galtung and Ruge Revisited', *Journalism Studies*, 2(2): 261–80.

Helm, D. (2012). 'Climate Policy: The Kyoto Approach Has Failed', *Nature*, 491: 663–5.

Hendriks, F. (1999). *Public Policy and Political Institutions: The Role of Culture in Traffic Policy*. Cheltenham, Northampton: Edward Elgar.

Hendriks, F. (2010). *Vital Democracy: A Theory of Democracy in Action*. Oxford, New York: Oxford University Press.

Hood, C. (1998). *The Art of the State: Culture, Rhetoric, and Public Management*. Oxford, New York: Clarendon Press.

Keane, J. (2003). *Global Civil Society?* Cambridge: Cambridge University Press.

Litsios, S. (2002). 'The Long and Difficult Road to Alma-Ata: A Personal Reflection', *International Journal of Health Services*, 32(4): 709–32.

Lukensmeyer, C. J., and Brigham, S. (2002). 'Taking Democracy to Scale: Creating a Town Hall Meeting for the Twenty-First Century', *National Civic Review*, 91(4): 351–66.

Mander, S. L., Bows, A., Anderson, K. L., Shackley, S., Agnolucci, P., and Ekins, P. (2008). 'The Tyndall Decarbonisation Scenarios. Part I: Development of a Backcasting Methodology with Stakeholder Participation', *Energy Policy*, 36(10): 3754–63.

Morelle, R. (2013) [website]. *Malaria Vaccine Shows Early Promise in Clinical Trials*. Retrieved from <http://www.bbc.co.uk/news/health-23607612> (accessed 17 August 2013).

Newell, K. W. (1988). 'Selective Primary Health Care: The Counter Revolution', *Social Science and Medicine*, 26(9): 903–6.

Pradhan, P. (1997). 'Government Set to Privatize Bara Forests: Others Cry Foul', *Kathmandu Post*, 21 February.

Prins, G., Galiana, I., Green, C., Grundmann, R., Hulme, M., Korhola, A., Laird, F., Nordhaus, T., Pielke, R., Rayner, S., Sareweitz, D., Shellenberger, M., Stehr, N., and Tezuka, H. (2010). *The Hartwell Paper: A New Direction for Climate Policy after the Crash of 2009*. Oxford, London: University of Oxford, London School of Economics.

Przeworski, A., Alvarez, M. E., Cheibub, J. A., and Limongi, F. (2000). *Democracy and Development: Political Institutions and Well-Being in the World, 1950–1990*. Cambridge, New York: Cambridge University Press.

Rayner, S. (2004). *The International Challenge of Climate Change: UK Leadership in the G8 and EU: Testimony given to the Environmental Audit Committee, 15 March*. London: House of Commons.

Rayner, S. (2010). 'How to Eat an Elephant: A Bottom-Up Approach to Climate Policy', *Climate Policy*, 10(6): 615–21.

Rayner, S., and Malone, E. L. (1997). 'Zen and the Art of Climate Maintenance', *Nature*, 390: 332–4.

Rittel, H. W. J., and Webber, M. M. (1973). 'Dilemmas in a General Theory of Planning', *Policy Sciences*, 4(2): 155–69.

Shackley, S. and Dütschke, E. (eds) (2012). *Carbon Dioxide Capture and Storage (CCS)*. Special Issue *Energy and Environment* 23 (2–3).

Shrestha, N. K., and Britt, C. D. (1996). 'Seeing the Forest for the Trees and the People', *Kathmandu Post,* 24 November.

Siegle, J. T., Weinstein, M. M., and Halperin, M. H. (2004). 'Why Democracies Excel', *Foreign Affairs*, 83(5): 57–71.

Snow, R. W., Guerra, C. A., Mutheu, J. J., Hay, S. I., and Krishna, S. (2008). 'International Funding for Malaria Control in Relation to Populations at Risk of Stable Plasmodium Falciparum Transmission', *PLoS Medicine*, 5(7): 1068–78.

Stiglitz, J. E. (2003). 'Democratizing the International Monetary Fund and the World Bank: Governance and Accountability', *Governance*, 16(1): 111–39.

Sunstein, C. R. (1995). 'Incompletely Theorized Agreements', *Harvard Law Review*, 108(7): 1733–72.

Thompson, M. (2008). *Organising and Disorganising: A Dynamic and Non-Linear Theory of Institutional Emergence and Its Implications*. Axminster: Triarchy Press.

Thompson, M., Ellis, R., and Wildavsky, A. B. (1990). *Cultural Theory*. Boulder: Westview Press.

Verweij, M. (2000). *Transboundary Environmental Problems and Cultural Theory: The Protection of the Rhine and the Great Lakes*. Houndmills, NY: Palgrave.

Verweij, M. (2003). 'Curbing Global Warming the Easy Way: An Alternative to the Kyoto Protocol', *Government and Opposition*, 38(2): 139–61.

Verweij, M. (2011). *Clumsy Solutions for a Wicked World: How to Improve Global Governance*. Houndmills, NY: Palgrave Macmillan.

Verweij, M., and Ney, S. (2012). 'Messy Institutions for Wicked Problems: How to Generate Clumsy Solutions'. Paper Presented at the 62nd Political Studies Association Annual International Conference in Belfast, 4 April.

Verweij, M. and Thompson, M. (eds) (2006). *Clumsy Solutions for a Complex World: Governance, Politics and Plural Perceptions*. Basingstoke, NY: Palgrave Macmillan.

Verweij, M., Douglas, M., Ellis, R., Engel, C., Hendriks, F., Lohmann, S., Ney, S., Rayner, S., and Thompson, M. (2006). 'Clumsy Solutions for a Complex World: The Case of Climate Change', *Public Administration*, 84(4): 817–43.

Weisbord, M. R., and Janoff, S. (2010). *Future Search: Getting the Whole System in the Room for Vision, Commitment, and Action*. San Francisco: Berrett-Koehler Publishers.

WHO (World Health Organization) (2000). 'WHO Expert Committee on Malaria: Twentieth Report'. WHO Technical Report Series No. 892. Geneva: WHO.

WHO (World Health Organization) [website]. *Malaria: Fact Sheet No. 94*. Retrieved from <http://www.who.int/mediacentre/factsheets/fs094/en/> (accessed 17 August 2013).

Wildavsky, A. B. (1994). 'How Cultural Theory Can Contribute to Understanding and Promoting Democracy, Science, and Development', in I. Serageldin, and J. Taboroff (eds), *Culture and Development in Africa*. Washington: The World Bank, 137–62.

Wu, H. D. (2000). 'Systemic Determinants of International News Coverage: A Comparison of 38 Countries', *Journal of Communication*, 50(2): 110–30.

11

Capacity and Constraint

Governance through International and Transnational Law

Nico Krisch[1]

Transboundary problems have long provided serious challenges for states' governance capacities, but their salience has increased radically over the last few decades. Besides the ever-increasing pressure to act on global environmental problems such as climate change, this is largely due to the rise of transnational security risks, especially terrorism, and the challenges that arise from increasingly liberalised and globalised markets. The scope and complexity of these problems place all aspects of states' governance capacity under strain: no state alone can deliver solutions to these problems or provide a sufficient regulatory framework on its own (see Lodge and Wegrich's introductory chapter in this volume). As any solution requires the involvement of many different actors, coordination becomes a key challenge; and a high degree of analytical capacity is necessary, not only to understand the problems but also to monitor the behaviour of actors and trace the operation of complex governance networks well beyond the boundaries of one's own jurisdiction.

As a result, the modern state not only needs to adapt its own administrative and regulatory structures to transboundary challenges; it also requires effective institutional structures for cooperation and governance on a regional and global scale. The classical instrument for international cooperation, international law, can only provide such structures under certain conditions and within strict limits. Governments have therefore turned to alternative

[1] I am grateful to Kai Wegrich and Martin Lodge as well as the participants in the authors' workshop at the Hertie School of Governance in April 2013 for their helpful comments on earlier versions of this contribution.

forms of transnational ordering, which in some cases have indeed led to more effective decision-making—key among them formal international institutions, informal government networks, extraterritorial regulation, and links with private forms of regulation. However, all of these tools come with drawbacks—some are more effective than others, and the more effective they are, the more they tend to entail a loss of control for national governments, regulators, and administrators. Domestic authorities have sought to readjust and develop new forms of influence in transnational regulatory contexts, some of them resulting in asymmetrical structures that increase the capacity of some countries' institutions while constraining those of others. In this chapter, I analyse the different forms of transnational law- and rule-making with respect to their varying impacts on, and links with, domestic governance institutions. I place a particular focus on one prominent example—the rise of informal institutions and transgovernmental networks in global regulation.

International law-making: potential and limitations

International law-making in its classical channels mainly proceeds through the conclusion of treaties, which require the consent of states to be binding. This mechanism reflects the decentralised structure of the international political order with its (formal) respect for the sovereign equality of states. In this structure, national governments have the right to choose what obligations they incur; traditionally, they also enjoyed significant leeway in interpreting and implementing these obligations. This left them much space to shape their own policies, but it also left international regimes relatively toothless in the face of opportunistic behaviour and non-compliance.

A central strategy for strengthening these regimes—and thus for making international cooperation effective—has been judicialisation (e.g. Stone Sweet, and Brunell 2013). Most prominent in the World Trade Organization (WTO), it delegates the monitoring and identification of treaty violations to an independent court or quasi-judicial body. This reduces domestic actors' policy space significantly, and not always in predictable ways. For example, as a result of the interpretative moves of the WTO's Dispute Settlement Body, European food safety regulators face increasing constraints on their ability to formulate their policies in line with public attitudes towards risk. Their precautionary approach on both hormones in beef and genetically modified organisms, triggered in part by earlier scandals, especially that around BSE, came under attack in the WTO, and in both cases European Union (EU) attempts at justifying their stance were largely unsuccessful (Pollack and Shaffer 2009). Even if this has not led to direct policy reversal in these cases

(Young 2012), the costs of non-compliance—both reputational and material—have been significant.

If judicialisation has made some regimes more effective, it has also provoked a certain backlash. As the precision of international norms and the level of delegation have grown, domestic actors have often felt overly limited in their options. Concerns about sovereignty costs, constitutional protections, and the democratic foundations of international law have come to the fore, particularly in the USA (Spiro 2000; Ku and Yoo 2012). Elsewhere, too, reluctance towards international law has grown. In Germany, for example, federal ministries are instructed, before working towards formal treaties, to 'examine whether a treaty is indeed indispensable or whether the same goal may also be attained through other means, especially through agreements below the threshold of an international treaty' (BMI 2011: §72).

Such reluctance has exacerbated existing limitations of international law as a problem-solving tool. The negotiation of treaties in large multilateral settings is burdensome and usually protracted, and typically needs to arrive at pareto-optimal solutions in order to draw states in. Uncertainty about the future makes governments reluctant to commit themselves in firm ways, and the need for domestic ratification of new treaties further prolongs the treaty-making process and brings in a domestic political calculus that (especially in more powerful countries) often leads to additional complications. In areas where widespread agreement is required for effective solutions—especially for certain global public goods problems—the requirement of individual state consent is a major hurdle that often leads to either inaction or weak policies and institutions (Trachtman 2013; Krisch 2014).

These limitations are most clearly on display in the area of climate change. The Kyoto Protocol suffered from the outset from the lack of US ratification, and negotiations on its extension beyond 2012—or a successor agreement—have proved arduous. In the eyes of many observers, the intergovernmental conferences, coupled with widespread civil society participation, have reached a size (in the case of the 2009 Copenhagen summit around 40,000 participants overall) that practically obviates effective decision-making (Victor 2011; Bodansky 2010). Even despite certain procedural innovations, such as the relaxation of the consensus requirement and the shift towards minilateral, small-group deals, negotiations have so far been unable to bridge major disagreements, especially over the kind and extent of required commitments from developing countries.

Possibly as a result of these difficulties, the conclusion of new multilateral treaties has declined significantly in recent decades—in spite of a growing awareness of the need to find global solutions to many problems (Denemark and Hoffmann 2008; Pauwelyn, Wessel, and Wouters 2012b). While this trend may display variation across issue areas, and may not apply in the same way to bilateral treaties (e.g. Bandelj and Mahutga 2013), in many contexts efforts at law- and decision-making have moved into other fora (see also Krisch 2014).

Creating capacity: the promise of formal international institutions

For much of the 20th century, formal international institutions were seen as the most obvious solution to the vagaries of the decentralised law- and decision-making process in the international order (Kennedy 1987; Mazower 2012). In order to be effective, however, international institutions require a far-reaching delegation of powers, which—depending as it does on state consent—is usually hard to come by (Hawkins et al. 2006). As a result, the creation of new institutions with firm decision-making powers on the global level has become exceedingly rare in many key policy areas (with an exception of strategies of judicialisation, as mentioned above).

More widespread has been the use of existing international institutions for new and broader purposes. One instance is the assumption of new powers of data gathering and information dissemination by the World Health Organization in the 2003 SARS crisis—powers later confirmed by its member states in a revision of the formal International Health Regulations (Fidler 2004). Yet the most prominent example for a broader use of existing institutions is the United Nations (UN) Security Council which, since 1990, has moved into an ever broader array of issue areas related to international security (Krisch 2012b, 2012a). The Council's broad scope of action is particularly visible in its counterterrorism measures, adopted with increasing vigour since 1998 (Rosand and Miller 2007). These measures include not only targeted sanctions against a great number of individuals, but also quasi-legislative measures on terrorism financing. As a matter of substance, the latter follow in the tracks of the earlier Convention on Terrorism Financing, but they were made binding by the Security Council on all UN member states (i.e. practically all states) despite the fact that ratification of the Convention by its signatories had been slow and weak up to that point. The Council has also come to adopt binding measures in areas of conflict prevention long seen as beyond its purview (True-Frost 2007); it has even begun to debate issues of climate change. In this respect, as in some of the other extensions of its remit, a significant number of states—especially developing countries—have voiced protest, as they insist on these matters being dealt with in the General Assembly or other, more inclusive fora. Yet the appeal of the Council lies in the fact that it allows for the adoption of globally binding rules in a small forum in which only nine votes out of 15 are (formally) required for a decision to be taken. For many actors interested in global regulatory capacity, the Security Council, with its low barriers for action, thus presents an attractive option.

An aspect of the expansion of international organisations' powers and functions has been the growth of what some commentators have called 'international bureaucracies' (Barnett and Finnemore 2004). The rule- and decision-making within these organisations often involves significant input by international civil servants who enjoy a certain degree of autonomy from their (state) principals, because of delegation or the expertise and moral authority they wield. Bureaucratic norms and cultures shape overall decision-making, especially in areas in which domestic governments have too little interest in exercising control.

International bureaucracies are, however, also helpful as tools for powerful countries to advance their interests. Such countries might seek to expand their regulatory capacity, often disguising their informal influence in the shadow of a seemingly impartial and relatively independent organisational staff and management, and thus 'laundering' their policies (Abbott and Snidal 1998). The workings of such structures of influence have been traced with particular clarity at the International Monetary Fund (IMF), where the USA has augmented its influence well beyond its (already considerable) voting share (Stone 2011).

A similar tendency can be observed in the UN Security Council's counterterrorism measures, which were widely seen as an effort by the USA to export its own policy agenda on a global scale (Alvarez 2003). The USA has been at the centre of most listings of terrorist suspects targeted by UN sanctions, especially in the early years after the 9/11 attacks. Its broader counterterrorism policies have left a decisive mark on those of the Security Council and the best practices identified by the Council's sub-organs. At the same time, the Council's Counter-Terrorism Committee and its executive body, the Counter-Terrorism Committee Executive Directorate (CTED), operate in a relatively consensual way, seeking to avoid the appearance of imposing rules on member states and instead cooperating with partner bodies in domestic governments as well as other international organisations (Heupel 2008; Messmer and Yordán 2011). Moreover, one of their main aims is the facilitation of technical assistance to states in order to create administrative and regulatory capacity for counterterrorism issues. These organs follow a 'managerial' approach that sees (potential) non-compliance as deriving from institutional inability (rather than resistance) on the part of national governments (Roele 2014). They also act in line with a broader trend toward international state building, in which typically western models of governance are reproduced as a template for institutional change in developing countries, and particularly in weak and crisis-ridden states (Chandler 2010).

Capacity through networks: the rise of informal institutions

Formal international institutions are difficult to create, and the powers of existing ones are not always easily stretched to include new policy areas. Binding decision-making powers are rare in international institutions in any event. Moreover, formal institutions typically (with the notable exception of the Security Council and the International Financial Institutions) operate on a basis of sovereign equality, granting all states an equal share, formally, of the vote (but see Cogan 2009). Attempts at modifying this structure in the design of formal institutions regularly provoke significant resistance. As a result, however, formal institutions often remain unwieldy and are not always appealing to powerful governments.

Functions, forms, and effects

An increasingly common alternative is provided by informal institutional settings (Vabulas and Snidal 2013), which typically produce only non-binding, informal norms (Pauwelyn, Wessel, and Wouters 2012a). These are not merely informal arrangements and norms that underlie formal ones (Helmke and Levitsky 2004; Stone 2011), but institutions that operate entirely (or largely) without a formal basis. The most common form of such institutions is that of government networks in which regulators from different countries come together to coordinate their actions. These have become attractive for their easy set-up, their institutional flexibility, their limited sovereignty costs, and the opportunity they provide to regulators to create transnational institutions of their own, independent from the classical channels of foreign affairs and potential concerns of other domestic actors (Slaughter 2004; Eilstrup-Sangiovanni 2009; Newman and Zaring 2012).

Informal institutions have varying forms and functions (see generally Vabulas and Snidal 2013). Some serve to exchange information and coordinate policy in a very general way, as in the original design of the G7 and G8 meetings or the BRICS group. Some help states to coordinate their negotiating positions with a view to other, often broader fora and institutions; the G77 at the United Nations, the G33 in the WTO context, or the Alliance of Small Island States (AOSIS) on climate change issues, are cases in point. Yet some informal institutions are also, to varying degrees, engaged in the production of rules and standards. The International Competition Network, for example, brings together competition authorities from across the globe in order to exchange views and experiences, but has also become active in standard setting through the elaboration of best practices and the peer-review system of mutual evaluations (Djelic 2011).

Rule-making through informal institutions has often been regarded as relatively ineffective because of the non-binding character of the norms produced and the absence of a formal delegation relationship that could give the respective institution a degree of independence and authority. In certain circumstances, though, informal standard setting is likely to have a significant impact, as the following examples illustrate:

- Coordination game situations appear particularly conducive to informal action (Verdier 2009: 122–6). Here, informal institutions can set a *focal point* which, if adhered to by a sufficient number of influential actors, will often drive others to accept it even if they would prefer a different substantive outcome. Product harmonisation through technical standards is the typical example here; in a liberalised market, the benefits of uniform standards often outweigh the costs of deviating from one's own preferred policy. (The fact that such standardisation is often performed by private organisations, such as the International Organization for Standardization (ISO) on the international level, signals already that bindingness only plays a limited role. Public regulatory networks, such as the International Organization of Securities Commissions (IOSCO) on securities regulation, benefit from the same effect (see Zaring 2005; Verdier 2009: 146).)
- Informal standards can also be effective if national regulators see them as welcome additions to their own *expertise* and capacity. Many policy problems today require particular bodies of knowledge and experience, which are often not available to national actors, especially in less affluent countries. Thus, global regulators may enjoy deference if they are seen as sufficiently well equipped and relatively impartial experts, even if their suggestions do not come in binding form (Avant, Finnemore, and Sell 2010).
- A third driving force for the effectiveness of informal standard setting is the *commitment* of regulators. In small settings, often characteristic of government networks, interactions are often based on mutual trust, and regulators will seek consistency between their international promises and their domestic regulatory action (Slaughter 2004: 198–200). Often equipped with powers of implementation, they can give standards teeth regardless of their binding or non-binding character (Eberlein and Newman 2008: 35–7).
- A fourth situation in which informal standard setting may be effective is that of a *linkage* with aid or market-access policies by powerful economies or international organisations. Through such conditionality, informal rules can become effective tools of regulation for all those for whom aid or

> market access are important benefits, which they will typically not forgo. The Financial Action Task Force (FATF), created by the G8 and the OECD to tackle money laundering (and later also terrorism financing), is a case in point here. Threats by the FATF to restrict access to member states' financial markets for (mostly third-party) jurisdictions not in compliance with its 'recommendations' have proved highly successful and have driven most of their targets to undertake significant policy adjustments (Sharman 2009).

Effectiveness depends, in part, on how broad the range of participants is. Trust is easier to generate in smaller settings, grounded in greater policy convergence, which makes agreement on common policies more likely and reduces the risk of later defection (Eilstrup-Sangiovanni 2009). The FATF's initial restriction of membership to OECD countries reflected this, but was later adjusted as broader inclusivity was seen as key to getting influential outsiders on board. However, with only 36 member jurisdictions, it seeks to maintain the benefits of a small negotiating circle, while gaining input from others through public consultations and regional satellite organisations (Roberge 2011). This reflects a 'club' approach to global regulation, for which informal institutions are often better suited than formal organisations with their orientation towards sovereign equality (Eilstrup-Sangiovanni 2009: 209f.). This suggests that informality benefits powerful states, able to form clubs in this way. However, weaker states may at times also seek and create informal institutions in order to form coalitions or to rebalance formal structures that are disadvantageous to them (Vabulas and Snidal 2013: 214).

Implications for governance capacity

From the perspective of national regulators, government networks hold significant advantages over other institutional forms. Yet they have limitations in scope—for cooperation problems without self-enforcing solutions (such as prisoner-dilemma situations), they may have difficulties in inducing compliance on their own but require other sources of enforcement such as powerful states or formal institutions (Verdier 2009). However, in situations in which they are effective, such networks enjoy the benefits of cooperation on transboundary problems with only limited constraints (at least formally: as previously described, the factual constraints especially for weaker countries may be severe). The non-binding character of informal standards allows countries a certain scope for manoeuvre and grants them the possibility of non-compliance when an issue becomes more salient and political costs become high (Abbott and Snidal 2000).

These networks also allow domestic regulators and administrators direct access to the international sphere. While formal international organisations today involve issue specialists from ministries and agencies other than the foreign service, classical diplomats and the international staff of international organisations will often play important roles. Networks, on the other hand, usually remain in the hands of the regulators in the issue area—they extend the scope of action of domestic institutions, rather than creating potentially competing, distinct bodies (Slaughter 2004).

For regulators, this requires new skills in intercultural negotiations and diplomacy, but also holds significant benefits. Cooperating through networks gives them access to information, expertise, and practical experience they may otherwise not have, especially when they come from smaller and developing jurisdictions (Newman and Zaring 2012: 259). It also allows them (or at least the more powerful players) to regain regulatory capacity lost to the forces of markets that escape political oversight by any one country. At the same time, the enmeshment in global regulatory networks also entails challenges for the identity and orientation of domestic administrative and regulatory institutions. The greater the share of 'globalised' regulatory affairs is, the more they mutate into parts of a broader whole, an 'international composite administration' (von Bogdandy and Dann 2008) or a 'global administrative space' (Kingsbury, Krisch, and Stewart 2005). This is likely to have repercussions for the structure of decision-making as well as for the mechanisms ensuring public accountability.

In terms of decision-making, international interactions can be expected to both favour and drive greater centralisation and hierarchy in the domestic (or regional) sphere. Influence in transnational networks, both public and private, appears to depend—apart from market power in general—on the ability to provide timely information and speak with a single voice, something that decentralised, pluralist domestic forms of regulation have difficulty providing (Posner 2009; Büthe and Mattli 2011).

In terms of accountability, government networks are often seen as advantageous over international delegation because they remain embedded in domestic political and governmental structures and are thus subject to local accountability mechanisms (Slaughter 2004). However, in order for such accountability mechanisms to be effective, they typically need to be moved to an earlier stage, providing accountability holders (legislators, stakeholders, or the public at large) with information during negotiation processes, not only after their conclusion when implementation into domestic regulation is at stake (Slaughter 2004: 235–7; Kingsbury, Krisch, and Stewart 2005; Berman 2012). Even so, the degree of influence of domestic audiences is often limited, especially in jurisdictions with relatively small negotiating power, which may have neither the clout to effectively introduce domestic concerns into the global network nor the (factual) freedom to reject standards once they are agreed upon. Moreover, this domestic influence will be complemented (and potentially overshadowed) by that of transnational accountability mechanisms, which typically give well-organised stakeholders a voice in the operations of the network itself (Chimni 2005).

An example: the Basel Committee on Banking Supervision

A typical example of a government network is the Basel Committee on Banking Supervision (BCBS), created in the 1970s to facilitate information exchange and coordination among financial regulators of 11 industrialised countries (Wood 2005; Young 2011). Triggered in part by different banking crises, from the 1980s onward the BCBS increasingly engaged in regulatory efforts, first in producing the Basel Accord on the capital adequacy of banks in 1988 and later through broader regulatory instruments. As the Committee's impact was more widely felt, participation claims by outsiders grew and led to an expansion of the Committee to institutions from 27 jurisdictions (including Brazil, India, China, South Africa, and Mexico). Growing visibility and contestation also provoked procedural changes in the direction of greater transparency and wider consultations in rule-making.

As with all informal institutions, the rules produced by the Basel Committee do not have binding force. Yet in the eyes of many observers, this fact does not make it less effective (Young 2011: 41). For participants, the pull towards compliance stems from their commitments to peers in the relatively small-group setting, even if compromises there have been costly. For example, in the late 1980s Japanese regulators were effectively coerced into a global agreement that damaged their banks' business strategies significantly; still, they implemented the accord (Singer 2004: 545ff.; but see also Verdier 2009: 137ff.). To outsiders, the Basel rules often provide focal points in a coordination game that are too costly to ignore, and they embody technical expertise in financial regulation that is often beyond reach for less well-resourced countries. Moreover, Basel standards are often used by the IMF for country assessments, thus providing additional incentives for compliance. In the context of global banking regulation, informal club structures—decision-making by some countries for a much broader setting—appear as a relatively effective alternative to formal international law, even if they create greater asymmetry among countries (see Ho 2002; Drezner 2007).

By all accounts, dominant influence in the Basel Committee has been exercised by regulators from the USA and the UK, home to key financial centres and thus close to the most advanced developments in banking practices (Singer 2004; Wood 2005; Baker 2010). Other member institutions played a lesser role, while regulators from outsider countries—i.e. most of the world—could make their voices heard only through the consultative process. Financial industry associations, in contrast, appear to have had a major impact on the design especially of the Basel II and III Accords in 2004 and 2009. Even if not all of their wishes were heeded in the transnational process (Young 2012), certain associations of large transnational banks enjoyed early and privileged access to regulators, creating blueprints and structures before other actors—smaller consumer banks, for example, or indeed many regulators—even knew of the regulatory initiatives (Lall 2012). Talk of 'regulatory capture' has become widespread around the Basel Committee, and it has been seen as a major source of the relative lack of stringency of Basel standards (Baker 2010; Lall 2012). In the case of the Basel II Accord, the particular influence of large transnational banks and the costs imposed on others led to significant unease domestically, especially in the USA where implementation has been delayed by conflict among domestic regulators, different kinds of banks, and Congress (Verdier 2012).

Standard setting in the Basel Committee, with all its different layers and actors, paints a good picture of the intricacies of the regulatory process in a government network, which imposes particular challenges on regulators but may also give them (at least some of them) new tools—to gain information and expertise as well as to re-establish regulatory capacity in global, liberalised markets. Yet it also reflects the difficulty in creating meaningful accountability processes in a sphere traditionally characterised by relative obscurity. Under public pressure due to the increasing visibility and impact of its work, the Basel Committee moved towards greater transparency and began to submit its proposals to public consultation in the late 1990s. In some national settings, including the USA, steps were taken to keep legislative committees informed about transnational harmonisation processes and to involve interested actors early on in these processes. This allowed for significant national input into the elaboration of the Basel II Accord (Barr and Miller 2006). Still, awareness of the implications of the Accord among a broader circle of actors only arose when the Accord was already in place. This did not obviate a lively debate about the right kind of implementation in the USA, but in countries with less leeway to deviate from global norms, such a debate would have likely come too late to affect regulatory outcomes substantially. Moreover, the relative weakness of domestic accountability—typically without a requirement of legislative ratification and instead focused on the implementation by regulators of their transnational commitments on the basis of existing statutory authority—makes the global process more consequential and makes capture more rewarding (and potentially likely) (Lall 2012: 615–18). The multi-actor, networked, and relatively centre-less structure of regulation in this mode renders classical accountability mechanisms increasingly ineffective and may give rise to other, less institutionalised, and potentially less powerful forms of 'spontaneous accountability' based on the mutual irritation of different actors and societal spheres (Ladeur 2012).

Extending domestic tools: extraterritorial regulation

A less cooperative, though sometimes more effective, way of tackling transboundary governance challenges is extraterritorial regulation. Mainly practised by the USA and the EU, extraterritorial regulation allows jurisdictions (individually or jointly) to create rules for acts taking place outside their own territories (Putnam 2009; Bradford 2012; Scott 2014). Under international law, exercises of extraterritoriality often create significant problems, and increasingly so in light of WTO disciplines (Ankersmit et al. 2012). At times, they spark significant political controversy, as in the European reaction to US attempts at enforcing its sanctions directed toward Cuba, Libya, and Iran against foreign companies operating outside the USA, or the recent outcry against EU attempts to subject international flights to its emissions trading system (Lowe 1997; Scott and Rajamani 2012). In other areas, though, a certain degree of extraterritoriality has met with, or acquired over time, broader acceptance, also because 'territory' has become an ever more indistinct concept in times of globalised markets and communication structures (Buxbaum 2009; Scott 2014). Extraterritorial action is also contemplated in a range of more recent treaties, including on corruption (Kaczmarek and Newman 2011; Magnuson 2013).

Extraterritorial regulation is not necessarily effective in all, or even many, circumstances. Governments do not usually have direct access to foreign territories, nor knowledge of events there, even if technological advances in data collection have expanded their intelligence capabilities (Suda 2013). Extraterritorial action depends on available information and intelligence, as well as on favourable market conditions that give the regulating entity sufficient clout over the targets of its regulation. This is typically the case if the regulatory body can use the threat of restricting market access to impose conditions on behaviour outside its own territory (Newman and Posner 2011: 595; Kaczmarek and Newman 2011: 749). As a result, the use of extraterritorial measures is normally restricted to the most powerful economies, and its reach limited to internationally active firms. Even if they can enhance regulatory impact, they presuppose extensive analytical and regulatory capacity and will often compromise the regulatory capacity of the affected foreign jurisdictions.

The paradigmatic case for extraterritorial regulation is the area of antitrust and competition (Gerber 2010). In the mid 20th century, the USA began applying its own rules to foreign conduct if that conduct had a significant 'effect' on the US market. This move was heavily criticised, but a few decades later, the EU came to adopt a similar approach. Because of the importance of US and EU markets for many foreign companies, enforcement of antitrust decisions has been relatively effective; it relies on the threat of restricting market access as well as on access to companies' assets within the USA and the EU. Partly because of the availability of this option, momentum towards a multilateral solution in the WTO context in the late 1990s faded. Today global cooperation is limited to a thin coordinating structure, the International Competition Network, in which the USA and the EU play a major role.

Creating links: public regulators and global private regulation

A different kind of challenge to states' governance capacities arises from the emergence of private authority in international affairs (Cutler, Haufler, and Porter 1999). Such authority, as with informal institutions, comes in many guises. At times it resembles that of classical international organisations when, as in the ISO, it is privately organised but consists of state-based member institutions. In other instances, for example with ICANN (the Internet Corporation for Assigned Names and Numbers), non-state institutions are delegated a position by a government (in this case the US government) to regulate a policy area or technology. In yet other cases, private authority stems from efforts at self-regulation by industries, or from efforts by civil society groups to create standards of a social or environmental kind designed to condition the operation of the global economy (see Haufler 2001; Vogel 2008; Büthe 2010; see also Matus's chapter in this volume).

Governments often have significant difficulties in dealing with such private structures. Many of them do not directly depend on governments for their operations, either because they have privileged access to infrastructure or because they target market actors directly. This may work without formal, legal implementation processes if those actors comply with private standards as a result of their own commitment (as in self-regulation), for reasons of competitiveness or reputational gains (as in quite a few sustainability schemes), or because they depend on a resource (such as the Internet in the case of ICANN) on which a private regulator may hold a monopoly (see Vogel 2008: 268ff.).

Governments and regulators have devised various forms of engagement with and impact on these structures. Some of them involve classical intergovernmental tools, such as government alliances to turn or integrate ICANN into a formal international organisation. While this effort has been unsuccessful thus far due to US resistance, it has resulted in a stronger role for the Government Advisory Committee (GAC) in the ICANN's governance, thus moving it closer to a 'public' entity (Cowhey and Mueller 2009: 185–8). Other strategies use state policies and existing international organisations to 'orchestrate' private regulators by facilitating their processes or lending legitimacy to their products. Especially when faced with multiple, competing private regulatory sites, governments have influenced rule choices by granting or withholding recognition or implementation through and links with domestic law and regulation. This has had significant effects in cases where private regulation depended on or benefited from government intervention (Abbott and Snidal 2009b).

Yet in many instances, global private regulation is intended to fill gaps where governments are unwilling or unable to regulate, and it is thus designed to operate outside, and parallel to, formal governmental channels. Many private schemes today not only produce rules and standards but also monitor implementation through their own certification schemes—for labour standards, sustainable forestry, and much else (Meidinger 2006). They have also developed their own forms of legitimation independent of governments (see also Macdonald and Macdonald 2010). For example, the Forest Stewardship Council—a civil-society-driven body promoting sustainable forestry standards—has institutionalised participation by business and civil society constituencies in a quasi-parliamentary fashion, and it has turned to transparent and consultative standard-setting processes in its work (see also Matus's chapter in this volume). In the context of global private regulation, governments and public regulators serve to complement the work of private institutions through policy monitoring and implementation. They may also strengthen private regimes, for example through links with public procurement. Yet overall, the state actors occupy a 'background role' (Abbott and Snidal 2009a: 83–7).

Capacities and constraints

Traditional legal and regulatory structures do not always fit the transboundary challenges of an ever more interdependent world. Cooperation through consent-based international agreements is slow, cumbersome, and often unsuccessful. Yet as we have seen in this chapter, new governance capacities are created through many other forms of global regulation—formal international institutions, government networks, extraterritorial regulation, and global private authorities. In one way or another, these forms operate without, or with a softened version of, the classical consent requirements. This makes for smoother functioning but also means that most of the norms produced in these forms do not bind states or other actors the way law traditionally does.

This informality has the advantage of being less threatening to states that are anxious to guard their sovereignty, and in many circumstances it may not even be less effective than binding rules. Effectiveness, as we have seen, typically depends on problem and market structures as well as the distribution of economic and political power. The different forms also offer distinct advantages beyond the mere creation of rules. Government networks often enhance the analytical capacities of participants by broadening the information base on problem characteristics, past regulatory experiences, and the interests of other participants. They also pull participants towards compliance by tying their commitments to a relatively small community of (international) peers. Extraterritorial regulation does not offer such benefits, but does allow regulators far greater freedom in the design of their policies. It is, however, of use only to a limited range of actors under quite particular conditions. Global private authorities operate in the (wide) gaps created in the absence of satisfactory public regulation, and have the advantage of strong society and market roots. Thus private authorities can provide information about potential hurdles for regulation as well as induce compliance through participation. In many contexts, though, reliance on private authorities may lead to low standards, or to a multiplicity of competing standards, the effects of which are difficult to assess.

The role of a national regulator or administrator in this picture is entirely different from that in the old command-and-control mode of regulation, and far more so even than results from the domestic turn to 'governance'. Regulators have become networkers: largely without the authority to set rules by themselves, they have to rely on communication and negotiation skills to bring together and influence their peers; they have to persuade and entice addressees within and outside their own jurisdiction to follow non-binding rules without the threat of formal enforcement; they have to find ways to influence the private institutions which, as we have seen, play an increasing role in global regulation (often) without involving public actors much; and they have to compete for regulatory share where other institutions—national, global, private, or public—operate in related fields (Black 2008).

This transforms but does not always weaken the role of national regulators. In the domestic political interplay, it may even strengthen them. Both parliaments and courts find it difficult to act on the international plane for structural reasons. If participation in international institutions usually favours 'executive multilateralism' (Zürn 2004), the centrality of the executive—at the governmental or regulatory level—in some of the other forms is even more prominent. The informality of many global processes, coupled with their sheer number and often seemingly technical nature, poses high hurdles for mobilisation and engagement with them. Even with increased transparency and consultation, participation beyond a small group of actors is typically found wanting. This provokes concerns about agencies or networks 'on the loose'. Yet given the dispersed and fluid character of authority in this complex regulatory interplay, as well as the fragmented character of a global 'public', classical tools for ensuring public accountability will often be of limited use.

In this picture of change, capacities and constraints are far from evenly distributed. For some regulators, the tools discussed in this chapter are a welcome addition to regulatory capacity; for others, they are mostly a constraint. The USA and the EU tend to be on the former side—they are the primary actors in extraterritorial regulation, and they are at the origin of what then become 'global' norms in many regulatory networks, both public and private (e.g. Posner 2009; Büthe and Mattli 2011). Among the 'rule-makers' in global regulation, they are increasingly joined by the BRICS countries and a select group of others, largely from the OECD context.

Yet this opening should not conceal the fact that most countries, especially developing ones, are at the receiving end of the process. Their institutions have little factual influence even if they have a seat at the table, as they lack the resources, expertise, and capacity to effectively shape global negotiations. They are short of sufficiently strong 'cooperation capacities' in an environment that is growing ever more complex, difficult to navigate, and dominated by resource-rich governments and transnational actors. In many settings, they do not even have a seat at the table—as we have seen, informality is far more conducive to exclusive, club structures than formal international institutions for which sovereign equality remains a strong regulative ideal. Governance capacity is not a zero-sum game among countries, and even those with little voice in global governance may benefit from common rules that allow them to re-regulate globalised markets. There is no doubt, though, that when we look at the capacity gains and losses in intergovernmental networks and transnational law, not all countries (and their regulators) are created equal.

References

Abbott, K. W., and Snidal, D. (1998). 'Why States Act through Formal International Organizations', *Journal of Conflict Resolution*, 42(1): 3–32.

Abbott, K. W., and Snidal, D. (2000). 'Hard and Soft Law in International Governance', *International Organization*, 54(3): 421–56.

Abbott, K. W., and Snidal, D. (2009a). 'The Governance Triangle: Regulatory Standards Institutions and the Shadow of the State', in W. Mattli, and N. Woods (eds), *The Politics of Global Regulation*. Princeton: Princeton University Press, 44–88.

Abbott, K. W., and Snidal, D. (2009b). 'Strengthening International Regulation Through Transnational New Governance: Overcoming the Orchestration Deficit', *Vanderbilt Journal of Transnational Law*, 42(2): 501–78.

Alvarez, J. E. (2003). 'Hegemonic International Law Revisited', *The American Journal of International Law*, 97(4): 873–88.

Ankersmit, L., Lawrence, J., and Davies, G. (2012). 'Diverging EU and WTO Perspectives on Extraterritorial Process Regulation', *Minnesota Journal of International Law Online*, 21(Spring): 14–94.

Avant, D. D., Finnemore, M., and Sell, S. K. (2010). 'Who Governs the Globe?' in D. D. Avant, M. Finnemore, and S. K. Sell (eds), *Who Governs the Globe?* Cambridge, New York: Cambridge University Press, 1–34.

Baker, A. (2010). 'Restraining Regulatory Capture? Anglo-America, Crisis Politics and Trajectories of Change in Global Financial Governance', *International Affairs*, 86(3): 647–63.

Bandelj, N., and Mahutga, M. C. (2013). 'Structures of Globalization: Evidence from the Worldwide Network of Bilateral Investment Treaties (1959–2009)', *International Journal of Comparative Sociology*, 54(2): 95–123.

Barnett, M. N., and Finnemore, M. (2004). *Rules for the World: International Organizations in Global Politics*. Ithaca, NY: Cornell University Press.

Barr, M. S., and Miller, G. P. (2006). 'Global Administrative Law: The View from Basel', *European Journal of International Law* 17(1): 15–46.

Berman, A. (2012). 'The Role of Domestic Administrative Law in the Accountability of Informal International Lawmaking: The Case of the ICH', in J. Pauwelyn, R. A. Wessel, and J. Wouters (eds), *Informal International Lawmaking*. Oxford: Oxford University Press, 468–99.

Black, J. (2008). 'Constructing and Contesting Legitimacy and Accountability in Polycentric Regulatory Regimes', *Regulation and Governance*, 2(2): 137–64.

BMI (Bundesministerium des Innern) (2011). *Gemeinsame Geschäftsordnung der Bundesministerien*. Berlin: Bundesministerium des Innern (BMI).

Bodansky, D. (2010). 'The Copenhagen Climate Change Accord: A Post-Mortem', *American Journal of International Law*, 104: 230–40.

Bradford, A. (2012). 'The Brussels Effect', *Northwestern University Law Review*, 107: 1–67.

Büthe, T. (ed.) (2010). *Private Regulation in the Global Economy: Symposium Issue Business and Politics 12(3).*

Büthe, T., and Mattli, W. (2011). *The New Global Rulers: The Privatization of Regulation in the World Economy*. Princeton: Princeton University Press.

Buxbaum, H. (2009). 'Territory, Territoriality, and the Resolution of Jurisdictional Conflict', *American Journal of Comparative Law*, 57: 631–75.

Chandler, D. (2010). *International Statebuilding: The Rise of Post-Liberal Governance*. London, New York: Routledge.

Chimni, B. S. (2005). 'Co-Option and Resistance: Two Faces of Global Administrative Law', *New York University Journal of International Law and Politics*, 37: 799–827.

Cogan, J. K. (2009). 'Representation and Power in International Organization: The Operational Constitution and Its Critics', *The American Journal of International Law*, 103(2): 209–63.

Cowhey, P., and Mueller, M. (2009). 'Delegation, Networks, and Internet Governance', in M. Kahler (ed.), *Networked Politics: Agency, Power, and Governance*. Ithaca: Cornell University Press, 173–93.

Cutler, A. C., Haufler, V., and Porter, T. (1999). *Private Authority and International Affairs*. Albany: State University of New York Press.

Denemark, R. A., and Hoffmann, M. J. (2008). 'Just Scraps of Paper? The Dynamics of Multilateral Treaty-Making', *Cooperation and Conflict*, 43(2): 185–219.

Djelic, M.-L. (2011). 'International Competition Network', in T. Hale, and D. Held (eds), *Handbook of Transnational Governance: Institutions and Innovations*. Cambridge, Malden: Polity, 80–8.

Drezner, D. W. (2007). *All Politics is Global: Explaining International Regulatory Regimes*. Princeton: Princeton University Press.

Eberlein, B., and Newman, A. L. (2008). 'Escaping the International Governance Dilemma? Incorporated Transgovernmental Networks in the European Union', *Governance*, 21(1): 25–52.

Eilstrup-Sangiovanni, M. (2009). 'Varieties of Cooperation: Government Networks in International Security', in M. Kahler (ed.), *Networked Politics: Agency, Power, and Governance*. Ithaca: Cornell University Press, 194–227.

Fidler, D. P. (2004). *SARS: Governance and the Globalization of Disease*. New York: Palgrave Macmillan.

Gerber, D. J. (2010). *Global Competition: Law, Markets and Globalization*. Oxford, New York: Oxford University Press.

Haufler, V. (2001). *A Public Role for the Private Sector: Industry Self-Regulation in a Global Economy*. Washington, DC: Carnegie Endowment for International Peace.

Hawkins, D. G., Lake, D. A., Nielson, D. L., and Tierney, M. J. (eds) (2006). *Delegation and Agency in International Organizations*. Cambridge, New York: Cambridge University Press.

Helmke, G., and Levitsky, S. (2004). 'Informal Institutions and Comparative Politics: A Research Agenda', *Perspectives on Politics*, 2(4): 725–40.

Heupel, M. (2008). 'Combining Hierarchical and Soft Modes of Governance: The UN Security Council's Approach to Terrorism and Weapons of Mass Destruction Proliferation after 9/11', *Cooperation and Conflict*, 43(1): 7–29.

Ho, D. E. (2002). 'Compliance and International Soft Law: Why Do Countries Implement the Basle Accord?' *Journal of International Economic Law*, 5(3): 647–88.

Kaczmarek, S. C., and Newman, A. L. (2011). 'The Long Arm of the Law: Extraterritoriality and the National Implementation of Foreign Bribery Legislation', *International Organization*, 65(4): 745–70.

Kennedy, D. (1987). 'The Move to Institutions', *Cardozo Law Review*, 8: 841–988.

Kingsbury, B., Krisch, N., and Stewart, R. B. (2005). 'The Emergence of Global Administrative Law', *Law and Contemporary Problems*, 68(3–4): 15–61.

Krisch, N. (2012a). 'Chapter VII Powers: The General Framework', in B. Simma, D.-E. Khan, G. Nolte, and A. Paulus (eds), *The Charter of the United Nations: A Commentary*. 3rd edn. Oxford: Oxford University Press, 1237–71.

Krisch, N. (2012b). 'Article 39', in B. Simma, D.-E. Khan, G. Nolte, and A. Paulus (eds), *The Charter of the United Nations: A Commentary*. 3rd edn. Oxford: Oxford University Press, 1272–96.

Krisch, N. (2014). 'The Decay of Consent: International Law in an Age of Global Public Goods', *American Journal of International Law*, 108(1): 1–40.

Ku, J., and Yoo, J. (2012). *Taming Globalization: International Law, the U.S. Constitution, and the New World Order*. Oxford, New York: Oxford University Press.

Ladeur, K.-H. (2012). 'The Emergence of Global Administrative Law and Transnational Regulation', *Transnational Legal Theory*, 3: 243–67.

Lall, R. (2012). 'From Failure to Failure: The Politics of International Banking Regulation', *Review of International Political Economy*, 19(4): 609–38.
Lowe, V. (1997). 'US Extraterritorial Jurisdiction: The Helms-Burton and d'Amato Acts', *International and Comparative Law Quarterly*, 46: 378–90.
Macdonald, K., and Macdonald, T. (2010). 'Democracy in a Pluralist Global Order: Corporate Power and Stakeholder Representation', *Ethics and International Affairs*, 24(1): 19–43.
Magnuson, W. (2013). 'International Corporate Bribery and Unilateral Enforcement', *Columbia Journal of Transnational Law*, 51: 360–417.
Mazower, M. (2012). *Governing the World: The History of an Idea*. London: Allen Lane.
Meidinger, E. (2006). 'The Administrative Law of Global Private-Public Regulation: the Case of Forestry', *European Journal of International Law*, 17(1): 47–87.
Messmer, W. B., and Yordán, C. L. (2011). 'A Partnership to Counter International Terrorism: The UN Security Council and the UN Member States', *Studies in Conflict and Terrorism*, 34(11): 843–61.
Newman, A. L., and Posner, E. (2011). 'International Interdependence and Regulatory Power: Authority, Mobility, and Markets', *European Journal of International Relations*, 17(4): 589–610.
Newman, A. L., and Zaring, D. (2012). 'Regulatory Networks: Power, Legitimacy, and Compliance', in J. L. Dunoff, and M. A. Pollack (eds), *Interdisciplinary Perspectives on International Law and International Relations: The State of the Art*. Cambridge: Cambridge University Press, 244–65.
Pauwelyn, J., Wessel, R. A., and Wouters, J. (eds) (2012a). *Informal International Lawmaking*. Oxford: Oxford University Press.
Pauwelyn, J., Wessel, R. A., and Wouters, J. (2012b). 'The Stagnation of International Law'. Working Paper No. 97. Leuven: Leuven Centre for Global Governance Studies.
Pollack, M. A., and Shaffer, G. C. (2009). *When Cooperation Fails: The International Law and Politics of Genetically Modified Foods*. Oxford, New York: Oxford University Press.
Posner, E. (2009). 'Making Rules for Global Finance: Transatlantic Regulatory Cooperation at the Turn of the Millennium', *International Organization*, 63(4): 665–99.
Putnam, T. L. (2009). 'Courts Without Borders: Domestic Sources of U.S. Extraterritoriality in the Regulatory Sphere', *International Organization*, 63(3): 459–90.
Roberge, I. (2011). 'Financial Action Task Force', in T. Hale, and D. Held (eds), *Handbook of Transnational Governance: Institutions and Innovations*. Cambridge, Malden: Polity, 45–9.
Roele, I. (2014). 'Disciplinary Power and the UN Security Council Counter Terrorism Committee', *Journal of Conflict and Security Law*, 19(1): 49–84.
Rosand, E., and Miller, A. (2007). 'Strengthening International Law and Global Implementation', in D. Cortright, and G. A. Lopez (eds), *Uniting against Terror: Cooperative Nonmilitary Responses to the Global Terrorist Threat*. Cambridge, Mass: MIT Press, 51–82.
Scott, J. (2014). 'Extraterritoriality and Territorial Extension in EU Law', *American Journal of Comparative Law*, 62(1): 87–125.
Scott, J., and Rajamani, L. (2012). 'EU Climate Change Unilateralism', *European Journal of International Law*, 23(2): 469–94.

Sharman, J. C. (2009). 'The Bark is the Bite: International Organizations and Blacklisting', *Review of International Political Economy*, 16(4): 573–96.
Singer, D. A. (2004). 'Capital Rules: The Domestic Politics of International Regulatory Harmonization', *International Organization*, 58(3): 531–65.
Slaughter, A.-M. (2004). *A New World Order*. Princeton: Princeton University Press.
Spiro, P. J. (2000). 'The New Sovereigntists: American Exceptionalism and Its False Prophets', *Foreign Affairs*, 79(6): 9–15.
Stone, R. W. (2011). *Controlling Institutions: International Organizations and the Global Economy*. Cambridge: Cambridge University Press.
Stone Sweet, A., and Brunell, T. L. (2013). 'Trustee Courts and the Evolution of International Regimes: The Politics of Majoritarian Activism in the ECHR, the EU, and the WTO', *Journal of Law and Courts*, 1: 61–88.
Suda, Y. (2013). 'Transatlantic Politics of Data Transfer: Extraterritoriality, Counter-Extraterritoriality and Counter-Terrorism', *Journal of Common Market Studies*, 51(4): 772–88.
Trachtman, J. P. (2013). *The Future of International Law: Global Government*. Cambridge: Cambridge University Press.
True-Frost, C. (2007). 'The Security Council and Norm Consumption', *New York University Journal of Legislation and Public Policy*, 40: 115–217.
Vabulas, F., and Snidal, D. (2013). 'Organization without Delegation: Informal Intergovernmental Organizations (IIGOs) and the Spectrum of Intergovernmental Arrangements', *The Review of International Organizations*, 8(2): 193–220.
Verdier, P.-H. (2009). 'Transnational Regulatory Networks and Their Limits', *Yale Journal of International Law*, 34(1): 113–72.
Verdier, P.-H. (2012). 'US Implementation of Basel II: Lessons for Informal International Lawmaking', in J. Pauwelyn, R. A. Wessel, and J. Wouters (eds), *Informal International Lawmaking*. Oxford: Oxford University Press: 437–67.
Victor, D. G. (2011). *Global Warming Gridlock: Creating More Effective Strategies for Protecting the Planet*. Cambridge: Cambridge University Press.
Vogel, D. (2008). 'Private Global Business Regulation', *Annual Review of Political Science*, 11(1): 261–82.
von Bogdandy, A., and Dann, P. (2008). 'International Composite Administration: Conceptualizing Multi-Level and Network Aspects in the Exercise of International Public Authority', *German Law Journal*, 9: 2013–39.
Wood, D. R. (2005). *Governing Global Banking: The Basel Committee and the Politics of Financial Globalisation*. Aldershot, Burlington: Ashgate.
Young, A. R. (2012). 'Less Than You Might Think: The Impact of WTO Rules on EU Policies', in O. Costa, and K. E. Jørgensen (eds), *The Influence of International Institutions on the EU: When Multilateralism hits Brussels*. New York: Palgrave Macmillan, 23–41.
Young, K. (2011). 'The Basel Committee on Banking Supervision', in T. Hale, and D. Held (eds), *Handbook of Transnational Governance: Institutions and Innovations*. Cambridge, Malden: Polity, 39–44.
Zaring, D. T. (2005). 'Informal Procedure, Hard and Soft, in International Administration', *Chicago Journal of International Law*, 5(2): 547–604.
Zürn, M. (2004). 'Global Governance and Legitimacy Problems', *Government and Opposition*, 39(2): 260–87.

12

Administrative Capacities in the EU

Consequences of Multi-level Policy-making

Eva G. Heidbreder

Thinking administrative capacities beyond the limits of the state

This chapter deals with two interrelated questions about administrative capacities 'beyond the state'. First, do supranational actors influence the demand for and promotion of specific administrative capacities? And, second, to what degree do national administrations adapt to such external demands and incentives? To answer these queries, I focus on the role of administrative capacities in a multi-level administrative setting that includes a supranational, national, and various subnational administrative layers.

The empirical case under scrutiny is the European Union (EU), which has developed extensive supranational policy-making without acquiring a single administration across all member states. It therefore offers a particularly rich test case to examine supranational administrative demands and (sub)state impacts. The scrutiny of EU policy-making allows us to discern how administrative capacities are defined in policy-making beyond the state, to analyse which instruments are developed to meet these capacity demands, and to understand the dynamics of the increasing importance of administrative capacity in multi-level policy-making systems.

Notably, the various actors within the EU concentrate on different notions of (sub)national administrative capacities. Public administrations are not the subject of a comprehensive supranational policy. The EU lacks both the legal competence and financial and human resources to develop any kind of binding top-down approach. Thus, this chapter is an attempt to provide an overview of the different policy areas and scattered instruments the European

Commission has developed incrementally, in order to ask whether there is a pattern underlying the rather detached activities that touch on the administrative capacities in the member states.

For international organisations more generally, the need for specific administrative capacities to implement and enforce supranational policies has not attracted much attention over the years. Instead, international administration focused primarily on the capacities required to set up and run an international secretariat (Weiss 1982). This lack of attention is closely linked to a lack of authority. Preserving the principle of full national administrative autonomy, actual capacities to indeed enforce international law have only been a marginal concern. This principle has prevailed also in the EU where more attention has been paid to the Commission as supranational bureau rather than the capacities of the member state bureaucracies.

Only in the mid 1990s was the lack of (sub)national administrative capacities defined as a potential threat to the effective application and protection of the common EU policy and legal framework. A definition of administrative capacities first emerged in the run-up to the eastern enlargement round in 2004–7 because it appeared unlikely that the large number of transformation states would be fully capable of applying the extensive body of EU law. Therefore, since the 1995 European Council in Madrid, the existence of 'administrative capacities' became an accession criterion in its own right. In collaboration with the Organisation for Economic Co-operation and Development (OECD), the European Commission formulated concrete checklists against which the overall 'horizontal' capacities of public administrations in the candidate states were examined. The capacities under scrutiny covered general administrative organisation and functioning in order to ensure that the acceding states would be capable of applying the expansive body of EU law.

Even though these demands on national administrative capacities to successfully participate in the supranational Union were first limited to the candidate states, they provided an indication of the de facto need for specific capacities and placed the topic on the EU agenda. Moreover, the demands identified at the time vis-à-vis the candidate states—namely, the ability to manage EU funds and policies and promote 'good administration' more generally—mirror roughly the priorities of the EU's administrative capacity agenda today. This turn of events provided first evidence for the strong demands supranational actors may place on national administrative capacities.

Nevertheless, the formulation of supranational capacity demands alone should not lead us to assume a direct effect on (sub)national administrations. The enlargement experience is telling also in this respect. Various studies confirm that the administrative reforms introduced under the pressure of pre-accession conditionality did not endure once the states had entered the

EU and the Commission lost its direct monitoring task (Meyer-Sahling 2009a, 2009b). In other words, even if there is high pressure to adapt administrative systems, national administrative practices and cultures are highly persistent and change—if at all—rather in an incremental and path-dependent manner that preserves national peculiarities.

To capture the meaning of administrative capacities in a multi-level polity, this chapter provides an overview of the definitions of administrative capacity the EU has developed since the mid 1990s and the instrumentation available to it to trigger or support change within national administrations. The focus is on the implications that policy-making in a multi-level system has for lower-level administrative actors. These implications are of relevance far beyond the EU since similar problems are to be expected also in other multi-level systems in the international arena.

The EU lacks legislative authority in the area of public administration and therefore the power to impose demands regarding horizontal administrative capacities in the member states. The analysis in this chapter unveils three different objectives pursued in putting administrative capacities on the supranational policy agenda that will be generalised as three types of administrative capacity objectives (good governance, management skills, administrative modernisation) at the end of this chapter. Each type can be linked to distinct demands arising from multi-level and transboundary policy-making that should apply more generally to policy-making beyond the state.

Challenge in the EU: an 'administrative expectations–capabilities gap'?

Drawing attention to administrative capacities in the EU, the first and preeminent question is: Whose capacities are we actually talking about? The general perception would bet on 'Brussels', meaning the European Commission and its fewer than 33,000 officials (European Commission 2013c) that serve as the Union's administrative executive. However, although national ministers in the Council of the EU mostly delegate the execution of EU policies to the European Commission, executive power rests formally with the member states. Three elements are hence decisive: the comparatively tiny size of the European Commission (as quasi-executive), its lack of resources (as implementing authority), and the general principle of administrative autonomy of the member state bureaucracies (as formally independent administrations). In sum, the EU is hence a system of quasi-executive federalism (*Vollzugsföderalismus*, as the Swiss system) in which policies are executed by national, regional, or local authorities inside the member states.

This system of multi-level policy execution creates deep-rooted tensions. Although the Commission is officially responsible for the correct implementation of EU law, it has no competences to instruct the de facto executing bodies that remain under national authority. To fulfil its duty and ensure correct policy implementation, the Commission can start a legal infringement procedure against a member state once policy implementation has fundamentally failed—it cannot pre-emptively regulate or control the independent national administrations. Therefore, the decisive unit of analysis we need to consider when talking about administrative capacities is the executing member state authorities, including the regional and local levels.

Considering EU policy-making, these actors have been rather neglected for a long time. The performance of member states was monitored primarily through a legal check-up that controlled for the transposition of EU law. Yet, since the mid 1990s, an understanding has grown that the mere transposition of EU legislation into national law is an insufficient indicator for policy compliance, which should entail effective implementation. Since then, capacities not only in candidate states but also in EU member states have become a matter of concern. I will argue in the following that these developments from a formal and largely legalistic to a more output-oriented approach reveal an incremental shift towards a different understanding of effective multi-level administration. Most importantly, once the negative externalities that inefficient or faulty administration in single states creates for the whole system are factored in, the demands on national administrative capacities change.

The relevance of this analysis goes beyond the specific EU case. Reviewing the incremental problem definition and instrument development in the EU may help to reveal more about the relevant administrative capacities in complex governance settings in which administrative policy execution involves actors from different, previously closed, state systems.

The remainder of the chapter illustrates the different instruments the EU has developed to address administrative capacities and the underlying objectives that led to the introduction of these instruments. On the one hand, there are a growing number of programmes and actions that directly promote *administrative and institutional capacity-building*. These initiatives first emerged in the context of eastern enlargement when it became clear that a lack of sufficient administrative capacities was a major obstacle for the candidate states to introduce and comply with the full body of EU law. Since then, technical and financial assistance schemes that support administrative capacities in candidate and member states exist, and their aims are presently being extended from assisting states to comply with EU policies (good governance) to better enabling states to profit from EU funding (management of EU funds and policies). These two objectives—promoting horizontal capacities for good administration and enhancing specific administrative resources to better manage EU funds—are linked to country-specific programming executed by the Directorates General on Employment and Regional Policy. However, we are also witnessing some more fundamental reorientation in the core Directorate General responsible for the internal market. Especially since the end of the 2000s, the emphasis on *correct policy execution* to exploit the full potential of the single market has gained momentum. The partial reorientation of Commission attention from developing new regulation to the effective enactment of existing regulation focuses efforts inevitably on administrative capacities inside the member states. Instead of explicit capacity-building instruments, different tools to create cooperation, information exchange, and networked solutions are implicitly also intended to trigger modernisation and administrative reform processes.

The next sections outline the different notions of administrative capacities that have emerged in a by-and-large detached manner from each other. Although they remain fairly unconnected inside the Commission, I will discuss the independently unfolding developments together in the final section of the chapter. The argument put forward is that the observable changes can be conceptualised in a larger framework of a maturing, multi-level administrative system, which is marked by specific functional capacity demands that come as part and parcel of multi-level policy-making. Given entrenched independent national systems, these demands do not, however, automatically lead to the establishment of an integrated administrative order but may also remain unanswered. In other words, needed capacities are lacking, which creates inefficiencies in the execution of multi-level policies.

Flanking policies: direct support for administrative capacities

Initially, policy implementation in the EU was exclusively in the hands of the member states' administrations. The principle of administrative autonomy granted the EU level no regulatory or organisational powers over national bureaucracies, and 'direct administration' through the Commission remained limited to few exceptions. However, to ensure effective and coherent policy implementation across the rising number of member states, today's multi-level administration builds de facto on various coordination mechanisms that sideline the strict application of exclusive administrative autonomy (Heidbreder 2011). As part of the incrementally growing interconnectedness of administrative actors at EU, national, regional, and local levels, administrative capacity has entered the policy agenda as an issue in its own right. I will discern three waves in which the topic was defined, redefined, and gradually expanded inside the Commission's programming schemes: the establishment of the topic on the agenda, the incorporation of policy tools in ordinary EU policy programming, and the strengthening of capacity-building through attempts to render supranational influence more binding.

Administrative capacities entering the agenda, 1995–2006: the big-bang enlargement[1]

As noted above, administrative capacities entered the EU policy agenda in the pre-accession phase of the Union's eastern enlargement (1993–2004/7). As part of the accession criteria, candidate states were obliged to adopt the Union's primary and secondary legislation, the so-called *acquis communautaire*, and to operate as stable democratic systems based on the rule of law. Beyond the so-called Copenhagen accession criteria, the Commission and member states realised soon after the pre-accession phase was initiated that administrative capacities were a serious obstacle for the transposition and implementation of the EU requirements. In addition, within the EU, the perception grew that dysfunctional public administrations were one of the key challenges for the transformation in the post-socialist states as such. As a consequence, the European Council of Madrid added administrative capacities as an additional accession criterion (European Council 1995). In light of the experiences during the tightly monitored pre-accession process, the conception of administrative capacities was soon expanded from the mere duty to comply with EU policies to the general quality of bureaucratic functioning as a precondition for good governance. Accordingly, while 'sectoral capacity was linked to particular parts of the acquis, horizontal capacity emerged as synonymous with administrative reforms' (Dimitrova 2005: 80).

The reform instruments in the soon-to-be member states were backed by pre-accession conditionality. In other words, the Directorate General (DG) Enlargement had leverage over the accession states since it evaluated annually the performance and reform success of the candidates—while it had no powers to monitor or push for reforms in the member states. Given the absence of genuine administrative standards in the EU's legal framework, checklists for the candidate states were drafted outside the EU rules in the framework of the OECD's Support for Improvement in Governance and Management (SIGMA) programme, formally an OECD programme but financed predominantly by the EU. The SIGMA baseline assessment was a 'response to the lack of specificity in horizontal administrative capacity assessment, combined with the perceived lack of accuracy by candidate states of previous

[1] The illustration of the period 1995–2004 refers in part to earlier work dealing with the repercussions of enlargement policy (Heidbreder 2011a: 61–80).

assessments' (Verheijen 2007: 17). Besides monitoring, technical assistance was offered within the framework of the Phare programme. Whilst most technical assistance was sourced out to external consultants, the EU initiated the twinning tool in 1998 to finance cooperation projects between public administrations of the member and candidate states. In addition, TAIEX (Technical Assistance and Information Exchange) was set up in 1996 to enable expertise sharing on EU legislation between the states.

Administrative capacities entered the EU agenda as part of its pre-accession strategy for two reasons. The first EU objective was to guarantee that the new member states would be able to meet the duty to comply with EU law. This objective soon grew into a second, larger, one, namely to support the transformation process the ex-socialist states were undergoing and thus to promote and stabilise good governance. The pre-accession strategy provided the Commission with leverage on the states since it evaluated progress and the readiness for accession of the candidates annually. This control element was backed up with technical and financial assistance from the EU to manage EU funds and policies.

Capacity-building and human resources, 2007–2013: the Social Funds' priorities

During the second phase, the assistance activities that had been developed as part of the pre-accession strategy were adapted and continued on a small scale, but expanded in scope. The reasons to keep administrative capacity-building on the agenda were twofold. On the one hand, the intended reforms in the candidate states showed at best limited success and appeared to be partly rolled back after accession (Verheijen 2007; Meyer-Sahling 2009a). On the other hand, it was recognised that problems identified in the candidate states were also obstacles in the member states, with Greece and Portugal explicitly asking for capacity-building support. The problem definition was thus expanded to potentially all member states for the programming period following accession (2007–13), which focuses on the so-called convergence regions (where GDP is less than 75 per cent of the EU average in the framework of cohesion policy). Since no formal EU competences over national public administrations were introduced, the approach is based on incentive-setting and assistance. The Commission stated that 'for the future programming period the strengthening of institutional and administrative capacity will be generalised and will be one of the main ESF [European Social Fund] priorities'. To that end, '[i]nstitutional and administrative capacity includes the ability of Member States and regions to contribute to the European Union's objectives and to fulfil the conditions and obligations arising from membership' (CEC 2007: 3ff.).

The instruments installed—already partly in place during the 2000–6 programming period—are financed by the European Social Fund (ESF, DG Employment). The ESF defines administrative capacities 'as the set of characteristics related to human capital in the public sector and to the performance and success of public policies' (Theisen et al. 2010: 14). To realise economic, social, and territorial cohesion, an emphasis is placed on human resources (public employment services, education and training systems, and other public administration). According to an elaborate stocktaking of all assistance aiming at capacity-building in all member states and target areas:

> [t]he focus on institutional and administrative capacity has increased in the 2007–2013 programming period. In 2007, 2008 and 2009, 5.5 million people from 17 EU Member States participated in ESF-funded priority axes addressing the topic... The selected priority axes represent up to 40 per cent of the total ESF budget.
>
> (European Commission 2010b: 8)

According to recent figures by the Commission for the 2007–13 period, member states approved indicatively 3.7 billion euros of investments into capacity-building actions. Of these investments '[t]he most important Heading/Category within ICB [institutional capacity-building] Theme is "Mechanisms for improving good policy and programme design, monitoring and evaluation", with 68% of the overall decided amount' (European Commission 2013b: 5).

The underlying reasoning behind the ESF involvement in capacity-building has remained similar to that during the eastern enlargement period: enhancing the overall performance of public services to promote good governance and providing assistance to manage EU funds. However, the mechanism to trigger administrative reforms is less influential than that for candidate states under the pre-accession criteria. For member states, capacity-building is encouraged through EU co-financing opportunities.

Still, the effects of EU financial and technical assistance are not without contradictions. With respect to the overall goal to improve good governance, the actual allocation of funds depends on the member states' agenda for ESF investments. As the rollback of reforms in the most recently admitted member states indicates, pre-accession reforms are not necessarily sustainable, and deep-cutting structural changes clash with entrenched national administrative cultures, structures, and interests. In addition, rising austerity pressures during the banking and financial crises have led member states to cut back investments in administrative reforms. In this context, technical assistance to manage EU funds and policies has also led to inverse effects. The tool has been widely used to buy in experts or top up wages to keep officials working on EU-related issues and to retain them in the public service. Technical assistance thus also has counterproductive effects on the actual goal of triggering substantive capacity-building in the member states because EU support is used to mend ad hoc shortcomings instead of building up effective internal resources.

Agenda shifts for administrative capacities, 2014–: attempts toward a tighter approach

For the programming period 2014–20, we can observe much continuation in content, combined with some innovations in the supranational steering toolbox. Inside the Commission, the two objectives—good governance and fund management—remain clearly separated, which is reinforced by the division of responsibility between different Directorates General. For the purpose of this chapter, they will be analysed side by side to capture the different facets of capacity demands multi-level policy-making entails. In the 2014–20 programming period, adaptations are introduced for both elements that offer chances to increase the supranational control over member states.

DG Employment continues to administer the ESF, whose administrative capacity objective remains a horizontal approach to promote the overall goal of good governance. Although the ESF instruments have not substantially changed, the introduction of the European Semester as a major instrument is seen as a possible tool to strengthen the Commission's potential leverage. The European Semester is the main tool to implement the EU's ten-year growth strategy as laid down in the Europe 2020 Programme (European Commission 2010a). Coordinated in a yearly cycle, the Commission analyses each member state's economic and structural reforms and offers recommendations for the upcoming 12 to 18 months in bilateral contracts between the Commission and each individual state. To ensure a more efficient use of EU funds, the strategic approach to realise the 2020 strategy is also reflected in the new multi-annual financial framework for the period after 2013.

In terms of both prioritisation and instruments, capacity-building has been strengthened. First, it is listed as one of 11 thematic priorities supported by EU funds. Second, ex ante conditionalities are to ensure a more efficient use of these funds. Ex ante conditionalities are fund-specific rules that give the Commission strengthened control functions over the allocation of resources because the 'fulfilment of those *ex ante* conditionalities should be assessed by the Commission in the framework of its assessment of the Partnership Contract and programmes. In cases where there is a failure to fulfil an *ex ante* conditionality, the Commission should have the power to suspend payments to the programme' (European Commission 2013a). For the Commission, these changes increase its actual leverage on member states, at least on ex ante programming. Since the underlying objectives are linked to the European Semester, which is legally binding because agreements have to be passed by the Council, the thematic objective could indeed lead to more impact—even though the Commission cannot sanction member states ex post if a state ultimately does not stick to the ex ante agreed conditions.

Turning to the management of EU funds, some institutional innovations have been introduced outside the ESF framework. A decisive conceptual shift is one of definition about capacities to absorb and manage EU funds. The question of whether a state has had the administrative capacity to retrieve EU funds has so far been handled as a mere state responsibility. More recently, the actual capacity to participate in and profit from EU programmes has emerged as a topic in the Commission. In response, DG for Regional and Urban Policy (DG Regio) has introduced in its agenda the absorption capacity of member states and regions, i.e. the ability to apply for, co-finance, and manage EU funds. DG Regio has adopted a definition of administrative capacity as:

> the ability and skill of central and local authorities to prepare suitable plans, programmes and projects in due time, to decide on programmes and projects, to arrange the co-ordination among principal partners, to cope with the administrative and reporting requirements, and to finance and supervise implementation properly, avoiding irregularities as far as possible.
>
> (Boeckhout et al. 2002: 2)

To accommodate the latest EU entrants, who have had massive difficulties in absorbing EU funds that range from 26.2 per cent of the funds available for Romania and 40 per cent for Bulgaria (Commission 13 June, cited by GIZ 2013; figures may still rise by the end of the programming period), DG Regio set up a new Competence Centre for Administrative Capacity-building, which has been operating since March 2013. DG Regio's competence centres provide the country units with issue-specific expertise to improve effectiveness and increase policy consistency across the different regions. In the words of a DG Regio official, the DG underwent a rethinking[2] towards:

[2] The shift from a mere concern with member state rule compliance to a shared responsibility for enabling all actors to produce the best EU policy output. In more detail: 'We have had a regular problem that member states who had difficulty—some member states including from the very beginning—have had difficulty fulfilling all the rules, which are very often their own rules, in using the money correctly in the timeframe allowed and didn't use the funding and procedures correctly. The official line as it was . . . until fairly recently very much "well, if they can't use the funds, that's their problem" and in case they do not get things solved, we do not think it is a good thing, but in the end if they do not use the funds, at least the EU tax payer at least has not lost out. However, with the arrival of the new member states in 2004, and most especially with Bulgaria and Romania in 2007, there is a move from being a question of "oh well, if they don't want it, so what" kind of business . . . we have realised that really our responsibility probably goes rather further and that rather than simply say "here is the money, if you can fulfil the rules . . . ", we have to help them and lead them through the path, give them advice. I always say, it is very similar to government social security administration where I can say, you get your social security if you can fulfil the rules and then very often they find out that actually they have to give some advice' (Interview 10, DG Regio, April 2013).

> "reality-based programming"... In the past we tried to focus very much on needs-based programming, where you look at what is really needed, and policy-based programming, where you look at what a policy like Europe 2020 dictates and try to adopt your programming. But now we are saying: that is all quite well, certainly you must not do things that are not needed or that are not in line with the policy, but also you must not propose things that we have not got any kind of hope of implementing.
>
> (Interview 10, DG Regio, April 2013)

In line with the mandate of the new competence centre in DG Regio, some loosening up in the co-financing rules for EU funds were introduced against the background of the financial crisis. Faced with rising concerns about administrative failures as a source of economic and political mismanagement in the member states, some within the Commission have started to change both attitude and efforts. Achieving a better absorption capacity in the regions and states is now an explicit goal for the next programming period. As part of the Commission's legislative initiatives on fiscal governance to tackle the enduring economic crisis (the so-called six- and two-pack regulatory packages), the legislative proposal to strengthen budgetary surveillance of member states suffering from serious financial instability mandates: 'A Member State subject to an adjustment programme experiencing insufficient administrative capacity or significant problems in the implementation of its adjustment programme shall seek technical assistance from the Commission' (European Commission 2011c: Art. 6.6, approved with amendments by EP on 23 March 2013). These regulations thus add a conditional element to states that receive substantial funds through the special financial instruments created during the economic and fiscal crisis.

To avoid competence overlaps between the DGs responsible for different aspects of capacity-building, two inter-service groups were set up. DG Regio—focusing on EU funds management—chairs the European Structural and Investment Funds Inter-Service Group on Reinforcing the Funds Capacity in Weaker Member States, which focuses on administrative capacity-building to improve participation in regional policies. DG Employment—responsible for horizontal capacities—chairs the Inter-Service Group on Institutional Capacity and Administrative Reform, which focuses on horizontal capacity-building. The groups consist of all DGs involved as well as the Secretariat General. DG Regio's activities in providing assistance to access and manage EU funds will be added to the continued activities of the ESF, which was reconfirmed in the new programming cycle in which both the ESF and the European Regional and Development Fund have administrative capacities as an objective (European Commission 2011a). The foci of DG Employment and

DG Regio remain clearly different, while the additional focus on administrative capacities as part of the two-pack[3] is an additional separate initiative. The establishment of the inter-service groups indicates coordination attempts, but they do not amount to a comprehensive integration into a single strategic approach addressing administrative capacities.

Rather, the incrementally growing attention to administrative capacities indicates the variety of capacity demands on national systems, which have been carved out in a fairly consistent line since the first agenda was set during the enlargement phase. The first demand that supranational policy-making entails is on effective management by national executing agencies. Only recently has this need for capacities been redefined as a common concern rather than as a matter of the individual states which might lose out on possible EU funding. The second demand is related, but more encompassing: namely, improvement of good governance more generally, which is considered a condition for a well-functioning common market.

The most ambiguous effect is created by technical assistance. While it is offered often in the form of buying in external expertise to manage EU funds and thus to support the first goal, it often creates the unintended side effect that it counteracts the establishment of sustainable good administration in itself. Both these incentive-setting and assisting sets of instruments reflect conditions for effective multi-level policy-making, to which we will now turn from another angle.

Completing the single market: indirect demands on administrative capacities

Very much apart from the direct concern with administrative capacities as a condition for good governance and as a necessity for correct fund management, administrative capacities have recently attracted increasing attention as a precondition for the successful completion of the single market under the auspice of DG Market and Services (DG Markt). Unlike the direct assistance offered by DG Employment and DG Regio, DG Markt touches indirectly on administrative capacities by putting enhanced emphasis on effective policy implementation. I will take up two aspects to illustrate the administrative capacity dimension. First, the refocused policy agenda and instruments promoted by DG Markt will be outlined briefly. Second, the technical innovations

[3] The term 'two-pack' is used as a shorthand for two legislative measures to complete the budgetary surveillance cycle and improve economic governance in the EU in reaction to the banking and fiscal crisis that were passed in May 2013 (see European Commission 2013d). The two-pack followed an earlier package of six measures, the so-called six-pack that comprised legislative measures to attain more fiscal discipline in the Euro states.

especially in the field of e-governance and the related redefinitions of capacities and European public service at large will be described.

The shift from regulation to policy execution, 2011–: the Single Market Act

Prompted by Commissioner Monti's report, *Strategy for the Single Market* (Monti 2010), the European Commission published *The Single Market Act: Twelve Levers to Boost Growth and Strengthen Confidence 'Working Together to Create New Growth'* in early 2011 (European Commission 2011b). This document has been instrumental in defining a strategic shift in the Commission's single market agenda that reorients much of the attention from a legal approach on regulation to a more applied approach to policy implementation and enforcement on the ground. Accordingly, even if administrative capacities are still formally treated as member state prerogatives, the measures and tools developed by the Commission affect all (sub)state administrations that are involved in implementing EU policies. Despite the scope of the approach that addresses the capacities of decentralised implementing executives, the Commission does not attain substantive new powers. Its responsibility is basically limited to that of providing communication infrastructure. This is reflected in the Commission's self-attributed role. When asked independently to describe their role in the 'governance of the single market', interviewees across all levels of DG Markt referred univocally to that of a facilitator. Rather than promoting the development of horizontal or specific management capacities in the states, DG Markt now provides coordination facilities that member states are obliged to use in order to improve policy execution in transnational administrative processes (for a more detailed overview, see Heidbreder 2014).

In more concrete terms, to improve policy enforcement, the Commission promotes joint, decentralised, and horizontally linked policy implementation, which is supported by new electronic tools. Instead of conferring administrative powers to Brussels, national administrations commit to cooperating horizontally during the implementation of single administrative acts. This is well exemplified by the implementation of the mutual recognition of professional qualifications (Heidbreder 2013). Granting free movement of labour, national administrations have long been obliged to recognise professional qualifications obtained in another member state. Yet, in practice regional and local authorities have often lacked the language skills and other resources to efficiently find and coordinate with their counterparts in another state. In the run-up to the introduction of the free movement of services, member states facing increasing demands requested administrative support from the EU. This request led to a legal obligation for member state administrations to cooperate in applying the Services Directive (European Parliament and the Council 2006). In addition to requiring member states to offer assistance to one another, the regulation also obliges states to use the Internal Market Information System (IMI), developed and provided by the Commission. In short, IMI is an easy-access electronic network tool, supported by an automatic translation service, which links relevant local, regional, and national authorities so that they can directly exchange information in an administrative procedure. In the case of professional qualifications, IMI allows the relevant authority to enter queries into IMI and receive a reply within a short period without special language skills.

What is unique about this tool and the approach promoted in the Single Market Act is that neither powers nor resources are reallocated from the national to the EU level. Instead, capacities on the regional and local levels are developed and interlinked. In order to effectively cooperate, states have to de facto build up new capacities and bring innovation into administrative management. Concretely, the Services Directive introduced the obligation for competent authorities to cooperate, which led observers and practitioners to expect massive reform and modernisation pressures, if not even a complete overhaul of national systems (see e. g. Schliesky 2008). In the words of a Commission official, administrative cooperation must be 'linked to national public administration modernisation. If you want to establish this kind of network you also need that all administrations are kind of flexible somehow' (Interview 11, DG Markt, April 2013).

Even if it is too early for a conclusive evaluation, it is safe to assume that the concentration on policy enforcement will inevitably imply administrative capacity-building on the (sub)state level. In the words of a Commission official:

> You need it, it is real life now—see professional qualifications, you have more and more people moving and you need it [IMI] . . . In Europe you can now travel for ten euros easily and you need six months and send a pile of papers and translate . . . It's not normal. [These are] real needs of people. You live in Europe and you still do this kind of 19th-century things [in administration].
>
> (Interview 11, DG Markt, April 2013)

The potential external impact is that previously independent, closed national bureaucracies have to adapt their procedures and create new capacities to eventually execute policies jointly across borders.

The introduction of new solutions: creating a European public service

The development of functioning electronic tools that offer genuine new solutions to long-standing, unresolved challenges, such as language barriers, is central to the innovations in the governance of the single market. A great number of stand-alone e-tools have been developed ad hoc. In order to gain an overview and develop a more comprehensive approach, the programme on Interoperability Solutions for European Public Administrations (ISA) has been set up under Commissioner and Vice-President of the Commission Maroš Šefčovič. In the context of improving interoperability on both a technical and substantive legal level, ISA has changed its terminology from e-governance, considered a general standard, to the concept of European public services. The inclusive definition states that 'European public services are cross-border public sector services supplied by public administrations, either to one another or to European businesses and citizens' (European Commission 2010c: 3, footnote 3).

As the programme title indicates, the main task is rendering public administrations technically compatible on all levels and across all member states of the EU. To this end, ISA provides technical support in programme development. In addition, ISA aims to be integrated into the policy development process across the different Commission services to better connect the patchwork of different solutions and tools developed mostly ad hoc in different DGs or by single member states. The capacity-building notion behind ISA integrates technical and policy agendas, as well as all actors involved in the European public services.[4]

In this vein, ISA also financed and developed IMI, which is now owned by DG Markt that runs the facilitating tool for the member states. In drawing from interviews across different DGs in the Commission, it is not clear whether ISA has been established as a fully participating and integrated partner in all matters of administrative capacity development. For instance, ISA is not explicitly listed as a regular participant in the inter-service group on administrative capacity-building run by DG Regio. However, ISA's current efforts to develop a coherent approach to the scattered technical tools and its success in offering tools that actually work (such as IMI) indicate the growing potential and relevance of ISA. The notion of technical and policy innovation as elements of a larger European public service is therefore likely to increase in importance in light of further demands to meet output-oriented objectives relating to the single market, cohesion policy, and necessary crisis-related reforms.

In view of external pressure for national public administrations to adapt, ISA can be seen as a strong potential catalyst for reform. First, the provision of

[4] In comparison to other initiatives that deal with e-governance in the Commission, such as the DAE or large-scale pilot programmes, ISA is the most comprehensive initiative that aims to create explicitly linkages between concrete administrative demands and policy/technical solutions based on the notion of European public services.

technical solutions that were previously unavailable or inefficient can be a decisive catalyst for modernisation and the introduction of new instruments. One example is the interest of German administrative bodies in introducing IMI to promote the digitalisation of back-office cooperation within and across Germany. Second, the use of new technologies can only be efficient if accompanied by sufficient changes in work practices and administrative organisation. Though some (Lenk 2009) have questioned whether the necessary reforms in thinking and organisational culture could be carried out, the explicit demand for certain capacities is ever more straightforward, given the obligation for administrative cooperation and the use of IMI. Reform resentments, lock-in effects, and path dependencies seriously hamper (sub)national adaptations, but they also imply persistent inefficiencies in multi-level and transnational policy execution.

Administrative capacity types: demands and instruments in multi-level policy-making

This chapter raised two interrelated questions about demands on administrative capacities and responses to these demands in the context of multi-level governance. Empirically, these questions were reviewed by examining the various notions of administrative capacities that can be found scattered across different Commission services and their respective policy instruments. The various activities the different DGs promote were incrementally established and eclectically expanded; indeed, they do not follow a comprehensive blueprint. This notwithstanding, reviewing the various EU initiatives allows us to distil a number of conceptual and theoretical findings that hint at underlying patterns of demands and responses.

Table 12.1 places the empirically observed instruments into a conceptual grid that attributes an underlying objective and specific supranational demands to the initiatives. Three general objectives can be distilled that cover theoretically related but conceptually distinct aspects of EU policy-making. First, the general objective of good governance can be identified. The legal background for the EU to get involved in this realm—despite formal administrative autonomy of the member states—is based on the understanding that good governance is generally necessary to ensure the smooth functioning of the common market. It is also related to the democratic principles stated in the first paragraphs of the Treaty of the European Union, as well as the 'right to good administration' contained in the Charter of Fundamental Rights and Freedoms that gained legal force with the introduction of the Lisbon Treaty in 2009.

Table 12.1. Administrative capacity demands and responses

Objective administrative capacity (*legal treaty link*)	EU demand on (sub) national capacity	Supranational instrument
Good governance (*condition for functioning single market*)	Functioning institutions	• Voluntary allocation of funds (ESF) • Programming oversight (ex-ante conditionalities/European Semester)
Effective management (*condition for protection of EU financial interest*)	Management capacities and resources	• Technical assistance (wage contributions, external expertise) • Mainstream administrative capacity in country approaches of DG Regio
Modernisation of public services (*condition for implementation/ compliance with EU law*)	Transnational/multi-level networks	• Cooperation obligations (legislation) • Electronic network tools (e.g. IMI) • Interoperability solutions (ISA)

Own source

More specifically, the EU expresses the demand for functioning (sub)national institutions. This demand was and continues to be very explicitly monitored in the enlargement context. For all member states, these demands are operationalised foremost in the ESF that offers funding for capacity-building. However, whether member states opt to use these funds has remained largely a matter of choice. The introduction of the European Semester and ex ante conditionalities offer more recent instruments that grant the supranational level more leverage because certain programming conditions have to be met to receive EU support in the first place. Since control is limited to ex ante programming, the actual effectiveness of the instruments remains to be verified.

The second underlying objective, the effective administrative management of EU resources, is less encompassing and focused more on skills. The legal basis for EU action is grounded in the Commission's competence and obligation to safeguard the common budget and common policies. The demand supranational policy-making creates is concretely the effective management of shared resources. Unlike policy-making within confined national boundaries, management failures in one member state produce negative externalities for the whole EU system. If, for instance, one national administration suffers from massive corruption, it will have negative effects on the whole EU budget and thus all 28 member states.

The notion that bad management in a single state has more encompassing negative effects has recently been expanded to the ability to use EU support. Lacking capacities to profit from EU funds becomes thus in itself seen as a source of negative externalities and, in turn, creating capacities to profit from EU funds is incorporated into the objective to promote effective management capacities. DG Regio has accordingly started to develop expertise on how to improve the absorption capacity of states. The main instrument to promote national management facilities has been technical assistance. However, this tool has also created the unintended effect that external management expertise is bought in instead of developing a sustainable administrative apparatus, let alone good governance. With the establishment of the new competence centre in DG Regio in 2013, the mainstreaming of administrative capacities into country approaches is an instrument to counteract such adverse effects and develop a more comprehensive capacity-building approach by focusing on both individual countries and the whole.

Finally, multi-level and transnational policy execution creates genuinely different demands on competent authorities that have to interact with peers in other member states executing complex administrative tasks that span across different national jurisdictions. As noted above, a case in point is the recognition of professional qualifications necessary to guarantee the free movement of labour and services. To effectively enforce these policies of the liberalised single market, the competent authority that has to recognise qualifications obtained in another member state depends on information, cooperation, and specific skills (most basically language skills) to correctly handle cross-border processes.

The Commission has identified the sheer lack of capacities of competent authorities as a major obstacle for the functioning of certain policies. The underlying modernisation objective is distinct from the good governance and management objectives. Legally anchored in the member state obligation to comply with EU law and implement EU policies, modernisation claims are linked to technical solutions facilitated by the supranational level. New network tools, most relevantly e-solutions, can only be fully exploited if they are backed by deep back-office reforms in the member states. The functional administrative needs entailed by the creation of the single market thus imply substantive administrative reorganisation—if effective policy execution is to be realised.

The chapter has shown that there are conceptually distinct demands that a multi-level administration such as the EU creates for its participating (sub) national administrative units. The reply to the question about which administrative capacities multi-level and transboundary policy-making requires can be condensed to three aspects: the need for stable administrative systems, the need for specific management skills, and the need to adapt both systems and skills to complex administrative procedures. Failure to respond to the demands linked to these objectives not only harms the individual state lacking capacities, but also creates (negative) externalities for the overall system.

The second question about how these demands have been accommodated is more difficult to answer. The empirical stocktaking of this chapter has assembled the various initiatives and instruments scattered over the different DGs in the European Commission. Whether and to what degree these instruments really result in changed administrative capacities remains a largely open question. It depends on the responsiveness of the member states and, in the end, their political will to prioritise effective multi-level policy-making over entrenched national structures and practices.

References

Boeckhout, S., Boot, L., Hollanders, M., Reincke, K.-J., and de Vet, J. M. (2002). 'Key Indicators for Candidate Countries to Effectively Manage the Structural Funds. Principal Report'. Rotterdam: NEI Research Consultant.

CEC (Commission of the European Communities) (2007). *Institutional Capacity: Public Administrations and Services in the European Social Fund 2007–2013*. Brussels: Commission of the European Communities (CEC).

Dimitrova, A. L. (2005). 'Europeanization and Civil Service Reform in Central and Eastern Europe', in F. Schimmelfennig, and U. Sedelmeier (eds), *The Europeanization of Central and Eastern Europe*. Ithaca: Cornell University Press, 71–90.

European Commission (2010a). 'Communication from the Commission: Europe 2020. A Strategy for Smart, Sustainable and Inclusive Growth'. COM (2010) 2020 final. Brussels: European Commission.

European Commission (2010b). 'The European Social Fund and Institutional Capacity of Public Bodies'. Summary Fiche. Brussels: European Commission.

European Commission (2010c). 'Towards Interoperability for European Public Services'. COM (2010) 744 final. Brussels.

European Commission (2011a). *Cohesion Policy 2014–2020: Investing in Growth and Jobs*. Luxembourg: European Union.

European Commission (2011b). 'Single Market Act: Twelve Levers to Boost Growth and Strengthen Confidence "Working Together to Create New Growth"'. COM (2011) 206 final. Brussels: European Commission.

European Commission (2011c). 'Strengthening of Economic and Budgetary Surveillance of Member States Experiencing or Threatened with Serious Difficulties with Respect to their Financial Stability in the Euro Area. Proposal for a Regulation of the European Parliament and of the Council Vol'. COM(2011) 819 final. Brussels: European Commission.

European Commission (2013a). 'Amended Proposal for a Regulation of the European Parliament and of the Council Laying Down Common Provisions on the European Regional Development Fund, the European Social Fund, the Cohesion Fund, the European Agricultural Fund for Rural Development and the European Maritime and Fisheries Fund covered by the Common Strategic Framework and Laying Down General Provisions on the European Regional Development Fund, the European Social Fund and the Cohesion Fund and repealing Council Regulation (EC) No 1083/2006'. COM(2013) 246 final. Brussels.

European Commission (2013b). 'Cohesion Policy: Strategic Report 2013. Factsheet: Institutional Capacity Building'. Brussels: European Commission.

European Commission (2013c). 'Key Figures Card: Staff Members'. Brussels: European Commission.

European Commission (2013d). '"Two-Pack" Enters into Force, Completing Budgetary Surveillance Cycle and Further Improving Economic Governance for the Euro Area'. Memo/13/457. Brussels: European Commission.

European Council (1995). 'Presidency Conclusions'. European Council Meeting in Madrid, 15 and 16 December. Madrid: European Council.

European Parliament and the Council (2006). 'Directive 2006/123/EC of 12 December 2006 on Services in the Internal Market'. Official Journal: L 376/36. Brussels.

GIZ (Deutsche Gesellschaft für Internationale Zusammenarbeit) (2013) [website]. *Absorption Rates*. Retrieved from <http://insideurope.eu/taxonomy/term/35> (accessed 20 August 2013).

Heidbreder, E. G. (2011). 'Structuring the European Administrative Space: Policy Instruments of Multi-Level Administration', *Journal of European Public Policy*, 18(5): 709–26.

Heidbreder, E. G. (2013). 'Regulating Capacity Building by Stealth: Pattern and Extent of EU Involvement in Public Administration', in P. Genschel, and M. Jachtenfuchs (eds), *Beyond the Regulatory Polity? The European Integration of Core State Powers*. Oxford: Oxford University Press, 145–65.

Heidbreder, E. G. (2014). 'Horizontal Capacity Pooling: Direct, Decentralised, Joint Policy Execution', in M. W. Bauer, and J. Trondal (eds), *The Palgrave Handbook of the European Administratve System*. Houndmills: Palgrave, Chapter 23.

Lenk, K. (2009). 'Organisationsänderung durch Wegsehen', *Verwaltung und Management*, 15(5): 241–50.

Meyer-Sahling, J.-H. (2009a). 'Sustainability of Civil Service Reforms in Central and Eastern Europe Five Years after EU Accession'. Sigma Papers No 44. Paris: OECD.

Meyer-Sahling, J.-H. (2009b). 'Varieties of Legacies: A Critical Review of Legacy Explanations of Public Administration Reform in East Central Europe', *International Review of Administrative Sciences*, 75(3): 509–28.

Monti, M. (2010). 'A New Strategy for the Single Market: At the Service of Europe's Economy and Society'. Report to the President of the European Commission José Manuel Barroso. Brussels.

Schliesky, U. (2008). *Die Umsetzung der EU-Dienstleistungsrichtlinie in der deutschen Verwaltung: Teil 1 Grundlagen*. Kiel: Lorenz-von-Stein-Institut.

Theisen, A.-M., Delmartino, M., Nunes, J., and Vilela, B. (2010). *The European Social Fund and Institutional Capacity of Public Bodies: Background Report*. Brussels: European Union.

Verheijen, A. J. G. (2007). *Administrative Capacity in the New EU Member States: The Limits of Innovation?* Washington, DC: The World Bank.

Weiss, T. G. (1982). 'International Bureaucracy: The Myth and Reality of the International Civil Service', *International Affairs*, 58(2): 287–306.

13

Collaborative Innovation and Governance Capacity

Eva Sørensen and Jacob Torfing

Introduction

The question of how to make public policies, organisations, and services more innovative has been on the top of the agenda among public leaders and governance researchers for a considerable time. Public innovation is perceived as the intelligent response to the key challenges to public governance: the fiscal crisis that puts severe constraints on governments' ability to meet the rising and changing demands of the citizens; the proliferation of 'wicked problems' that cannot be solved by standard solutions or by spending more money; the persisting problems with executing public policies; and the increasing political, social, and cultural globalisation that calls for the development of new institutional forms of transnational governance.

While the traditional public governance approach to public sector innovation identified office-seeking and voter-maximising political leaders as the main driver of innovation (Polsby 1984), the New Public Management reform programme has seen the strategic leadership of public managers and public–private competition as the key sources of public innovation. More recently, however, the leadership- and competition-driven approaches to public innovation have been supplemented by a collaborative approach that aims to overcome the increasing organisational and institutional fragmentation associated with New Public Management. The growing interest in collaboration as a driver of public innovation is visible in recent governance research (Hartley 2005; Bommert 2010; Osborne 2010) as well as in many of the public sector reform programmes that have appeared in the last decade (Australian National Audit Office 2009; HM Government Cabinet Office 2010; OECD 2010).

The basic idea of collaborative innovation is that problem-focused collaboration between relevant actors from different organisations, sectors, and levels can contribute to the formulation, implementation, and diffusion of innovative ideas that transform not only public policies and services, but also the organisational forms and routinised processes through which they are produced and delivered (Eggers and Singh 2009). Hence, collaboration between public and private actors with relevant innovation assets can help to define the problems or challenges at hand in new and better ways; spur the generation of ideas through mutual learning; select the most promising ones for prototyping and testing through a negotiated assessment of potential benefits and risks; create joint ownership of new and bold solutions; mobilise and coordinate resources in the implementation phase; and disseminate knowledge of innovative solutions and their effects (Sørensen and Torfing 2011). There are many examples of how multi-actor collaboration enhances public innovation. In Denmark ministerial departments have worked together and collaborated with experts and private stakeholders in order to develop a new and innovative climate policy. In the city of Oakland, California, the Policy Department collaborates with local government agencies and community organisations to curb gang-related violence. In Britain the National Health Service has brought together growing numbers of managers and professionals to develop, adapt, and implement health-care innovations, and the Talking Heads Network assembles more than 10,000 head teachers in an inter-organisational community of practice that plays a key role in the diffusion of innovation in primary education (Mulgan and Albury 2003).

Studies of public innovation and collaborative governance confirm that collaboration between public and private stakeholders has much to offer in terms of enhancing public innovation (Roberts and King 1996; Sørensen and Torfing 2011, 2012), but they also reveal a number of barriers that must be overcome if we are to realise the full innovation potential of collaborative forms of governance (Halvorsen et al. 2005). Many of these barriers are rooted in bureaucratic institutional factors such as formal rules and routines, rigid budget and accounting systems, top-down steering based on command and control, and horizontal specialisation that leads to the formation of mental and organisational silos. Another set of barriers concerns the culture of public organisations that often lack a strategic focus on innovation, procedures for exploring and exploiting new solutions and handling risks, and incentives for managers and employees to collaborate and innovate. A final set of barriers stems from the deep-seated role perceptions of the public and private actors that prevent them from engaging in an open-ended and collaborative search for new and creative solutions.

It is a key task for public leaders and managers to remove these barriers while simultaneously enhancing the drivers of collaborative innovation. This type of hands-off innovation management must be combined with hands-on innovation management that aims to convene, facilitate, and catalyse collaborative innovation in and through close interaction with the relevant and affected actors from the public, private, and third sectors. In undertaking their new and important role as innovation managers, political and administrative leaders in the public sector will need a radically different set of skills and capacities compared to those required for their traditional role as bureaucratic leaders and for the more recent emphasis on strategic leadership and management in the context of public–private competition. While the traditional forms of public leadership and management are about instructing and controlling public employees in order to ensure that they do things right and are motivated to do a good job, innovation management is about creating processes that allow for novel and different things to emerge. The task of governing 'emergence' rather than 'facticity' requires a new set of leadership and management characteristics and skills: one must be a good communicator and experienced conflict mediator, while also being visionary, curious, courageous, and capable of tolerating ambiguity.

This chapter considers why public innovation has moved to the top of the public sector reform agenda. It points out how collaborative forms of governance can contribute to enhancing public innovation, identifies a number of barriers to collaborative innovation, and clarifies how public leaders can remove such barriers and strengthen the drivers of collaborative innovation. Finally, it discusses how we can enhance the public sector's capacity for collaborative innovation and which skills are required in order to lead, manage, and engage in processes of collaborative innovation.

Governance challenges that call for public innovation

As evidenced in several studies of public policy, there are many contingent factors that influence why certain topics, issues, and ideas momentarily move to the centre stage of public policy-making (Cohen, March, and Olsen 1972; Kingdon 1984; Pollitt and Bouckaert 2004). The factors that are cited in the literature are a mixture of structural pressures, the emergence and spread of new ideas and problem definitions, interaction between strategic actors, and the surfacing of favourable opportunities and occasions for decision-making. Therefore, one should be cautious when seeking to explain why public innovation has moved to the top of the political agenda in most western democracies. While recognising that political agendas are ultimately formulated by strategic actors who are exploiting a particular 'window of opportunity' to respond to structural pressures and advance new topics and ideas in ways that appear to be legitimate (DiMaggio and Powell 1983; Kingdon 1984), we shall point to four structural conditions that seem to have prompted the growing interest in enhancing public innovation: the fiscal crisis, the proliferation of 'wicked problems', the recent focus on policy execution problems, and the globalisation of public governance.

As pointed out by Christopher Hood (2010) in a recent report to the Swedish government, three possible responses are available to elected governments aiming to deal with the global fiscal crisis. First, elected politicians can make strategic decisions about where to cut and where not to cut the public budget in order to make ends meet. This option involves the politicians in a painful and undoubtedly unpopular process of political prioritising. Second, in order to avoid being blamed for making public budget cuts, politicians can instead decide to make across-the-board cuts that reduce public expenditure by the same percentage in all areas of government. This means that the hard choice about how to cut public budgets is devolved to public managers who will be forced either to limit the citizens' access to public welfare or to reduce the number of public employees and make the remaining workforce work harder. None of these strategies is very attractive because they all reduce the availability and quality of public welfare provision.

The third response to the fiscal crisis is to enhance public innovation. Public innovation is an attractive alternative to both politically prioritised spending cuts and blind across-the-board cuts because it breaks with the idea that lower expenditure will inevitably lead to less public welfare. Despite the fact that public innovation will sometimes foster better, but also more expensive, solutions, it holds the promise that it can give us more and better solutions and welfare services for the same, and even fewer, public resources. For example, approximately 5.5 offenders can be electronically monitored for the cost of incarcerating one offender behind bars, and the lower costs are matched by a higher service quality since the offenders can stay with their families and maintain their jobs while serving their sentences (Eggers, Baker, and Vaughn 2012).

Another structural condition that calls for innovation has been pointed out by governance researchers such as Jan Kooiman (2003) and Joop Koppenjan and Erik-Hans Klijn (2004). They argue that public authorities face a growing number of 'wicked problems' that cannot be solved by standard solutions or by increasing the public funding of the existing measures. Wicked problems are complicated to solve because there is uncertainty about the precise nature of the problem, disagreement about how to solve it, conflicting demands concerning the solution, and difficulties with measuring the effects of new policy initiatives (Rittel and Webber 1973; see also Chapter 10 in this volume). Wicked problems such as child obesity, gang-related crime, long-term unemployment, airport expansion, and climate change are all characterised by a high level of complexity. Any efforts to solve them must take this complexity into account and aim to find new and creative solutions that meet the conflicting demands while mobilising popular and political support. For example, the problem of how to build low-cost and high-quality dwellings within a short time horizon for people living in an area devastated by a huge earthquake was solved by quickly building the ground floor of houses that could later be completed by the homeowners themselves by adding a second floor and a new roof.

A third structural condition relates to the fact that political-administrative systems in advanced industrialised societies suffer from persistent policy execution problems that are evidenced by the failure to implement new policy designs. These problems are by no means new, but they become more and more visible due to the introduction of elaborate systems of performance management. For a long time, policy execution problems have been viewed as a result of implementation problems deriving from the resistance of professional front-line personnel to new policy initiatives (Pressman and Wildavsky 1973; Lipsky 1980). The solution recommended by New Public Management is to use a combination of sticks, carrots, and sermons in order to motivate the front line to implement the new policy designs in the way that they are meant to be implemented.

However, an interesting new explanation for the persistence of policy execution problems is that the real problem lies with the policy design rather than with the front-line personnel. The reason new policies are not implemented is often that they are poorly designed. The lack of communication between the political and administrative policy-makers and those who are in charge of implementing the new policies and have a regular contact with the relevant and affected actors results in inadequate and flawed policy designs that rest on insufficient knowledge about the nature of the problem and the feasibility of different problem-solving strategies (Macmillan and Cain 2010). In the absence of relevant and practical knowledge about the nature of a problem and what might help to solve it, public policies are designed on the basis of a mixture of tradition and political ideology, neither of which is particularly helpful in a rapidly changing world.

If this diagnosis is right, the only way to solve the increasingly visible policy execution problems is to produce better policy designs through a sustained dialogue between policy-makers and service providers. In light of the attempt by New Public Management to separate political–strategic 'steering' from administrative 'rowing' (Osborne and Gaebler 1992), the facilitation of such a dialogue will require the development of new and innovative governance procedures. In Denmark the government has experimented with the creation of 'governance labs' in which decision-makers from all levels of government, from ministries to front-line personnel, are brought together to discuss particular problems and challenges and find novel solutions that can be implemented and will work in practice.

Finally, national governments are currently facing a growing number of problems and challenges that they cannot solve on their own and that therefore require global forms of governance. Examples of such problems are human trafficking, terrorism, pandemics, financial instability, food safety, and global warming. The mushrooming of transnational institutions and networks indicates that there is increasing recognition of the need to develop regional and other forms of transnational governance arenas among governments and sometimes also NGOs. However, recent experiences attest to the fact that it is difficult to find the right institutional set-up for producing efficient governance solutions (Zürn 2000; Djelic and Sahlin-Andersson 2006; Enderlein, Wälti, and Zürn 2010). The problem is that the transnational forms of governance challenge the fundamental feature of political institutionalisation in the 19th and 20th centuries: the sovereignty of the nation state. Hence, the field of transnational governance faces a mounting demand for organisational innovations that both enhance the cross-national capacity to effectively deal with international and borderless policy problems and leave considerable space for national self-determination. The Open Method of Coordination developed in the European Union is an interesting example, as it facilitates the development of common policy goals and policy guidelines backed by naming and shaming procedures while insisting that nation states are fully responsible for reaching the goals and solving the problems.

As we have seen, the four structural governance challenges call for different kinds of public innovation: the economic crisis calls for public service innovation; the proliferation of wicked problems calls for policy innovation; the policy execution problems call for procedural innovation of the policy-making process; and the growth in global governance ambitions requires organisational innovation. Exactly how political and administrative policy entrepreneurs will react to these structural challenges is difficult to say and subject to variation, depending on differing social and political conditions. However, the costs of failing to respond to the structural challenges will grow over time, and the pressure on public authorities to begin the uncertain innovation journey will increase.

Collaboration as driver of public innovation

Demands for a more innovative public sector were first voiced in and by the New Public Management reform programmes that emerged in the USA, the UK, and the Antipodes in the late 1980s and early 1990s and gradually spread to the rest of the western world (Osborne and Gaebler 1992; Pollitt and

Bouckaert 2004). New Public Management found academic inspiration in public choice theory that criticised large public bureaucracies for being ossified and resistant to change, partly because of a lack of demand-side pressures and strategic leadership, and partly because of the presence of inflexible rules and strong coalitions between users and professionals (Downs 1967; Niskanen 1987). Enhanced competition between public agencies and private contractors and a stronger emphasis on strategic management, which could ensure a flexible usage of rules and resources, were introduced in order to enhance efficiency through rationalisation and public innovation (Hood 1991).

Two decades of New Public Management have contributed to making the public sector more flexible and competitive; nevertheless hierarchical and compartmentalised systems of rules and regulations still hamper innovation. Furthermore, research shows that the forms of strategic leadership and performance management that New Public Management brought about tend to establish new barriers to innovation as public organisations become more risk averse (Hartley 2005; Moynihan 2008; Ansell and Torfing 2014). Finally, whereas public–private competition might enhance the pressure to innovate, it does not provide a method for producing innovation and often acts as a barrier to knowledge exchange (Hartley, Sørensen, and Torfing 2013).

Due to the barriers to innovation in traditional public hierarchies and the shortcomings of New Public Management, there has been a growing interest in collaboration as a driver of public innovation (O'Toole 1997; Newman, Raine, and Skelcher 2001; Nambisan 2008; Bommert 2010). The interest in collaborative innovation is shared by distinguished scholars in the field of business innovation who claim that strategic inter-firm alliances and network-based innovation systems are important drivers of innovation in private firms (Lundvall 1985; Teece 1992; Powell and Grodal 2005). The argument behind the recommendation for collaborative innovation in both the public and private sectors is that collaboration among a variety of relevant actors disturbs embedded worldviews and stimulates the development of new, more complex, and holistic understandings of the problems or challenges at hand. Collaboration also facilitates knowledge sharing and enables the cross-fertilisation of ideas. Finally, it improves the estimation of benefits and risks of alternative solutions, ensures the mobilisation of relevant resources, and produces a sense of ownership of bold ideas, which enhances the chances of their successful implementation and diffusion (Sørensen and Torfing 2011).

One of the best examples of collaborative innovation from our own studies in the strategic research project on Collaborative Innovation in the Public Sector (CLIPS) is the creation of a local Resource Centre that offers leisure activities to at-risk youth in a deprived neighbourhood in Copenhagen. The municipality has collaborated with civil society and community organisations to create a much needed service that is provided by a handful of public employees and a large number of volunteers from the local neighbourhood. The local Resource Centre has had multiple effects: crime rates have fallen, the quality of life of local youth has improved, the local community has been empowered, and a new link between generations has been forged. The innovative involvement of local volunteers has cut the cost of running the new Resource Centre, as compared with similar projects (Torfing and Krogh 2013).

When discussing the prospects of collaborative innovation, it is important not to equate collaboration with the attempt to create a total consensus. In fact, the demand for unanimous consent tends to prevent innovation, or at least radical innovation, as it often involves settling on the lowest common denominator that fails to break with common wisdom or established practices. Instead, collaboration alludes to processes through which two or more actors deploy their competences, skills, and resources in transforming a shared object while constructively managing their differences (Gray 1989). Thus, the goal of collaboration is not the formation of an all-encompassing consensus that leaves no residue, but to reach an agreement about how to respond to the problem or challenge at hand. Seen from this perspective, collaborative innovation hinges on the ability to exploit the differences and disputes between the actors as a driver for developing new understandings of the problem and unconventional solutions. In other words, collaboration is a driver of innovation when it helps to reveal the insufficiency of existing strategies and practices and facilitates a creative search for new ones.

Although collaboration has the advantage of bringing together actors with relevant innovation assets (knowledge, ideas, skills, implementation capacity, etc.) across the institutional and organisational boundaries that normally separate them (Bommert 2010), we do not see collaboration as a substitute for other innovation drivers, but rather perceive it as a valuable supplement to hierarchy and competition. While top-down leadership is well suited for putting innovation onto the political agenda and competition provides an incentive for actors to innovate, collaboration provides an efficient method for producing innovations (Hartley, Sørensen, and Torfing 2013). As such, the attempt to spur public innovation in response to the above-mentioned governance challenges is predicated on finding the right combination between hierarchical, competitive, and collaborative forms of governance (Sørensen 2012).

Methods and tools for collaborative innovation

There has been a growing interest in the role and impact of the new forms of interactive governance that tend to supplement and supplant the traditional hierarchical forms of government that are based on imperative commands

(Torfing et al. 2012). The most prominent examples of the new forms of governance are quasi-markets, partnerships, and governance networks. All three forms can be seen as methods and tools for collaborative innovation as they bring together public and private actors in a collaborative process that aims to solve emerging problems and challenges in new ways. However, as we shall see, the scope for innovation in these new forms of governance differs.

Although the three forms of governance tend to combine elements of hierarchy, competition, and collaboration, they all promote collaboration between public authorities and private stakeholders that might help to foster innovative solutions. *Quasi-markets*, for example, aim to contract out public services to private providers that are recruited through open tender. They facilitate collaborative innovation in public service provision to the extent that they are regulated by 'relational contracts' that oblige public purchasers and private providers to engage in ongoing negotiations about the form, content, quality, and payment of the services that are produced and delivered by the private contractor. Whereas the first generation of contracts between public purchasers and private providers provided a detailed and more or less non-negotiable description of the terms for the private contractors' production and delivery of public services that effectively eliminated the possibility of service innovation, the second generation of relational contracts only outlines the basic parameters of the agreement and sets up procedures for recurrent, trust-based negotiations of the nature and form of the services specified in the contract. This kind of contract opens a space for collaborative innovation and is particularly suitable in the case of long-term projects where the conditions change over time and the goal is constant service improvement through incremental innovation (Lubienski 2009). However, the contractual regulation of the collaboration between the public and private actors tends to limit the scope for collaborative innovation in order to ensure a high degree of top-down control and maintain the terms of the original agreement between the public monopsonist and the private providers. Hence, there are limits to what can be negotiated by whom, how, and when. The use of quasi-markets as drivers of public innovation requires that public authorities have the capacity to formulate long-term contracts that, on the one hand, ensure public leadership and control and, on the other hand, leave sufficient room for collaborative innovation.

Partnerships leave more space for collaboration and innovation because they are less tightly regulated. Public–private partnerships (PPPs), through which public authorities form partnerships either with private firms or with civil society organisations, are based on the premise that the partners will work together closely in an attempt to solve more or less explicit governance tasks. The understanding is sometimes codified into a contract that defines the mutual obligations and/or sharing of benefits and risks within the partnership

(Hodge and Greve 2007). However, since the contract is less detailed and less strict, the scope for collaboration is greater due to and is propelled by a desire for mutual gains derived from the exploitation of complementary resources.

Since collaborative partnering is an important source of public innovation, there is an increasing interest in what has been termed 'public–private innovation partnerships' (PPIs). However, the EU rules for contracting with private partners tend to act as a barrier to the establishment of PPIs. Private partners involved in the idea phase may not win the open tender to deliver the service in the implementation phase and therefore risk losing everything that they have invested in the joint innovation process. While the risk of not winning the tender is a serious disincentive for private firms to partner with public authorities, examples of successful PPIs exist. Nonetheless, the development of a clear and transparent procedure for the formation of PPIs may help to overcome present barriers and spur collaborative innovation. The challenge for public authorities when seeking to promote collaborative innovation in partnerships is to find a way of working together with individual private actors while keeping the door open for future collaboration with other private partners.

Governance networks bring together relevant and affected actors in negotiated interaction through which they exchange and/or pool their resources in order to foster more effective, democratic, or innovative solutions to specific governance problems. Governance networks have in common that they are based on the participants' recognition of their mutual dependence, but they tend to differ with regard to their composition, form, and purpose (Sørensen and Torfing 2007). Some governance networks are intra-organisational and comprised of public actors from different levels and offices within the same organisation, whereas others are inter-organisational and may include a number of private stakeholders. Some networks are formal whereas others are informal, and some are exclusive with few participants while others are inclusive and large. Finally, while some networks are merely advisory, others have a delegated autonomy to make important policy decisions.

The innovative potential of governance networks is derived from the sustained collaboration between interdependent actors with different experiences, perspectives, and ideas (Dente, Bobbio, and Spada 2005). The absence of contractual regulations creates a flexible structure within which both the substantial content of the problem and the overall objectives and the rules of the game can be negotiated. Therefore, public authorities who engage in and seek to manage governance networks must have the capacity to influence the negotiated interactions in the network without reverting to traditional forms of command and control. In other words, public managers must be able to meta-govern governance networks (Sørensen and Torfing 2009), for example, through a strategic construction of interdependencies that designate them as key actors in the networks they aim to govern.

In sum, quasi-markets, partnerships, and governance networks represent different institutional designs, which have the varying potential to enhance public innovation by opening a space for multi-actor collaboration in the field of public policy-making and service provision. However, these three forms of interactive governance also call for specific governance capacities on the part of public authorities and public managers.

Barriers to collaborative innovation

Empirical experiences with quasi-markets, partnerships, and governance networks from the last two decades indicate that institutional arenas for collaborative governance play an important role in advancing public innovation while they may also enhance the effectiveness and democratic quality of public governance (Borins 2001; Marcussen and Torfing 2007). Research also identifies barriers, however, that hamper the capacity of interactive governance arrangements to produce collaborative innovation. Three types of barriers appear to be particularly pronounced. The first set concerns the many constraints on collaborative innovation imposed by the traditional bureaucratic organisation of public administration; the second set relates to the risk-aversive culture of public organisations; and the third emanates from the deep-seated role perceptions that prevent public and private actors from engaging in collaborative innovation.

The bureaucratic organisation of public administration imposes several constraints on collaborative innovation. Firstly, the growing number of formal rules and explicit routines, combined with hierarchical steering and a meritocratic career system, tend to reduce the willingness to deviate from the rule book, experiment, and take risks. Secondly, the horizontal compartmentalisation of the public sector into different administrative silos, each of which is populated by different more or less autonomous professions, tends to prevent problem-driven collaboration. Thirdly, the mental and organisational silos in the public sector are sustained by the public budgeting and accounting systems that make each and every public agency responsible for staying within the limits of its budget frame and seldom allocate resources for cross-cutting problem-solving. The elaborate system of performance management also encourages public agencies to focus on meeting their own performance targets rather than spending time collaborating with other agencies. Finally, the development of positive feedback loops between the public services and regulations, the organisational set-up, the competences and skills of the employees, and the expectations and benefits of the users tend to create lock-ins and path dependences that make it very difficult to transform the public sector.

Another set of barriers to collaborative innovation is the lack of an innovation culture that is based on a strategic focus on innovation at the level of public leadership and management, regular feedback from, and dialogue with, users and other stakeholders, stable procedures for exploring and exploiting new ideas, and methods for managing and negotiating risks. The culture of public organisations tends to be highly risk aversive, as there seems to be a general lack of incentives for innovation. Rewards for innovation are few and far between, and an initial dip in performance following the introduction of innovative solutions will be punished by the performance management system. Furthermore, public agencies risk becoming targets of budget cuts if they succeed in producing innovations that make it possible to do more for less.

A final set of barriers to collaborative innovation concerns the deep-seated role perceptions of the public and private actors that prevent them from reaping the fruits of collaboration. Elected politicians often see themselves as sovereign decision-makers who have all the power and all the responsibility and therefore have no need for engaging in time-consuming, tiresome discussions with lay actors. Public administrators tend to see themselves either as technocrats who only trust their own technical knowledge or as professionals who have a privileged insight into what constitutes 'good quality' and 'correct solutions' within their specific domain. Citizens are construed first as weak, passive, and subordinated 'clients', and later as empowered, rational, and demanding 'customers', neither of which are expected to contribute to the production of public governance solutions. Finally, private firms and NGOs are viewed as lobbyists who are expected to pursue their own specific interests rather than contribute to the promotion of the larger public good. All these role perceptions function as barriers to collaborative innovation.

To conclude, the bureaucratic constraints must be removed, an innovative culture must be built, and the role perceptions of the public and private actors must be changed if we want to spur collaborative innovation in the face of mounting challenges that confront the public sector. To enhance innovation, we must transform governance and build new institutional capacities.

Building institutional capacities

Some ground clearing is needed in order to enhance collaborative innovation in the public sector. However, removing the barriers that we have just delineated is not enough. Public authorities will also have to pursue a more positive agenda that focuses on how they can systematically improve the capacity of the public sector to collaborate and innovate. Building and reinforcing institutional capacities that enable the public sector to support and enhance collaborative innovation require reform in five different areas.

Developing public leadership

New Public Management gave public leaders and managers responsibility for developing the public sector and making it more dynamic and efficient. However, the idea that top-level leaders and managers should single-handedly transform the public sector is flawed since there is a limit to the number of creative ideas any given person can have. Even when new ideas emerge, top-down administrative reforms and service innovations are unlikely to succeed due to lack of ownership and outright resistance at the level of implementation. Hence, transformational leadership should give way to post-transformational, distributive leadership that focuses on how public leaders and managers encourage others to take responsibility for transforming public organisations and contributing to policy and service innovation (Parry and Bryman 2006). Top-level public leaders should set the agenda, delegate power, and motivate middle managers and public employees to create more public innovation. Such a move requires a shift from a control-oriented leadership to a more trust-based leadership. The middle managers will also have to change their behaviour since they will be in charge of convening public and private actors with relevant innovation assets, facilitating collaboration by developing a common frame of reference and mediating conflicts, and catalysing innovation by creating appropriate disturbances that force the collaborators to think outside of the box (Ansell and Gash 2007, 2012).

The skills and competences needed to lead and manage processes of collaborative innovation include being good at communicating, developing visionary ideas, and building consensus. Strong technical knowledge, attention to detail, and power are less important. Last but not least, both top-level and middle managers will have to develop skills and tools for managing risks. Innovation is an open-ended search process filled with all kinds of risks that cannot be eliminated, but only managed and negotiated. Risk management and risk negotiation will, therefore, be a key competence for public leaders and managers (Brown and Osborne 2013). Other skills required for managing collaborative innovation include being curious, imaginative, and visionary; having the ability to bring different people together to collaborate in a constructive and forward-looking way; and having the integrity and courage to go against the grain and implement new solutions that break with acquired habits and common knowledge in a particular area.

Changing the institutional structure of public organisations

Public organisations can become more innovative by setting up routines for exploring and exploiting new and creative ideas. This endeavour should be supported by the development of specific tools and procedures for organising and driving innovation processes. Therefore, the structure of public organisations will also need to be changed. Collaborative innovation is likely to thrive in public organisations that disperse decision-making autonomy to the lower hierarchical levels and promote vertical communication and dialogue in order to ensure support for innovative projects at the executive level. In order to facilitate collaborative innovation along the horizontal axis, public organisations should promote the use of skunkworks that aim to create spaces outside, but close to, daily operations. This would permit public employees from different organisations and organisational units to collaborate in order to develop and test new ideas in practice (Eggers and Singh 2009). Hence, we do not necessarily have to abolish specialisation and functional differentiation, but we should find new and unbureaucratic ways to drill holes in the administrative silos and encourage interdepartmental dialogue. Collaborative innovation will also benefit from the development of borderless organisations that open up towards their external environment and invite private actors to participate in collaborative arenas. Finally, the construction of an interorganisational 'cloud' of dedicated change agents with special skills and competences to organise and drive collaborative innovation processes will help public organisations to manage transformative processes despite shortage of policy entrepreneurs and process consultants (Deloitte 2012).

Building a strong innovation culture

Reforms of the organisational structure must be followed by deliberate attempts to build a strong culture of innovation. The first step is to put collaborative innovation at the top of the agenda and insist that public innovation requires a permanent and systematic effort to meet challenges with innovative solutions. The promotion of a broadly communicated innovation agenda should be followed by the development of an executive innovation strategy that defines where the organisation should aim to become a first mover and where it should be a second mover. The next step is to develop and gradually refine common language enabling the members of the organisation to talk about collaborative innovation and understand each other when they aim to develop solutions across professions, administrative units, and organisational boundaries. The common language used to address innovation issues will benefit from the integration of key elements of design thinking that emphasise the importance of designing and testing prototypes at the operational level in constant dialogue with other employees, service users, and private stakeholders (Bason 2010). Following this thinking, methods and routines should be crafted for defining problems and challenges, seeking inspiration, generating new and bold ideas, selecting and testing the most promising ones, and scaling-up and diffusing the innovative solutions that seem to work. The last step is to encourage and reward new and creative inventions, as well as successful attempts to adopt and adapt other organisations' most successful innovations. Public organisations can gain a lot from drawing from other organisations' innovations because they save the development costs while having the full benefit of well-tried solutions. Cultivation of inter-organisational networks that facilitate uploading and downloading of innovative ideas and solutions is important in this regard.

Using human relations management to enhance collaborative innovation

Human relations management can also be used to enhance the capacity for collaborative innovation, for example by enhancing diversity among the employees in terms of gender, age, ethnicity, professional background, etc. Diversity can enhance innovation, especially if there are a sufficient number of boundary-spanners who can facilitate dialogue and act as translators and mediators between groups of employees that have different ways of thinking about and dealing with particular problems. The creation of possibilities for internal mobility amongst the employees has the same effect as increased diversity. Different perspectives challenge and disturb each other and create synergies that spur innovation. It is also important to recruit and nurture creative talents. Public organisations are used to hiring employees who are efficient, reliable, and do things in the right way, but if they want to spur innovation, they will have to recruit and develop creative talents. However, nurturing and retaining creative talents are a huge challenge for public managers because creative and entrepreneurial employees tend to problematise the rules and norms of the organisation, are impatient when it comes to realising new ideas, and bad at collaborating with others. The last human relations tool concerns the organisation of work. Encouragement of problem-driven teamwork with a low degree of structuration tends to spur collaborative innovation. Communities of practice that focus on recurring problems and emerging challenges draw on their common frame of reference and competences and skills to find innovative solutions (Wenger 1998). Yet, while innovation may be facilitated by communities of practice, more radical innovations frequently emerge at the interstices between communities (Swan, Scarbrough, and Robertson 2002). As such, there seem to be good reasons for enhancing collaboration between different communities of practice so that they can challenge and inspire each other, and produce more disruptive innovations.

Advancing new forms of learning

Learning and innovation are two sides of the same coin, but collaborative innovation presupposes the development of new kinds of learning. Mutual learning through which different actors develop, discuss, contest, and revise their understandings, ideas, and visions is important for the development of a common frame of reference that can facilitate collaborative innovation. Reflexive learning that reflects upon and contests common wisdom in the light of new experiences and emerging problems is important for the development of new ideas and solutions that go beyond the existing problem-solving processes based on trial and error (Engeström 2008). However, in order to create more radical innovation, public organisations must find ways to stimulate transformative learning that questions the tacit assumptions underlying our existing paradigms and aim to understand and comprehend the unknown by inventing new narratives and visions (Mezirow 2000).

Conclusion

In this chapter we have shown that new governance challenges require the public sector to become more innovative and that public innovation can be spurred by collaboration. Our argument calls for further rapprochement between the growing research on public innovation and the burgeoning research on collaborative governance. Until now, these two bodies of literature have developed side by side without much interaction. However, it is obvious that both governance researchers and students of public innovation can learn from each other and develop a new interdisciplinary field of research that focuses on how the barriers to collaborative innovation can be eliminated and new institutional capacities supporting collaborative innovation can be developed.

The efforts of top-level public leaders and managers play a key role in developing a public sector that is more capable of meeting new problems and challenges with innovative solutions that are fashioned in and through multi-actor collaboration. However, as we have indicated above, their leadership role must be transformed since the role prescribed by New Public Management will not be appropriate. We no longer need the transformative leaders of the 1980s and 1990s who used their integrity, charisma, and entrepreneurial spirit to turn around ineffective and ossified public organisations. Instead we need public leaders and managers who can recruit, motivate, and support teams of public and private innovators that bring together different kinds of knowledge, perspectives, and ideas in the pursuit of public innovation.

Future attempts to reap the benefits of collaborative innovation call for an alternative to the forms of public governance associated with New Public Management. Hence, in order to enhance collaborative innovation, public–private competition should be replaced with public–private collaboration, changing the focus on inputs and outputs to a focus on processes and outcomes. A transformation of public governance along these lines of thinking is recommended by proponents of New Public Governance (Osborne 2006, 2010). New Public Governance is by no means a fully fledged governance paradigm, but it incorporates new and emerging trends that must be further developed if we are to succeed in boosting public innovation.

References

Ansell, C., and Gash, A. (2007). 'Collaborative Governance in Theory and Practice', *Journal of Public Administration Research and Theory*, 18(4): 543–71.

Ansell, C., and Gash, A. (2012). 'Stewards, Mediators and Catalysts: Toward a Model of Collaborative Leadership', *The Innovation Journal*, 17(1): 1–21.

Ansell, C., and Torfing, J. (eds) (2014). *Public Innovation through Collaboration and Design*. Abingdon and New York: Routledge.

Australian National Audit Office (2009). *Innovation in the Public Sector: Enabling Better Performance, Driving New Directions*. Canberra: Australian National Audit Office.

Bason, C. (2010). *Leading Public Sector Innovation*. London: Polity Press.

Bommert, B. (2010). 'Collaborative Innovation in the Public Sector', *International Public Management Review*, 11(1): 15–33.

Borins, S. (2001). 'Encouraging Innovation in the Public Sector', *Journal of Intellectual Capital*, 2(3): 310–9.

Brown, L., and Osborne, S. P. (2013). 'Risk and Innovation: Towards a Framework for Risk Governance in Public Services', *Public Management Review*, 15(2): 186–208.

Cohen, M. D., March, J. G., and Olsen, J. P. (1972). 'A Garbage Can Model of Organizational Choice', *Administrative Science Quarterly*, 17(1): 1–25.

Deloitte (2012). *GovCloud: The Future of Government Work*. Washington, DC: Deloitte.

Dente, B., Bobbio, L., and Spada, A. (2005). 'Government or Governance of Urban Innovation?' *DIPS*, 162(3): 41–52.

DiMaggio, P., and Powell, W. W. (1983). 'The Iron Cage Revisited: Institutional Isomorphism and Collective Rationality in Organizational Fields', *American Sociological Review*, 48(2): 147–60.

Djelic, M.-L. and Sahlin-Andersson, K. (eds) (2006). *Transnational Governance: Institutional Dynamics of Regulation*. Cambridge, New York: Cambridge University Press.

Downs, A. (1967). *Inside Bureaucracy*. Boston: Little Brown.

Eggers, W. D., and Singh, S. K. (2009). *The Public Innovator's Playbook: Nurturing Bold Ideas in Government.* Washington, DC: Harvard Kennedy School.

Eggers, W. D., Baker, L., and Vaughn, A. (2012). *The Public Sector, Disrupted: How Disruptive Innovation Can Help Government Achieve More for Less.* Washington, DC: Deloitte.

Enderlein, H., Wälti, S. and Zürn, M. (eds) (2010). *Handbook on Multi-Level Governance.* Cheltenham, Northampton: Edward Elgar.

Engeström, Y. (2008). *From Teams to Knots: Activity-Theoretical Studies of Collaboration and Learning at Work.* Cambridge, New York: Cambridge University Press.

Gray, B. (1989). *Collaborating: Finding Common Ground for Multiparty Problems.* San Francisco: Jossey-Bass.

Halvorsen, T., Hauknes, J., Miles, I., and Røste, R. (2005). 'On the Difference between Public and Private Sector Innovation'. Publin Report D9. Oslo: Publin.

Hartley, J. (2005). 'Innovation in Governance and Public Service: Past and Present', *Public Money and Management,* 25(1): 27–34.

Hartley, J., Sørensen, E., and Torfing, J. (2013). 'Collaborative Innovation: A Viable Alternative to Market-competition and Organizational Entrepreneurship?' *Public Administration Review,* 73(6): 821–30.

HM Government Cabinet Office (2010). *The Civil Service Reform Plan.* London: HM Government.

Hodge, G. A., and Greve, C. (2007). 'Public-Private Partnerships: An International Performance Review', *Public Administration Review,* 67(3): 545–58.

Hood, C. (1991). 'A Public Management for All Seasons?' *Public Administration,* 69(1): 3–19.

Hood, C. (2010). *Reflections on Public Service Reform in a Cold Fiscal Climate.* London: 2020 Public Services Trust.

Kingdon, J. W. (1984). *Agendas, Alternatives, and Public Policies.* Boston: Little Brown.

Kooiman, J. (2003). *Governing as Governance.* Thousand Oaks: Sage.

Koppenjan, J., and Klijn, E.-H. (2004). *Managing Uncertainties in Networks: Public Private Controversies.* London: Routledge.

Lipsky, M. (1980). *Street-Level Bureaucracy: Dilemmas of the Individual in Public Services.* New York: Russell Sage Foundation.

Lubienski, C. (2009). 'Do Quasi-markets Foster Innovation in Education? A Comparative Perspective'. OECD Education Working Papers No 25. Paris: OECD.

Lundvall, B.-Å. (1985). *Product Innovation and User-Producer Interaction.* Aalborg: Aalborg University Press.

Macmillan, P., and Cain, T. (2010). *Closing the Gap: Eliminating the Disconnect between Policy Design and Execution.* Washington, DC: Deloitte.

Marcussen, M. and Torfing, J. (eds) (2007). *Democratic Network Governance in Europe.* Basingstoke, New York: Palgrave Macmillan.

Mezirow, J. (ed.) (2000). *Learning as Transformation: Critical Perspectives on a Theory in Progress.* San Francisco: Jossey-Bass.

Moynihan, D. P. (2008). *The Dynamics of Performance Management: Constructing Information and Reform.* Washington, DC: Georgetown University Press.

Mulgan, G., and Albury, D. (2003). *Innovation in the Public Sector*. London: Prime Minister's Strategy Unit.

Nambisan, S. (2008). *Transforming Government through Collaborative Innovation*. Washington, DC: IBM Center for Business of Government.

Newman, J., Raine, J., and Skelcher, C. (2001). 'Transforming Local Government: Innovation and Modernization', *Public Money and Management*, 21(2): 61–8.

Niskanen, W. A. (1987). 'Bureaucracy', in C. K. Rowley, and G. Tullock (eds), *Democracy and Public Choice: Essays in Honor of Gordon Tullock*. Oxford, New York: Blackwell, 135–40.

O'Toole, L. J. (1997). 'Implementing Public Innovations in Network Settings', *Administration and Society*, 29(2): 115–38.

OECD (Organisation for Economic Co-operation and Development) (2010). *The OECD Innovation Strategy: Getting a Head Start on Tomorrow*. Paris: OECD.

Osborne, D., and Gaebler, T. (1992). *Reinventing Government: How the Entrepreneurial Spirit is Transforming the Public Sector*. Reading: Addison-Wesley.

Osborne, S. P. (2006). 'The New Public Governance?' *Public Management Review*, 8(3): 377–87.

Osborne, S. P. (ed.) (2010). *The New Public Governance? Emerging Perspectives on the Theory and Practice of Public Governance*. London, New York: Routledge.

Parry, K. W., and Bryman, A. (2006). 'Leadership in Organizations', in S. Clegg, C. Hardy, T. B. Lawrence, and Nord, Walter, R. (eds), *The Sage Handbook of Organization Studies*. 2nd edn. London, Thousand Oaks: Sage Publications, 447–68.

Pollitt, C., and Bouckaert, G. (2004). *Public Management Reform: A Comparative Analysis*. Oxford, New York: Oxford University Press.

Polsby, N. W. (1984). *Political Innovation in America: The Politics of Policy Initiation*. New Haven: Yale University Press.

Powell, W. W., and Grodal, S. (2005). 'Networks of Innovators', in J. Fagerberg, D. C. Mowery, and R. R. Nelson (eds), *The Oxford Handbook of Innovation*. Oxford, New York: Oxford University Press, 56–85.

Pressman, J. L., and Wildavsky, A. B. (1973). *Implementation: How Great Expectations in Washington Are Dashed in Oakland*. Berkeley: University of California Press.

Rittel, H. W. J., and Webber, M. M. (1973). 'Dilemmas in a General Theory of Planning', *Policy Sciences*, 4(2): 155–69.

Roberts, N. C., and King, P. J. (1996). *Transforming Public Policy: Dynamics of Policy Entrepreneurship and Innovation*. 1st edn. San Francisco, CA: Jossey-Bass Publishers.

Sørensen, E. (2012). 'Governance and Innovation in the Public Sector', in D. Levy-Faur (eds), *The Oxford Handbook of Governance*. New York: Oxford University Press, 215–27.

Sørensen, E. and Torfing, J. (eds) (2007). *Theories of Democratic Network Governance*. Basingstoke: Palgrave Macmillan.

Sørensen, E., and Torfing, J. (2009). 'Making Governance Networks Effective and Democratic through Metagovernance', *Public Administration*, 87(2): 234–58.

Sørensen, E., and Torfing, J. (2011). 'Enhancing Collaborative Innovation in the Public Sector', *Administration and Society*, 43(8): 842–68.

Sørensen, E. and Torfing, J. (eds) (2012). *Collaborative Innovation in the Public Sector*. Special Issue 'The Innovation Journal' 17(1).

Swan, J., Scarbrough, H., and Robertson, M. (2002). 'The Construction of "Communities of Practice" in the Management of Innovation', *Management Learning*, 33(4): 477–96.

Teece, D. J. (1992). 'Competition, Cooperation, and Innovation', *Journal of Economic Behaviour and Organization*, 18(1): 1–25.

Torfing, J., and Krogh, A. H. (2013). *Samarbejdsdrevet innovation i bandeindsatsen*. Copenhagen: DJOEF Publishers.

Torfing, J., Peters, B. G., Pierre, J., and Sørensen, E. (2012). *Interactive Governance: Advancing the Paradigm*. Oxford, New York: Oxford University Press.

Wenger, E. (1998). *Communities of Practice: Learning, Meaning, and Identity*. Cambridge, New York: Cambridge University Press.

Zürn, M. (2000). 'Democratic Governance Beyond the Nation-State: The EU and Other International Institutions', *European Journal of International Relations*, 6(2): 183–221.

14

Capacity, Innovation, and their Interaction in Multi-stakeholder Sustainability Initiatives

Kira Matus

Introduction

Over the past 15 years, there has been an explosion of multi-stakeholder sustainability initiatives (MSIs)—programmes that include voluntary standards and certifications (both third party and second party, or firm/industry led), sustainability roundtables, and a variety of venues to share best practices. This trend is part of a larger move, as described by a number of scholars, towards systems of 'governance', and away from more traditional systems of government when it comes to the regulation of natural resources, the environment, and their impact on livelihoods and quality of life (Cashore 2002; Falkner 2003). Many regulatory scholars place these initiatives on one end of a spectrum of regulatory tools whose other end would be command-and-control-style policies (with market-based mechanisms someplace in between) (Matus 2010; Roberts 2011).

There have been a number of explanations for the increasing popularity of these types of regulatory approaches, including arguments that they are better suited to deal with transboundary issues, allow for the costs to be borne by those who value the benefits, and are more able to perform in areas where more traditional regulatory capacity is less able to deliver environmental protection, resource management, and social and economic improvements (see also Krisch's chapter in this volume). Thus, one of the major arguments advanced in support of private governance systems is not that they are the best or the only solution, but rather that they are especially well suited to operate when the technical and financial capacities of the state are insufficient to support a public, domestic programme. The multi-stakeholder, expert-based process for standard development and use of independent third-party certifiers may also confer an increased level of legitimacy around the sustainability profile of a given certified product.

Another key argument in favour of non-state sustainability governance regimes is that they provide important venues for innovation—technical, administrative, and regulatory—in ways that would be difficult in traditional regulatory systems. At best, they are (or it is argued that they could be) more nimble, flexible, and responsive; they can encourage programmes of continuous improvement, and may be better served to deal with the complex challenges presented by human–environmental systems. The ability to both capture and cultivate innovation is part of this argued flexibility.

The reality of whether MSIs can fill capacity gaps, as well as act as laboratories for technical and regulatory innovation, has been complex, and at times problematic (Auld, Gulbrandsen, and McDermott 2008; Auld 2010). In fact, capacity and innovation are highly interwoven features of this system. These systems themselves require different types of capacities (technical, administrative, and authoritative) from a wide range of actors, which range from small, local farmers, and firms, to large enterprises, multinational corporations, a variety of government actors, third-party bodies, supply chain actors, and consumers spanning major retailers and individual households. Innovation itself, including successful learning, as well as dissemination and uptake of new technologies and approaches, requires a great deal of technical and managerial capacity on the part of developers and adopters (Matus et al. 2012).

Most work evaluating the impacts of standards, certifications, and other private governance systems for sustainability has rightly focused on the direct impacts on sustainable development outcomes—improved livelihoods, social conditions, and environmental quality (including water quality, soil quality, and biodiversity). Still, there is a growing recognition that these systems have a wider set of indirect impacts that may have larger repercussions than the more commonly evaluated direct metrics (Steering Committee of the State-of-Knowledge Assessment of Standards and Certification 2012). This chapter will explore two mechanisms—capacity and innovation—and the way that these two elements are connected and can reinforce, or undermine, each other. The next section of this chapter will consider what 'capacity' means in the context of governance systems that operate outside, or parallel to, more conventional government regulatory systems. This includes the kinds of capacities, as well as whose capacities, these systems require for success. It also includes how these systems may impact, for better or for worse, capacities of different actors over time. The third section will then explore the different kinds of innovation that are demanded, but also result from non-state systems of governance for sustainability. And finally, the chapter will conclude by examining what is known about the relationship between the two, and how both capacity and innovation are important impacts and determinants of efforts to better govern human–environmental systems.

Capacity—whose, and what types?

One of the long-standing challenges of environmental governance is that many key problems cross political boundaries, from watersheds that span multiple localities, fisheries in international waters, to global atmospheric issues such as the ozone layer and climate change. Beyond the inherently transboundary nature of particular ecosystems, there is also a variety of challenges from globalisation, which have accelerated trends in natural resource extraction (with all of the potentially negative impacts associated with these activities) to be used someplace far away and then disposed of someplace else altogether. Thus, the environmental impacts of consumption behaviour in one part of the world may have other impacts in areas distant in space, time, or both.

This has long been recognised as a strain on the regulatory capacities of governments on a variety of levels. One of the most obvious challenges has come from the international arena, where legal institutions are less well established than at the national level, and where formal, binding agreements can take years (or decades) to emerge. Even then, they may lack the authority to compel translation into national law. Many national governments have only limited abilities to influence many of these processes, as has been well demonstrated in the latest round of climate negotiations, where the nations facing the greatest impacts often have the weakest voice and influence in the proceedings. Scholars, practitioners, and regulators have all raised concerns about the capacity of the international governance system to develop, enforce, and maintain regulatory programmes that are able to successfully deal with transboundary issues of sustainability.

There is a second capacity issue in this sphere, which is not unique to sustainability problems: the variation in national and local regulatory capacity in critical areas. Regulation rests upon five core activities: (1) the decision to set standards in a problem area, (2) the creation of the standard, (3) the process of gathering information about the regulated entities and feeding it back into standard setting and enforcement, (4) enforcement of the standards, and (5) behavioural change on the part of those subject to regulation. In certification, the existence of systems that can perform all five functions is seen as an issue in developing countries that are heavily economically dependent on natural resource extraction. Some of the more established systems of standards, certification, and labelling, such as the Forest Stewardship Council (FSC), Fairtrade,

Table 14.1. Examples of multi-stakeholder initiatives

Organisation	Programme description
Forest Stewardship Council (FSC)	Founded in 1994, the FSC is a standard and ecolabel system that focuses on sustainable forestry management practices. As of November 2013, over 187 million ha of forest worldwide have been certified to FSC standards.
Marine Stewardship Council (MSC)	Founded in 1997, MSC is a standard and ecolabel system that focuses on sustainable seafood. As of 2013, over 10% of the global wild harvest of fish came from MSC-certified fisheries.
Rainforest Alliance (RA)	Founded in 1987, the Rainforest Alliance is focused on the preservation of biodiversity and sustainable livelihoods. It has standards for agriculture (cattle, cocoa, coffee, flowers, fruits, tea, and palm oil), forestry, and tourism.
International Federation of Organic Agriculture Movement (IFOAM)	Organic certifications focus on sustainable agriculture practices. Organic certifications are nationally based, and some are government run, while others are private. The umbrella organisation for national programmes is the International Federation of Organic Agriculture Movement (IFOAM), which was founded in 1972.
Fairtrade International	Founded in 1997, Fairtrade International (FLO) joined up a number of nationally-based fair trade organisations, some in existence since the 1950s, whose aim is to create better equity in international trade, with a focus on vulnerable and marginalised producers and workers. Global sales of Fairtrade-labeled products were €3.4 billion in 2008.
LEED	Founded in 1993, the US Green Building Council develops and runs the Leadership in Energy & Environmental Design (LEED) standard and label. The first LEED standards were promulgated in 2000, and as of 2012, there were 102,742 participating projects (9.9 billion square feet).

and the Marine Stewardship Council (MSC), were designed, at least in part, to address the real challenges of environmental protection in less developed, often southern nations (see Table 14.1 for more examples of these organisations). Many of the countries targeted by these programmes have limited capacity, financial and technical, to build rigorous programmes to provide environmental protection. China is well known for having, on paper, some of the most advanced and forward-thinking environmental protection laws in existence. But the actual administration of these programmes has been challenging, due to political and organisational structures, limited resources, and varied local enforcement (Economy 2004). While the US Environmental Protection Agency (EPA) has nearly 19,000 employees, China's Ministry of Environmental Protection (MEP) has only a few hundred employees at the national level (U.S. Census Bureau 2011).

Finally, environmental regulation can require technical capacity on the part of the regulated. For many environmental programmes, this translates to the need for expertise at very fine levels—farm, fisherman, factory, retailer—in order to ensure compliance with various technical standards. This has proven to be a challenge in many parts of the world, both developed and developing. While more sophisticated regulatory systems are able to provide active systems of guidance (agricultural and technical extension programmes, nationally supported research agendas, financial support for R&D and investment), these sorts of support are not universally available. Inability to translate standards into practice, even in the face of robust administration and enforcement, is another significant barrier to effective environmental governance.

In theory, private governance systems should be well placed to deal with these sorts of local, national, and international capacity gaps. For example, part of the Kyoto Protocol included a programme called the Clean Development Mechanism (CDM). The goal of CDM was to encourage developed nations to invest in clean technologies in developing nations, in return for emissions reduction credits. Many aspects of the programme were initially controversial, and investor willingness to participate quickly evaporated. In response, the World Wildlife Fund spearheaded the creation of the CDM Gold Standard programme. CDM Gold has been effective in allowing the CDM to operate by addressing key problems that arose from the international agreement that established the programme, without requiring a long, and potentially ineffective, international renegotiation (Steering Committee of the State-of-Knowledge Assessment of Standards and Certification 2012: 78).

In order to play a role in filling capacity gaps, private governance systems must perform tangible regulatory functions. Fundamentally, the capacity to enact regulation involves the use of resources. These include financial resources, organisational resources, authority, and knowledge (Hood 2007; Howlett 2011). Non-governmental systems act as a transfer mechanism which allows for the movement of key resources to areas where they are needed without facing the geographical and institutional restraints faced by governments. For private systems, which exist largely outside formal government structures, financial, organisational, and knowledge resources are dominant. Unlike nation states, such private systems have little in the way of formal authority or coercive power. Their appeal relies on the benefits they confer on participants, largely though market incentives or the transfer of knowledge and expertise.

This transfer of resources and capacity can be seen in the structures and activities of many of the leading agricultural, voluntary third-party certification programmes, such as the FSC, the MSC, Rainforest Alliance, and Fairtrade. These certification programmes have organisational structures that include international representation from multiple stakeholders. Standard-setting activities include technical experts, and the organisations work extensively with trained external auditors to ensure compliance. When farmers or firms engage in these programmes, the organisational and informational resources of the programme are a large determinant of successful implementation. Knowledge and organisational resources, in turn, have a large impact on the overall administrative capacity of these programmes, which need to be able to engage with producers who agree to adhere to their standards, and also to adjust and adapt the standards to deal with changing contexts as they grow in geographic scope and overall scale.

How effective are these sustainability certifications at transferring resources and capacities from the developed to the developing world, as many intended? Studies of the uptake and impacts of the oldest and most developed of these systems, which were largely focused on natural resources (agriculture and fisheries), has shown that despite their efforts, the largest initial uptake often occurred in areas that already have well-established regulatory capacity. For example, only 17 per cent of FSC-certified forests were in tropical areas as of 2006 (Cashore et al. 2006), and as of 2012, North America and Europe account for 83 per cent of FSC-certified forests. Canada had the largest area of forest land covered by certification, and Brazil, which has the highest certified forest acreage in the southern hemisphere, has just 15 per cent of the Canadian total (FSC 2012). Similarly, the majority of MSC-certified fisheries are in Europe and North America (Marine Stewardship Council). This calls into question the extent to which private governance is currently able to enhance the sustainable use of natural resources in areas that do not already have strong environmental regulatory capacity.

The case of FSC certification in Bolivia provides interesting material for exploring the interaction of traditional regulatory capacity, local/firm capacity, and certification. Bolivia has been a leader in the certification of tropical forests. As of 2004, Bolivia accounted for 38 per cent of FSC-certified tropical forests, and 60 per cent of its timber for export was certified (Ebeling and Yasué 2009). This, on the face of it, presents a bit of a puzzle. Bolivia has significantly greater uptake of forest certification than other countries in Latin America, such as Ecuador, despite being poorer and having higher levels of corruption (Ebeling and Yasué 2009). Yet closer inspection shows, among other factors, greater capacity at both the government and firm level than in Ecuador. For example, Bolivia introduced a stringent Forest Act, whose provisions were very close to FSC, reducing the additional cost of FSC compliance for firms. The Bolivian Forestry Superintendence is relatively effective, and has limited corruption. Furthermore, the Bolivian forestry industry is dominated by a small number of large, exporting firms with at least some (but in many cases significant) awareness of FSC and other certification programmes, and their value in key export markets like Europe. Finally, at the same time as the Forest Act came into force, extension and capacity-building programmes were undertaken by NGOs, which helped many producers achieve Bolivian legal requirements along with certification requirements (Nebela et al. 2005; Ebeling and Yasué 2009). What this case indicates, at least on a preliminary basis, is that countries with stronger regulatory and firm capacity were better able to engage in certification activities.

Beyond agriculture, one major area where non-governmental certification programmes have advanced recently is the textile industry. Many of the leaders in this space have been in upmarket, developed world firms with strong sustainability values. The Sustainable Apparel Coalition (SAC)—a large coalition of major brands representing approximately 30 per cent of the global apparel and footwear supply chain—is in the process of developing an industry-wide voluntary standard, the Higg Index. The goal of the Higg Index is to help firms reduce the quantity of material and energy used in manufacturing, improve the quality of their products and production processes (e.g. reduce toxicity), and improve the livelihoods of those employed in manufacturing.

The current version of the index, Higg Index 1.0, jointly developed by some of the SAC's members, allows brand comparison based on environmental performance of apparel products, and pushes to have 'a single, much simpler and more effective standard for [the] industry' (Chouinard, Ellison, and Ridgeway 2011). Future versions are expected to include footwear products, and social and labour impacts. The SAC is also considering developing an index verification process or protocol (Allwood 2006; Chouinard, Ellison, and Ridgeway 2011; Golden, Subramanian, and Zimmerman 2011; LeBlanc 2012; Steering Committee of the State-of-Knowledge Assessment of Standards and Certification 2012; Sustainable Apparel Coalition [website]). While this is an interesting initiative, which could have a significant effect on an industry with considerable environmental and social impacts, major capacity challenges still exist. The firms signing on to the Higg Index are large, multinational firms. By contrast, their suppliers are typically located in less developed countries, where firms fight for the tiniest advantage and where investment in environmental and social aspects of production is limited by both technical and financial capacity. This problem is present not just in the firms that are involved in the processing of fibres, weaving of cloth, and cutting and assembling of clothing, but even in the chemical firms that produce the dyes, pigments, and finishing chemicals that are used in very large quantities in the industry.

Certification programmes encounter a number of capacity challenges, including the ability of the organisations that create and manage them to develop and adapt appropriate baseline standards; the ability to adapt these standards to different local contexts (as well as to expand scope to different kinds of fisheries, forests, supply chains, crops, etc.); and even their own access to resources. Due to their voluntary nature, certification programmes also must grapple with the ability of adopters to adhere to the technical demands of their standards. Overall, organisational capacity to undertake regulatory activities, such as monitoring and enforcement, is closely related to the availability of financial resources.

The capacity of different types of actors to engage in certification and other types of voluntary programmes has proven to be an important area of consideration for these programmes. The capacity of the regulated to comply with regulations (and the cost of this compliance) is always a consideration. However, in voluntary systems, capacity of the target group is a key consideration in how the standards are set, and their eventual effectiveness. The need to ensure enough uptake to make the programme viable can require setting standards at a level that may be too low to have the desired environmental and social impacts (Steering Committee of the State-of-Knowledge Assessment of Standards and Certification 2012). Unlike compulsory regulation, there is no direct authority that can be brought to bear to make firms invest in the capacity required to comply; instead, incentives and aid often need to be supplied.

The issue of the technical capacity of the regulated has become even more complex as these non-governmental programmes have moved beyond primary production, and into manufactured supply chains. For example, products in the electronics space involve global supply chains where firms are contracting and subcontracting to a large number of firms. Thus, ensuring the compliance of all actors, or even having data on the practices employed by these suppliers, can be challenging.

Organisationally, some programmes have struggled to ensure a supply of trained auditors, especially in developing countries (Steering Committee of the State-of-Knowledge Assessment of Standards and Certification 2012). The auditing component is especially crucial for non-governmental systems. The legitimacy of the various programmes relies on consistent, reputable decisions by these groups, as they provide the enforcement and information feedback functions of the system. But as certification programmes grow, it has been hard to maintain a large enough supply and also deal with the conflicts of interest that can arise when the groups paying the auditors (firms, farmers, etc.) have different interests than the certification organisations. Auditors are also an important link in many systems because they often have the closest relationship with the actors undergoing certification. As such, they have, in some cases, become de facto extension agents (since they have an interest in helping their clients secure, and continue to adhere to, certification).

Financial resources also play a role in the capacity of these systems to be successful regulatory systems. The first generation of business models for certification programmes focused on using the willingness of consumers to pay a price premium for certified products to pay the costs of implementing and managing these systems, thus transferring financial resources from richer areas to those with fewer financial resources to invest in environmentally responsible practices. Since these programmes are private, and cannot rely on state support, they also require sources of revenues. The ability of these programmes to be financially self-sustaining has been a challenge, and many of them, including the FSC and the MSC, have relied heavily on philanthropic donations, especially in the early years of the programmes when fees from certification and label rights, and other income sources were minimal. The ISEAL Alliance, a global membership organisation for sustainability certifications, has identified financing as the number-one challenge facing its members, in terms of ensuring the viability of these programmes (Steering Committee of the State-of-Knowledge Assessment of Standards and Certification 2012: 13, 17).

A final consideration is the impacts of individual systems on other forms of governance, both public and private. In reality, certification and other private governance systems are never the sole regulatory institution active in a given area. There is a variety of public and private governance activities that overlap in different ways. As will be discussed later in this chapter, innovations in these systems of governance, as well as technical innovations, may in fact lead to direct capacity improvements, which could also spill over into other firms, farms, and government institutions that are not direct participants in these programmes. Many of the certifications overlap—it is not unheard of for coffee growers to be certified by two or more independent sustainability certification programmes. This means that private systems may be in competition with each other—and can be supported or undermined by traditional regulatory statutes as well.

There is some evidence that capacity spillovers are more than just a theoretical benefit. The FSC in Bolivia and the Higg Index are both examples where some aspects of these systems have aided capacity development at the firm, forest, and farm levels. The more recent development of MSIs, such as the Roundtable on Sustainable Palm Oil, as well as legality verification programmes in the forest industry, are both examples of improving capacity at broader levels. Legality verification, which certifies that timber was harvested legally according to the regulations of its country of origin, has been criticised in some quarters as being too lax a standard because it does not hold any of these countries to minimum sustainability standards. But the argument in favour of these programmes is that it is an improvement on current situations and provides an important intersection between public and private governance that can build regulatory capacity and traditional authority in areas where they are weak (Cashore and Stone 2012).

Since experience has shown that areas where there is stronger overall regulatory capacity have better outcomes from non-governmental programmes, programmes such as this could be an important element in improving the effectiveness of environmental governance regimes of all types. A study of Reducing Emissions from Deforestation and Forest Degradation (REDD+) projects[1] in Peru found that a number of certifiers are active participants, including the Climate, Community and Biodiversity Alliance (CCBA), the Voluntary Carbon Standard (VCS), and the Rainforest Alliance. Many of the REDD+ programmes studied are pursuing certification in one of these programmes, and many individuals from these organisations in Peru have been key actors in building the system to enable REDD+ projects (Hajek et al. 2011). The capacity of certifiers to help legitimise the projects, as well as their resource capacity to work with other projects, is a clear example of a capacity spillover.

What these examples demonstrate is that despite the vision of using a variety of non-governmental regulatory systems to fill in major capacity gaps in the management of environmental resources, they are not, in fact, impervious to the same challenges that have driven their development. Those programmes that have operated in higher-capacity areas, or have engaged in capacity-building exercises, have had more success. But it seems clear that non-government certifications alone struggle to have significant impacts in areas where capacities—regulatory and technical—are lacking. However, the ability of these programmes to disseminate best practices and invest resources in capacity-building exercises has also proven that these challenges are not insurmountable.

Innovation: technical and governance

Non-governmental sustainability regulatory systems involve innovation of a number of types—both governance and technical. They create a market for a variety of innovations that promote sustainable development, and take advantage of different technological advances to open up new spaces and methods to become more effective in scale, scope, and impact. For the sake of this discussion, innovation will include the second and third phases of technological change as described by Schumpeter—both the commercial introduction and diffusion of technologies (Ruttan 1959). It will also adopt Harvey Brooks's definition of technology as 'knowledge of how to fulfil certain human purposes in a specifiable and reproducible way' (Brooks 1980). This definition allows us to consider technology as a broader concept rather than as

[1] REDD+ is a deforestation programme that uses market incentives to reduce carbon dioxide emissions from deforestation. REDD+ activities can be undertaken by any combination of public, private, and NGO actors. The main REDD+ programmes are the Forest Carbon Partnership Facility (World Bank), the UN-REDD Programme, and Norway's International Climate and Forest Initiative. Unlike the CDM programme, developing countries cannot use REDD activities to offset their emissions.

a mere physical artefact. Following Brian Arthur's work, we include devices and techniques, methods, or processes, as well as 'assemblages of practices and components' and the 'collection of devices and engineering practices available to a culture' (Arthur 2009: 28). Finally, the innovations of particular interest here can be specifically defined as 'technologies for sustainable development' (or sustainable development technologies (SDTs)) with the potential to help meet 'the needs of the present without compromising the ability of future generations to meet their own needs' (Brundtland and World Commission on Environment and Development 1987). The benefit of this set of conceptualisations is that both the governance systems and the technologies required to meet particular standards can be referred to as technologies under Arthur's definition, somewhat simplifying the discussion.

One way to consider the direct impacts of these systems on the problems they seek to address is a function of two major elements: whether the standards themselves work and the level of uptake of the standards. Thus the overall impact is heavily reliant on the development and diffusion of two sets of innovations, i.e. technologies that allow for improvement of livelihoods while reducing negative environmental impacts (more good with less bad), and also on the overarching policy regime itself, which we can think of as sets of governance techniques. While the relationship between these systems and innovation can be examined from any number of angles, two are of particular interest here, and will be linked with capacity issues in the final section. The first is how technological innovations have been used to *enable* more effective private governance. And the second, less discussed, is how private governance systems have become important *drivers* of technological innovation.

The interaction of innovation and private governance has mostly focused on how technological advances enable the expansion, and improve the effectiveness of, different kinds of private governance systems. For example, in forestry, the development of genetic techniques, along with radio-frequency identification (RFID) technology, has enabled much more effective supply chain tracking efforts (Cashore and Stone 2012). Improved analytical techniques make it more difficult (though not impossible) to pass off counterfeit goods as certified. The combination of geographic information system (GIS) and satellite technologies and advances in genomics, proteomics, metabolomics, and transcriptomics to provide cellular-level identification improves the ability to monitor practices, especially in terms of agriculture and fisheries certifications (Migone and Howlett 2012).

More generally, the availability of greater numbers of sustainable options improves both effectiveness and uptake of these systems. When producers consider becoming certified, one major concern is the cost of compliance (Steering Committee of the State-of-Knowledge Assessment of Standards and Certification 2012). A major aspect of this is how much investment in technology will be required. Thus, the greater the number of effective, cost-competitive options available, the more likely firms, farmers, fishermen, and other producers will be able to engage in these programmes.

Innovations in the governance systems themselves also enable the uptake and improved effectiveness of non-governmental regulatory systems. Many of these are hybrids in which governments are involved to various degrees. These include programmes like legality verification for timber and the integration of voluntary third-party standards into EU sustainable biofuels regulations. Other innovations in this family of regulatory approaches include the development of new kinds of industry-association tools and standards, often with NGO and civil society input (e.g. Sustainable Apparel Coalition's Higg Index), and the efforts, spearheaded in part by the World Wildlife Fund, to establish roundtables for key commodities. These roundtables include firms, governments, and civil society groups in order to establish sustainability standards throughout these products' global supply chains. The most well-established of these is the Roundtable on Sustainable Palm Oil (RSPO), which had already certified 15 per cent of the global palm oil supply (RSPO: World Index) only four years after the first certification was issued in 2008 (RSPO: Milestones). RSPO, and other roundtables of this sort, are part of a new generation of certification programmes that increasingly take a supply chain, systems perspective—not just focusing on producers and consumers. These innovations to the 'techniques' of non-governmental systems also appear to have important impacts on their uptake and overall effectiveness vis-à-vis other types of regulatory systems.

The availability of cost-effective, sustainable technologies for producers has frequently been addressed in studies of these systems, but the impact that they have on technological innovation has not been examined nearly as closely. While there is certainly literature to support regulatory pull on investments in innovation (OECD 2011), it does not focus particularly on voluntary regulatory systems. However, it is clear that they have had an impact in at least a few areas. One case of interest is the development of green building practices and products, driven by the LEED and similar green building standards. Combined with public procurement policies in many jurisdictions that require public buildings to be LEED certified, the growth in this space catalysed by the programme has created a market for expertise and technologies that allow for increasingly cost-effective ways to meet the standard (which, in turn, makes it more attractive for even more firms to certify, increasing the market, and so on).[2] This can lead to a phenomenon like Portland, Oregon's green

[2] EPA Star, which is voluntary, but run by the US government, is considered to be at least partially responsible for major improvements in the energy efficiency of appliances, as it created market incentives for innovation in this space through consumer awareness of operating costs.

building cluster, which attracts significant expertise to the area, is supported by local and state government initiatives, and represents a growing segment of the regional economy (Allen and Potiowsky 2008).

The example of increased traceability in supply chains can also be viewed from this perspective. The need to have better control over processes and actions by suppliers with whom firms may have little or no direct interaction is also creating space for new technological innovations, including analytical testing, and ways to transmit data without jeopardising confidential information. It may also create demand pull for innovations in particular sectors—such as green production processes for microchips to fulfil E-Peat (greener electronics), or greener dyes and pigments in the textile industry.

Innovation can occur in 'high tech' areas, heavy manufacturing activities, and even agriculture and aquaculture practices. More study is required to understand if, and how, certification programmes have been impacting the development and diffusion of various practices in some of the areas with well-developed certification programmes, including tropical forest crops (coffee, cocoa, and tea), forestry, fisheries, and aquaculture. Another area of consideration is the role of these programmes in creating demand for new technologies and diffusing them. This not only includes direct diffusion via uptake of those engaged with non-governmental systems, but also the spillovers due to copying, local learning, network effects, and other mechanisms, which could result in substantial uptake of particular technologies within a wider group of potential users, much like the REDD+ example discussed in the previous section.[3]

For both agricultural and technology-heavy activities, there is a worry that technology standards (as opposed to outcome-based standards) could in fact become barriers to innovation, due to lock-in by potential users. This same concern is present in government regulation as well, though it is unclear to what extent the concern is warranted.

Conclusions: interaction between capacity and innovation

In studies of governance systems, capacity and innovation are often examined separately despite awareness that they are also very closely linked. When studying the uptake of technological innovation, the capacity of users to search, select, and integrate new technologies (technically, strategically, and managerially) is a major consideration. In studies of administrative capacity, the ability to learn, innovate, and deal with new technologies (administrative and technical) can play an important role in regulatory effectiveness. In better understanding

[3] This is a particularly interesting area for future research.

the uptake and effectiveness of non-governmental systems, as well as their future potential, capacity and innovation are key, intertwined elements.

Innovation and capacity can create a potentially virtuous cycle. In some cases, governance innovations can overcome capacity gaps, one of the underlying premises of many non-governmental systems. Technological innovations can also be used to overcome these capacity challenges—as seen in the development of RFID tracking systems that allow for origin and legality to be traced, even in places where the local administrative systems are unwilling or unable to enforce government regulations. On the flip side, innovations are more easily diffused—be they novel systems of governance, or particular technologies that support sustainable development when there is existing capacity in place. Improvements in capacity, be they governmental or non-governmental, make it easier to incentivise and implement innovations—which can, in turn, eventually improve capacities—and so on in an upward, positive spiral.

As many scholars of systems of governance of human–environmental systems have clearly shown, there are no such things as panaceas. Governance (as opposed to government) is not an effective system for all sustainability problems in all places. Despite large growth over the last 15 years and attention received from practitioners and scholars, its uptake remains relatively low, and the total impacts unknown and difficult to quantify. Private governance approaches to sustainable development are not immune to the capacity challenges that face traditional, public regulatory programmes. Technology, despite all of its benefits, has a long history of unintended consequences, and technologies that support sustainable development continue to face significant barriers to development and implementation (Matus et al. 2012).

The reality of these systems to deliver improved capacity, and to incentivise effective governance and technological innovations and thus contribute to more sustainable development, has proven to be complex. The evidence is mixed, at best, as to whether they can be used to fill gaps in administrative capacity. In South America, forestry certification has been much more successful in places where government regulators had public legitimacy and some level of technical capacity. Uptake of many standards by smaller or less technically sophisticated users has been challenging, and many have, at least initially, favoured those users with relatively greater internal technical capability, or the financial resources to hire outside experts.

Legitimacy is another major consideration. Third-party certification may help improve the legitimacy of MSIs, but auditors, like public regulators, are not immune to capture and face the same shortage of trained personnel that challenge many governments. The financial models of most MSIs, which are dependent on a combination of philanthropy and licensing fees, are different, but usually no less problematic, than those faced by many government programmes. MSIs rely on price premiums in the market which may not exist and can be highly variable. In addition, the need for certified producers to pay for their audits creates principal–agent problems with the supposedly independent third-party certifiers. Finally, the success of these programmes relies solely on their perceived legitimacy, which requires that they deliver value to producers alongside positive sustainability outcomes. If they fail to deliver—for example, if their standards are deemed too lax by consumers, or too stringent and costly for most producers—then they will be unable to command market share and maintain their legitimacy. Since the programmes are voluntary, problems with administrative capacity and legitimacy could destroy the viability of any given programme as a governance system.

Nevertheless, the spillovers from indirect impacts of these systems on both capacity and innovation are important areas for study. Improved technology and user capacity make for better ability to comply on the part of the regulated. Furthermore, experience with these systems and related innovations may also allow regulators to enter in more traditional roles. The development of expertise, proven standards, and techniques for measurement, enforcement, and implementation may allow for the development of government programmes that have potential for wider-reaching activities (and thus potentially greater outcomes). In other words, in some cases, these systems, through their impacts on capacity and innovation, could be key stepping stones in the development of effective, government management of the human–environment system. To capture these effects, impact studies of MSIs should consider a variety of indirect impacts beyond environmental and economic outcomes. While capacity and innovation can be difficult to quantify, they may also prove to be part of an important set of dynamics linking public and private governance activities.

What, then, is the future of MSIs? The prognosis appears to be mixed. There is little evidence that these efforts, on their own, can substitute for regulation by governments to support sustainable development. Levels of uptake, ability to deliver positive outcomes, and durability remain elusive on the scales required to address the most pressing issues of sustainable development. Yet they have a clear value. In global arenas where there is no single government institution with the authority to regulate across boundaries, MSIs can be important tools to add flexibility and supplement the capacity of international institutions. They can be useful for harmonising the flow of information, such as through complex supply chains. In some cases, they can fill in specific gaps, such as gaps in technical capacity that can make it difficult for regulators to set standards. But use of MSI-developed standards can present a trade-off for a government's legitimacy and authority, which should be carefully considered. Finally, MSIs are important parts of the innovation process to support sustainable development. They create venues for the demonstration of new technologies and methods of governance, and, as they grow, may in turn spur demand for further innovation. They may also, over time, change underlying norms in such a way as to support regulatory efforts by governments, ultimately improving the effectiveness of public governance.

References

Allen, J. H., and Potiowsky, T. (2008). 'Portland's Green Building Cluster: Economic Trends and Impacts', *Economic Development Quarterly*, 22(4): 303–15.

Allwood, J. M. (2006). *Well Dressed? The Present and Future Sustainability of Clothing and Textiles in the United Kingdom*. Cambridge: University of Cambridge Institute for Manufacturing.

Arthur, W. B. (2009). *The Nature of Technology: What It Is and How It Evolves*. New York: Free Press.

Auld, G. (2010). 'Assessing Certification as Governance: Effects and Broader Consequences for Coffee', *The Journal of Environment and Development*, 19(2): 215–41.

Auld, G., Gulbrandsen, L. H., and McDermott, C. L. (2008). 'Certification Schemes and the Impacts on Forests and Forestry', *Annual Review of Environment and Resources*, 33(1): 187–211.

Brooks, H. (1980). 'Technology, Evolution, and Purpose', *Daedalus*, 109: 65–81.

Brundtland and World Commission on Environment and Development (1987). *Our Common Future*. New York: Oxford University Press.

Cashore, B. (2002). 'Legitimacy and the Privatization of Environmental Governance: How Non-State Market-Driven (NSMD) Governance Systems Gain Rule-Making Authority', *Governance*, 15(4): 503–29.

Cashore, B., and Stone, M. (2012). 'Can Legality Verification Rescue Global Forest Governance? Analyzing the Potential of Public and Private Policy Intersection to Ameliorate Forest Challenges in Southeast Asia', *Forest Policy and Economics*, 18: 13–22.

Cashore, B., Gale, F., Meidinger, E., and Newsom, D. (2006). 'Introduction: Forest Certification in Analytical and Historical Perspective', in B. Cashore, F. Gale, E. Meidinger, and D. Newsom (eds), *Confronting Sustainability: Forest Certification in Developing and Transitioning Countries*. New Haven: Yale School of Forestry and Environmental Studies, 7–24.

Chouinard, Y., Ellison, J., and Ridgeway, R. (2011). 'The Sustainable Economy', *Harvard Business Review* 89: 52–62.

Ebeling, J., and Yasué, M. (2009). 'The Effectiveness of Market-Based Conservation in the Tropics: Forest Certification in Ecuador and Bolivia', *Journal of Environmental Management*, 90(2): 1145–53.

Economy, E. (2004). *The River Runs Black: The Environmental Challenge to China's Future*. Ithaca: Cornell University Press.

Falkner, R. (2003). 'Private Environmental Governance and International Relations: Exploring the Links', *Global Environmental Politics*, 3: 72–87.

FSC (Forest Stewardship Council) (2012). Facts and Figures on FSC Growth and Markets. Bonn: FSC.

Golden, J. S., Subramanian, V., and Zimmerman, J. B. (2011). 'Sustainability and Commerce Trends', *Journal of Industrial Ecology*, 15(6): 821–4.

Hajek, F., Ventresca, M. J., Scriven, J., and Castro, A. (2011). 'Regime-Building for REDD+: Evidence from a Cluster of Local Initiatives in South-Eastern Peru', *Environmental Science and Policy*, 14(2): 201–15.

Hood, C. (2007). 'Intellectual Obsolescence and Intellectual Makeovers: Reflections on the Tools of Government after Two Decades', *Governance*, 20(1): 127–44.

Howlett, M. (2011). *Designing Public Policies: Principles and Instruments*. Abingdon, New York: Routledge.

LeBlanc, S. (2012). *Sustainable Fashion Design: Oxymoron No More?* New York: Business for Social Responsibility (BSR).

Marine Stewardship Council [website]. *Certified Fisheries on the Map*. Retrieved from <http://www.msc.org/track-a-fishery/fisheries-in-the-program/certified/certified-fisheries-on-the-map> (accessed 2 September 2013).

Matus, K. J. (2010). 'Standardization, Certification, and Labelling: A Background Paper for the Roundtable on Sustainability Workshop January 19–21, 2009', *Certifiably Sustainable? The Role of Third-Party Certification Systems*. Washington, DC: National Academies Press, 79–104.

Matus, K. J., Clark, W. C., Anastas, P. T., and Zimmerman, J. B. (2012). 'Barriers to the Implementation of Green Chemistry in the United States', *Environmental Science & Technology*, 46(20): 10892–9.

Migone, A., and Howlett, M. (2012). 'From Paper Trails to DNA Barcodes: Enhancing Traceability in Forest and Fishery Certification', *National Resources Journal*, 52: 421–41.

Nebela, G., Quevedob, L., Jacobsena, J. B., and Hellesa, F. (2005). 'Development and Economic Significance of Forest Certification: The Case of FSC in Bolivia', *Forest Policy and Economics*, 7: 175–86.

OECD (Organisation for Economic Co-operation and Development) (2011). 'Sustainable Chemistry: Evidence on Innovation from Patent Data'. Series on Risk Management No. 25. Paris: OECD.

Roberts, T. M. (2011). 'Innovations in Governance: A Functional Typology of Private Governance Institutions', *Duke Environmental Law and Policy Forum*, 22: 37–144.

Roundtable on Sustainable Palm Oil [website]. 'Milestones'. Retrieved from <http://www.rspo.org/en/milestones> (accessed 20 January 2014).

Roundtable on Sustainable Palm Oil [website]. 'RSPO Worldwide Impact'. Retrieved from <http://www.rspo.org/en/RSPO_Worldwide_Impact> (accessed 20 January 2014).

Ruttan, V. W. (1959). 'Usher and Schumpeter on Invention, Innovation, and Technological Change', *The Quarterly Journal of Economics*, 73(4): 596.

Steering Committee of the State-of-Knowledge Assessment of Standards and Certification (2012). *Toward Sustainability: The Roles and Limitations of Certification*. Washington, DC: RESOLVE, Inc.

Sustainable Apparel Coalition [website]. 'The Higg Index—Overview'. Retrieved from <http://www.apparelcoalition.org/higgindex/> (accessed 20 January 2014).

U.S. Census Bureau (2011). *Statistical Abstract of the United States, 2012*. 131st edn. Washington, DC: U.S. Census Bureau.

15

Conclusion

Problem-solving Capacity and the Modern State

Martin Lodge and Kai Wegrich

This volume has sought to contribute to one of the most defining questions in contemporary politics: are modern states capable to deal with key immediate and long-term governance challenges? In addressing this question, this volume has focused on the role of administrative capacities as a site of and source for innovative practices to address governance challenges.

As noted in the introductory chapter, doubts about the problem-solving capacities of states are hardly new. Political systems are said to be unable to generate long-term solutions as short-termist and blame-avoiding politicians seek to win elections (Hood 2010), as entrenched interests are keen to extract selective benefits, and as public sector cutbacks are being announced and resisted (see Hood and Wright 1981). Furthermore, capitalist systems generate (side) effects for welfare states that can no longer be compensated for, as the revenue base is dwindling away, whether through tax competition, mobile capital, or, more likely, the collapse of the tax base because of demographic change. In addition, volatile electorates are said to make governing in hard times even more difficult and unstable (see Lodge and Wegrich 2012b; Lodge 2013). Debates as to how to balance calls for long-term stability with a preference to facilitate flexibility to changing circumstances have been at the heart of (the study of) politics for decades. Similarly, concerns about the capture of certain aspects of the state by certain select interests, as well the fear of the involvement of the state in ever more social domains, have been a well-established feature in the literature.

The contemporary climate, however, is characterised by a number of unique features that distinguish it from its predecessors. One feature is the nature of the modern state itself, which is said to have undergone a considerable transformation. For some, the modern state is an offspring of the Weberian age of industrialisation. Accordingly, the state is characterised by a shift towards rule-based governing and an emphasis on being distinct from the private sector. This contrasts with the image of a state in an age of 'post-industrial' and digitalised economies. Such transformation of the economy also requires states to adjust to such 'postmodern' terms by relying more extensively on power sharing through markets and networks. This is said to require a loss of distinctiveness from the private sector and a more discretionary approach towards rules. We suggest, however, that the 'state' has remained central regardless of the increasing prominence of networks and other non-hierarchical forms of governing (Hill and Lynn 2005). As authors interested in 'publicness' have suggested, many activities are characterised by considerable state involvement, and therefore reflect somewhat different accountability requirements than others (Bozeman and Moulton 2011).

In other words, to come to an informed view about whether states have problem-solving capacities, it is important to understand the actual challenges that states face, both in terms of external demands (i.e. how to address declining birth rates, how to attract private investment in utilities) and in terms of understanding underlying administrative prerequisites. A focus on administrative capacities allows for an in-depth look at the link between the change of contexts and demands that states face and their ability to generate and support problem-solving capacity through administrative means.

Among the unique features of the modern state are the nature and extent of dispersed authority. Of course, what commonly is defined as public services (such as health, education, or even utilities) has historically been produced by third-party actors, such as churches, political parties, or private firms. However, what is different in the contemporary age is the degree of dispersion of state authority, first of all, in transnational settings, second, in national government settings where a period of 'agencification' over the past three decades has increased the number and diversity of non-ministerial bodies, and third, a period of proclaimed growth in 'collaboration' (Ansell and Gash 2008).

A further feature that distinguishes this age from previous ones is reflected in the type of criticism that involves the modern state. The state of the 2010s is one that that is characterised by depleted resources (Lodge 2013). It lacks financial resources as mounting debt burdens and fear of repercussions by financial markets constrain the space for spending. Demographic change raises the spectre of ever growing demands on health and welfare budgets at a time when the revenue base of states is declining. Climate change is said to contribute to extreme weather events with, potentially, devastating consequences. In addition, the state is said to lack the authority to impose its will, the organisational resources to 'do something', and the capability to communicate information to its population.

This perception of depleted resources has gone hand in hand with a sense that the contemporary orthodoxies of governing have also failed. That is, after decades in which it has been popular to denounce 'hierarchy' (e.g. Gunningham, Grabosky, and Sinclair 1998; Coglianese and Lazer 2003; Sabel and Zeitlin 2008), it has also become apparent that so-called 'non-hierarchical' means of governing are far from fail-safe as private actors lack motivation and capacity to govern themselves, and as states are unlikely to bind themselves to benchmarking and other 'soft' instruments when these are not in their own electoral or economic interest (Lodge 2007; Gunningham and Sinclair 2009). In the end, both state and non-state actors are said to be incapable and unmotivated to tackle contemporary governance challenges.

The failure of 'non-hierarchical' modes of governing relates to a further distinct feature of the early 21st century, namely the nature of contemporary statehood itself. The so-called governance turn in the social sciences has highlighted that 'the state' cannot be understood as a monolithic actor, but rather as an ill-defined entity of highly diverse mechanisms and interests that operate on multiple logics (Lodge and Wegrich 2011). In addition, steering is rarely, if ever, about a hierarchical relationship between a 'subject' that steers and an 'object' that is being steered (Mayntz 1987). Instead, a key theme has been that public policies emerge in the context of mediation and interaction among institutionalised settings of state and non-state actors (Mayntz and Scharpf 1995). Accordingly these settings also shape the way in which implementation is organised, whether through hierarchy, markets, or networks.

The interest in modes of governance (i.e. markets, hierarchies, and networks) as well as actor constellations encouraged a decline in interest in the nature of the state, the way in which bureaucracies were organised, and how bureaucracies contributed (or not) to problem-solving. The key source for problem-solving was seen to lie in non-state actors, from the local to the transnational level. This interest in non-state solutions to public problems led, on the one hand, to an interest in the study of market-based private sector provision of services (and its regulation; see Majone 1997). On the other hand, there was also a growing interest in the way in which societal actors, such as non-governmental organisations (NGOs), voluntary organisations, and other non-profit outfits organised to contribute to public policies (Salamon 2002). While the (normative and analytical) focus of these two literatures was rather distinct, they displayed a rather similar view regarding bureaucracy. Both of them regarded bureaucracy as an impediment to innovative approaches to governing, while non-state actors were seen to be 'closer' to the actual problem at hand, better informed, more responsive, efficient, and effective. Whereas the literature on NGOs and networks has shown little interest in public sector reform, the literature advocating marketisation also put forward managerialist prescriptions for public sector reform (often (mis-)labelled as New Public Management) (Hood 1991, 1994).

If the story ended here, one could argue that this volume's interest in administrative capacities is distinctly unfashionable. However, just as 1980s pop songs, haircuts, and moustaches have made a return in popular fashion, an interest in bureaucracy has witnessed resurgence in the social sciences. One source for this renewed interest has been the advocacy of the importance of 'Weberianisation' of bureaucracy to reduce corruption, to enhance competency, and to generate economic and social progress (Evans and Rauch 1999). Similarly, Weberianisation has been a key theme in the literature on the Europeanisation of central and eastern European bureaucracies post 1989 in the context of European Union accession agreements (Meyer-Sahling, Lowe, and van Stolk 2012). A second source has been scholars critical of earlier managerial reforms. The literature on 'post NPM' (Christensen and Lægreid 2006; Lodge and Gill 2011) has suggested that there has been a counter-trend towards growing public service distinctiveness in the face of failure in privatised public service provision. Nevertheless, while this rediscovery of bureaucracy (Olsen 2006) did point to some features that were supposed to advance capacity (such as 'merit appointments'), little attention has been placed on the skills and competencies that are actually expected of bureaucrats (Hood and Lodge 2004, 2005). In other words, the search for 'measurement' and the consequent urge to concentrate on 'merit appointment' have meant that very little interest has been paid to the actual features of and demands on bureaucracies that are associated with this particular age of governance.

This volume contributes to the discussion on the problem-solving capacity of the modern state in two ways. One, it emphasises the importance of a differentiated understanding of administrative capacities so as to advance discussions about the role of bureaucracy in a setting that is characterised by extensive dispersion, as suggested by the governance literature. Second, it suggests that the problem-solving capacity of governance systems depends on the presence of administrative capacities. The next section summarises some of the key points of this volume. The following section then points to the wider contribution of this volume to the contemporary literature on governance. Finally, this concluding chapter considers different 'recipes' for enhancing administrative capacities.

This volume

To contribute to the discussion on the problem-solving capacities of the modern state, this volume has discussed administrative capacities through a range of perspectives. First of all, this volume looked at key administrative capacities on their own. We distinguished coordination, delivery, analytical, and regulatory capacities. As noted in the introductory chapter, these four capacities are intended to capture the variety of demands placed on public bureaucracies. Approaching the concern with problem-solving capacity through the lens of (four) administrative capacities allows us to explore the critical role of particular administrative capacities on their own, and in combination with each other. Any innovation requires administrative capacity, and therefore administrative capacity is central to any problem-solving. Furthermore, the emphasis on administrative capacities adds to discussions about 'wicked problems' in public administration. It does so by encouraging researchers and practitioners not to hide behind the inevitable world of complex trade-offs, but to consider the consequences of such contexts by thinking carefully about different administrative capacities.

The chapters by Hupe and Hill, Wegrich and Štimac, Lodge, and Parrado suggested that demands on these four capacities have changed considerably. For example, delivery capacity has changed as the direct involvement of states in the production and execution of services has been reduced due to outsourcing and privatisation. Hammerschmid et al. suggest that at least some of the managerial tools that have been introduced into the public sector have had, overall, positive effects on administrative capacity. At the same time, delivery capacity is still required as a back-up when private providers either fail or are perceived to fail in performing their functions. Analytical capacities have become increasingly contested in an age of distrust in authority, globalisation of knowledge, easy access to Internet-based knowledge claims, and high degrees of complexity and uncertainty (see Beck 1992, 1997; Power 1997). Similarly, the age of governance has also placed a growing emphasis on regulatory capacity and the capacity and motivation of regulatees to co-regulate (Lodge and Wegrich 2012c). Coordination capacities are challenged by the dispersed nature of contemporary governing, whereas analytical capacities do not just come in different guises (i.e. different types of analysis are requested by politics, by (transnational) rule systems, and by other 'stakeholders'), but sources of knowledge are disputed by 'lay' opinion as well as by different disciplines or 'traditions' within disciplines. Therefore, administrative capacities at large need to be understood as a mixture of (at least) these four subtypes that are required in any governing system. The different challenges and demands on administrative capacity will vary across particular issues, domains, and national governing systems; however, they need to be considered in order to come to a better appreciation of the continuing role of 'the state' in contemporary governance.

This book's second part dealt with fundamental governance challenges that are likely to place a considerable cost burden on states. If the financial crisis that began in 2008 succeeded in placing considerable financial legacies on various states, the cost pressures of climate change and demography are likely to reflect far greater cost drivers. Attempts at policy innovation to deal with these challenges are considered by Lenschow and Jordana in the area of environmental and infrastructure regulation, respectively, and by Kreyenfeld and Rasner in the field of family and pensions policy. The search for problem-solving capacity appears in many guises, in terms of organisational forms (such as regulatory agencies) and in the form of policy instruments. These chapters also highlight how policy innovations' intended outcomes are highly contingent on private choices; for example, in the area of private decisions regarding reproduction.

The search for policy innovation raises many challenges in terms of design as well. One is the search for finding resource non-intensive instruments to steer behaviours in ways that might alleviate cost pressures. Another is innovation in terms of dealing with uncertainty about the future, especially in terms of the often-proclaimed breakthrough technologies that are supposed to reduce production costs of, say, elder care. A third one is innovation in administrative capacities themselves. It is noticeable that much of the debate in public policy has been about the development of 'innovative' instruments to deal with policy challenges, but far less attention has been paid to the administrative prerequisites so that these instruments can realise their potential effect. Indeed, many of the diagnosed problems with these 'innovative' instruments stem from the fact that little attention has been paid to underlying assumptions and prerequisites. For some, this might be surprising. For others, this might be part of the inevitable argumentative character of public management thinking where winning rhetorical strategies require ambivalence and ambiguity (Hood and Jackson 1991). This volume suggests that the proper place for scholarship is to unpack this ambivalence and ambiguity in reform recipes.

The volume's third part focused on a traditional interest in the governance literature, namely how non-state and transnational regimes might be seen as extending (or undermining) problem-solving capacity. This volume questions whether, and if so how, administrative capacities play a role in facilitating regimes driven by non-state actors. Such regimes are, at times, established and managed among non-state actors and often take on a transnational character (see Krisch, Matus). In many such arrangements states play an 'orchestrating' role (Abbott and Snidal 2009). The chapters in this part, in particular the chapter by Sørensen and Torfing on collaborative innovation, highlight varieties of 'orchestration', whether it is in the sense of facilitating settings that allow for the generation of hybrid regimes, or in the sense of offering conditions for non-state actors to perform their varied responsibilities and grant them legitimacy. These chapters all point to the significant capacity requirements to enable the functioning of such non-state innovations. Somewhat different is the setting of European Union multi-level governance. As discussed by Heidbreder, administrative capacity is central to many of the contemporary debates in EU governance.

Furthermore, this part has also noted how some governance strategies can be more resourceful than others. Contemporary accounts have noted how networks and hybrids display greater resilience in terms of responding to unexpected challenges than those arrangements that are said to be 'simple' and 'elegant'. As observed, hybrid, or clumsy, instruments and arrangements seem widespread across the different areas under consideration in this volume. How hybrids emerge and whether such clumsiness can be engineered, or whether it is only possible to establish the background conditions for such arrangements to emerge are open questions (see Verweij).

In sum, this book contributes to debates about the problem-solving capacities of the state by reflecting on the resources that are available within and beyond the state. In addition, this volume highlights the considerable challenges that contemporary states face. The challenges of demography, climate change, and financial crisis do not impact all states in the same way (Lodge and Hood 2012); however, they do have considerable implications for the way in which discussions about governance can evolve. Furthermore, they also limit the set of options for developing administrative capacities.

Governance, contemporary challenges, and administrative capacity

As noted in the introductory chapter, debates about the future of the state have evolved around the notion of 'governance'. Governance is seen as a rescue to government: it offers superior problem-solving capacities, it is supposed to be less hard-edged than managerial approaches to governing, and it is also supposedly more legitimate and participatory. Non-state actors are seen as providing resources to support the problem-solving capacity of states (often those that states either never had or no longer have) and as establishing governance arrangements without much or any involvement of states themselves. However, this debate about governance as a possibility of non-traditional resources to play a role in policy-making beyond the boundaries of the 'traditional' state reflects on a diversity of debates. We consider in turn three debates involving governance in this section, namely, the first on whether states have been 'hollowed out' or 'filled in', the second on legitimacy, and the third on public sector reform programmes.

'Hollowed out' or 'filled in'?

One of the traditional arguments regarding governance has been that the state has been 'hollowed out' (Rhodes 1997; Matthews 2012). According to this argument, the state has handed over its key tools that previously allowed it to steer the economy and society. Authority has been transferred to the private sector, to international organisations, and to fragmented administrative bodies. No central steering capacity remains, thereby creating the image of the 'hollow state'. Governance thus takes place in a highly dispersed context in which authority is shared and fragmented, and where therefore the exercise of hierarchy is, at most, limited. The 'hollowed out' state is thus powerless to face forthcoming crises; it lacks resources to act and memory to respond intelligently.

The chapters of this volume do not paint a picture of the 'hollowed out' state in the sense of lack of activity or concern. States do seek to play a role in addressing governance challenges, and they do have an impact. However, whether they achieve intended outcomes is a different question. Our interest in administrative capacity adds to the 'hollowing out' debate by concentrating on those oversight and coordination functions that are said to be at the heart of the governance debate, while also considering those administrative capacities that are seen to have been diluted or complexified, namely those of delivery and analysis. This volume suggests that both delivery and analytical capacities are of continued centrality to contemporary statehood. For example, delivery capacities remain central as private providers fail (outright or in delivering specified outputs), or are no longer seen as capable of handling sensitive activities (such as airport security). Of course, a continued role (and a return to such a role) in delivery does not necessarily represent a rejection of the 'hollowed out' perspective. It may, after all, be the case that administrative capacities have been blunted in a 'hollowed out' world that is characterised by a dispersion of authority to diverse agencies, the outsourcing and privatisation of service delivery, and internationalisation (as well as growing legal complexity).

However, the 'hollowed out' perspective is problematic for a number of reasons. First, it paints a picture of a status quo ante that hardly ever existed. It is questionable whether states ever had a 'central' capacity to intervene in economic and social life and succeeded in changing outcomes everywhere. It is equally questionable whether there was ever a 'non-hollowed out' state in which governmental activity was not shared with non-state actors and where the impact of state action was not dependent on compliant non-state actors. Second, even the most hollowed out or dispersed activities still rely on the 'state' for legitimisation, for resources, for the supply of information, and so on. In particular, the 'hollowed out' perspective has difficulty in accounting for the continued (if not even more pronounced) significance of regulatory and coordination capacities that have been highlighted in this volume. In other words, the 'hollowed out' state might be a good description of the dispersed nature of contemporary governing. However, whether it depicts a state of the world in which the 'state' is unable to affect these dispersed activities and organisations through its resources is an open question.

The chapters in this volume point to the continued centrality of state actors across select policy domains. They also offer examples of missed opportunities or unintended effects of particular interventions (cf. Margetts, 6, and Hood 2010). However, such examples hardly amount to evidence of a loss of state capacity overall. It rather points to the highly complex environment in which state action takes place. Indeed, examples of unintended effects should give rise to a reconsideration of administrative capacities. Furthermore, while it may very well be the case that the contemporary setting of governing makes hierarchical intervention ever more problematic as states increasingly rely on co-governing and internationalisation, such co-governing is hardly new and administration has always been reliant on the acceptance of authority by citizens, firms, and other societal organisations.[1]

The contrasting, second image of governance is that of the 'filled in' state (cf. Matthews 2012). The view of the 'filled in' state highlights two aspects. One is that states have continued power to step in and reverse 'hollowing out'. The responses to the post-2008 financial crisis were widely argued to signal that states were the only shows in town when the going got tough. The state was said to 'be back'. However, subsequent developments suggest that the state hardly was 'filled in' as it tried to divest itself of nationalised banking systems, industry bailout provisions, and other mounting debt burdens that resulted from the crisis response. For some, the politics of austerity signalled a world of politics in which the threat of financial market responses to 'irresponsible' state finances was seen as a key reason for states to tackle their budget deficits and to slim their staffing costs. The 'tax state' is certainly under pressure from a number of sources. One is the declining tax base due to shrinking workforces and increasingly mobile business. Another is the shrinking discretionary basis for expenditures as more and more social policies appear as mandatory expenditures in national budgets. As Streeck and Mertens (2013) have shown, the extent to which mandatory expenditures have grown as a proportion of discretionary ones points to a decline in the way in which governments can flexibly respond to challenges (for some, this may, of course, be a good thing).

[1] Indeed, for Max Weber, the exercise of legitimate authority required the acceptance among the subjects of the state that the state had legitimacy to use coercion.

Therefore, even though the 'filled in' state may appear initially persuasive as an account of the immediate post-2008 crisis response by states in the industrialised and industrialising world, other arguments suggest that this might very well be seen as the final wave of a dinosaur's tail. Large-scale nationalisation and bailouts of banking sectors would certainly have been classified as 'unthinkable' (among practitioners and researchers alike) only a few months before the financial crisis hit. Arguably less unthinkable were other 'recovery' measures, such as schemes to encourage drivers to exchange 'old bangers' for new cars. Such measures were far more representative of well-known industrial policy measures of early generations. They therefore represented a 'back to the future'-type response, the key aspect being that administrative capacities hardly existed to deal with these interventionist measures. However, as the financial crisis turned into a sovereign debt crisis and heads of European governments jetted from one crisis summit to another, it seemed that states were far from being 'filled in' but were witnessing a high degree of dependence on volatile financial markets again.

A different 'filling in' argument is that states have just become more intelligent in steering actors. In other words, the 'loss' of capacity that has been highlighted by the 'hollowing out' perspective can be argued to be actually a sharpening and focusing in terms of capacity. It might be, after all, far cheaper (to the state) to regulate private providers of public services than to own and organise the provision oneself. Much debate about capacity reflects a view that emphasises direct governmental action, namely the resources of finance and organisation. States intervene through large-scale financial interventions or through outright nationalisation to stabilise economies and industries. If these are indeed the only resources, then one might follow Wolfgang Streeck and colleagues in arguing that the contemporary capitalist state is bound to fail. However, if one assumes that states are also able to 'steer', for example, through information or through oversight rather than merely through material cash transfers or direct ownership and production, then questioning the limits of the 'filled in' state becomes more problematic. It might be argued that a world of highly diversified information channels, of distrust of state propaganda (or 'information'), and of highly complex organisational and individual arrangements leads to considerable challenges for any attempt at steering or directing behaviours. However, merely to argue that state capacity to affect behaviour is limited because of a lack of discretionary expenditure ignores some of the inherent resources of the state (although whether the power to direct and steer remains as central as in previous periods is also an empirical question).

Legitimacy

A separate debate in the governance literature focuses on questions of legitimacy. The problem-solving capacity of networked and 'bottom-up' arrangements are said to easily outgun the capacities of planned and centrally executed 'top-down' programmes. The effectiveness and inclusiveness of these measures are therefore said to offer a different form of legitimacy than the kind of legitimacy that is associated with legislation-based state action as whipped through elected parliaments. The focus on administrative capacities could be accused of taking a particularly 'top-down' perspective in that it puts the 'state' at the heart of the analysis. Our intention is not to celebrate the state and bureaucracy as some form of superior entity. Instead, we argue that observers fascinated by markets and networks as well as Weberian bureaucracies need to think more carefully about what it is about bureaucracies that generates particular outputs or outcomes, and what it is about bureaucracies that politicians and publics expect.

Furthermore, we are not suggesting that having 'more' coordination, analytical, regulatory, and delivery capacities would automatically lead to more or better problem-solving. First of all, it is not obvious what 'more' or 'better' is, given the often competing doctrines about how to design resourceful administrative arrangements. It is one of the tragedies of the contemporary fascination with performance measurements, league tables, and benchmarking that little attention is paid to issues of the validity and reliability of particular measures and indicators. In particular, too little attention has been paid to the normative construction that goes into the generation of measurements and data. Ultimately, what 'good' governance is remains a value choice (for an early attempt, see von Justi 1759).

A focus on administrative capacities centres the debate on the less fancy, but far more important, questions that bureaucracy watchers in the world of practice and research should be asking, namely, 'What do we expect bureaucracy actually to be able to do?' For some, especially politicians, such questions might be difficult to answer, as bureaucracy offers an ideal blame magnet when things go wrong. For others, bureaucracy is purely about the promotion of professional norms. Outside interference is seen as unwelcome meddling and regarded as a threat to quality and commitment (for an early variant of this argument in the field of civil-military relations, see Huntington 1957). However, state actors are in a highly interdependent relationship with each other and with non-state actors. Therefore the exercise of most of these capacities will always be contingent on non-state actors. Furthermore, how 'more' capacities should be organised and developed also depends on the institutional structure of the state.

In other words, a focus on administrative capacities is not about 'top-down' intervention. Instead, it suggests that for any form of governance arrangement to operate, it is essential to consider the administrative prerequisites and to consider how they link to existing capacities and motivations within and outside the state. For the world of practice, this means that discussions should focus on a problem-centred approach (Simon 1946). Such an approach would therefore ask what the particular challenges are, and then consider various solutions in view of the required administrative capacities. Similarly, the world of research could do well in returning to an agenda such as that set out by Herbert Simon (1946) rather than pursuing a fascination with formal documents that suggest that formal hierarchy matters. Such a view has been increasingly popular in the wake of the rise of the principal–agent literature with its argument that formal provisions matter in tying down agents and principals alike (see McCubbins, Noll, and Weingast 1987; Epstein and O'Halloran 1999; Huber and Shipan 2002)

Legitimacy, however, is not just about effectiveness, but also about participation. This volume has admittedly neglected this aspect in the contemporary governance discussion. However, a focus on administrative capacities also contributes to these debates. Questions regarding access and decision rules require administration, and such arrangements are unlikely to emerge spontaneously. Therefore, although we do not focus explicitly on the implications of different understandings of democracy and participation on problem-solving in the contemporary state, a focus on administrative capacities nevertheless points to an essential, if often neglected, aspect of this debate. It raises the question as to who should be involved—and how—when it comes to reflecting on the role of bureaucracy in democracy.

Public sector reform programmes

The final governance-related debate under consideration refers to wider administrative reform doctrines. Readers may be asking why this book has not looked at competing doctrines of state organisation to account for degrees and understandings of capacity. Such debates have been widespread; for example, the literature on central and eastern Europe has often emphasised the importance of 'Weberianisation' of bureaucracy, others have been more interested in the advantages and disadvantages of the so-called New Public Management, while others have been keen to put forward labels to announce the arrival of a new paradigm such as 'public value', 'public governance', or 'post NPM' (Jann and Wegrich 2010; Benington and Moore 2011; Lodge and Gill 2011). Others, again, may have decided to look at organisational structures of government to identify islands of 'innovation'.

Our focus here is not on announcing or denouncing paradigms. As noted, whether bureaucracies perform better or worse when they are more or less rule-bound, or when they are more or less distinct from other labour markets, is an empirical and a normative question. What matters, however, is that the implications for administrative capacity should be at the heart of the analysis when it comes to endorsing one set of arguments rather than others. One way of using the administrative capacities perspective in the context of these debates is to ask what the capacity implications of those reforms actually are—both in terms of what they require and in terms of how they impact on pre-existing capacities. In that sense, the administrative capacities perspective is an antidote to the cyclical nature of administrative reform debates and doctrines that tend to stress some administrative values and neglect others, thereby over time inevitably leading to disappointment as other, temporarily repressed, values grow in public importance (cf. Hood 1998, 1991).

Recipes for governance innovation

One key interest in the literature on public policy is to account for different ways in which states respond to economic policy challenges. In the 1970s, this meant that the central capacities of the French state were compared favourably with those of a declining United Kingdom (Hayward 1976). Such accounts were challenged during the 1980s when the policy programmes of Conservative governments were linked to the 'strong' unitary state features of the UK Westminster system. This was contrasted with the more fragmented, and therefore 'reform unfriendly', political systems of continental Europe. Similarly shifting debates can be had about electoral reform (proportional representation being praised for encouraging stability and consensus, plurality vote for decisive action), corruption (decentralisation being seen as both good and bad in reducing perceived levels of corruption), and civil service capacities ('experts' seen as unwilling to reform and see the 'big picture', while generalists are condemned as 'amateurs').

That apparently contradictory arguments are being advanced to deal with the same problem should hardly come as a surprise to public administration watchers (Simon 1946; Hood and Jackson 1991). It should serve as a warning sign against the reform rhetoric that regularly appears in government, think tank, or international organisational documentation. This volume has taken a different angle to this debate, as noted in the introductory chapter. We suggest that any debate about governance innovation should be concerned with the underlying prerequisites. One essential prerequisite has been at the heart of this volume, namely the requirements placed on bureaucracy. As noted, there are many different ways in which analytical, coordination, regulatory, and delivery capacities can be conceptualised and understood. At their core, however, they are united by forcing the question about what role public administration can play within a chosen set of governance arrangements. Here we concentrate on four potential variants as to how to think about different conceptions of administrative capacities.

One perspective suggests that administrative capacities should be protected through insulation and rule-boundedness. Such arrangements already exist in the world of regulation and central banking, where the idea of insulation from electoral politics has been widely endorsed over the past three decades or so. Similar ideas could be developed in terms of analysis, where stand-alone 'think tanks' and 'evaluation units' could be seen as one way to advance administrative capacity. Similarly, one of the key ideas behind the rise of 'executive agencies' that were separated out from the 'normal' policy-making functions of ministerial departments was to create more insulated 'executive' capacities in government that would not be neglected by wider political concerns. In short, this recipe would argue that greater insulation coupled with clear mandates would allow for greater administrative capacity.

A different perspective suggests that there is a need for less separation from wider society. Administrative capacities should therefore be provided mainly by non-state actors, such as private actors. Delivery could be largely driven by private providers competing away surplus profits in a competitive marketplace, analysis would be provided by competing think tanks that fought hard on the marketplace for ideas, coordination would be spontaneous and driven by entrepreneurs established to combine different areas, and regulation would be provided through benchmarking and different classification or certification regimes that allowed customer-citizens a real choice in terms of the kind of goods and services they wished to consume. Potentially, some forms of 'crowdsourcing' could be used to tap the brains of the many in order to make up for the limited capacity of the state to offer analytical insights.

A third perspective would argue that administrative capacities are best provided through highly decentralised and participatory mechanisms. Administrative capacities would take on a distinct form—namely, coordinating mostly at the local level; ensuring delivery, rather than necessarily delivering oneself; regulating service at different levels, but mostly in terms of emphasising participation in decision-making rather than economic analysis; and analysing future trends in terms of local sustainability, not national electoral advantage.

Finally, a fourth perspective would place its emphasis on considering the conditions under which problem-solving under uncertainty can take place. Accordingly, the emphasis is not so much on the 'strategic' leadership dimension at the top of organisations, and not at the street level of minute-by-minute front-line interaction between subjects and bureaucrats, but in the middle (Roe 2013). It is at the mid level of bureaucracy where key issues regarding administrative capacities can be advanced. Such a recommendation is, of course, highly unfashionable. After all, 'cutting' bureaucracy was largely about eliminating the 'middle' in (public and private) organisations, thereby, ironically, cutting away exactly that critical element of slack that allows not just for the 'translation' between leadership intentions and front-level execution, but also for institutional memory and reflection. Thus, what matters is that sufficient 'slack' exists to encourage system-wide considerations that are sufficiently close to the 'ground' to be empirically grounded, but also sufficiently detached from the daily grind of front-line experience so as to allow for a more comprehensive perspective.

In sum, we do not advocate any single perspective towards advancing administrative capacities. Instead, we are arguing that all these perspectives have their place and need to be considered as they have distinct implications for the way in which administration is aligned in its relationship with politics, society, and the economy. In particular, as noted by Verweij in this volume, it is widely argued that endorsing any one solution at the exclusion of others may be 'elegant', but also highly vulnerable. Thus, the more discussions regarding administrative capacities are willing to consider rival perspectives, the more likely it is that a more informed debate will emerge and a less inferior option will be chosen.

Conclusion

This volume does not pretend to have easy answers to the question of the problem-solving capacity of the contemporary state. It does not offer a unified 'theory' or an argument that suggests either that we are all seeing the demise of the contemporary state or that governance via non-state actors and/or the reliance on transnational arrangements is going to come to the rescue of the state. Instead, our argument is that the worlds of research and practice should pay more attention to the importance of administrative capacities.

For the world of research, there are a number of implications from this argument. One is that those interested in 'the state' need to pay more attention to the role of bureaucracy, and in particular to its various capacities. For those interested in the study of bureaucracy, it suggests a move beyond the description of reform announcements or the analysis of formal provisions and towards the study of what bureaucracies actually do, and what they are expected to do by other actors in the political system. Such a problem-centred perspective (Simon 1946) may be resource intensive, but it connects to a number of different intellectual and research traditions. Similarly, a focus on administrative capacity also addresses issues in the wider 'non-hierarchical governance' discussion (Sabel and Zeitlin 2008) which, as yet, has paid only limited interest to the implications of their hyped-up and ultimately futile explorations for the study of administration (Lodge 2007). Furthermore, the discussion about innovation emerging from societal organisations would be advanced by incorporating a refined perspective on bureaucracy into their research agendas.

For the world of practice, a focus on administrative capacities is a direct challenge to those who advocate that bureaucracy should be 'fit for purpose' without clarifying what actually the 'purpose' is supposed to be. There are a number of reasons as to why political and other actors may not wish to engage in a debate about 'purpose'. In particular, the wider context of executive politics is characterised by key tensions that have contradictory implications for administrative capacities (Lodge and Wegrich 2012a).

One such tension is between the functional demand for transboundary solutions to governance problems and contemporary politics that are shaped by increasingly 'national' campaign rhetorics that deny not just the capability of transnational arrangements, but their outright legitimacy. Another tension is between the call for consistency and control and the functional process of ever increasing differentiation that leads to specialisation. A third tension, one that has been long diagnosed in the study of liberal democracy, is the tension between long-term sustainability and short-term electoral politics. As debates about energy politics have shown, party politics that seek votes in calling for 'cheap energy prices' do not necessarily lead to long-term sustainable policy outcomes. However, this tension also highlights the question as to why some areas, such as central banking, have seen an acceptance of arrangements that take certain decisions outside the direct realm of electoral politics, whereas other areas are more contested, such as energy policy.

We have argued that bureaucracy has four key 'purposes' and that therefore contemporary discussion should start by acknowledging those roles. It is not enough to condemn bureaucracy for its incompetence, or to develop 'one size fits all' competency frameworks. Rather, what is required to make a meaningful contribution is to consider the problems that administration (public and private) encounters, including those 'unmentionable' ones that include political masters. This volume has concentrated on coordination, analytical, delivery, and regulatory capacities. There is no 'perfect' combination among these capacities, but to advance capacity, the worlds of research and practice would do well to use them as a starting point for any discussion.

In sum, and as we argued also in *The Governance Report 2014* (Hertie School of Governance 2014), considering administrative capacities as one key element to contribute to the problem-solving capacity of the contemporary state reflects a view of problem-solving that accepts limitations and boundaries, and therefore demands critical reflection rather than enthusiastic endorsement of reform templates. It suggests that a debate about the role of bureaucracy in the context of contemporary politics and economics is critical in developing capacity. In other words, states are capable of being involved in problem-solving, but they need to consider the role of administration. Such debates are not in need of reform templates that offer easy answers to meaningless questions. Rather, administrative capacity, and overall problem-solving capacity in general, will be enhanced by confronting the realities of governing in dispersed settings. Not more, but also, not less.

References

Abbott, K. W., and Snidal, D. (2009). 'Strengthening International Regulation Through Transnational New Governance: Overcoming the Orchestration Deficit', *Vanderbilt Journal of Transnational Law*, 42(2): 501–78.

Ansell, C., and Gash, A. (2008). 'Collaborative Governance in Theory and Practice', *Journal of Public Administration Research and Theory*, 18(4): 543–71.

Beck, U. (1992). *Risk Society: Towards a New Modernity*. London, Newbury Park: Sage Publications.

Beck, U. (1997). 'Subpolitics: Ecology and the Disintegration of Institutional Power', *Organization and Environment*, 10(1): 52–65.

Benington, J., and Moore, M. H. (2011). *Public Value: Theory and Practice*. Basingstoke: Palgrave Macmillan.

Bozeman, B., and Moulton, S. (2011). 'Integrative Publicness: A Framework for Public Management Strategy and Performance', *Journal of Public Administration Research and Theory*, 21(Supplement 3): i363–80.

Christensen, T., and Lægreid, P. (2006). *Autonomy and Regulation: Coping with Agencies in the Modern State*. Cheltenham, Northampton: Edward Elgar.

Coglianese, C., and Lazer, D. (2003). 'Management-Based Regulation: Prescribing Private Management to Achieve Public Goals', *Law and Society Review*, 37(4): 691–730.

Epstein, D., and O'Halloran, S. (1999). *Delegating Powers: A Transaction Cost Politics Approach to Policy Making Under Separate Powers*. Cambridge, New York: Cambridge University Press.

Evans, P., and Rauch, J. E. (1999). 'Bureaucracy and Growth: A Cross-National Analysis of the Effects of "Weberian" State Structures on Economic Growth', *American Sociological Review*, 64(5): 748–65.

Gunningham, N., and Sinclair, D. (2009). 'Organizational Trust and the Limits of Management-Based Regulation', *Law and Society Review*, 43(4): 865–900.

Gunningham, N., Grabosky, P. N., and Sinclair, D. (1998). *Smart Regulation: Designing Environmental Policy*. Oxford, New York: Clarendon Press.

Hayward, J. (1976). 'Institutional Inertia and Political Impetus in France and Britain', *European Journal of Political Research*, 4(4): 341–59.

Hertie School of Governance (ed.) (2014). *The Governance Report 2014*. Oxford: Oxford University Press.

Hill, C. J., and Lynn, L. E. (2005). 'Is Hierarchical Governance in Decline? Evidence from Empirical Research', *Journal of Public Administration Research and Theory*, 15(2): 173–95.

Hood, C. (1991). 'A Public Management for All Seasons?' *Public Administration*, 69(1): 3–19.

Hood, C. (1994). *Explaining Economic Policy Reversals*. Buckingham, Philadelphia: Open University Press.

Hood, C. (1998). *The Art of the State: Culture, Rhetoric, and Public Management*. Oxford, New York: Clarendon Press.

Hood, C. (2010). *The Blame Game: Spin, Bureaucracy, and Self-Preservation in Government*. Princeton: Princeton University Press.

Hood, C., and Jackson, M. W. (1991). *Administrative Argument*. Aldershot, Hants, England, Brookfield: Dartmouth Publications.

Hood, C., and Lodge, M. (2004). 'Competency, Bureaucracy, and Public Management Reform: A Comparative Analysis', *Governance*, 17(3): 313–33.

Hood, C., and Lodge, M. (2005). 'Aesop with Variations: Civil Service Competency as A Case of German Tortoise and British Hare?' *Public Administration*, 83(4): 805–22.

Hood, C., and Wright, M. (1981). *Big Government in Hard Times*. Oxford: Robertson.

Huber, J. D., and Shipan, C. R. (2002). *Deliberate Discretion? The Institutional Foundations of Bureaucratic Autonomy*. Cambridge: Cambridge University Press.

Huntington, S. P. (1957). *The Soldier and the State: The Theory and Politics of Civil-Military Relations*. Cambridge, MA: Belknap Press of Harvard University Press.

Jann, W., and Wegrich, K. (2010). 'Governance und Verwaltungspolitik. Leitbilder und Reformkonzepte', in A. Benz, and N. Dose (eds), *Governance-Regieren in komplexen Regelsystemen. Eine Einführung*. 2nd edn. Wiesbaden: VS Verlag für Sozialwissenschaften, 175–200.

Lodge, M. (2007). 'Comparing Non-Hierarchical Governance in Action: The Open Method of Co-ordination in Pensions and Information Society', *Journal of Common Market Studies*, 45(2): 343–65.

Lodge, M. (2013). 'Crisis, Resources and the State: Executive Politics in the Age of the Depleted State', *Political Studies Review*, 11(3): 378–90.

Lodge, M., and Gill, D. (2011). 'Toward a New Era of Administrative Reform? The Myth of Post-NPM in New Zealand', *Governance*, 24(1): 141–66.

Lodge, M., and Hood, C. (2012). 'Into the Age of Multiple Austerities? Public Management and Public Service Bargains across OECD Countries', *Governance*, 25(1): 79–101.

Lodge, M., and Wegrich, K. (2011). 'Governance as Contested Logics of Control: Europeanized Meat Inspection Regimes in Denmark and Germany', *Journal of European Public Policy*, 18(1): 90–105.

Lodge, M., and Wegrich, K. (2012a). 'Public Administration and Executive Politics: Perennial Questions in Changing Contexts', *Public Policy and Administration*, 27(3): 212–29.

Lodge, M., and Wegrich, K. (2012b). 'Conclusion: Executive Politics in a Changing Climate', in M. Lodge, and K. Wegrich (eds), *Executive Politics in Times of Crisis*. Basingstoke: Palgrave Macmillan, 284–96.

Lodge, M. and Wegrich, K. (2012c). 'Executive Politics and Policy Instruments', in M. Lodge and K. Wegrich (eds), *Executive Politics in Times of Crisis*. Basingstoke: Palgrave Macmillan, 118–35.

Majone, G. (1997). 'From the Positive to the Regulatory State: Causes and Consequences of Changes in the Mode of Governance', *Journal of Public Policy*, 17(2): 139–67.

Margetts, H., 6, P., and Hood, C. (2010). *Paradoxes of Modernization: Unintended Consequences of Public Policy Reform*. Oxford, New York: Oxford University Press.

Matthews, F. (2012). 'Governance, Governing, and the Capacity of Executives in Times of Crisis', in M. Lodge and K. Wegrich (eds), *Executive Politics in Times of Crisis*. Basingstoke: Palgrave Macmillan.

Mayntz, R. (1987). 'Politische Steuerung und gesellschaftliche Steuerungsprobleme. Anmerkungen zu einem theoretischen Paradigma', *Jahrbuch zur Staats- und Verwaltungswissenschaft*, 1: 89–110.

Mayntz, R., and Scharpf, F. W. (1995). *Gesellschaftliche Selbstregelung und politische Steuerung*. Frankfurt, New York: Campus.

McCubbins, M. D., Noll, R. D., and Weingast, B. R. (1987). 'Administrative Procedures as Instruments of Political Control', *Journal of Law, Economics and Organization*, 3(2): 243–77.

Meyer-Sahling, J.-H., Lowe, V., and van Stolk, C. (2012). 'Towards NPM-ization of the Post-Communist State? Attitudes of Public Officials towards Models of Bureaucracy in Central and Eastern Europe', in M. Lodge and K. Wegrich (eds), *Executive Politics in Times of Crisis*. Basingstoke: Palgrave Macmillan, 99–117.

Olsen, J. P. (2006). 'Maybe It Is Time to Rediscover Bureaucracy', *Journal of Public Administration Research and Theory*, 16(1): 1–24.

Power, M. (1997). *The Audit Society: Rituals of Verification*. Oxford: New York: Oxford University Press.

Rhodes, R. A. W. (1997). *Understanding Governance: Policy Networks, Governance, Reflexivity, and Accountability*. Buckingham: Open University Press.

Roe, E. (2013). *Making the Most of Mess: Reliability and Policy in Today's Management Challenges*. Durham, London: Duke University Press.

Sabel, C. F., and Zeitlin, J. (2008). 'Learning from Difference: The New Architecture of Experimentalist Governance in the EU', *European Law Journal*, 14(3): 271–327.

Salamon, L. M. (ed.) (2002). *The Tools of Government: A Guide to the New Governance*. Oxford, New York: Oxford University Press.

Simon, H. A. (1946). 'The Proverbs of Administration', *Public Administration Review*, 6(1): 53–67.

Streeck, W., and Mertens, D. (2013). 'Public Finance and the Decline of State Capacity in Democratic Capitalism', in W. Streeck, and A. Schäfer (eds), *Politics in the Age of Austerity*. Cambridge: Polity, 26–58.

von Justi, J. (1759). *Grundsätze der Policey-Wissenschaften*. Göttingen: Verlag der Wittwe Vandenhöck.

Index

Bold entries refer to figures or tables.

Index